Conflict in
Korea

Conflict in Korea

An Encyclopedia

James Hoare
and Susan Pares

ABC-CLIO

Santa Barbara, California
Denver, Colorado
Oxford, England

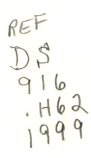
Library of Congress Cataloging-in-Publication Data

Hoare, James.
    Conflict in Korea : an encyclopedia / James Hoare and Susan Pares.
        p.   cm.
    Includes bibliographical references and index
    ISBN 0-87436-978-9 (alk. paper)
    1. Korea--History--20th century.   2. Korea--History--Partition, 1945
3. Korean War, 1950–1953--Causes.   I. Pares, Susan.
II. Title.
DS916.H62 1999   99-15211
951.904--dc21   CIP

ABC-CLIO, Inc.
130 Cremona Drive, P.O. Box 1911
Santa Barbara, California 93116-1911

Typography by Straight Line Design.
This book is printed on acid-free paper.
Manufactured in the United States of America.

Contents

Conflict in Korea:
An Encyclopedia

Preface

This encyclopedia has been some two years in the making, and it has led us into some interesting byways. Originally, we were approached to see if we knew anybody who might be interested in preparing such a work. We put forward various people, but no one was willing. At that point, Dr. Robert Neville of ABC-CLIO suggested that we might take on the task. We agreed, and have enjoyed learning in detail about this subject.

As befits an encyclopedia, the work is presented as entries arranged alphabetically. Cross-references, where appropriate, lead users to related entries; and almost every entry is followed by a list of works consulted, given in author-date form. These abbreviated references are expanded in the Bibliography, itself divided into books and annuals, newspapers, and periodicals. The Chronology aims to fix the key dates.

"Korean conflict" signifies not only the Korean War, even though that war has been undoubtedly the bloodiest and most terrible episode in the conflict. This encyclopedia is thus *not* an encyclopedia of the war, but aims to take a longer view of the conflict that has divided the Korea Peninsula since 1945 and that can trace its origins to developments earlier in the twentieth century both inside and outside Korea. The war ended in an armistice in 1953. No treaty of peace has ever been signed, and the spirit of conflict continues to this day, though now, nearly fifty years after the outbreak of hostilities in 1950, a change in the balance of strength between the two Koreas is having its effect on the intensity of the conflict.

The contest between two political and economic systems has been played out unrelentingly through propaganda, diplomacy, and sometimes terrorism and has extended into many unexpected areas of life. Koreans have been caught up first and foremost in the struggle, but the Korean conflict has sometimes stretched far beyond the Korea Peninsula, touching the lives of many, from liberation in 1945 onward. Physical violence has been matched by ideological bitterness between the two Koreas and their supporters and by dissenting views among non-Koreans over the significance and interpretation of the conflict. Specific causes of the conflict can sometimes be identified, but its roots, as is so often the case, must be traced back to human intransigence. Division and war have cost the Korean people, North and South, dearly in this century. We can only hope that the twenty-first century brings better prospects for all Koreans and that the wounds of the past can at last be healed.

Note on Personal Names and Romanization

The practice among Koreans and Chinese in listing their names is to put the family name first, followed by the given names, thus Kim Il Sung and Zhou Enlai. This style is used in both speech and writing and is the system followed in this encylopedia. In particular, where a Korean or Chinese name appears as a headword for an entry, the name has been written without a comma separating the family name from the given name or names.

Romanization of Korean words and names can follow several patterns. The standard romanization into an English form is that devised in 1939 by two American scholars, G. M. McCune and Edwin Reischauer. A modified version of their system has been used in this book for most Korean words. The traditional way of transcribing personal names generally separates the given name into its component parts, linking them with a hyphen, as in Pak Hon-yong. (Sometimes there is only one given name, as in Nam Il.) The tendency with the names of important people seems now to be to present them in three separate parts, giving Kim Dae Jung. Koreans familiar with the need for a romanized form of their name may choose their own romanization, hence names such as Syngman Rhee and Park Chung Hee.

In transcribing Chinese words and names, the pinyin romanization now standard in the People's Republic of China has been used, except for a few names, such as Chiang Kai-shek, where a particular form has become universally recognized by non-Chinese.

Acknowledgments

A work such as this has to depend a lot on other people's scholarship. We owe a particular debt to the following works: *Historical Dictionary of the Korean War* (1991) edited by James I. Matray; *Historical Dictionary of the Republic of Korea* (1993) by Andrew C. Nahm; *The History of the United Nations Forces in the Korean War* (1972–1977) published by the Ministry of National Defense, Republic of Korea; and *Korean War Almanac* (1990) by Harry G. Summers, Jr. Our debt to these and to many other works is shown, we hope adequately, in the references and the Bibliography.

A number of individuals have helped on various points—some great, some small. They include Sid Brown, *Morning Star* newspaper, London; James Foley, Centre for Korean Studies, School of East Asian Studies, University of Sheffield, U.K.; Mrs. Y. S. Park and her colleagues, Information Section, British Embassy, Seoul; Brigadier Colin Parr, Defense Attaché, British Embassy, Seoul; Dr. Horace G. Underwood, Yonsei University, Seoul; and Colonel Zhou Yi, Defense Attaché's Office, Embassy of the People's Republic of China, London. There are many others, in P'yongyang, Seoul, and elsewhere, who have contributed to our understanding of the complex issues with which this book deals, but who for a variety of reasons would prefer not to be named. We thank them as well, while understanding their concerns.

Inevitably, libraries, archives, and museums have been essential to our work. We would like to thank the staffs of the Library of the School of Oriental and African Studies, University of London; the British Library; the Foreign and Commonwealth Office Library; the Photograph Archive of the Imperial War Museum, London; the War Memorial in Seoul; and the Victorious Fatherland Liberation War Museum in P'yongyang. On-line access to the Library of Congress and to the Bodleian Library, Oxford, has also proved useful. We should also thank all those, whether governments, Korean War veterans, scholars, or database compilers, who have made available on the Internet so much material about the Korean conflict and about the two Koreas today. Korean sites seem to be among the easiest to access and the most user-friendly of all those available, and this has helped our work in many ways.

The views expressed are our own, and do not necessarily represent those of Her Majesty's Government.

James Hoare
Susan Pares
London, March 1999

Introduction

Geographic Setting

The Korea Peninsula curves out from the landmass of Northeast Asia, dividing the Yellow Sea (more usually known in Korea as the West Sea) from what the Koreans call the East Sea, but which is more likely to appear on non-Korean maps as the Sea of Japan. Although the peninsula was a single political entity for more than a thousand years, since 1948 it has been divided into two states: the Democratic People's Republic of Korea (North Korea) in the northern half of the peninsula and the Republic of Korea (South Korea) in the south. This political division does not affect the essential geographic unity of the peninsula.

To the north is a long border with China, mainly formed by the Yalu (Amnok in Korean) and the Tumen (Tuman in Korean) Rivers, and a short frontier with Russia, where the Tumen dissolves into marshy bogland. The border with China is some 640 miles (1,025 kilometers), whereas that with Russia is just over 9 miles (15 kilometers). The total area of the peninsula, including more than 3,500 islands, is some 82,242 square miles (221,000 square kilometers), approximately the size of mainland Britain. Land reclamation is steadily augmenting this total in both North and South Korea. The peninsula is about 688 miles (1,100 kilometers) long, and the average width is about 170 miles (250 kilometers). The shortest distance to Japan is 130 miles (206 kilometers). Korean schoolchildren were once taught that the peninsula is shaped like a rabbit; now, in tougher times, they learn that it resembles a tiger.

The peninsula is rugged, and the combination of jagged low hills, swift-flowing streams, and deep valleys makes it spectacularly beautiful in places such as the Diamond (Kumgang) Mountains, mostly in North Korea, and the Chiri Mountains in central South Korea. The east coast has steep cliffs and few islands. On the west, the seas are shallow, with huge tidal variations and many islands. Off the southern coast, drowned valleys have also produced a large number of islands. Overall, only approximately 20 percent of the land is suitable for agriculture. The best agricultural land is to be found on the western side, and this has been steadily increased in a process of land reclamation, both North and South, which goes back at least to Japanese colonial times in the early twentieth century. Because of the quality of the land, the western side of the peninsula has also been the area of most population concentration.

The climate is varied. It is semitropical on the southern island of Cheju, but in the rest of the peninsula it ranges from subzero winter temperatures to summer monsoons. Spring and autumn, with clear skies and bright sunshine, are generally regarded as the best seasons. The natural vegetation for most of the peninsula is deciduous forest, but very little of this survives. Generally, this natural vegetation has given way to agriculture or to secondary forests, with paddy rice farming the most widespread form of agriculture wherever the land allows it. Since the 1960s, the growing season has been extended by the use of plastic covers to cultivate winter vegetables. In the far south of the peninsula and on Cheju Island, the natural vegetation is subtropical. On Cheju, it is possible to grow citrus fruits, and the production of oranges and tangerines has become an important feature of the local economy since the 1970s.

Origins and Early History

Koreans trace their historical origins to the Neolithic Age (ca. 5000–1000 B.C.), when the mythical founder of the Korean state, the half-human, half-divine Tan'gun, is supposed to have reigned. The ancestors of today's Koreans inhabited not only the Korea Peninsula, but were also spread widely over what is now northeastern China, while there were also Chinese colonies on the peninsula. In reality, it is at the end of Korea's Iron Age in the early centuries of the Christian era that the first recognizable states began to emerge on the peninsula. This is known as the Three Kingdoms period. The kingdoms were Paekche, Koguryo, and Silla. Some historians believe that there was a fourth kingdom, Kaya. Silla succeeded in uniting most of the peninsula in 668 A.D. with the help of China's Tang Dynasty. Despite this support, Silla refused to be drawn into the Chinese state system and thus helped create a sense of separate identity among the peoples on the Korea Peninsula from the Chinese. The Silla links with Tang China nevertheless remained strong, and Chinese political, cultural, and religious influences were spread widely among the Silla aristocracy. Silla's capital at Kyongju in the southeast of the peninsula was laid out on Chinese lines. From China came Confucian and Buddhist teachings, both of which were readily adopted by the Koreans. The Koreans were also influenced by Chinese architecture, but developed it in their own way, as they did other arts such as metalwork.

Silla's decline began with power slipping away from the center to local magnates, and, for a brief period around the beginning of the tenth century, there was a revival of three separate kingdoms. This division did not last, and soon Silla was succeeded by the Koryo kingdom (918–1392 A.D.), from which, through China, the West derived the name "Korea." The capital was moved to the center of the peninsula, to what is now Kaesong. Koryo's rulers drew on a wider aristocratic base than did Silla's and allowed for a degree of mobility between lesser and upper noble classes. Confucian doctrine, with a strong emphasis on obedience, reinforced aristocratic rule, but Buddhism and native shaman rites were also held in high esteem, particularly at times of danger. During the Koryo period, the border of the Korean state was settled along the Tumen and Yalu Rivers. It was a time of remarkable artistic achievement in ceramics, painting, poetry, sculpture, and printing. Although developing their own techniques, Korean artists and craftspeople continued to draw on and refine those from China and passed on much of their knowledge to Japan. Even when royal rule was replaced by military rule for much of the twelfth century, the artists continued their work.

The new border in the north brought the Koreans into conflict with the Mongol people whose state of Liao was to the north of the Tumen River. As China fell apart under Mongol pressure, Koryo deemed it sensible to pay tribute to Liao and other Mongol states, rather than to the remnants of the Song Dynasty, which held on in the south of China. Koryo's international position deteriorated further when the Mongols established the Yuan Dynasty in China in 1271. Mongol pressure to incorporate the Koreans into their empire increased, and Korean troops were compelled to join the Mongol forces in attempts to invade Japan in 1274 and 1281. All this put a huge strain on Koryo society, as the peasants were expected to increase production to meet the costs of fighting.

The close links between the Koryo kings and the Mongol emperors were emphasized by the practice whereby the Korean crown prince, the heir apparent, took a Mongol bride and lived in the Mongol capital of Dadu, or Khanbaliq (modern Beijing), before ascending the throne. Even the collapse of the Yuan Dynasty brought little relief, as the fighting in China spread periodically into the Korea Peninsula. Added to these raids by what were, in effect, Chinese bandits were more systematic attacks by Japanese pirates—in reality probably a mixture of Japanese, Chinese, and Korean pirates—in the late fourteenth century. Diplomatic attempts to stop these failed, and instead the raids increased the importance of the Koryo military. Meanwhile, the ruling classes were split over whether Koryo should continue to support the failing Yuan in China or switch its allegiance to the rising native Chinese Ming Dynasty. One Koryo general, Yi Song-gye, who favored the Ming, staged a coup d'état and proclaimed himself king of a new Choson, or Yi, Dynasty in 1392.

The Yi Dynasty ruled Korea until 1910. The capital was moved the short distance from Kaesong to Hanyang (modern Seoul), which became the economic, social, and political center of the country—a position it held in a unified Korea until 1945 and that it still holds in modern South Korea. Buddhism, favored by Koryo, now took second place to the doctrines of Confucianism. Established in Korea since approximately the fourth century A.D., Confucianism placed a strong emphasis on social order and education and now came to dominate most aspects of Korean life. Its influence remains strong in both

Koreas today. Korea's new rulers gained advantages by breaking the power of the Buddhist monasteries, many of which had grown strong and rich under Koryo. Buddhism did not disappear, but it faded from the central position that it had once occupied. For much of the Yi Dynasty, Korean links to China were at their strongest, surviving even the transition from the Ming to the non-Chinese Manchu Qing Dynasty in 1644 and lasting until China's defeat by Japan in 1895.

During the late fifteenth and early sixteenth centuries, periodic unrest in the areas neighboring Korea brought problems. Japanese pirates raided Korea's coasts. The Koreans protested, but political turmoil in Japan again meant that there was no central authority that could control these raiders. When Japan again experienced stability at the end of the sixteenth century, Korea still suffered as the Japanese ruler Hideyoshi attempted to attack China through Korea. The Imjin War, as Hideyoshi's invasion became known, lasted from 1592 to 1597, devastated the peninsula, and ended with Hideyoshi's death. The war left a legacy of strong anti-Japanese feeling in its wake. That was not all. The pressures in China as the Ming Dynasty drew to a close at the end of the sixteenth century spilled over into Korea, just as the Mongol incursions had done four hundred years before. Under attack from the Manchu, the court fled from Seoul to the nearby island of Kanghwa, as its predecessor had done when the Mongols attacked.

In such circumstances, it is perhaps not surprising that from the seventeenth century onward Korea increasingly tended to turn in upon itself. It was never entirely isolated from the outside world, but it tended to treat it with considerable wariness. Regular diplomatic missions were sent to Beijing, relations were maintained with the Tokugawa rulers who had succeeded Hideyoshi in Japan, and the Japanese established a permanent trading establishment in the far south of the country at Tongnae, now part of the port of Pusan. Trade continued, and by the late nineteenth century many Koreans were using Western goods bought from Chinese and Japanese peddlers. Roman Catholicism, introduced through China and developed at first by Koreans on their own without outside assistance, found a niche and eventually led to a clandestine French missionary presence in the country beginning in the 1830s.

Korean authorities were aware of the international links of the Roman Catholic Church and tried to destroy its presence on Korean soil. Both native and foreign Catholics suffered terrible persecutions, yet the Catholic faith survived.

Opening to the Outside World

The firm Korean refusal to contemplate change to what were seen as the time-honored ways of behavior meant that the country was in a poor position to resist Western and Japanese overtures in the latter years of the nineteenth century. Western attempts at trade were rebuffed, sometimes with force. A U.S. merchant ship, the *General Sherman*, which was leased to a British company and included a British Protestant missionary among its passengers, attempted to sail up the Taedong River in 1866. The ship became trapped and was attacked. It was burnt and all aboard killed. A U.S. naval expedition sent to punish those responsible was ignominiously defeated at Kanghwa Island in 1871 by the Koreans.

The persecution of Catholic missionaries and their congregations intensified because such groups were seen as dangerous forerunners for Western military might. The French too sent an expedition, which fared little better than the U.S. one. These Korean victories tended to create a false sense of security, which proved no match for a more determined approach. This came in 1876, when the Japanese forced Korea to sign its first modern treaty, an echo of similar treaties forced on China and Japan in the previous forty years. The Koreans looked to China for support, but the Chinese, battered by years of Western pressure, had little constructive advice to offer. Western countries quickly followed the Japanese example, and the "opening" of Korea began—to traders, diplomats, and missionaries, as well as to new ways of thought.

During the next thirty years, a nominally independent Korea found itself at the mercy of the great powers around it. As well as China and Japan, Korea now faced Western pressures. The British and the Americans were strongly represented in China and Japan, and their merchants were looking for new sources for profits. Russia reached Korea's borders in 1860. This worried the British, who saw an advance by Russia as a threat to British imperial interests. Several ports in Korea were opened to Western trade, but the Korean ports never achieved the same importance as the ports opened in China and Japan. Competition between China and Japan for control of the Korea Peninsula ended with the Japanese triumph following their defeat of China in 1895 in a war that saw much fighting on the Korea Peninsula, although officially Korea was neutral. Japanese and Russian rivalry in East Asia led them into a contest for dominance over the peninsula, a struggle that in turn ended with the defeat of Russia in 1905 in another war fought partially on Korean soil. The Russian defeat and the Anglo-Japanese Alliance of 1902, together with the indifference of the United States, paved the way for the Japanese to establish control over the peninsula. Korea became a Japanese protectorate in 1905, and Japanese control over the kingdom grew steadily stronger in the following years. Many Koreans remained unhappy with what had happened to their country, and some fought the Japanese, but such opposition was ruthlessly suppressed. In 1909, a Korean patriot assassinated the first Japanese Resident-General, Prince Ito Hirobumi, at Harbin. The following year, the Japanese completed the process of takeover, annexing the peninsula as a colony after its thousand years of independence.

Korea as a Japanese Colony

Thirty-five years of harsh colonial rule followed. Korean resentment at Japanese control led to a number of uprisings and protests, the largest of which was the *samil* (March First) uprising of 1919. As before, all such opposition was savagely crushed, reinforcing already established anti-Japanese feeling and leaving an abiding bitterness among Koreans. At the same time, Korean opposition to the Japanese developed outside the country, in China and in the West. In northeast China, then generally known in the West as Manchuria, where the Japanese puppet state of Manzhouguo was established in 1932, guerrilla bands harassed the Japanese, often carrying out raids in Korea itself. In Shanghai, members of a Korean government in exile schemed and plotted for the day of their return to Korea. Both activities were of marginal importance in the colonial period, but were to have a considerable impact later.

In recent years, new research has shown that Japanese rule brought incidental benefits. These included the development of a modern administrative system; the promotion of education, new roads, and railways; and the beginning of industrialization. Such changes, however, were primarily designed to benefit Japan. Road and rail links, for example, facilitated Japanese trade; Korean interests came in a poor second. After the outbreak of full-scale hostilities between China and Japan in 1937, the demands on Korea became ever greater as Japan moved steadily toward a total war footing. Now even Korean names were forbidden, huge economic requirements were placed on the peninsula, and Koreans were pressed into service for the war effort. They included many women, known euphemistically as "comfort women," who were forced to become prostitutes for Japanese forces in China and later in Southeast Asia. Korean women were not the only ones to suffer such humiliation, but they were one of the major groups involved. Some Koreans benefited from Japan's wartime needs. A number of Koreans, including the future president of South Korea, Park Chung Hee, were selected for officer training, whereas some of those engaged in agriculture or manufacturing gained as the war progressed. For most Koreans, however, the war meant harder work and fewer rewards.

Division and Civil War

The end of World War II brought freedom from Japanese rule, but it was hardly the liberation the Koreans expected. Korean hopes for the restoration of a unified independent state were not realized. There had been little Allied planning for the sudden collapse of Japan or for the future of Korea, and the division of the peninsula at the 38th parallel into Soviet and U.S. zones was initially for the purpose of effecting the Japanese surrender. Even as the war in the Pacific ended, however, there were those on the U.S. side who perhaps thought that a more enduring division might be to U.S. advantage. In particular, it was believed that it could be useful to have Seoul under U.S. control.

What had officially been seen as a temporary arrangement quickly set into permanent division when the two superpowers failed to agree on a unified government for Korea. At the same time, political attitudes were hardening in both North and South. Two separate states emerged in 1948: the

Republic of Korea, proclaimed on 15 August, with the U.S.-educated veteran independence campaigner, Syngman Rhee, as its president; and the Democratic People's Republic of Korea on 9 September, led by a relatively unknown former guerrilla leader, Kim Il Sung, who was head of the Communist Party and premier. Each state still celebrates its National Day on these dates. In broad terms, North Korea's leadership came from the guerrilla bands that had operated from Communist-controlled areas in China and the Soviet Union in colonial days and from Koreans settled in the Soviet Union. In South Korea, the top leadership came from exile groups in the then Nationalist China and the United States.

Both Korean states claimed the allegiance of all Koreans, and each called for early reunification and indulged in much military jockeying for position along the 38th parallel between 1948 and 1950. Communist guerrilla fighters kept up campaigns in mountainous areas of the South. The potential for a wider armed conflict was always present, although the South Koreans were weaker in military terms than were the North Koreans. Although the U.S. occupation forces had begun the process of creating a South Korean army, this was not complete by the time U.S. forces withdrew from Korea. The South Korean army had little armor and artillery and no air force. The North Koreans had large stocks of equipment left behind at the departure of Soviet forces in December 1948, including T-34 tanks, Yak-9 fighters, and Il-10 bombers. They had been able to incorporate into their new army large numbers of experienced Koreans who had fought with the Chinese Red Army in the civil war in China. The Chinese Communist victory over the Nationalists and the establishment of the People's Republic of China (PRC) in October 1949 meant that many of these experienced soldiers were free to return to Korea. Soviet advisers had remained behind to help train these forces.

It was against this background that North Korea, with the tacit agreement of both the Soviet Union and the newly established PRC, and with promises of more equipment and supplies from the former, attempted to achieve reunification by force in June 1950. The bid was nearly successful, but was stopped by U.S. and UN intervention and in the end only perpetuated the peninsula's division, which continues to this day. North Korea's very existence was threatened by UN successes, and its survival was possible only because the PRC entered the war during October–November 1950 to save it from total defeat at the hands of the UN forces. After three years of fighting, the war ended on 27 July 1953 with an armistice agreement signed on the one side by North Korea and the Chinese People's Volunteers and on the other by the UN commander. Under its terms, a Military Armistice Commission, made up of representatives of the two sides, would supervise the armistice arrangements. The South Korean president, Syngman Rhee, regarded the armistice as a betrayal and refused to sign it. After some U.S. pressure, he did, however, agree to abide by it. At Geneva in 1954, a major international conference convened to try to settle the problem of Korean unification (and to deal with Indochina), but failed to reach agreement. Korea remained divided.

The armistice agreement, therefore, is the only agreed arrangement for the peninsula, and it remains in force to this day. The North Koreans have regularly called for its replacement by a peace treaty between themselves and the United States. They have always argued that their real opponent in the war was the United States, rather than the United Nations, and they tend to dismiss the other participants as lackeys of the United States. In North Korea's view, because South Korea was not a party to the armistice, it should not be a party to a peace treaty, a position opposed by South Korea and the United States, which remains the South's military backer. After 1991, when the UN Command (UNC) appointed a South Korean general as its head, the North Koreans largely withdrew cooperation with the UN side of the Military Armistice Commission, though they agreed in June 1998 to resume talks, provided an American headed the UNC team.

The Korean War left both Korean states devastated. Millions were dead, homes were destroyed, and families split. For most of the next twenty years, both North and South Korea put most effort into rebuilding and reconstruction. The wish for reunification did not disappear, but it was subordinate to the process of state building and economic development.

North Korea

Until the early 1970s, North Korea probably had the economic edge over the South, as it rapidly industrialized with Soviet and East European assistance. Its success was not accomplished, however, without huge political and social cost. Ordinary civil society disappeared, as all social organs were taken over by the state. In political terms, Kim Il Sung, the former guerrilla leader and Soviet protégé, gradually eliminated his main rivals in a style reminiscent of Joseph Stalin, the Soviet leader, so that by the early 1970s, Kim was the unchallenged leader of North Korea. The result was one of the most tightly ruled political units in the world, with power centered on Kim and a small group of supporters drawn from his own family or from those who had fought with him in the guerrilla war against Japan. Together these formed the core of the Korean Workers' Party. Unable to decide on an appropriate successor, Kim eventually selected his son Kim Jong Il for this role in about 1973. The son remained in the background for another ten years, being trained for the succession in a series of party and government posts, and was referred to only as "The Party Center." Beginning in the early 1980s, he appeared in public. While his father's title was always translated into English as the "Great Leader," the younger Kim's title was "Dear Leader." He remained a more shadowy figure than his father, but he was known for his interest in the arts, for his links with the military, and, according to the more lurid stories, for heavy drinking and outbreaks of temper. When Kim Il Sung died in 1994, Kim Jong Il succeeded him in practice, but not in title. It was not until 1997, when he became secretary-general of the Korean Workers' Party, that he formally assumed any of his father's titles. In September 1998, he also became effective head of state, but not president. The constitution was changed so that the presidential title was reserved for Kim Il Sung, whereas Kim Jong Il ruled as head of the military.

The North Korean economy began to falter in the 1970s. Equipment supplied or bought in the 1950s and early 1960s began to wear out, and the North Koreans were badly hit by the fall in commodity prices, which occurred after the 1973 world oil crisis. North Korea bought some new equipment, but, finding that it could not pay for it, became the first Communist state to default on its debts. Increasingly, the North Korean economy was kept going, despite claims of independence, by subsidies (partly disguised as trade offered at "friendship prices") from its two chief allies, China and the Soviet Union. China's move toward a market economy after 1978, the end of communism in Eastern Europe in the late 1980s, which also brought about the end of the economic system known as COMECON,* and the collapse of the Soviet Union in the early 1990s all adversely affected North Korea. Its foreign trade disintegrated and its whole economic system began to slow down.

To make matters worse, floods, drought, and a tidal wave between 1995 and 1997 caused immense damage to agriculture. Unable to feed its people, and with little idea of what to do next, the North Korean government appealed for international humanitarian aid. When the appeal was successful, the North Koreans appealed for more and by 1998 seemed to assume that aid would be forthcoming whatever they did. Although some trade with South Korea has replaced that lost with the fall of the Soviet Union, and China still appears to trade at subsidized prices and to give aid, it is clear that the North Korean economy is in a very weak state. Officially claimed figures for an income of $700–$1,000 per capita, which appeared in the 1970s, have been revised down to some $450, but even that may be exaggerated. The one industrial area where there are still signs of activity is in the production of military equipment, including missiles. Some of this is for the North's own use, but North Korea also exports both weapons and missiles. So far, however, despite widespread claims that North Korea's economic problems would inevitably lead to political upheaval and perhaps the collapse of the ruling elite, there is no sign that this is the case. The regime is nonetheless isolated, as its former Communist allies have followed new political and economic paths.

South Korea

The South seemed less politically stable after 1953 than the North. Syngman Rhee became steadily

---

*COMECON was the term generally used in the West for the Council for Mutual Economic Assistance, founded in 1949, which was the economic equivalent of the Warsaw Pact. It linked the Soviet Union and the Communist countries of Eastern Europe in a mutual trading community. Although North Korea was never a member of COMECON, its economy was closely tied in with it. COMECON was dissolved in June 1991.

more autocratic and flagrant in his abuse of the electoral system. Although he was voted into a fourth presidential term in 1960, blatant electoral fraud led to massive student demonstrations throughout South Korea, and Rhee was eventually forced to resign, going into exile in Hawaii, where he died in 1965. A short-lived period of somewhat chaotic democracy followed, cut abruptly short by a military coup d'état under the leadership of Major General Park Chung Hee. A period of military dominance in politics began and lasted almost unbroken until 1992. South Korea's front-line position in the Cold War ensured it the continued backing of its main supporter, the United States. Park civilianized himself, as did his fellow coup associates, and ran for president on three occasions. As the years passed, however, his rule became increasingly autocratic, provoking widespread opposition. A dispute between Park and the director of the Korean Central Intelligence Agency (KCIA) over how to handle this opposition led the KCIA director to assassinate the president in October 1979.

Another brief democratic interlude followed until General Chun Doo Hwan seized power in mid-1980. Chun continued much the same policies as Park Chung Hee, except that Chun introduced a constitution that allowed only one term to the presidency. Despite some hesitations, in the end he abided by his own rules and stepped down in 1988. Under his successor, Roh Tae Woo, another former general, many of the restrictions of earlier years were relaxed. South Koreans could now read more or less what they liked, watch most films and plays (though strict controls continued on material from Japan), and were allowed to travel abroad. Politically too, there were changes, with Roh joining forces with a veteran opposition leader, Kim Young Sam, as well as with more conservative politicians, to ensure continued government dominance of the National Assembly.

Kim Young Sam was elected president in 1992. The first civilian president since 1960, Kim duly succeeded Roh in February 1993. Kim began well, with a major onslaught on corruption, but his reforming zeal did not last, and by 1994 he seemed to have run out of ideas about policy. At the same time, scandals, some involving his son, began to link him to the sources of corruption that he officially opposed.

Although at first he resisted attempts to bring his predecessors to account for their respective roles in seizing power in 1980 and for corruption, he was eventually forced to do so by popular pressure. By 1997, he was widely seen as a weak and ineffective president. Although Kim Young Sam tried to prevent it, the December 1997 presidential election brought another former dissident to power. This was Kim Dae Jung, long seen by South Korea's military rulers as a dangerous opponent—he nearly beat Park Chung Hee in the 1971 elections, and Park never forgave him. With Kim's election, South Korea moved a stage further down the road to democracy, for this was the first time that a candidate had succeeded in winning the presidency without the support of the government machine.

It was ironic that Kim Dae Jung's election coincided with the biggest financial crisis that South Korea has ever experienced. Until then, the "miracle on the Han" (Seoul's main river) had become a byword internationally for successful economic development. It had not always seemed so. The division of the peninsula in 1945 and the Korean War left the southern part of the peninsula with a number of handicaps, cut off from such industrialization as had existed under the Japanese and from supplies of power in the North. The South was traditionally the agricultural center of the country, with little experience with industry. The Korean War caused much damage to buildings and to land—though this was greater in the North—and created a massive refugee problem because more people went south than went north in the course of the war. This was not entirely a political statement; many just fled from the heavy bombing that the North suffered.

Syngman Rhee was not much interested in economic matters and was content to rely on U.S. subsidies to keep his country going. Although recent research has indicated that the Rhee years were less of an economic black hole than they once seemed, nevertheless, South Korea's situation was widely viewed as completely hopeless in the 1950s. In 1961, its gross national product (GNP) per capita was officially estimated at $148, which made it among the lowest in the world.

The military rulers who took over in 1961 had no particular solution to the economic problems that South Korea faced, except perhaps that, unlike

Rhee, they recognized that there was a problem. From 1962 onward, drawing on Japanese colonial practices and experiences in Korea and prewar Manchuria, the military rulers began a series of five-year plans designed to make the South stronger than the North. Eventually, these plans began to deliver high growth rates, which were to last until the early 1980s. The political uncertainty following the death of President Park then led to a faltering in economic advance for a time, but it resumed after 1981. The original foundations of this growth lay on import substitution and light industry, especially textiles. Soon the concentration was on heavy industry, with strong emphasis on steel production, chemical manufacture, and shipbuilding. To these was added automobile production beginning in the mid-1970s. Later, the South Korean industrial conglomerates, known as *chaebol* and roughly modeled on the Japanese *zaibatsu*, would branch out into new areas including computers and other electronic products. At all times, the export market was targeted; domestic consumers and workers were promised rewards, but only at some vague future date.

Economic strength, therefore, was not achieved without social cost. The requirement for a strong economic base was justified under Park Chung Hee by the need to be able to meet any challenge from North Korea. Workers' rights and personal freedoms generally were limited, often on the pretext of the need to combat the "threat from the North." There were benefits, as GNP per capita rose to $1,500 by about 1980 and to $10,000 by the mid-1980s, but the benefits were not always equitably distributed. Under Park Chung Hee, however, one potential imbalance was corrected. Under the banner of the *saemaul undong*, or new community movement, some attempt was made to ensure that the rural population did not lose out too much as the country urbanized. Cheap cement enabled villages to construct roads, assembly halls, and other amenities, which assured their inhabitants that not all economic benefits were going to the towns. Especially under Park's successor, President Chun Doo Hwan, the *saemaul* movement also attempted to provide an ideology to counteract the North's communism. This was less successful than its provision of economic benefits, not least because Chun chose his younger brother to run it. This prompted charges of

nepotism, to which were soon added claims of corruption.

GNP continued to rise under Roh Tae Woo and Kim Young Sam, and South Korea joined the Organization for Economic Co-operation and Development in 1997. Even as it did so, however, there were signs of difficulty. At first, these seemed mainly to affect smaller *chaebol*. In July 1997, however, Kia Motors, the country's third-largest automobile manufacturer, sought government assistance, as it could not meet its short-term loan requirements. By October, it was bankrupt, and when the banks refused further loans, the government stepped in to nationalize it, fearful of the social consequences of not doing so in a country with virtually no social security system.

Before long, international credit rating agencies began to reduce South Korea's rating. By mid-November 1997, the South Korean currency had dropped below 1,000 won equalling $1. On 21 November 1997, the government finally approached the International Monetary Fund (IMF), seeking $20 billion to help it meet short-term debt. Shortly afterward, the IMF granted South Korea $57 billion, the largest sum it had ever provided. At that stage, South Korean external debt was estimated at $156.9 billion. The won fell again against the dollar, though it bounced back, but by June 1998 there could be little doubt that the South Korean economy was in recession, with increasing unemployment and a fall in real gross domestic product and in per capita GNP.

In this time of crisis, government leadership at first seemed lacking. Rumors abounded that President Kim Young Sam had been virtually unaware of the crisis until mid-November 1997 and uncertain what to do thereafter. His successor, Kim Dae Jung, had seemed equally confused at first, but was soon making a better impression as he used his prestige to persuade trade unions and the giant conglomerates of the need to accept the IMF's package. Once in office, he made strenuous efforts to persuade the unions to accept redundancies, while pressuring the *chaebol* into reform. The South Korean economic miracle has clearly suffered a major blow, but many of the fundamentals that made it successful in the first instance remain in place, and it will probably recover over time.

Prospects for Reunification

Fifty years after the emergence of two Korean states, both at the outset pledging to bring about reunification, the peninsula remains divided. Each side maintains large armed forces, estimated at one million in the North, with a population of approximately 22 million, and 660,000 in the South, with a population of some 46 million. There are also some 37,000 U.S. troops in the South. The North has over the years mounted a series of terrorist attacks on the South. These reached a peak in the late 1960s and included an attempted commando raid in January 1968 on the Blue House, the South Korean presidential palace.

An attempt in 1973 to assassinate President Park killed his wife. A bomb explosion in Rangoon in 1983, which missed President Chun, killed a number of his senior ministers and advisers. In 1987, in an apparent bid to disrupt the 1988 Olympic Games, due to be held in Seoul, North Korean agents planted a bomb on a Korean Air plane, which blew up over the Andaman Sea, killing all on board.

Despite all this, the two sides have made periodic attempts to discuss the issue of reunification, so far without much progress. Following the improvement in Sino-U.S. ties after President Richard Nixon's visit to China in 1972, the two Koreas began to talk for the first time since the end of the Korean War and appeared to reach an agreement when they issued identical communiqués on 4 July 1972. The talks and the high hopes ended in mutual recrimination and were not revived until the changed circumstances of the late 1980s. Following another series of high-level talks, a number of North-South agreements were signed in 1991 and seemed to offer hope for the future, but, once again, the initiative failed. A planned summit between South Korea's President Kim Young Sam and North Korean President Kim Il Sung in July 1994 was aborted when Kim Il Sung died.

Thereafter, the North took offense at the South's failure to send condolences on Kim's death, and relations reverted to their usual level of hostility. North Korea's growing economic problems after the collapse of the Soviet Union in 1991 led to some contact, as did the U.S. and South Korean wish to prevent any North Korean nuclear weapons program. President Kim Dae Jung has made a number of small conciliatory moves, but, as the two Koreas enter the twenty-first century, the hostilities that have marked their relationship for most of the past fifty years continue to be the dominant feature of their relations.

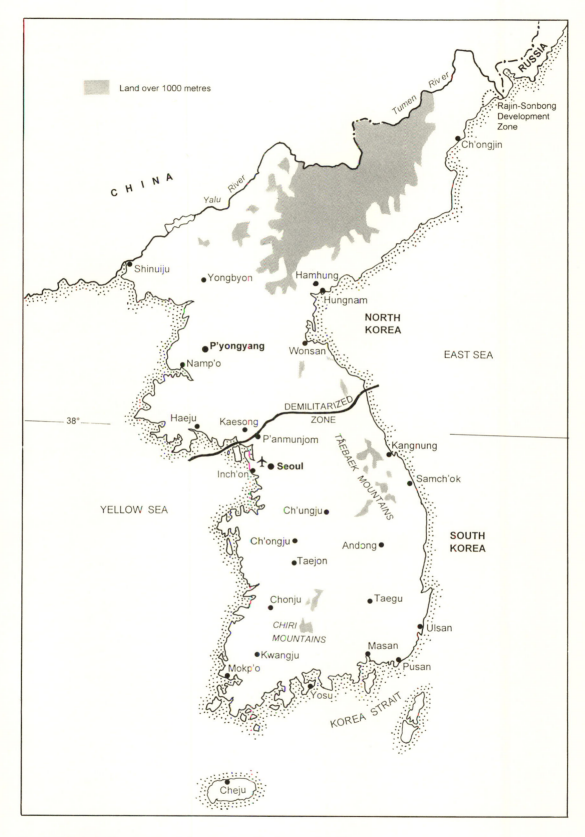

Map 1. Principal cities, towns, and sites mentioned in the encyclopedia.

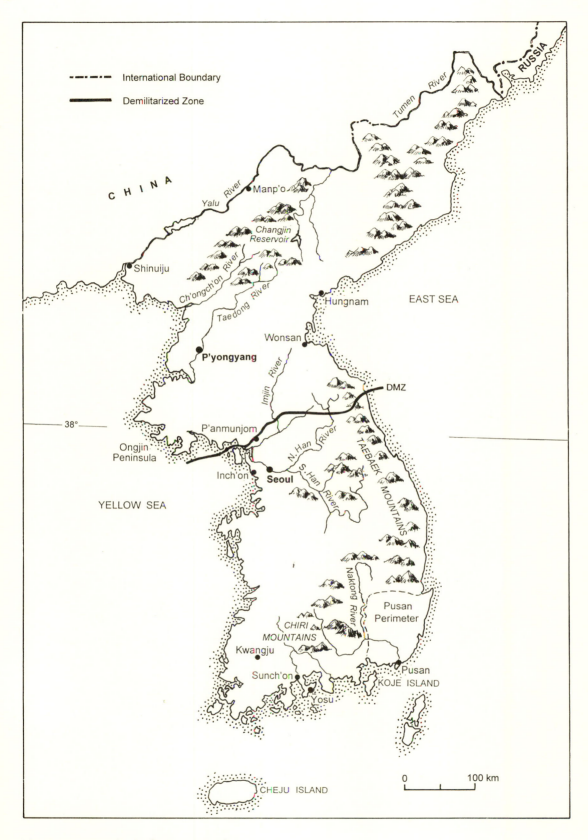

Map 2. Important sites in the Korean Conflict.

Conflict in Korea

ABDUCTIONS

Both North and South Korea have resorted to abduction. In their sweep south in 1950, North Korean forces detained individuals and groups that they deemed politically suspect or whose services they required, such as doctors. Among those seized and taken north were the writer and nationalist leader Yi Kwang-su, convicted after liberation of collaboration with the Japanese, and another nationalist activist, **Kim Kyu-shik**. Both are presumed to have died in the North.

Once established, the North Korean state seems to have practiced abduction as a means of securing specialized services. In 1978, Shin Sang-ok, a South Korean film director, and his wife, Ch'oe Un-hi, a film actor, were abducted from Hong Kong to North Korea reportedly on the orders of **Kim Jong Il** to allow him to use their expertise in the development of the North Korean film industry. The couple stayed as advisers to Kim until they defected back to South Korea in 1985. Foreigners may also have been detained in North Korea to train North Korean agents in the manners of their society, presumably to allow the latter to pass themselves off as non-Koreans. Kim Hyon-hui, implicated in the **Korean Air flight KA858 bombing** of November 1987, after her capture revealed that she had lived for two years with a Japanese woman, reportedly kidnapped, to learn Japanese ways. Such claims, if true, suggest an elaborate, long-term campaign of disruption.

Ambiguity can surround apparent cases of abduction. In April 1979, Ko Sang-mun, a South Korean teacher undergoing training in Norway, instead of going to the South Korean embassy in Oslo, apparently went by mistake to the North Korean embassy, where he was detained and later taken to North Korea. P'yongyang radio subsequently announced that Ko had defected. Similar uncertainty surrounds Lee Jae-hwan, a South Korean studying in the United States, who disappeared in 1987 while on a visit to Austria. His family believe he was abducted; North Korea insists he

A

defected voluntarily. In July 1995, An Sung-won, a minister of the South Korean Full Gospel Church on a missionary tour in the Yanbian Korean Autonomous District of China on the Sino-Korean border, was abducted by a group of North Koreans. A month later, he appeared on North Korean television, claiming he had defected voluntarily. Whether abduction or defection, such incidents have often happened in third countries.

There is little doubt about the circumstances in which, since the late 1950s, sometimes large groups of South Korean fishermen and their boats have been seized by North Korean patrols and taken to the North on the grounds that these vessels were fishing in North Korean waters. Often both men and vessels have been released back to the South only after months in custody. South Korea claims that many fishermen are still held in the North. On land, villagers living in the southern half of the **Demilitarized Zone** who stray across the Military Demarcation Line may be described as "abducted" by North Korean guards before being returned. It does seem, however, that North Korean agents penetrating South Korean territory may have abducted civilians, as is said to have happened in August 1978 to three South Korean youths abducted from beaches. In July 1997, South Korea sought the cooperation of the United Nations High Commissioner for Human Rights (UNHCHR) in repatriating the Reverend An Sung-won and in November 1997 was considering a similar appeal to the UNHCHR for help in tracing the three abducted youths. In January 1999, South Korean government statistics were released, which claimed around 3,750 South Koreans had been abducted by the North since the end of the Korean War in 1953. Of these, 441 were still detained. The South Korean National Intelligence Service, reporting on the situation, listed 22 of them as being in prison camps and named 15 of these.

South Korea has on occasion resorted to abduction as a means of bringing suspects under its jurisdiction. In the summer of 1967, the Korean Central Intelligence Agency (KCIA) abducted 17 members of an alleged North Korean spy ring, said to have been based in the former East Berlin, that included the celebrated composer **Yun I-sang**, and brought them via then West Berlin to Seoul for trial. Other South Koreans abroad have been known to disappear; the suspicion is that they have been detained by South Korean intelligence and returned to South Korea. The KCIA's most notorious operation was in August 1973, when its officers seized **Kim Dae Jung**, then an opposition leader, now president, in a Tokyo hotel room and removed him by sea to South Korea. *See also:* Defections; Demilitarized Zone (DMZ); Infiltration; North-South Boundaries; Yun I-sang. *References:* Bermudez 1988; Macdonald 1996; Nahm 1993; *Newsreview,* 6 February 1999; *White Paper* 1997.

ACHESON, DEAN GOODERHAM (1893–1971)
Dean Acheson was U.S. secretary of state at the outbreak of the **Korean War** in June 1950. Acheson was born in Middletown, Connecticut, and graduated from Yale and Harvard. He became undersecretary of the treasury in 1933 and joined the Department of State in 1941. In 1949, he became secretary of state. In a speech to the Washington Press Club in January 1950, he excluded Korea and Taiwan from the U.S. Pacific defense perimeter; later, some saw this as a factor leading to the Korean War, although the U.S. decision to withdraw troops from Korea in 1949 was a more powerful signal. After June 1950, Acheson played a major role in defining U.S. policy and enjoyed the support of President **Harry S Truman**, whose decision to recall General **Douglas MacArthur** in April 1951 Acheson backed. After leaving office, Acheson was a foreign policy adviser to a number of presidents. *References:* Acheson 1969, 1971.

AERIAL BOMBING
Although some spectacular air battles took place over the Korea Peninsula during the **Korean War**

between UN and Communist aircraft, the **United Nations Command** forces enjoyed superiority in the air from the earliest stages. This allowed the UN air forces, principally the U.S. Far Eastern Air Force operating from Japan, to bomb North Korea with little restriction, and by April 1951, the Air Force announced that few recognizable military targets were left in North Korea. Strategic bombing nonetheless continued, with attacks on the hydroelectric dams and power stations on the **Yalu** and Tumen Rivers, to prevent supplies from reaching the North Korean/Chinese troops. This strategy failed, as did attempts in the summer of 1952 to use bombing to force the Communist side to accept the UN position on **prisoners of war** at the **armistice** negotiations. The bombing campaigns and the indiscriminate attacks on military and civilian targets were heavily criticized at the time and have remained a source of much bitterness in North Korea ever since. *References:* Futrell 1961, revised edition 1983; Jackson 1973, 1988; Michener 1953.

AERIAL SURVEILLANCE
Observation and reconnaissance aircraft of the U.S. and South Korean air forces, some unmanned and many equipped to take aerial photographs, are deployed regularly along the Military Demarcation Line (MDL) running down the middle of the **Demilitarized Zone** (DMZ). Mindful of the North's surprise attack in June 1950, the South and the **United Nations Command** keep the front line between the two states under constant observation with the aim of detecting any buildup of troops and equipment on the northern side and any signs of road and tunnel construction. Coastal areas are also kept under surveillance, and patrols are carried out over the waters east and west of the peninsula. North Korea protests regularly about such activities and sometimes retaliates by firing on aircraft in the DMZ or over sea.

The South Korean Defense Ministry revealed in November 1997 that a remote-controlled reconnaissance aircraft was being developed by South Korean heavy industry. *See also:* United States Navy Reconnaissance Plane EC-121 (1969).

AGENCY FOR NATIONAL SECURITY PLANNING (ANSP)
See **National Intelligence Service (NIS).**

AIR RAID DRILLS
See **Curfews and Civil Defense Measures.**

AIRCRAFT HIJACKINGS
On two occasions, civilian aircraft have been hijacked from South to North Korea. On 16 February 1958, a Korean National Airlines DC-3 passenger plane was diverted to the North while on an internal South Korean flight. The 34 passengers on board included a member of the National Assembly, a U.S. officer, and three crew. Three weeks later, on 6 March 1958, 26 passengers were returned through **P'anmunjom**, but the hijackers and aircraft remained in the North. Eleven years later, a Korean Air Lines YS-11 aircraft, likewise on a domestic flight, was hijacked on 11 December 1969 to the North. It was carrying 51 passengers, all South Korean nation-als, of whom 39 were released to the UNC authorities at P'anmunjom on 14 February 1970. South Korea claims that the crew is still held captive.

In April 1958, an unsuccessful attempt was made to hijack a C-46-593 transport aircraft of the South Korean Air Force to the North.
See also: North Korean Use of Terrorism.
References: History: VI, 1977; *Newsreview,* 6 February 1999; Yi 1973.

ANTI-COMMUNIST LAW (1961)
See **National Security Law.**

ARMISTICE
On 27 July 1953, the **Korean War** ended with the signing of an armistice at the negotiation site of **P'anmunjom**. The signatories were Marshal **Kim Il Sung** and General **Nam Il** for the **North Korean People's Army** (NKPA); **Peng Dehuai**, commander of the **Chinese People's Volunteers**; and General **Mark Clark** and Lieutenant-General William

United Nations Command delegates to the armistice negotiations, Kaesong, 13 August 1951. Admiral C. Turner Joy of the U.S. Navy is in the center of the lineup; General Paik Sun-yup of the South Korean Army is next to him (fourth from left). (Imperial War Museum HU 61451)

Delegates from the North Korean People's Army and the Chinese People's Volunteers at the preliminary meeting to the Kaesong armistice talks, 8 July 1951. Although no identification is provided, the group almost certainly includes General Nam Il (NKPA), Xie Fang (CPV), and General Lee Sang Cho (NKPA). (Imperial War Museum HU50471)

Harrison for the **United Nations Command** (UNC). Only Nam Il and Harrison actually attended at P'anmunjom to sign; the others signed at their respective headquarters. There were no signatories for the South Korean forces.

The armistice document comprised five articles. Article I fixed a Military Demarcation Line within a **Demilitarized Zone** (DMZ) with the purpose of physically separating the two opposing sides. Control over entry into the DMZ and over activities within it was entrusted to a **Military Armistice Commission** (MAC) and to the commanders of the three sets of forces concerned. Article II laid out concrete arrangements for the cease-fire and armistice. The principal aim of these arrangements was to monitor and restrict troop levels and levels of armaments within the peninsula and to ensure the smooth functioning of the MAC, of a **Neutral Nations Supervisory Commission**, and of their subordinate organizations. Article II further prescribed the composition, functions, authority, and duties of the MAC, of the **Joint Observer Teams** assisting it, of the

Neutral Nations Supervisory Commission, and of its supporting **Neutral Nations Inspection Teams**.

Article III dealt with the issue of **prisoners of war**. Before the armistice was signed, agreement had been reached on the terms of repatriation for the troops of the three commands. Article III of the armistice detailed the arrangements for exchange of prisoners of war and of civilian detainees, responsibility for whom was entrusted to a **Neutral Nations Repatriation Commission**, a **Committee for Repatriation of Prisoners of War**, a **Committee for Assisting the Return of Displaced Civilians**, and joint Red Cross teams. (All were to be dissolved upon completion of their duties.)

The preamble to the armistice document had made clear its purely military nature. The final two articles emphasized again the need for a lasting political settlement of the Korean question, recommending (Article IV) that a high-level political conference attended by all sides be held within three months of signature and pointing out (Article V) that the terms of the armistice should remain in effect "until expressly superseded either by mutually acceptable amendments and additions or by provision in an appropriate agreement for a peaceful settlement at a political level between both sides."

The document, signed on 27 July 1953, was the outcome of protracted and often bitter negotiations that had been initiated two years before. After a year's fighting, the two sides—the UNC and the North Korean and Chinese commands—had ground to a stalemate and were ready to consider a Soviet proposal of 23 June 1951 for a cease-fire. The first talks opened on 10 July 1951 at **Kaesong**, within territory controlled by the North Koreans, but were suspended on 22 August 1951 after both sides had violated the area's neutrality. Negotiations resumed on 25 October 1951 at a site at P'anmunjom, just south of the Communist line of actual control and halfway between the two sides' headquarters at Kaesong (North Korea/China) and Munsan (UNC). From 8 October 1952 until 26 April 1953, full-scale talks were again broken off, but received new impetus, possibly as a result of the death of the Soviet leader **Joseph Stalin** on 5 March 1953. Nevertheless, discussions on the exchange of sick and wounded prisoners of war went on at liaison officer level during the

period of suspension; the exchange took place in Operation **Little Switch** between 20 April and 3 May 1953. Throughout the two years of negotiations, hostilities never ceased north and south of the **38th parallel**, and UNC bombing raids continued against North Korean targets, with the aim of wearing down the North's resistance.

The principal areas of negotiation were the demarcation of a cease-fire line and demilitarized zone, the formation and composition of bodies authorized to supervise the cease-fire and the entry of troops and weapons into Korea, the release and exchange of prisoners of war, and recommendations to be made to the governments concerned. A number of issues introduced by one side or the other were eliminated from the final agreement. The thorniest problem was that of the repatriation of prisoners of war. The UNC pressed for voluntary measures, whereby prisoners would have a choice over which state they would be repatriated to. The North Korean/Chinese side insisted on adherence to the provisions of the 1949 **Geneva Convention**, which stipulated speedy and compulsory repatriation to a prisoner's country of origin. The presence of prisoners among the North Korean troops cap-

This Giles cartoon entitled "Korea Armistice" originally appeared in the London paper Daily Express *on 28 July 1953. The caption reads, "Gently, Gently…." (Express Newspapers, London)*

tured by the UNC who were originally from South Korea but had voluntarily or involuntarily joined the NKPA and of former Nationalist Chinese troops among the Chinese soldiers captured encouraged the UNC to insist on voluntary repatriation. Eventually, after the United States had hinted at nuclear reprisals against China, the North Koreans and Chinese accepted the voluntary principle.

The South Korean president, **Syngman Rhee**, bitterly resisted the armistice on the grounds that it would render impossible the unification of the Korea Peninsula on his terms and would leave Chinese troops on Korean soil. South Korea had placed its armed forces under the UNC in 1950, so strictly could not be a party to the armistice, but Rhee in any case would not have agreed to it. He attempted to sabotage negotiations by ordering the release on 18 June 1953 of 27,000 North Korean detainees who had refused repatriation, but three weeks later undertook not to disrupt further the final agreement. North Korea has argued that it and the United States should alone discuss a permanent peace for the peninsula, and that the South is not entitled to a place in any further negotiations, a position that the United States resists.

The political discussions recommended by the authors of the armistice were held within the framework of the 1954 **Geneva Conference**, but achieved no settlement. The 1953 agreement still remains in effect and has governed much of the subsequent development of events in the Korea Peninsula.

See also: Cease-fire Proposals; Demilitarized Zone (DMZ); Dulles, John Foster; Geneva Conference (1954); Joint Observer Teams; Kaesong; Military Armistice Commission (MAC); Neutral Nations Inspection Teams; Neutral Nations Repatriation Commission; Neutral Nations Supervisory Commission; P'anmunjom; Prisoners of War; Repatriation of Prisoners of War; 38th and Other Parallels.

References: Bailey 1992; Foot 1990; Hermes 1966; Mattray 1991; Vatcher 1958.

ASSASSINATIONS AND ATTEMPTED ASSASSINATIONS

The use of assassination as a tool to eliminate rivals and troublesome individuals and to promote political aims has a long history in Korea. In the fifteenth century, at least two of the Choson Dynasty kings had competitors to the throne assassinated within their own families. Assassination has particularly characterized periods of instability, as in the last quarter of the nineteenth century, when domestic reform was on the agenda and China, Japan, and Russia maneuvered for control of Korea. In December 1884, a group of young reformers, eager to see conservative leaders removed, assassinated seven of them in an attempted coup d'état. Japanese support, which they had hoped to rely on, did not materialize, and the plot failed. In October 1895, Queen Min, wife of King Kojong, was murdered by disaffected Korean troops with the connivance of Japanese advisers. She had been thought to favor cooperation with Russia. Those who had supported Japan's maneuvers to control Korea came to be viewed as enemies of the Korean people. D. W. Stevens, an American adviser placed by the Japanese in the Korean Ministry of Foreign Affairs, was killed in 1908 in San Francisco by two Korean expatriates. The Japanese statesman Ito Hirobumi, who in 1905 helped to conclude the protectorate treaty, was shot in Harbin in Manchuria in October 1909 by An Chung-gun.

In the post-1945 era, assassination continued to be viewed as a means of removing opponents or resolving seemingly intolerable situations. The troubled years 1945–1948, when the peninsula swung toward division, were a time of intense infighting between right and left and between factions within these two wings. These years were marked by the killing of four political leaders: in September 1945, Hyon Chun-hyok, secretary of the North Korean Branch Bureau of the **Korean Communist Party**; in December 1945, Song Chin-u, a founder of the **Korean Democratic Party** (KDP); in July 1947, Yo Un-hyong, head of the 1945 **Korean People's Republic**; and in December 1947, Chang Tok-su, likewise a member of the KDP. Song and Chang had remained in Korea during the colonial period and been active within the moderate nationalist group.

During the three decades after 1948, politics in South Korea were still marred by assassinations and attempted killings. In June 1949, **Kim Ku**, leader of the **Korean Independence Party** and for a while collaborator with **Syngman Rhee**, was assassinated. (Kim's alleged killer was himself apparently assassinated in October 1996.) In June 1952 and again in October 1955, attempts were made on President Rhee's own life. In September 1956, an unsuccessful assassination attempt was directed against Chang Myon, then vice-president–elect of South Korea. In August 1973, during the **Park Chung Hee** era, the Korean Central Intelligence Agency (KCIA) was thwarted in an attempt to dispose of **Kim Dae Jung**, long-standing leader of the opposition, who in 1997 was elected president of South Korea. President Park's life was ended in October 1979 when he was shot by the then head of the KCIA.

An earlier attempt on Park's life had been made by Mun Se-kwang, a Korean living in Japan, where he was a member of a pro–North Korean residents' group. At a meeting on 15 August 1974 in Seoul attended by Park and his wife, Yuk Yong-su, Mun aimed at the president, but mortally wounded his wife. It was claimed afterward that he was acting on North Korean instructions. The incident sharpened South Korean apprehensions over **Japanese contacts with North Korea.**

The 1974 attempt, attributed to North Korean instigation, reflected the North's continuing use of assassination as part of a wider campaign of terror. It has aimed at the top, doubtless hoping, if successful, to throw government and society in the South into confusion and to spark popular support for political change. Its most daring attempt, which failed, was to send a team of commandos from the North into Seoul in January 1968 in a raid targeted on the **Blue House**, the presidential residence. The team was intercepted. Their prime aim was to assassinate President Park. Two and a half years later, in June 1970, two North Korean agents attempted to place explosives on the roof of the entrance gate to the National Cemetery in Seoul, where President Park was to attend a ceremony. That assassination bid also failed. Similar tactics, however, were employed to deadlier effect in the **Rangoon bombing** in October 1983, when a North Korean team concealed explosives at the Burmese national memorial, killing 17 South Korean officials. President **Chun Doo Hwan**, the chief target of the attack, escaped injury.

The secretive nature of North Korean politics makes it hard to know if assassination has been employed by the regime there as a means of control over its internal political opponents. Where elimination of such opponents has taken place, this has tended to be through show trials and judicial executions. It is impossible to judge whether South Korea has ever made assassination forays into the North. *See also:* North Korean Use of Terrorism.

ATTLEE, CLEMENT RICHARD (1883–1967)

Clement Richard Attlee, Britain's second Labour prime minister, and later Lord Attlee, was born in Putney, Surrey, in 1883. He was often known by the shorter version of his first name, as Clem Attlee. He was a social worker and served in World War I before entering politics. He became leader of the opposition Labour Party in 1935, and served as deputy prime minister in **Winston Churchill**'s World War II coalition government. Attlee became prime minister when Labour won the 1945 general election. Although the Labour Party was a socialist party, its leadership was strongly anti-Communist in outlook, and Britain did not recognize the Democratic People's Republic of Korea (North Korea) on its establishment in 1948. Diplomatic relations were established with the Republic of Korea (South Korea) early in 1949.

By the time of the outbreak of the **Korean War** in 1950, Attlee's ministerial team, reelected in February 1950, was old and tired. The government responded to U.S. requests for help in Korea with general support for the doctrine of collective security through the United Nations. To Attlee and his colleagues, especially the foreign secretary, Ernest Bevin, the Korean conflict was proof of Soviet worldwide aggressive policies. Although Britain already had extensive overseas military commitments, and his military advisers were reluctant to see these increase, Attlee agreed to send British naval and ground forces to Korea. He remained concerned, however, that the war should not spread and that the United States should not be distracted from what he thought were the main danger areas, Europe and the Middle East.

Following the Chinese intervention in November 1950, the Labour government became concerned at General **Douglas MacArthur**'s conduct of the war and at the apparent U.S. threat to use nuclear weapons in Korea. Attlee visited Washington to seek reassurances on these matters. Although the

U.S. response was less than satisfactory, Attlee presented the visit as a success. The debate over the Korean War and the economic consequences that it had for Britain led to splits in the Labour Party that lasted several years. Those splits were one factor in the defeat of the Labour government in the October 1951 general election. Attlee, who remained leader of the Labour Party until 1955, took no further direct interest in Korea, but in 1954 led a Labour Party delegation to the **People's Republic of China,** which helped to improve relations damaged by the Korean War.

References: Attlee 1961; Bullock 1983; Harris 1982; MacDonald 1990.

AUSTRALIAN FORCES IN THE KOREAN WAR

Almost as soon as the **Korean War** began in June 1950, the Australian government, then headed by Prime Minister Robert Menzies, came under strong U.S. pressure to contribute forces to the conflict. Although the first official Australian reaction to the news in Korea was to point to Australia's existing commitments, once the Australian Cabinet heard that Britain would contribute to support the UN in Korea, it did likewise. Australia became the first country after the United States to dispatch forces from all three services to Korea. The Royal Australian Navy sent a frigate and a destroyer to Korean waters on 29 June 1950, the Air Force sent No. 77 Fighter Squadron on 30 June, and on 26 July, an infantry battalion drawn from Australian occupation forces in Japan arrived in Korea.

Australian naval forces formed part of the general blockade of the North Korean coast. The blockade operated from late 1950 until the end of the war in July 1953. Australian air forces operated with the UN Command, No. 77 Squadron's World War II vintage propeller-drive Mustangs eventually being replaced by British-built Meteor-8 jets. These proved inferior to the U.S. F-86 Sabre jets, which subsequently became standard in Australian Air Force units, though long after the end of the Korean conflict. Australian ground forces formed part of the 28th Commonwealth Brigade, along with British and New Zealand forces, and in July 1951 were incorporated into the **First Commonwealth Division.** They took a major part in the fighting at **Kap'yong** in April 1951, and were later prominent in

fighting on the **Hook** from October 1952 until the end of the war in July 1953.

After the war ended, Australian forces remained in Korea, although in steadily reducing numbers, until April 1957, when the last eight Australian military personnel were withdrawn from Korea. At the same time, the Australian government announced its continued commitment to South Korea, but declined to restate the **Sixteen-Nation Declaration (1953).** Thereafter, although Australian naval ships occasionally visited South Korea, the only remaining element of Australia's military commitment was a liaison officer accredited to the Commonwealth Liaison Mission in **Seoul.** When Australia opened an embassy in Seoul in 1962, the newly appointed Australian defense attaché assumed this post, an arrangement that still continues.

At its height, Australian involvement in the Korean War had numbered more than 5,000 men, together with military equipment, two destroyers or frigates, one aircraft carrier, and a fighter squadron. Australian casualties were 261 killed, 1,034 wounded, and 37 missing or assumed to be **prisoners of war.**

See also: Australian Involvement in Korea; First Commonwealth Division in the Korean War; New Zealand Forces in the Korean War.

References: Barclay 1954; Grey 1988; McCormack 1983; O'Neill 1981, 1985; Rees 1964.

AUSTRALIAN INVOLVEMENT IN KOREA

Before World War II, Australian involvement in Korea was limited to the activities of an Australian Presbyterian mission operating in the south of the peninsula. Australian diplomatic, consular, and trade matters were otherwise handled by British officials. From 1947 onward, however, Australia's interests in Korea increased. Australia played a major role in the 1947 **United Nations Temporary Commission on Korea** and its successor, the 1948 **United Nations Commission on Korea.** As did most Western countries, Australia extended diplomatic recognition to the Republic of Korea following its establishment in 1948, although it was not until 1962 that Australia established an embassy in **Seoul.** During the **Korean War,** Australia sent forces from all three services, and this participation played an important part in the country's development of an independent foreign policy.

While maintaining relations with South Korea, Australia established diplomatic relations with North Korea in 1974, and the two countries exchanged embassies. However, the link was short-lived, being broken off in the autumn of 1975. Since then, although Australia has continued to recognize the North, it has rejected North Korean attempts to reestablish embassies.

See also: Australian Forces in the Korean War; Diplomatic Recognition; United Nations Commission for Unification and Rehabilitation of Korea (UNCURK).

References: Buzo 1981; McCormack 1983; O'Neill 1981, 1985.

AX MURDERS (1976)

The phrase "ax murders" commonly describes the confrontation on 18 August 1976 between members of the **United Nations Command** (UNC) Support Group and the **North Korean People's Army** (NKPA) over trimming a tree in the Joint Security Area (JSA) at **P'anmunjom**, which ended in the death of two U.S. Army officers. The immediate effect of the incident was to raise the level of alert both north and south of the **Demilitarized Zone**. Negotiations between the two sides defused the situation and resulted in the imposition of tighter control on movement within the JSA.

The focus of the incident was a poplar tree growing between two UNC posts in the area south of the Military Demarcation Line (MDL) within the JSA. In full leaf, the tree blocked the view between the two posts. Tree trimming was carried out routinely within the JSA. An earlier attempt to cut back the offending tree had brought an NKPA request to desist, but had not led to an immediate security officers' meeting, as was customary when potential disagreements arose. In view of the earlier warning, the UNC work team that set out on 18 August 1976 was accompanied by a UNC Support Group contingent, consisting of two U.S. Army officers, one South Korean officer, and eight other guards. The "on-scene" officer in command was instructed to seek an on-the-spot security officers' meeting if a confrontation arose.

The UNC workforce was soon joined by an NKPA group led by Lieutenant Pak Chul. Trimming began, but was halted when Pak requested the U.S. Army officer in charge, Captain Arthur Bonifas, to suspend work to allow the status of the tree to be discussed at a security officers' meeting. Bonifas refused. Lieutenant Pak sent for reinforcements. When they arrived, swelling the North Korean contingent to approximately thirty, Pak again demanded that work cease. On further refusal, he is reported to have shouted "Kill the Americans!" and then to have knocked Bonifas to the ground, where he was beaten to death by NKPA guards. The other U.S. Army officer, Lieutenant Mark Barrett, was also attacked and killed. The axes brought in to trim the tree were used during the attack. Injuries were reported sustained on both sides. The fight was over in four minutes, broken up when the UNC truck driver moved his vehicle forward above the body of Captain Bonifas to protect him from further attack.

A meeting of the **Military Armistice Commission** (MAC) on 6 September 1976 negotiated the removal of four NKPA observation posts from south of the MDL and clearer marking of the line itself within the JSA. Whereas both sides had previously had free access to the entire JSA, in recognition of its neutral status, after the ax murders it was decided that henceforth only MAC personnel or those from the **Neutral Nations Supervisory Commission** would be authorized to cross the MDL. NKPA guards, who had formerly entered the JSA by a common point of entry, no longer did so and entered from the northern side.

The poplar tree was cut down by UNC forces on 21 August 1976.

See also: Demilitarized Zone (DMZ); P'anmunjom.

References: Kirkbride 1984; 1985: 19, 60; 1994: 44–51.

BACTERIOLOGICAL AND CHEMICAL WARFARE

Accusations that the United States had used bacteriological and chemical weapons against the population of North Korea and **Northeast China** formed one of the bitterest controversies of the **Korean War**. For a year from February 1952, Soviet, Chinese, and North Korean leaders and media frequently repeated charges, first, that epidemics of contagious illnesses had broken out in areas occupied by troops of the **United Nations Command** (UNC) before they withdrew south in late 1950 and early 1951, and then that U.S. military aircraft and personnel, developing Japanese experiments of World War II, had dropped, first, poison gas, and then biologically toxic materials—infected insects and shells filled with bacteriological agents—over enemy territory. The Chinese premier, **Zhou Enlai**, in a broadcast of 8 March 1952, hinted that any captured U.S. Air Force personnel thought to have helped to spread disease over China would be treated as war criminals. Accounts by UNC **prisoners of war** (POWs) of their detention indicate that pressure was put on captured U.S. airmen to confess to participation in such activities. Statements made by a number of U.S. POWs were said to be confessions of the use of germ warfare. These confessions were refuted by the United States in April 1953.

Offers by the International Committee of the Red Cross and the World Health Organization to investigate claims of sickness in North Korea and China were not taken up. Instead, two other investigations were made in 1952 into the situation in those areas. The first was in March by a delegation from the International Association of Democratic Lawyers; the second, in August, by an International Scientific Commission. Both agreed that the case against the United States was clear. Whether true or false, the accusations played a large part in international criticism of the UNC, and the United States in particular, and were strongly promoted by journalists such as **Wilfrid Burchett** and **Alan Winnington**.

Neither at the time nor later was it possible to

B

determine the veracity of the charges against the United States of deploying chemical and biological warfare, but the charges were not new. Similar claims had been made in 1949 about U.S. use of such methods in Eastern Europe, but no evidence was ever produced. However, it appears that the United States had been pursuing research into both types of warfare since the end of World War II, if not before, and it is possible the U.S. military might have considered their use in Korea. There is, however, no clear evidence that they did use such methods. Later studies suggest that at that time the U.S. military may not have solved problems of the safe handling of toxic materials and their successful projection against an enemy. Epidemics of disease were recorded in North Korea during the war, which might have been a result of malnutrition, deprivation, and destruction of the infrastructure, as much as of deliberately spread infection. On the North Koreans' own admission, the germ warfare campaign proved ineffective. The truth will probably remain obscure.

See also: Propaganda Warfare.

References: Halliday and Cumings 1988; Hermes 1966; Kiernan 1986; Kim 1979; Lone and McCormack 1993; Macksey 1993.

BELFAST, HMS

See **United Kingdom and Korea.**

BELGIAN FORCES IN THE KOREAN WAR

Belgian troops, present in Korea from January 1951 to June 1955, incorporated at times a platoon of approximately 44 Luxembourg soldiers. Following the Belgian government's decision of 25 August 1950 to commit forces to Korea, a Belgian volunteer infantry battalion was raised, to which was added a

Luxembourg infantry platoon. When thus combined, the troops were known as the BELUX Battalion. This unit, under the command of Lieutenant-Colonel Albert Crahay, was attached variously to the U.S. 3rd Infantry Division and the British 29th Infantry Brigade, itself under the operational control of the U.S. division. The Belgian/BELUX Battalion's heaviest action was in April 1951 at the battle of the **Imjin River**, for which it received citations, and in October 1951 at Haktang-ni, north of Chorwon.

The battalion was disbanded in 1955. At peak strength, it numbered approximately 945 men. The three rifle companies were divided into French- and Flemish-speaking companies, with the Luxembourg platoon, when present, incorporated into a French-speaking company. During 1951, up to 100 Korean soldiers supplied by the Korean Service Corps were taken into the battalion, primarily as porters and stretcher-bearers. Eventually, some of these men moved into front-line military duties; others served as drivers and mechanics. In 1952, they numbered 250. Although paid and administered by the South Korean military, they could be promoted up to non-commissioned rank within the battalion, though with authority over only other Korean soldiers. Generally, each company had one Korean sergeant.

Altogether, 3,498 Belgian and 89 Luxembourg soldiers passed through the ranks of the battalion. Belgian casualties were 101 dead, 350 wounded, five missing in action, and one dead in captivity. One prisoner was repatriated in 1953. Luxembourgian deaths numbered two. Two Belgian nurses worked in Japan.

The Belgian government also supplied several DC-4 air transports to the Korean campaign.

See also: Imjin River, Battle of (1951); Korean Augmentation to the United States Army (KATUSA); Koreans Attached to the Commonwealth Forces (KATCOM).

References: Blair 1987; Crahay 1967; History: III, 1974 and VI, 1977; Summers 1990.

BIG SWITCH (1953)

Known as Big Switch, the final exchange of **prisoners of war** (POWs) between the **United Nations Command** (UNC) and the North Korean/Chinese side followed the signing of the **armistice** agreement on 27 July 1953. From 5 August to 6 September, a total of 88,596 POWs passed in convoys between the two sides at the exchange point at **P'anmunjom**: 70,183 North Koreans, who included 60,788 male POWs, 473 female POWs, 23 children, and 8,899 civilian internees; 5,640 Chinese POWs, including one female POW; and 12,773 UNC POWs, of whom the greater number were 7,862 Koreans returning to the South, and 3,597 U.S. POWs (all figures in Hermes 1966:514). Those refusing repatriation were turned over to the **Neutral Nations Repatriation Commission** on 23 September 1953 for a two-month period of explanation before making a final decision. Some 2,200 UNC POWs, it was thought, may have still been in North Korean and Chinese camps at the time of the armistice and not released. As in **Little Switch,** returning Communist POWs threw away the clothing, boots, and other goods they had been issued by the UNC before they were handed over, either in an attempt to maintain that they had been badly treated or to assert their contempt for their captors.

See also: Repatriation of Prisoners of War.
References: Farrar-Hockley 1954; Hermes 1966.

BLAKE, GEORGE (1922–)

George Blake was head of station, or chief, of the British Secret Intelligence Service (SIS) unit in **Seoul** at the time of the outbreak of the **Korean War** in June 1950. The SIS was tasked with monitoring developments in the Soviet maritime provinces and with reporting on North Korean activity should there be an invasion. Blake and his assistant, Norman Owen, decided to remain following the North Korean attack and were taken into captivity. Blake claims that while he was a prisoner he became convinced of the justice of socialism and offered his services to the Soviet Union. Released in April 1953, Blake returned to SIS work, but was arrested in 1961 and sentenced to 42 years' imprisonment for spying. In 1966, he escaped from London's Wormwood Scrubs prison and has lived in Moscow since then. His story has been the subject of a novel and television play in South Korea.

See also: Foreign Civilian Detainees in the Korean War.
Reference: Blake 1990.

BLOCKADE OF KOREAN COASTS

From the early autumn of 1950, an organized

United Nations (UN) blockade of the Korean coasts aimed at establishing control of the seas around the Korea Peninsula. In general, this task was undertaken by U.S. ships, but from time to time, other forces under the United Nations Command and South Korean naval units were also involved. The blockade was not only aimed at preventing supplies from reaching North Korea by sea, but was also designed to ensure that UN and South Korean access was kept open. Through bombardment and the use of carrier-based attack aircraft, as well as ship-launched commando raids, the blockading forces were able to strike at the North Korean and Chinese People's Volunteer troops behind the lines. In addition, these forces engaged in successful minesweeping operations around a number of Korean ports.

See also: Embargo.
References: Field 1962; Hallion 1986.

BLOODY AND HEARTBREAK RIDGES, BATTLES OF (1951)

Journalists termed the fierce fighting that took place during the summer and autumn of 1951 in the eastern-central area of the front, after the beginning of armistice discussions in July of that year, as the battles of Bloody and Heartbreak Ridges. The ridges were a series of jagged north-south hills. The tactical aim of the engagements was to keep up the fighting morale of United Nations Command (UNC) forces; to consolidate the UN hold on the area known as the Punchbowl, itself the center of heavy fighting in July and August 1951; and to drive the enemy away from the Hwachon Reservoir, which supplied the South Korean capital, Seoul, with drinking water and hydroelectric power. The strategic purpose was to put pressure on the Communists to engage in substantive negotiations in the armistice talks.

The U.S. 2nd Division seized Bloody Ridge after a heavy contest in August, driving North Korean forces back to Heartbreak Ridge. Realizing that the North Koreans and the Chinese People's Volunteers fighting with them had well-placed artillery, the U.S. 2nd Division began the attack on the North Korean forces. What they did not know, however, was that the enemy forces were strongly entrenched in the approaches to Heartbreak Ridge and could bring considerable firepower to bear. The U.S. forces were also unprepared for the new willingness to fight

shown by the North Korean forces, now re-formed after the defeats of late 1950 and early 1951. After two weeks of direct frontal assaults, the UNC switched tactics to concentrate on outflanking the North Korean–Chinese forces by taking the surrounding hills. At the same time, the UN forces made extensive use of artillery and air attacks. These tactics succeeded where the frontal assault had failed, and Heartbreak Ridge was finally taken on 13 October 1951. It remained in UNC hands throughout the remainder of the war, despite an attack by North Korean forces in November 1952.

The battle left the U.S. 2nd Division with some 3,700 casualties, while the supporting 23rd Regiment and its attached French battalion suffered approximately 1,800. North Korean and Chinese losses were also heavy, with estimates as high as 25,000 killed and wounded. The UN losses were regarded as a high cost for relatively little gain, and there were no more such direct assaults by the UNC. A film, Heartbreak Ridge, based on the fighting, appeared in 1986.

See also: French Forces in the Korean War; Punchbowl; United States Forces in the Korean War.
References: Bergot 1983; Hermes 1966; Matray 1991.

BLUE HOUSE

The presidential residence in Seoul, known since 1960 as the Blue House (Korean: Chongwa Dae) because of its blue roof tiles, is closely associated with the person of the president of the Republic of Korea. As such, it was the target of a North Korean army commando unit, which on 20 January 1968 reached a point 800 meters from the Blue House before being challenged. The 31-man team had crossed the Demilitarized Zone undetected. Its mission was to assassinate President Park Chung Hee. In ensuing gunfights, 30 of the unit were killed or missing. South Korean military and civilian losses were 68 killed and 66 wounded. In addition, three members of the U.S. armed forces were killed and three wounded.

See also: North Korean Use of Terrorism.
References: Bermudez 1988; Bolger 1991.

BOMB AND OTHER ATTACKS

Spectacular North Korean attacks used explosive devices against President Chun Doo Hwan and his party in the **Rangoon bombing** of 1983 and planted them on a Korean Air Lines plane in 1987. North Korean agents were said to have placed a time bomb in June 1970 in the gateway of the National Cemetery in **Seoul**, targeting President **Park Chung Hee** who was scheduled to visit there. The device exploded prematurely, killing one agent. Bomb attacks in 1968, on the Korean International Telecommunications Center, and in 1984, on the U.S. Cultural Center in **Taegu**, were also attributed to North Korean agents, as was a bomb explosion at Seoul Airport in September 1986, five days before the opening of the Asian Games in the capital.

In July 1974, a Korean Air Lines plane carrying 152 passengers came under North Korean antiaircraft fire from north of the **Han River** as it attempted an emergency landing at Seoul Airport.

See also: Korean Air Flight KA858 Bombing (1987); Rangoon Bombing (1983).

References: History: VI, 1977; Kirkbride 1994.

"BUG-OUTS"

Bug-outs was the pejorative term used in the U.S. Army, and taken up with enthusiasm by other soldiers in Korea, to describe unauthorized retreats of U.S. forces in the face of the enemy in the early phases of the **Korean War**. These retreats were a particularly acute problem in the early weeks of the fighting, when ill-prepared troops from the U.S. Eighth Army, whose previous experience was routine garrison duty in Japan, were hastily thrown into battle and found themselves facing a determined North Korean opponent. Not surprisingly, they often broke and ran. Although, when **United Nations** (UN) forces went on the offensive in September 1950, the problem seemed to have solved itself, it reemerged when the **Chinese People's Volunteers** entered the war in October 1950. After initially resisting the Chinese, many U.S. units fled south in disorganization, abandoning equipment as they went, in what became known as the "big bug-out." The main problem may have been poor standards of command, rather than any deficiencies among the enlisted men. Most U.S. forces, when forced to retreat, did so in orderly fashion. When General **Matthew Ridgway** assumed command of the Eighth Army in December 1950, he worked hard and successfully to restore discipline among his troops.

References: Appleman 1961; Ridgway 1967.

BURCHETT, WILFRID (1911–1983)

Wilfrid Burchett was an Australian journalist of radical views. He was not a member of any Communist party, but wrote consistently for left-wing publications. After extensive reporting assignments in Eastern Europe and the Pacific area, including reporting on the effects of the atomic bomb dropped on Hiroshima, Japan, on 6 August 1945, Burchett went to the **People's Republic of China** in 1951. From there, he asked his newspaper, the Paris-based *Ce Soir*, to let him cover the **armistice** talks that started at **Kaesong** on 10 July 1951 between the **United Nations Command** (UNC) and the North Korean/Chinese side. He was accredited to the Communist side, one of only two English-speaking correspondents attached to the Communists—the British journalist **Alan Winnington** was the other. The two men coauthored two pamphlets, *Koje Unscreened* (1953), describing conditions at the **Koje Island prisoner of war camp**, and *Plain Perfidy* (1954), which protested against the UNC handling of the processes for the **repatriation of prisoners of war**. Burchett also expressed his views on the Korean conflict in *This Monstrous War* (1952) and in several other books. Like Winnington, Burchett fell afoul of his government, which argued that he had participated in the interrogation and indoctrination of Australian **prisoners of war** (POWs). Official displeasure led to his being banned from Australia in 1954 and to a refusal to renew his Australian passport in 1956. From then until his passport was restored in 1972, he traveled on temporary papers issued by friendly governments. In 1974, he brought a case for defamation against a right-wing Australian parliamentarian who had accused him of being a Soviet agent; the hearing was inconclusive.

There is no doubt that Burchett met Australian, British, and U.S. POWs in the camps in North Korea, including U.S. airmen who had already made statements admitting implication in germ warfare, and that he questioned them about their stories, but it is not clear that he joined in interrogation of them. *Ce Soir* carried his reports alleging U.S. use of **bacteriological and chemical warfare** against North Korea and China. Burchett also reported on the devastating effects of U.S. bombing of North Korea. He pointed to UNC violations of the neutrality of the Kaesong truce site and claimed that the UNC was faking maps of its claims on the military demarcation line under discussion in the armistice talks. At Kaesong and later at **P'anmunjom**, he and Winnington received much clearer briefing from the North Korean/Chinese delegates on the progress of the talks than was provided to the correspondents accredited to the UNC team. As a result, these journalists frequently secured their information from Burchett and Winnington, despite General **Matthew Ridgway**'s attempts in February 1952 to forbid contacts between the UNC and Communist correspondents. The two men undertook to help secure for two major Western news agencies photographs of U.S. POWs in their camps and of General **William Dean** of the U.S. Army, captured at **Taejon** in August 1950. Burchett and Winnington's contribution to these exclusive news stories further irritated the UNC side.

See also: Armistice; Bacteriological and Chemical Warfare; Press Correspondents in the Korean War; Winnington, Alan.

References: Burchett 1952, 1968, 1969, 1981; Kiernan 1986; Knightley 1975; Lone and McCormack 1993; Winnington and Burchett 1953, 1954.

CAIRO CONFERENCE (1943)

The Cairo Conference was a two-part summit meeting held in Cairo, Egypt, in November 1943, in the course of World War II, between U.S. President **Franklin D. Roosevelt**, British Prime Minister **Winston Churchill,** and Chinese leader **Chiang Kaishek.** At its conclusion, the participants issued a statement on 1 December 1943, known as the Cairo Declaration, which laid down Allied war aims against Japan. It called for Japan's unconditional surrender and for Japan to give up all territory acquired since 1875. Regarding Korea, a Japanese colony since 1910, the declaration said that the "great powers, mindful of the enslavement of the Korean people, are determined that in due course Korea shall become free and independent." The Soviet leader, **Joseph Stalin,** did not attend the Cairo Conference, but at the Tehran Conference (also November 1943) agreed that Korea should be independent.

The terms of the Cairo Declaration were reaffirmed at the **Potsdam Conference** in 1945.
Reference: Foreign Relations 1961.

CAMERON, MARK JAMES WALTER (1911–1985)

The British journalist and writer James Cameron was sent by *Picture Post*, an illustrated British weekly magazine, in 1950 to cover the **Korean War.** He was accompanied by a photographer, Bert Hardy, who produced memorable pictures of the **Inch'on landing** (September 1950) and of the effects of attack and bombing on Korean citizens. Cameron and Hardy sent only three stories. The third one, which described in words and photographs the plight of political prisoners captured by the South Koreans, was judged too sensitive by the conservative proprietor of *Picture Post*, Edward Hulton, to be carried. The then editor of the magazine, Tom Hopkinson, protested and was sacked when he refused to resign. *Picture Post* then ran through a series of editors and was finally closed in 1957.

Cameron's indignation at the arbitrary and cruel treatment of the prisoners he saw in **Pusan** was echoed in the doubts and sometimes anger of other Western observers, who began to question the reasons for foreign involvement in the war.
See also: Press Correspondents in the Korean War.
References: Cameron 1967, 1974; Halliday and Cumings 1988: 70, 92, 98–99, 100, 102; Hopkinson 1970; Knightley 1975.

CANADIAN FORCES IN THE KOREAN WAR

Before the outbreak of the **Korean War** in June 1950, Canada had been involved since 1947 in the maneuvering on the Korean question at the **United Nations.** There was a Canadian representative on the **United Nations Temporary Commission on Korea,** for instance, although not on its successor, the **United Nations Commission on Korea.** For this reason, and on the grounds of the need for Western solidarity against Communist aggression, the United States called on Canada for support in Korea in June 1950. After initial hesitation because of domestic considerations, Canada contributed forces from all three services to the Korean War.

Royal Canadian Navy vessels arrived in Korean waters at the end of July 1950 and went into action when HMCS *Cayuga* bombarded Yosu on the **Pusan Perimeter** on 15 August 1950. Canadian vessels had escort duties at Inch'on and **Wonsan** in the autumn of 1950, but their most important role was in the evacuation from the North Korean port of Chinnamp'o during the retreat following the intervention of the **Chinese People's Volunteers** in October 1950.

The main contribution to the air combat, also beginning in July 1950, was provided by Royal Canadian Air Force (RCAF) No. 426 Transport

Local people greet troops from Princess Patricia's Canadian Light Infantry passing through a Korean village in early 1952. (Imperial War Museum MH 33052)

Squadron, under the operational control of the U.S. Military Air Transport Service. When the Canadians first arrived, they were thrown straight into the hectic struggle to supply the Pusan Perimeter, but by early 1951 the pattern settled down into a regular series of supply runs. The RCAF lost no aircraft or crew during their service in Korea. Besides the transport squadron, some 22 RCAF fighter pilots fought with U.S. units. One pilot was shot down, but was taken prisoner and repatriated at the end of the war.

Canadian ground forces, which included Princess Patricia's Canadian Light Infantry and Lord Strathcona's Horse, arrived in December 1950 and took a prominent role in the battles with the Chinese that marked the spring of 1951. These units formed part of the forces that held the Chinese along the **Imjin River** and at **Kap'yong** during that spring. Despite some initial reluctance, the 25th Canadian Brigade became part of the **First Commonwealth Division** on its formation in July 1951. There was concern in Canada when Canadian troops from this division were sent to handle riots at the **Koje Island prisoner of war camp** during May–June 1952 without any consultation with the Canadian government. The incident passed, but the government remained unhappy at the way its troops had been used.

A total of some 21,900 Canadian infantry served in Korea in the war. Canadian forces were at their peak, at just over 8,000, in January 1952, but more than 7,000 Canadians were still in Korea at the **armistice** in July 1953. More than 300 were killed or died of wounds, approximately 1,200 were wounded, and 32 became **prisoners of war**. The ground forces remained longer in Korea than the other units, but the last major infantry groups withdrew in April 1955. A last Canadian unit, a medical team, left Korea in June 1957.

See also: Inch'on Landing (1950); Namp'o; Pusan and the Pusan Perimeter.

References: Barclay 1954; Farrar-Hockley 1954; Grey 1988; History: II, 1973; Melady 1983; O'Neill 1981, 1985; Wood 1966.

CAPITOL BUILDING

In 1948, the Capitol Building in **Seoul** became a symbol of the Republic of Korea when President **Syngman Rhee** proclaimed the establishment of the new republic from its steps. During the **Korean War**, North Korean forces sacked it while retreating in September 1950 before the **United Nations** counterattack. It was used to mark the return of Seoul to the South Korean government after the recapture of the city in 1950.

Despite these associations, many Koreans had ambivalent feelings about the Capitol Building. Completed by the Japanese in 1926 in Western classical style, it served until 1945 as the seat of colonial administration and, as such, symbolized also Japanese dominance of Korea. Rhee refused to use it and left it derelict. After 1961, President **Park Chung Hee**'s government restored it as main government offices. Later used as the National Museum of Korea, it was demolished in 1996.

See also: Seoul.

CARTER, JAMES (JIMMY) EARL (1924–)

Jimmy Carter, president of the United States from 1977 to 1981, was born in Plains, Georgia, in 1924. After service in the U.S. Navy, Carter entered politics for the Democratic Party and served one term as president until he was decisively beaten in 1981 by the Republican Party candidate, Ronald Reagan. Carter began his presidency with a pledge to remove U.S. ground forces from the Korea Peninsula. He also disliked the authoritarian policies of South Korea's president, **Park Chung Hee,** and the South Korean government came under strong criticism for

Former U.S. president Jimmy Carter chats with North Korean leader Kim Il Sung, whom he met in North Korea in June 1994 for discussions on resolving problems arising from the North Korean nuclear program. (Pyongyang Times)

its human rights breaches. This new approach on the part of a U.S. president led to some praise from North Korea for his policies, and it was reported that North Korean President **Kim Il Sung** described Carter in 1977 as "a man of justice." However, after a visit to **Seoul** in June 1979, Carter was persuaded not to reduce troop levels in Korea, though his administration continued to criticize the South Korean record on human rights. In the last days of his presidency, Carter intervened to persuade Park's successor, **Chun Doo Hwan**, not to execute the dissident opposition leader, **Kim Dae Jung**. This approach was continued by Reagan.

After leaving the presidency, Carter continued to take an interest in Korea. In June 1994, at the height of the crisis between the United States and North Korea over the **North Korean nuclear program**, Carter accepted a long-standing invitation to visit **P'yongyang**. While there, he negotiated an agreement with Kim Il Sung whereby North Korea would halt its nuclear program and begin discussions on the matter with the United States. Although Kim Il Sung died the following month, Carter's agreement held, and the crisis passed.

See also: North Korean Nuclear Program; United States Military Presence in South Korea since 1953.

References: Cumings 1997; Oberdorfer 1997; Sigal 1998.

CASSELS, ARCHIBALD JAMES HACKETT
(1907–)

Major-General James Cassels was commander of the **First Commonwealth Division** in Korea. Cassels was born in 1907. He graduated from the British military academy in 1926 and served in India and in World War II. As commander of the 51st Highland Division during 1944–1945, he was the youngest divisional commander in the British army. He also gained experience working with Canadian forces. Later, he served in Palestine, and from 1950 to 1951 he was chief military liaison officer (defense attaché-equivalent) in Australia. When the First Commonwealth Division was formed in Korea in 1951, Major-General Cassels became its commander. His was not an easy task. He had to weld together different forces, taking account of the concerns of their governments, and had to get along with successive commanders of the U.S. First Corps, who often had very different ideas of how the war should

be conducted. Cassels introduced the **Koreans Attached to the Commonwealth Forces** (KATCOM) system. When he left in 1952, the division had become a cohesive force. After commands in Malaya and Germany, he was chief of the general staff from 1965 to 1968.

See also: Australian Forces in the Korean War; Canadian Forces in the Korean War; First Commonweath Division in the Korean War; Koreans Attached to the Commonwealth Forces (KATCOM).

References: Barclay 1954; Farrar-Hockley 1990, 1995; Grey 1988; McGibbon 1996; O'Neill 1981, 1985.

CEASE-FIRE PROPOSALS

Various attempts to secure a cease-fire in the **Korean War** preceded the **armistice** negotiations initiated between the **United Nations Command** (UNC) and the North Korean/Chinese command on 10 July 1951 and concluded on 27 July 1953. On three occasions, in July, August, and October 1950, Indian Prime Minister **Jawaharlal Nehru** and the Indian representative at the **United Nations** (UN), **Sir Benegal Narsing Rau**, proposed initiatives to defuse the situation in Korea. These culminated in the formation of a cease-fire committee composed of representatives from Iran, Canada, and India, with Arab-Asian backing. The committee, formed on 14 December 1950 by a majority vote of the UN General Assembly, was to investigate ways of securing a withdrawal of all non-Korean forces from the peninsula and ensuring a unified, independent state. Among proposals considered was a conference, to be attended by the United States, the Soviet Union, the **People's Republic of China** (PRC), and Britain, which would discuss issues beyond the immediate cessation of fighting. The committee's formal proposal on 13 January 1951 to the PRC was rejected by the Chinese premier, **Zhou Enlai**, who sought to link a cease-fire to the withdrawal of the United States from **Taiwan** and the seating of the PRC at the United Nations in place of Nationalist China. The cease-fire committee gave way at the end of January 1951 to a UN Good Offices Committee, formed of Iran, Mexico, and Sweden, tasked with exploring possible ways of achieving a cease-fire.

The first year of the Korean War was a time of movement in the peninsula. It seemed, first, to the UNC and then to the Communist command that military conquest might achieve political goals. Each side was eager to dominate on the basis of military and territorial strength and neither wished to be forced to negotiate from a position of weakness. Only when it became clear in the late spring of 1951 that neither side could hope for outright victory did the incentive for a cease-fire emerge. Rumors in May 1951 that the **Union of Soviet Socialist Republics** (USSR) might favor a cease-fire were clarified in a radio broadcast of 23 June 1951 by Jacob Malik, the permanent Soviet representative at the UN, who indicated that the USSR would support a withdrawal of troops from the **38th parallel.** This was followed up on 30 June by a broadcast on Radio Tokyo by the UNC commander-in-chief, General **Matthew Ridgway**, to his Communist counterpart, in which Ridgway expressed UNC willingness to negotiate, since he was informed that the Communist side might "wish a meeting to discuss an armistice." The answer accepting Ridgway's proposals came back on 1 July via Radio P'yongyang from **Kim Il Sung**, commander of the **North Korean People's Army**, and **Peng Dehuai**, commander of the **Chinese People's Volunteers.**

At the first contact, on 8 July 1951, Admiral **Charles Turner Joy**, representing the UNC, made it clear that only military matters would be discussed in the negotiations and that, until a cease-fire was concluded, hostilities would continue. Indeed, two more years of fighting followed, as each side tried to secure the most advantageous line of demarcation and acquire further stretches of territory.

See also: Armistice.

References: Farrar-Hockley 1995; Matray 1991; Schnabel 1972.

CENSORSHIP

In North Korea, all newspapers function as organs of party institutions, radio and television are managed as outlets for propaganda, and state-run publishing houses handle all book and periodical production. Media emphasis is placed on the promotion of official doctrine and support for state leaders and policies. Radio and television sets are said to be fixed to official channels, to prevent North Korean citizens from receiving any other broadcast or televised material.

Censorship in South Korea has never been so severe, but the determination to ensure that the official line prevails has led at times to repressive measures against the press, particularly in the initial stages of successive presidencies from **Syngman Rhee** to **Park Chung Hee** and **Chun Doo Hwan**. Newspapers and journals have been closed and journalists dismissed, as in 1948–1949, 1962, and 1980. Areas especially targeted are reproduction of North Korean material, favorable reports of the Northern regime, and criticism of the South Korean government. Only after **Roh Tae Woo**'s presidency of 1987 did government control of press and publication ease significantly.

See also: Korean Central News Agency (KCNA); Naewoe News Agency; Yonhap News Agency.

CENTRAL INTELLIGENCE AGENCY (UNITED STATES)

The Central Intelligence Agency (CIA) is the principal intelligence gathering and analysis agency of the U.S. government and also its principal counterintelligence agency. The CIA was created in 1947, but its origins lay in the World War II Office of Strategic Services. During the period immediately before the **Korean War**, CIA reports indicated that North Korea, with backing from the **Union of Soviet Socialist Republics** and the **People's Republic of China** (PRC), might attempt to unify the peninsula by force. Once the war began, CIA reporting and analysis concluded that, although any attempt to unify the peninsula after the landing at **Inch'on** might provoke the Chinese to intervene, this was unlikely. When the Chinese did intervene, the CIA maintained that it would be difficult for the United States to bring sufficient military or economic pressure on China to change its policies. This contradicted General **Douglas MacArthur**'s view that the United States should wage a direct war against the PRC.

See also: Willoughby, Charles A.

CHAEBOL

The large business conglomerates, or *chaebol,* of South Korea are a distinctive component of the economy. Many started out, and continue to operate, as family-run concerns. Some are international names—Hyundai, Samsung, Daewoo, LG (formerly Lucky Goldstar). Several have histories reaching back into the Japanese colonial era; Samsung, for instance, began in 1938 as a small export firm. During the rapid industrialization of the 1960s and 1970s, the *chaebol*, diversifying into manufacturing and trade, worked closely with successive governments to build up the South Korean economy.

The rivalry between North and South has partly taken the form of developing differing economic systems. The *chaebol* symbolize South Korea's commitment to a capitalist system, albeit under government control, in contrast to the centrally planned economy of the North. The *chaebol* have also contributed substantially to the Republic of Korea's economic success. At the same time, a number of *chaebol* have shown interest in developing links with North Korea. *Reference* Kang 1996.

CHANGJIN RESERVOIR (1950)

The Changjin Reservoir in northeastern Korea forms part of the elaborate hydroelectric schemes begun by the Japanese. It lies north of Hungnam, some 75 miles (121 kilometers) south of the **Yalu River.** To participants in the **Korean War,** it was generally known by its Japanese name, Chosin. During November–December 1950, it was the scene of a major fighting withdrawal by U.S. forces, including the U.S. 1st Marine Division and the 3rd and 7th Infantry Divisions, to Hungnam after the **Chinese People's Volunteers** had launched their second intervention. Although the U.S. units involved suffered heavy casualties and the action was technically a defeat, the withdrawal was conducted in a manner that contrasted so favorably with the "**bug-outs**" farther south that, like Dunkirk in World War II, it took on a heroic character.

The survivors, including British and South Korean forces, have formed their own veterans' organization, the Chosin Few, and there is a growing body of literature about the action.

References: Appleman 1987; "The Chinese Failure at Chosin" (World Wide Web site); Hammel 1994; Matray 1991; Montrose and Canzona 1957; Summers 1990.

CHEJU ISLAND

Cheju Island, the main island and a province of the Republic of Korea, lies off the south coast of the Korean mainland. Though often remote from the mainstream of Korean affairs, it was the scene of a major uprising against U.S. occupation forces in 1948 and, during the **Korean War**, of a revolt in October 1952 by Chinese **prisoners of war** (POWs) sent there after the May–June 1952 Koje Island incident.

The 1948 revolt was partly a backlash against the large number of right-wing groups that had moved onto the island the year before to combat leftist-leaning political organizations, particularly the Communist South Korean Workers' Party (established in 1946). On 3 April 1948, well-planned groups of armed guerrillas moved out from bases that they had established on Mount Halla, the extinct volcano that dominates Cheju, to attack police stations and other public buildings. There was already much dissatisfaction on the island over the U.S. occupation forces' decision to go ahead with separate South Korean elections on the basis of a **United Nations** (UN) resolution of 14 November 1947, and the guerrilla groups were able to exploit this to gather support.

The rebellion was to last over a year, well beyond the proclamation of the Republic of Korea in August 1948. At an early stage, the U.S. military governor of South Korea, General **William Dean**, visited the island and instructed that force should be kept to a minimum. However, the resulting secret talks between the South Korean Constabulary, the forerunner of the South Korean Army, and the guerrillas broke down as attacks on alleged leftists by right-wing groups and the police grew severer.

After faltering in the summer and early autumn of 1948, the rebellion was revived in October 1948 by the mutiny at **Yosu-Sunch'on** on the mainland among Constabulary forces waiting to be transferred to the island. (Among those involved was Major **Park Chung Hee**, later president.) This new phase of the fighting, marked by more effective organization among the guerrilla bands, which by then probably had closer links to North Korea, lasted well into 1949. But the newly established government of President **Syngman Rhee** was determined to reimpose control and, using the Yosu-Sunch'on events as a pretext for introducing the first **National Security Law** in November 1948, began a major drive against the rebels on Cheju. Massive numbers were arrested, villagers were brought into protective areas, and killing was widespread. By April 1949, the rebellion was over, though sporadic guerrilla fighting would continue on Cheju and in other parts of South Korea until the mid-1950s. The cost was high; estimates of the numbers killed on both sides range between 15,000 and 60,000, and there was massive destruction of property, especially in the rural areas. Only in May 1949, one year after the rest of the country, were the people of Cheju able to vote in the elections for representatives for the constituent assembly in **Seoul**.

In 1952, following the breakup of the North Korean–Chinese POW rebellion in **Koje Island prisoner of war camp** during May–June 1952, Chinese POWs seeking repatriation were moved to new camps on Cheju. There they continued to demonstrate against their detention, refused to obey UN forces' orders, and began a plot to kill the officer in command of the camp. When this was discovered, the POWs began a violent protest on 1 October 1952. UN troops entering the camps to restore order were attacked with stones, clubs, and spears. In the conflict, 51 prisoners were killed and 90 wounded, and a number of UN soldiers were also wounded. These events led to protests by the Communist negotiating teams at **P'anmunjom** that excessive force had been used unnecessarily. The protests were ignored.

See also: Yosu-Sunch'on Rebellion (1948).

References: Halliday and Cumings 1988; Merrill 1982, 1989.

CHEN KENG (1904–1961)

General Chen Keng was born in central China in 1904. He joined the Chinese Communist Party in 1922, studied at the Whampoa Military Academy during 1924–1925, and then spent some time in Moscow. Between 1937 and 1950, he was a successful field commander in the southwest, becoming commander of the Yunnan Military Region in 1950. In 1951, he went to Korea with **Deng Hua** as a deputy to **Peng Dehuai**, commander of the **Chinese People's Volunteers**. Although rarely mentioned during this period, he is known to have stayed in Korea until just after the **armistice** in 1953, when he returned to China. He then served as a member of the National Defense Council, became a four-star general in 1955, and was deputy chief-of-staff of the **People's Liberation Army**. He was also vice-minister for National Defense from 1959 until his death in 1961.

Reference: Klein and Clark 1971.

CHIANG KAI-SHEK (1887–1975)

Chiang Kai-shek was president of the Republic of China from 1926 to 1975, with occasional short gaps. Chiang Kai-shek is the Cantonese version of his name, which is romanized as Jiang Jieshi in pinyin and Chiang Chieh-shih in the older Wade-Giles system. He was born in China's Zhejiang Province in 1887. Following the fall of the Manchu Dynasty in 1911, he became a revolutionary leader, emerging in the 1920s as a close associate of Sun Yat-sen, the founder of the Republic of China. After Sun's death in 1925, Chiang became leader of the Guomindang, or Nationalist Party, and president of the Republic. In 1926, he began a campaign to unify China. At first allied with the Chinese Communist Party, he turned against it in 1927, and for the rest of his life he was firmly anti-Communist. During World War II, he was treated as one of the "Big Four" leaders, together with **Franklin D. Roosevelt**, **Winston Churchill**, and **Joseph Stalin**. Chiang made a bid for a Chinese role in postwar Korea, but this was disregarded by the others.

In 1949, having lost to the Chinese Communists in the civil war, which began in 1946, Chiang retreated to **Taiwan**, from where he claimed he would return to the mainland. However, in 1950 it seemed more likely that the Communists would take Taiwan, until the outbreak of the **Korean War** prompted U.S. President **Harry S Truman** to order the U.S. Seventh Fleet to patrol the Taiwan Strait to prevent an invasion of Taiwan. Chiang offered troops to serve in Korea, but the offer was not accepted. At the **armistice** in 1953, more than 14,000 Chinese prisoners refused repatriation to the **People's Republic of China** (PRC), preferring to go to Taiwan. One of the first actions of **Dwight D. Eisenhower** on becoming U.S. president in 1953 was to "unleash" Chiang to allow him to launch an attack on the Chinese mainland, but this never materialized. Until his death in 1975, Chiang maintained close relations with the South Korean governments of **Syngman Rhee** and **Park Chung Hee**, who shared his strong anti-communism, a policy continued by Chiang's successors until South Korea established diplomatic relations with the PRC in 1992.

See also: Cairo Conference (1943); Prisoners of War; Repatriation of Prisoners of War; United States Forces in the Korean War.

CHINA
See **People's Republic of China (PRC); Taiwan.**

CHINESE INVOLVEMENT IN KOREA
(1919–1948)
After the collapse of the March First Independence uprising of 1919 against Japanese colonial rule, many Korean Nationalists fled to China. In April 1919, a **Korean Provisional Government**, which survived with varying fortunes until 1945, was established in Shanghai. Korean exiles were scattered throughout China in Shanghai, Beijing, and Guangzhou (Canton), and in the north, west, and southwest of the country. They were also divided politically. Their differences reflected varying ideas on how best to end the foreign domination of their country, but also included various ideologies. Korean left-wing groups were already forming in China by 1919, alongside both moderate and extreme Nationalist groups. The left-right division was reflected in a similar ideological split emerging simultaneously in China, where the First United Front, a period of political and military cooperation between the Chinese Nationalist Party and the Chinese Communist Party (CCP), ended in 1927, when the Nationalists turned against the Communists. (The two sides formed a Second United Front in 1937 against Japanese aggression, but after Japan's defeat in 1945, they fought a civil war from 1946 that ended with a Communist victory in 1949.)

Relations between the various Korean groups and their Chinese hosts were always shifting and dependent on the fortunes of the latter. Each side, Korean and Chinese, sought to gain what advantage it could from alliance with the other. Attempts by Korean factions from left and right to achieve their own united front failed, and divisions remained. **Kim Ku**, who for a while maintained a close relationship with the Nationalist government that extended to military training for Koreans, pursued assassination and bombings against Japanese targets. The more moderate **Kim Kyu-shik** and Kim Won-bong formed the Korean National Revolutionary Party, and Kim Won-bong organized the Korean Volunteer Force (KVF). He too liaised with the Chinese Nationalists, whom he followed after they withdrew to Chongqing (Chungking) in western China in 1937.

In 1940, non-Communist Korean resistance activists joined in the Nationalists' war effort with the formation of the Korean Restoration Army.

In northern China, the CCP, based at Yan'an (Yenan) in Shaanxi Province, conducted its own military campaigns against the Japanese. In these, it had the support of Korean Communists such as **Mu Chong**. In 1941, Mu gained control of the KVF, which he reorganized the following year as the Korean Volunteer Army (KVA). Also in 1942, the North China Korean Independence League was formed from an earlier youth federation. The Korean Communists associated with the CCP became known as the Yan'an faction. After 1945, they joined CCP forces fighting the Nationalists in **Northeast China**, but were not permitted to bring their military arm, the KVA, with them on their return to North Korea after liberation. Their impact on the Korean political scene was consequently much reduced.

The Korean resistance movement in China was too scattered and too disunited to offer any serious confrontation to the Japanese occupation of Korea. Rather, the post-1945 divisions were already apparent within the movement, yet, ironically, none of the leaders it raised from right or left was ultimately able to direct postwar events in the peninsula.

See also: Chiang Kai-shek; Japanese Colonial Period in Korea (1910–1945); Left-Wing Political Factions.
References: Eckert 1990; Fairbank 1992; Scalapino and Lee 1972; Yang 1994.

CHINESE PEOPLE'S VOLUNTEERS
The Chinese forces that fought in the **Korean War** from October 1950 until the **armistice** of 27 July 1953 were not, in theory, made up of units of the **People's Liberation Army** (PLA), but were "volunteers" who had answered the North Korean appeal for assistance. There were indeed some volunteers, especially from among the Korean communities in **Northeast China**, but the reality was that most of the Chinese People's Volunteers (CPV) were PLA officers and men obeying orders to fight in Korea. The use of the term "volunteers" was designed to allow the government of the **People's Republic of China** (PRC) to present itself as not formally involved in Korea and to avoid direct confrontation between the United States and China.

The PRC's leaders were aware of plans by the North Korean leader **Kim Il Sung** to invade the South and appear to have given their approval, even though, with the Chinese civil war just ended, they would have preferred a period of peace to rebuild the economy and to consolidate their victory. Given the history of Korea, the PRC leaders were aware that conflict on the peninsula was likely to involve China, and in the spring of 1950 they began to plan accordingly. During May–June 1950, the 4th Field Army, under General Lin Biao, moved from the central south to its home base in the northeast of China, adjoining Korea. While this was perhaps a natural development, with the end of the civil war, and with similar regroupings to places of origin by other Chinese armies, it may also have been undertaken with Korea in mind. Yet the Chinese made no move as the North Korean forces swept south in June and July 1950, and Chinese reporting of the early stages of the war was low-key. When U.S. actions touched Chinese interests, however, China reacted with anger. Following the announcement by U.S. President **Harry S Truman** on 27 July 1950 that he was placing the U.S. Seventh Fleet in the Taiwan Strait, the Chinese premier, **Zhou Enlai**, formally condemned the move as a direct U.S. intervention in Chinese affairs which would not be ignored. From now on, the Chinese appear to have assumed that conflict with the United States was inevitable.

This growing Chinese belief was reflected in military planning. In mid-July 1950, the Central Military Commission of the Chinese Communist Party, the highest military body in the country, had issued instructions that a "Northeast Border Force" should be organized at Shenyang and Andong. This force would become the core of the CPV. When **United Nations** (UN) forces crossed the **38th parallel** after the amphibious landing at **Inch'on** in September 1950, the Chinese began to hint through Indian diplomatic channels that they would intervene. As the UN pushed further north in October, against a progressively disintegrating North Korean army, the hints increased but were ignored by UN Commander-in-Chief **Douglas MacArthur** and his advisers. MacArthur equally ignored intelligence reports that pointed to a Chinese military buildup close to the border with North Korea.

The Chinese were indeed not only hinting at action but also preparing for it. During October 1950, Chinese troops, organized into army groups and moving at night, began to cross the **Yalu River** into North Korea. By the end of the month, there were some 180,000 of them, under the command of a veteran PLA leader, **Peng Dehuai**. On 26 October, Chinese forces attacked South Korean units on the Yalu River and at other points below the border. A week later, the Chinese media made the first references to Chinese volunteers operating in Korea. The North Koreans announced on 7 November that Chinese volunteers had been in action since 25 October, and the Chinese Ministry of Foreign Affairs confirmed their presence in Korea on 11 November. At the same time, in China itself a campaign to "Resist America, Aid Korea" began in support of the volunteers. The campaign was used also to intensify controls on the population and to mount an attack on domestic opposition to Communist rule.

After inflicting a severe blow on UN forces, the Chinese drew back on 7 November. When, however, MacArthur launched the **Home for Christmas** offensive, designed to end the war, on 24 November, the Chinese hit back two days later along the entire front, in what became known as the first Chinese offensive. UN forces retreated in disarray, eventually regrouping south of the South Korean capital, **Seoul**, in January 1951. The UN counterattack drove the CPV back across the 38th parallel, and when the Chinese attacked again in April 1951, they were held. What proved to be the final Chinese offensive was launched against Seoul in June 1951. It failed, and negotiations began to end the conflict. The war settled down to a stalemate, although with periodic rounds of heavy fighting from the summer of 1951 until the armistice was signed two years later. Peng Dehuai signed on behalf of the CPV.

All units of the PLA were represented in Korea. CPV pilots flew MiG-15 jets against UN fighters, and Chinese artillery was used to devastating effect in the last engagement of the war in late June and early July 1953, but it was the ordinary infantry who were best known, establishing a reputation as tough fighters. In the early stages of their intervention, they fought with little in the way of supplies and with a motley collection of weapons acquired during the war against the Japanese and the Chinese civil war. However, despite frequent contemporary references to "Chinese hordes," with the implication of disorganized masses, they were always disciplined units, with a proper system of commands. As time passed, a regular system of rotation of forces was introduced, supply lines improved, and weapons became more standardized. It is estimated that as many as 700,000 Chinese were in Korea at the height of the fighting during May–June 1951 and that the figure may have reached 800,000 in summer 1952. The Chinese issued no official details of casualties, but a recent figure from a Chinese source (Yue 1998) of 360,000 casualties suggests that UN estimates at the end of the fighting of around 380,000 dead and wounded among the CPV may have not been too exaggerated.

The CPV remained in Korea until October 1958 and took a prominent part in North Korea's postwar reconstruction. CPV representatives continued to attend **Military Armistice Commission** (MAC) meetings until the outbreak of the Cultural Revolution in China in 1966, but resumed attendance in the 1970s. The CPV finally withdrew, at North Korean request, in September 1994. By that time, the Chinese had long since ceased to pretend that those attending the MAC meetings were anything but PLA officers.

See also: Chinese Involvement in Korea (1919–1948); Peng Dehuai; Repatriation of Prisoners of War; Taiwan.

References: Cold War International History Project Bulletin 1995/1996; Gittings 1967; Hao and Zhai 1990; Spurr 1988; Whiting 1960, reprinted 1968; Yue 1998.

CHIRI MOUNTAINS

A group of high, heavily wooded peaks, the Chiri Mountains lie at the southern tip of the Sobaek range, which runs in a northeasterly to southwesterly direction down the middle of the southern end of the peninsula. The Chiri Mountains, on the borders of South Kyongsang and North and South Cholla provinces, long kept a reputation for stubborn guerrilla activity, carrying on the Korean tradition whereby dissidents and outcasts take to the mountains for refuge.

The central-southern region of South Korea, as Cumings (1990) has shown, responded enthusiastically to the movement to establish **People's**

Committees. When these were disbanded toward the end of 1946 by the occupying **United States Army Military Government in Korea** and rightist organizations, discontent began to take hold and flared up again in the 1948 rebellions in **Cheju Island** and the Yosu-Sunch'on area. Many of those defeated in the **Yosu-Sunch'on Rebellion** fled to the nearby Chiri Mountains. By early 1949, the U.S. **Central Intelligence Agency** was placing the total number of guerrillas in the South (excluding Cheju) at between 3,500 and 6,000. These fighters operated principally out of mountainous areas such as the Chiri, which, remote from roads and railways, were less accessible to the National Police units sent to suppress them. There was little coordination between the various guerrilla groups and, despite claims to the contrary, little evidence of outside direction or arming. The guerrillas lived off what they could request or take from neighboring villages. Their main target was the police, who responded by clearing whole villages of their population, with the intention of depriving the fighters of their popular base.

This phase of the guerrilla movement in the South peaked in the summer of 1949. Thereafter, a vigorous police campaign conducted during the winter months of 1949 with the backing of U.S. counterinsurgency experts brought it under control. However, the North Korean occupation of the South from mid-June to mid-September 1950 encouraged those guerrilla fighters who remained to reemerge in support of the Communist invaders. North Korean soldiers subsequently trapped in the South as their units retreated north after the **Inch'on landing** swelled guerrilla ranks to an estimated 8,000. Throughout the early stages of the Korean War, guerrillas continued to harass **United Nations Command** (UNC) and South Korean forces behind the UNC lines, threatening transport, communications, and supplies. A further pacification campaign, termed Operation Ratkiller, was launched from early December 1951 to mid-March 1952, led in its first phase by General **Paik Sun-yup.** South Korean troops and police converged twice on the Chiri Mountains and succeeded in killing and capturing large numbers of guerrillas and bandits. Guerrilla activity, however, persisted in the mountains until 1955, well after the end of the war.

The Chiri Mountains, still a remote area, now form a national park.

See also: Cheju Island; T'aebaek Mountains; Yosu-Sunch'on Rebellion (1948).

References: Cumings 1990; Halliday and Cumings 1988; Hermes 1966; Merrill 1983.

CHO MAN-SHIK (1882–ca. 1950)

A moderate, Christian, nationalist leader from **P'yongyang**, Cho Man-shik was among the organizers of the March First 1919 uprising against Japanese colonial rule and was imprisoned for his role in that uprising. Cho graduated in 1913 from Waseda University in Japan, where he absorbed the teachings of the Indian nationalist leader M. K. Gandhi, who advocated tactics of nonviolence and noncooperation toward the British administration in India and policies of production and consumption of native goods. Cho aimed at a similar economic self-sufficiency in Korea, where the local manufacturing economy was threatened by strong Japanese competition. In 1920, he founded the Society for the Promotion of Korean (or Native) Production, which led in 1922 to the Korean Production Movement, launched with the hope of persuading Koreans to organize consumer cooperatives, buy Korean-produced goods, and reject imports. The intention was not to boycott Japanese goods, but to encourage a preference for Korean products and thereby to create a spiritual effect on national unity. The movement initially enjoyed support from Korean manufacturers, intellectuals, and popular and religious organizations, even though Korean-produced goods were sometimes more expensive than imported ones. The movement reached its peak in 1923, but lost impetus thereafter. The Japanese authorities responded with tariff restructuring and subsidies and concessions to Korean businessmen. These moves diluted enthusiasm for Cho's campaign. The movement was also targeted by left-wing critics, who claimed that it was bolstering Korean business and thus consolidating the hold of imperialism and Japanese capitalism in Korea. These critics further complained that the movement's leadership lay with a foreign-educated elite and offered no role to the masses. The movement, an initiative of the moderate, gradualist approach to Korean independence,

struggled until 1937, when all such organizations were ordered to disband.

During 1922–1923, Cho had also associated himself with another similar initiative, the abortive project for a national university for Korea. He remained in the country throughout the Japanese occupation, but with his reputation untarnished, and in August 1945 was invited by the Japanese to assist in the maintenance of order in the north after they withdrew. This he did and was named finance minister in the short-lived **Korean People's Republic**. He led the northern branch of the Committee for the Preparation of Korean Independence and in November 1945 founded the northern **Korean Democratic Party** (KDP). He fell from favor, however, with the Soviet occupation forces, who insisted, against his protests, on including an equal number of Communists in new political bodies. Matters came to a head when, during December 1945–January 1946, Cho voiced his opposition to the proposals for a **Joint Commission on Trusteeship** issuing from the **Moscow Agreement**. After a public confrontation with the Soviet command in January 1946, Cho was taken into protective custody, from which he never emerged, and his KDP followers fled south. Cho was soon denounced as a Japanese collaborator. He was still alive in June 1950, when he was offered in exchange for two Communists in South Korean custody. The deal fell through, however, and it is thought that he was executed shortly thereafter.

See also: Japanese Colonial Period in Korea (1910–1945); Nationalism.

References: Cumings 1981 and 1990; Lone and McCormack 1993; Robinson 1988; Scalapino and Lee 1972; Wells 1985.

CH'OE HYON (1907–1982)

Ch'oe Hyon's career from anti-Japanese guerrilla fighter in the northeast and other parts of China in the late 1930s to posts in the **North Korean People's Army** in the late 1940s, membership of the Politburo of the **Korean Workers' Party**, and positions as minister of communications (1958–1962) and minister for the People's Armed Forces (1972–1977) in the government of North Korea illustrated the advantages to be gained from a close relationship with the North Korean leader **Kim Il**

Sung. In common with other former guerrilla campaigners such as **Kim Ch'aek** and Ch'oe Yong-gon (1900–1976), who also attained high office in party, state, and government organs, Ch'oe Hyon joined forces with Kim Il Sung and, like him, withdrew into the Soviet Union during 1940–1941, returning with the Soviet army to Korea in 1945. His loyalty to Kim secured him a place in the party and military hierarchy throughout the rest of his career.
References: Scalapino and Lee 1972; Suh 1981.

CH'ONGCH'ON RIVER

The Ch'ongch'on River flows from its source in the west-central mountains of North Korea in a south-westerly direction to the Yellow Sea, which it enters at Shinanju. During the **Korean War**, it acted as a marker for troops under the **United Nations Command** (UNC) in their push north in October 1950 toward the **Yalu River**. The area north of the Ch'ongch'on was one of the first points at which UNC forces made initial contact with troops of the **Chinese People's Volunteers** on the first Chinese offensive in the peninsula; the lower reaches of the river were the scene of considerable fighting during October–November 1950. The Ch'ongch'on later served as a border in the air contest between UNC and North Korean fighter aircraft.
References: Blair 1987; Farrar-Hockley 1990, 1995; Schnabel 1972.

CHOSIN RESERVOIR

See **Changjin Reservoir** (1950).

CHUN DOO HWAN (1932–)

Chun Doo Hwan was president of South Korea from 1980 to 1987. He was born in 1932 in North Kyongsang Province, in what is now South Korea. In 1950, he enrolled in the **Taegu** Technical Middle School, but in 1951 transferred to the (South) Korean Military Academy (KMA). He graduated in 1955, among those who had completed the first full KMA course. He held various army appointments before becoming a member of **Park Chung Hee's** Supreme Council for National Reconstruction, set up after the 1961 military coup. Chun was then the personnel section chief of the newly formed Korean Central Intelligence Agency (KCIA), before becoming a battalion commander of the Capital Garrison

Command in 1967. Subsequent posts included that as commander of the 29th Regiment of Korean troops committed to the **Vietnam War** and as commander of the First Paratrooper Special Force in the early 1970s.

By 1979, Chun was commander of the Defense Security Command, in charge of army intelligence. In this role, he was tasked with investigating the assassination of President Park in October 1979. On 12 December 1979, Chun staged a coup d'état, arresting the Martial Law administrator, General Chung Sung-hwa, and seizing control of the armed forces. The following year, Chun made himself acting director of the KCIA and chairman of the Standing Committee for National Security Measures. In these capacities, he was responsible for the decision to send special forces in May 1980 to suppress the rebellion in **Kwangju** in the southwest of the country.

Following the resignation of President Choi Kyu Hah, who had succeeded President Park, Chun in turn became acting president in August 1980 and was duly elected president in February 1981 under a modified version of Park Chung Hee's **Yushin Constitution**. This limited the presidential term of office to seven years, and Chun made great play of his intention to step down after his single term. Chun was not a popular figure and had few achievements to his credit. He was blamed for the events in Kwangju and for his harsh suppression of former politicians and his hostility to the media, shown by drastic curbs on journalists and by the suppression or forced amalgamations of newspapers and radio and television companies. He also pursued a vendetta against the veteran opposition leaders **Kim Dae Jung** and **Kim Young Sam**. In addition, while Chun was himself seen as personally honest, members of his family, including his wife and his younger brother, were widely regarded as corrupt. During his period in office, he paid particular attention to foreign affairs and made a number of attempts to negotiate with North Korea, but with little success. He was the presumed target of the 1983 **Rangoon bombing** attack, seen as the work of North Korean agents, and which killed several of his closest advisers. Despite this, he accepted the North Korean offer of flood aid in 1984, though it was an initiative that in the end led nowhere. In domestic terms, his period in office

Former presidents Chun Doo Hwan and Roh Tae Woo, 26 August 1996, pictured at the opening of their trial in Seoul for mutiny and treason. Chun was sentenced to death and Roh received a lengthy prison sentence. Both men were later reprieved. (Korean Herald)

was marked by some relaxation of the tight restrictions that had prevailed under the Yushin Constitution, but he insisted that most important was his pledge to hand over power to his successor in 1987.

However, under growing opposition pressure, he agreed in April 1986 that there could be a debate on constitutional revision. When this had failed to produce results by April 1987, Chun announced that further debate was suspended and that the next presidential election, due at the end of the year, would be based on the arrangements laid down in the existing constitution. There followed much political unrest,

including, eventually, middle-class demonstrations, which attracted world attention. Faced with such bad publicity immediately preceding the 1988 Seoul Olympics, Chun's preferred successor, **Roh Tae Woo**, intervened in June 1987. Roh proposed a package of political reforms, including the direct election of the president. Chun accepted this package and the crisis was defused. When he duly stepped down, to be succeeded by Roh, in February 1988, Chun received little credit for this "first peaceful transfer of power." Indeed, so strong was the criticism of the corruption that had surrounded his presidency that he felt compelled to make a public apology, before retiring with his wife to self-imposed exile in a remote Buddhist monastery.

Following the election of former dissident Kim Young Sam as president in 1992, there were renewed calls for an investigation of Chun's presidency and, in particular, his role in the Kwangju incident. In 1993, former General Chung Sung-hwa brought a case of mutiny to the courts against both Chun and Roh. The prosecution agreed that the 1979 incident was a mutiny, but declined to take action. Popular protest continued, and in December 1995 both Chun and Roh were arrested. To the initial charges of bribery and corruption were soon added treason and mutiny. Both were convicted in 1996, with Chun sentenced to death and Roh to 22 years and six months' imprisonment, together with heavy fines. Both sentences were reduced on appeal (Chun to life and Roh to 17 years). Following the 1997 presidential election, President Kim Young Sam, with the approval of the incoming president, Kim Dae Jung, released both Chun and Roh from prison, though the heavy fines still stood.

Chun was much criticized by North Korea for his actions in 1979 and during his term in office. But although the North Koreans repeatedly called for his punishment, they may well have felt that the way in which a former president was treated on leaving office indicated that the North Korean elite might expect little mercy if the peninsula were to be unified on South Korean terms.

References: Clark 1988; Kim and Whan 1988.

CHUNG JU-YUNG (1915–)

One of South Korea's most prominent businessmen and the founder of the giant Hyundai group, Chung Ju-yung was born in 1915 in what is now North Korea. As well as having industrial interests, Chung was active in many other areas of South Korean life and stood, unsuccessfully, as a presidential candidate in 1992. From the beginning of President **Roh Tae Woo**'s *Nordpolitik,* Chung began to develop contacts with North Korea in the hope of extending Hyundai's operations into the North. He has long pursued a project to create a North-South tourist industry, and finally succeeded in organizing visits to the Diamond (Kumgang) Mountains in North Korea in 1998. In addition, in June and October 1998, following North Korea's continued appeal for

humanitarian assistance after three years of natural disasters, Chung succeeded in delivering two consignments each of 501 head of cattle to the North as aid through the **Demilitarized Zone** at **P'anmunjom**. Chung met **Kim Jong Il** during a visit to **P'yongyang** in October 1998.

CHURCHILL, SIR WINSTON LEONARD SPENCER (1874–1965)

Winston Churchill was twice British prime minister, from 1940 to 1945 during World War II and again from 1951 to 1955. He was born in 1874 into a long-established aristocratic family, although his mother was American, and Churchill always prided himself on his links with the United States. After a brief military career, he entered parliament in 1900 and remained a political figure for the rest of his life. While in opposition, he supported the decision by the Labour government of **Clement Attlee** to send British forces to Korea. As prime minister from October 1951, Churchill accepted that, since World War II, the United States was the leading Western power in Asia. Both he and his foreign secretary, Anthony Eden, were generally supportive of U.S. actions in Korea, though like Attlee, they preferred to see a limited war and were concerned that Korea would distract U.S. attention from Europe and the Middle East.

References: Farrar-Hockley 1990, 1995; Foot 1985; MacDonald 1990.

CIA

See **Central Intelligence Agency (United States)**.

CLARK, MARK WAYNE (1896–1984)

Mark Clark was born in New York in 1896. He graduated from the U.S. Military Academy at West Point in 1917 and saw service in France during the last months of World War I. In World War II, he was deputy commander-in-chief to General **Dwight D. Eisenhower** and later commander of U.S. forces in Italy. After the war, Clark commanded U.S. troops in Austria, where he became known for strong anti-Communist views. In 1950, he was appointed commander of the U.S. Army field forces and became responsible for training U.S. troops for duty in Korea. In that capacity, he visited the Korean front line in February 1951.

In May 1952, Clark became commander-in-chief, Far Eastern Command, and commander-in-chief of the **United Nations** forces in Korea, replacing General **Matthew Ridgway**. Clark arrived in the midst of such issues as the aftermath of the riots in **Koje Island prisoner of war camp**, and much of his time was taken up with political rather than military problems. The former included the protracted **armistice** negotiations and difficulties with South Korean President **Syngman Rhee**, who was bitterly opposed to anything short of the complete defeat of North Korea and the **Chinese People's Volunteers**. Although Clark's personal views were not unlike those of Rhee, Clark kept to his orders and was even prepared to overthrow Rhee if necessary. Operation Everready, however, proved unnecessary, and Clark signed the armistice agreement on 27 July 1953 in his capacity as commander-in-chief of the **United Nations Command**, claiming later that he did so with a heavy heart as the first U.S. soldier to end a war short of victory. These words, which come from his account of his time in Korea, *From the Danube to the Yalu*, feature prominently in the Museum of the Victorious Fatherland Liberation War in **P'yongyang** as evidence that the North Korean forces beat the United States in the war. Clark retired in October 1953 and for eleven years headed a military school in Charleston, South Carolina, becoming noted for his strongly expressed anti-Communist views and for arguing that Korea led to the **Vietnam War**.
Reference: Clark 1954.

COLOMBIAN FORCES IN THE KOREAN WAR

Colombia contributed an army infantry battalion and a frigate to the **United Nations Command**. The Batallón Colombia, 1,060 strong when it arrived in Korea on 15 June 1951, was attached first to the U.S. 24th Division and then in 1952 to the U.S. 7th Division for the Old Baldy and **Pork Chop Hill** Operations (1951–1953). A total of 4,314 men served in the battalion, which was rotated four times before it left Korea on 29 October 1954. Casualties were 131 dead, 448 wounded, and 69 missing in action, of whom 28 were repatriated. The battalion enjoyed a high reputation.

The *Almirante Padilla*, one of the three frigates composing the Colombian navy, arrived on 8 May

1951 for patrolling and convoy escort duties. It was rotated with the two other frigates in five tours of duty up to 11 October 1955. More than 1,000 naval officers and men served in Korea, with no casualties.
See also: Korean War (1950–1953).
References: History: III, 1974 and VI, 1977; Matray 1991; Summers 1990; Thomas 1986.

COMBINED FORCES COMMAND (REPUBLIC OF KOREA–UNITED STATES)

Established in November 1978, the Republic of Korea–United States Combined Forces Command brought together South Korean and U.S. forces under the control of the commander of U.S. forces in Korea, who is also the commander of the **United Nations Command** in Korea. A South Korean general was designated as deputy commander. In theory, this arrangement placed virtually all South Korean military forces under a U.S. commander, even though at the time of its introduction U.S. President **Jimmy Carter** had announced plans to withdraw all U.S. troops from Korea. The creation of the command has been heavily criticized by North Korea as an example of South Korea's subordination to the United States. In practice, U.S. control over South Korean forces has been limited. When the latter have felt the need to act without U.S. agreement, such as in December 1979, they have done so, and the United States has made no formal response.
See also: Chun Doo Hwan; Roh Tae Woo.

COMMITTEE FOR ASSISTING THE RETURN OF DISPLACED CIVILIANS

The Committee for Assisting the Return of Displaced Civilians, authorized in paragraph 59 of the **armistice** document signed on 27 July 1953, dealt specifically with the needs of civilians displaced during the **Korean War**. Two groups were identified. The first consisted of those who, on 24 June 1950, on the eve of the North's invasion of the South, had been resident on one side of the Military Demarcation Line (MDL) established by the armistice, had ended the war in territory under the military command of the opposing side, and on the conclusion of fighting wished to return home. The second comprised civilians of foreign nationality who, at the end of the war, likewise found themselves north or south of the MDL in territory controlled by either the **United Nations Command** or the North Korean/Chinese command and wished to return to the other side. The armistice called on the commander within each area to "permit and assist" civilian residents wanting to go home and foreign nationals who wished to return to territory under the military control of the other side and to publicize "widely" the provisions of paragraph 59. The civil authorities were also asked to give "necessary guidance and assistance" to both categories of civilians.

The Committee for Assisting the Return of Displaced Civilians consisted of four military officers, two drawn from each of the two military commands, and was under the general direction of the **Military Armistice Commission**. Its duties were to coordinate arrangements for the return of civilians and to provide practical assistance. It held its first meeting on 11 December 1953, reviewed applications for repatriation during January and February 1954, and had concluded its duties by 1 March 1954, after which it was disbanded.

The wording of the armistice agreement at this point was not directed at civilian internees, who were included in the arrangements for **prisoners of war** (POWs). The intention was clearly to help families and individuals, who had fled north or south, to return to their original homes. In the event (as Kim Choong Soon [1988: 99] has shown), Korean applications came only from the South. Of an initial 76 individuals who by 18 February had expressed a wish to return to the North, 37 were finally returned on 1 March, the remainder having changed their minds or been detected as North Korean spies. No Korean names were put forward by the North, which instead released 19 foreign nationals—eleven Turks and eight Russians. These two groups had been among those foreigners captured by the North Koreans in July 1950 when they invaded the South and subsequently held in camps in the far north. Some of the foreign detainees were released in April 1953 via China and the Soviet Union and the others thereafter. The Turkish group consisted almost entirely of one large family, many of them children; the Russians were in fact stateless and mainly elderly.

With the repatriation of POWs and civilians, the line dividing the peninsula was effectively sealed.

Any further movements of population thereafter had to be clandestine.

See also: Foreign Civilian Detainees in the Korean War; Korean Civilian Prisoners in the Korean War.
References: Hermes 1966; Kim Choong Soon 1988.

COMMITTEE FOR REPATRIATION OF PRISONERS OF WAR

The Committee for Repatriation of Prisoners of War, formed of equal numbers—three from each side—of military officers drawn from the **United Nations Command** (UNC) and the North Korean/Chinese command, was authorized in the **armistice** document of 27 July 1953 to supervise the actual handing over by both sides of their **prisoners of war** (POWs). Large numbers of POWs were involved—some 66,900 North Koreans and Chinese, and approximately 12,770 South Koreans and UNC troops. The committee was required to coordinate the arrival and reception of prisoners at **P'anmunjom**, the point of exchange; to supervise the work of joint Red Cross teams set up to minister to the needs of POWs; to arrange security; and to ensure that the process of exchange was completed within the time limit of 60 days stipulated in the armistice. The committee worked under the general direction of the **Military Armistice Commission**. Once its task was completed, it was disbanded.

See also: Repatriation of Prisoners of War.
Reference: Hermes 1966.

CONFUCIANISM

Korean society, particularly in the South, but also in the North, is often described as Confucian. South Korea is a secular, capitalist state, whereas North Korea remains one of the world's last Communist states; yet the two still share deeply rooted beliefs on how social and political life should be conducted that draw on a long tradition of Confucianist principles. Chief among these is the concept of social harmony, to be achieved through a proper understanding by all members of society of their relationship to each other. A hierarchical rather than an equal distribution of roles is accepted, epitomized in the relations between ruler and ruled, father and son, elder sibling and younger, husband and wife. In each relationship, the first named expects obedience from the second, but must in turn give protection and guidance. Only the last of the "five relation-ships," that between friends, suggests a level of equality, when it enjoins friends to be honest with each other. In principle, the needs of the individual in a Confucian society are subordinated to the common good.

Such beliefs have had an effect on the expectations of both rulers and ruled in Korea that has endured into the present century. Men such as **Syngman Rhee**, **Park Chung Hee**, and even **Chun Doo Hwan**, all presidents of South Korea, and President **Kim Il Sung** in the North, sought loyalty and obedience from those around them and from the population at large. Such a style of autocratic leadership did not encourage compromise with either domestic political opponents or the rival Korean state. Ultimately, South Korean leaders who were unable to quell political turbulence were removed. In the different political system of the North, Kim Il Sung outmaneuvered his opponents, while relying on a group of contemporaries who had fought alongside him from the 1930s to provide a base of loyal intimates. Kim, in return for national unity centered around himself, took seriously the task of guiding his people through a series of instructions on all aspects of their lives. His son, **Kim Jong Il**, is following the same path. Within the context of the Korea Peninsula, the willingness of leaders and governments of both North and South to exercise strong and pervasive control has probably intensified the general level of tension while denying either side the chance to take advantage of weakness in the other.

The teachings of the Chinese philosopher Confucius (551–479 B.C.) had entered Korea by the fourth century A.D. Respected alongside Buddhism for centuries and taken as the basis of the education of scholars and officials, Confucianism in a stricter form eventually ousted Buddhism from the late fourteenth century to provide the moral and organizational foundation of Korean government and society. Confucianist doctrines and practices have fallen away over the past century, but a bedrock of assumptions and attitudes has remained.

References: Howard, Pares, and English 1996; Yang 1994.

CPV

See **Chinese People's Volunteers.**

CROSS-RECOGNITION

Following the opening of North-South Korean contacts during 1971–1972 and South Korean president **Park Chung Hee**'s statement in June 1973 that South Korea would no longer break off diplomatic relations with countries that established relations with North Korea, the idea of mutual diplomatic cross-recognition of the two Koreas by their major supporters enjoyed some international support.

The idea seems to have been first developed by a U.S. official, Morton Abramovitz, in 1971. It was taken up by the then U.S. secretary of state, Henry Kissinger, and regularly reemerged during the 1970s and 1980s. Hungary's establishment of diplomatic relations with South Korea in 1989, followed by changes in Eastern European and Soviet attitudes, and China's decision to establish relations with South Korea in 1992, however, were not matched by progress in U.S. and Japanese negotiations with North Korea, which remained slight. While South Korea achieved its goal, the North failed to keep pace.

See also: Diplomatic Recognition; Red Cross North-South Talks.

References: Abramovitz 1971; Kim 1992.

CUMINGS, BRUCE GLEN (1943–)

U.S. academic Bruce Cumings is the foremost Western scholar on the origins of the **Korean War**. Born in 1943, Cumings spent a year as a Peace Corps volunteer in South Korea before completing his Ph.D. at Columbia in 1975. He has since held a series of academic posts. His writings on East Asia include a general history of Korea, *Korea's Place in the Sun* (1997), but he is best known for his two-volume *The Origins of the Korean War*. Volume I, "Liberation and the Emergence of Separate Regimes, 1945–47," appeared in 1981, and volume II, "The Roaring of the Cataract, 1947–50," appeared in 1990. These archive-based studies have aroused controversy, especially in South Korea, for Cumings challenges the view that the outbreak of the Korean War was solely a North Korean responsibility. Although new material from the former Soviet Union and China undermines some of his arguments, much remains valid, and the two volumes are essential reading for an understanding of Korea between 1945 and 1950.

References: Cumings 1981, 1990, 1992, 1997.

CURFEWS AND CIVIL DEFENSE MEASURES
The high level of fighting preparedness of the South Korean forces in the face of possible North Korean attack has been backed by civil defense measures. A wide-scale midnight to 4 A.M. curfew, imposed by the U.S. military administration in September 1945, was maintained by successive South Korean governments until January 1982 as a check on the movements of North Korean infiltrators. Night curfews between the same hours may still be imposed on a local basis. Since January 1972, regular daytime civil air raid defense drills have been held, at first monthly, but from 1993, only three times a year. Nighttime blackout drills are also held periodically.

The severity of North Korean terrorist attacks in the mid-1960s prompted the formation in April 1968 of a Homeland Reserve Force under army direction. The Civil Defense Law of September 1975 authorized the creation of a civil defense corps, charged primarily with air-raid defense and disaster rescue work, and of a students' national defense corps.

See also: North Korean People's Army (NKPA); North Korean Use of Terrorism; South Korean Armed Forces.

References: Bolger 1991; Kirkbride 1994.

CZECHOSLOVAKIA
See Neutral Nations Supervisory Commission.

D

DANISH INVOLVEMENT IN THE KOREAN WAR

Denmark sent no combatants to the Korean War, but between March 1951 and August 1953 the Danish Red Cross ship *Jutlandia* undertook three tours of duty in Korean waters. The 100-member medical team, working on the hospital ship or in medical units in the forward area, mainly treated **United Nations** (UN) troop casualties, but eventually also cared for civilians. The ship's ambulance helicopter assisted in evacuations, and the ship itself transported patients to hospitals in Japan.

The *Jutlandia*'s principal port was **Pusan**, but it often moved to other areas. In a first proposal for **armistice** discussions, broadcast on 30 June 1951 to the commander of the Communist forces, the UN commander-in-chief, General **Matthew Ridgway**, suggested "a Danish Hospital ship in Wonsan harbor" as the meeting place—a clear reference to the *Jutlandia*. The Communist side counterproposed with **Kaesong**, where the first talks took place.

References: History: III, 1974 and VI, 1977; Schnabel 1972.

DEAN, WILLIAM FRISCHE (1899–1981)

William Dean was born in Carlyle, Illinois, in 1899. He was commissioned in the U.S. Army in 1923. By 1941, he was a lieutenant-colonel, and by the end of World War II in 1945, he had become a major-general. In October 1947, he went to Korea as military governor of the U.S.-occupied southern half of Korea and deputy to Lieutenant-General **John Hodge**, commander of the U.S. occupation forces in Korea. Dean transferred to Japan in January 1949 and assumed command of the U.S. 24th Division in Kyushu in the south of Japan in October 1949. At the outbreak of the **Korean War** in June 1950, Dean's forces were the nearest U.S. troops available and were rushed to Korea to try to stop the North Korean advance. However, in the battle to hold **Taejon**, the troops, ill-prepared, lightly armed, and lacking experienced officers, proved no match for the North Korean forces. Dean took charge of the battle himself, but a forward thrust failed. He made a last attempt to hold the line, but eventually ordered his men to withdraw south on 20 July. In the confusion of the retreat, he was separated from his men and evaded capture until 25 August 1950. He was the highest ranked U.S. officer to fall into enemy hands in the course of the war. For most of the next three years, he was held in solitary confinement and treated no better than other **prisoners of war**. In his account of his captivity, he noted how ill-prepared he was to be taken prisoner. He was not released until 3 September 1953. He returned to the United States and was commander of the U.S. Sixth Army in San Francisco until he retired in 1955.

For his efforts to stop the North Korean advance, he was awarded the Medal of Honor in January 1951.

References: Dean 1954; Rees 1964.

DEFECTIONS

Ever since the **Korean War**, a flow of defections from the North to the South has been balanced by a smaller but persistent trickle of defections to the North, generally presented there as motivated by ideological principles (whatever the true reasons) and often explained away by the South as **abductions**. The South Korean Unification Ministry revealed in October 1998 that, from the end of the Korean War in 1953 up to that date, 923 North Koreans had defected to South Korea. Of those, 199 had died or emigrated. According to a 1994 government poll of defectors, some had not intended defection, but, as agents operating in the South, had surrendered to the authorities there or had been arrested and had subsequently changed allegiance. After a dip in numbers in the 1970s, the volume of defections rose again in the 1980s and 1990s, with 142 defectors arriving in 1996 and 1997 and a further 52 in the first ten months of 1998.

The majority of North Koreans defecting to the South have been young people in their twenties and thirties, generally arriving on their own. The ability to travel inside North Korea or to leave the country on work has almost certainly been an important factor in their decision to go. Such mobility has to some extent been determined by profession, and it is not surprising that of the group of defectors polled in 1994, soldiers constituted the largest section, followed by party and government officials, students, loggers, and technicians. Farmers and fishermen were frequent defectors in the 1960s, but apparently not since then. The 1994 poll revealed further that the capital, **P'yongyang**, was the point of departure for the greatest number of defectors (possibly reflecting the high proportion of party and government officials and students), and many of these defected by way of a third country (often in the course of official duties or study overseas). South Hwanghae Province, bordering on the **Han River** estuary and with a long coastline, produced the next largest group of defectors, many of whom left by sea or crossed the **Demilitarized Zone** (DMZ). Some, such as soldiers and journalists, whose duties took them right to the DMZ, swam across the Han estuary or even made a dash for the south at **P'anmunjom**. A direct route across the DMZ is still being used. In the 1960s, escape by foot or by sea was the most frequent means of defection. North P'yongan and North Hamgyong Provinces, lying at the western and eastern ends, respectively, of the Sino-Korean border, yielded another important group. As this border has become progressively porous in the 1990s, it has developed into the more common route of escape from North Korea into China or Russia. Some defectors may spend a period of years in China before reaching South Korea.

Public announcements, particularly of early defections, spoke of ideological choice and commitment to the free world, but there has generally been a material or personal aspect to the decision to defect. The 1994 poll indicated that one-quarter of those questioned may have defected for political or ideological reasons; the rest, because of social and personal problems. One category of potential defectors, North Korean air pilots, was openly encouraged in April 1953 by General **Mark Clark**, commander-in-chief, **United Nations Command**, who used propaganda leaflets to offer a reward of $100,000 and political asylum to the first North Korean pilot to deliver to the South an undamaged MiG-15 plane (the Soviet-designed fighter aircraft used by the Chinese and North Koreans), and $50,000 and political asylum to succeeding pilots who defected with their military planes. The first reward was claimed in September 1953 by No Kum-sok, who was followed by several other North Korean pilots. Financial rewards on a sliding scale and resettlement grants have been offered to all defectors accepted by South Korea. Military equipment has commanded the highest rate. Another pilot, Yi Ung-pyong, who in 1983 brought his MiG-19 to the South, received one billion won (then roughly $1.25 million). **Hwang Jang-yop**, a former high-ranking official in the **Korean Workers' Party** of North Korea, who defected in February 1997, received 247 million won (then worth about $275,000), of which 100 million was in recognition of the information that he had brought with him on the North.

Some "defections" are involuntary, as when North Korean soldiers drift into South Korean waters; these men are repatriated. On occasion, through an elaborate ploy, North Korea has managed to pass off as a defection an agent into the South. The most spectacular case was that of Yi Su-gun, deputy head of the (North) **Korean Central News Agency**, who in March 1967 made a "dash for freedom" at P'anmunjom, where he had been covering a meeting of the **Military Armistice Commission**. (He was eventually detected and executed.) Defectors arriving now in South Korea may be sequestered and questioned closely by the security services in an attempt to establish their authenticity, and may be kept under surveillance.

The pattern of defections from North Korea since the mid-1990s has changed, with occasional large family groups, including elderly members, small children, and pregnant women, arriving in the South in addition to the customary young single people. Some of these families escaped by boat from China or North Korea, aided financially by family members living outside the North who were able to meet them in China. Fears of an influx have already been expressed in South Korea. With an eye to the integration of defectors, the South Korean government in July 1997 introduced a new act that spoke for the first time of "escapees" rather than "defectors"; reduced the former two-year mandatory period of residence in a resettlement center to one year, with emphasis on job training and adjustment to life in the South; sought to discourage new arrivals from congregating in **Seoul**; and cut the scale of resettlement payments and rewards. The construction of two new resettlement centers is planned. The new act commits the South Korean government to accepting those who have attempted to enter the South at personal risk, as, for instance, by sea; but it is clear that those who apply to enter South Korea from a third country face selection. In mid-1997, an estimated 1,500 North Korean defectors were in third countries, of whom 500 may have applied to enter the South.

Defectors from North Korea since the mid-1990s have included several high-ranking party, government, and military officials. Hwang Jang-yop's defection in Beijing in February 1997 was followed by that of two North Korean diplomats, the brothers Jang Sung-gil, ambassador to Cairo, and Jang Sung-ho, head of the North Korean trade mission in Paris, who both left their posts in August 1997 to seek asylum in the United States. Hwang and the Jang brothers have been debriefed by both U.S. and South Korean security services. Although such defections represent a triumph for the South, they pose problems for it in its negotiations with the North and in its dealings with third countries. Defectors are now providing information on South Koreans abducted by the North, or who have defected to North Korea.

Defection may bring momentary relief, but the general understanding is that, in both North and South, defectors are only moderately successful at establishing themselves in the new society. Those in the South may find it difficult to secure work and social contacts. Some of those in the North, it is reported, face interrogation and may ultimately face detention in a prison camp.

See also Demilitarized Zone (DMZ); Hwang Jang-yop; P'anmunjom.

References: History: VI, 1977; Kirkbride 1994; *Newsreview,* 7 January 1995, 1 February 1997, 17 May 1997, 7 and 21 June 1997, 30 August 1997, 20 September 1997, 4 and 11 October 1997, 24 October 1998, 7 November 1998, 6 February 1999; Yi 1973.

DEMILITARIZED ZONE (DMZ)

The Demilitarized Zone is a strip of land, cutting across the entire width of the Korea Peninsula, which separates the two states to its north and south and their respective armies. The DMZ does not follow the **38th parallel**, but instead the line of actual control at the end of the fighting in 1953. It runs northeast from the **Han River** estuary in the west, slicing the 38th parallel 25 miles (40 kilometers) north of Seoul, and then continuing in an easterly direction before turning northeast again to end at the East Sea. It stretches 151 miles (240 kilometers) on land, with an additional 40 miles (60 kilometers) in the Han River estuary. It is 2.5 miles (4 kilometers) wide, extending 1.2 miles (2 kilometers) on each side of the Military Demarcation Line (MDL) running along the middle. This line forms the boundary between the two Koreas and is indicated by 1,291 yellow signs marked in Korean and English on one side, Korean and Chinese on the other.

The DMZ was established under the first article of the 1953 **armistice** agreement. Both sides had accorded high priority to the creation of such a zone as a basic condition for the cessation of hostilities. The armistice agreement requires that the movement of soldiers, police, and civilians into the zone, and the introduction of weapons and the construction of military installations, be tightly controlled. Nonetheless, each side has built military facilities and, at times, has brought what the other side considers excessive armaments into the zone. A number of defensive barriers, such as mine fields, barbed-wire entanglements, and antitank walls, have been erected within the zone. A further defensive line, the Civilian Control Line, has been constructed south of the zone in South Korean territory; and it must be assumed that the northern perimeter of the DMZ is reinforced by a further tightly controlled corridor on the North Korean side. Responsibility for the security of the DMZ was at one time shared between U.S. Army troops and South Korean forces, but, since October 1991, has been solely in the hands of South Korean forces. The zone is constantly patrolled and has never ceased to be tense along its length, with clashes, sometimes fatal, occurring at intervals between personnel of the two sides. The **United Nations Command** (UNC) through the **Military Armistice**

Commission has charged the North with numerous armed intrusions into the southern half of the DMZ and sometimes even south of the zone into South Korean territory. The volume of North Korean violations was particularly high between 1968 and 1970. North Korea in turn has complained to the UNC that its military personnel have at times penetrated into the northern half of the DMZ. In December 1979, a UNC three-man patrol, confused by foggy conditions, crossed north over the MDL. The U.S. soldier leading the patrol was killed by North Korean guards. By contrast, two residents of the village in the southern half of the zone (see below) who strayed across the MDL in October 1997 were released after four days' detention.

The large number of land mines, estimated at around one million, laid since the Korean War within the DMZ and between the DMZ and the Civilian Control Line south of it, have caused death or injury to both soldiers and civilians. In the period 1992–September 1998, according to South Korean sources, 41 servicemen and civilians were killed by mines, and 46 were injured. In September 1997, the U.S. government gave, as one of its reasons for refusing to sign an international treaty banning the production and use of antipersonnel mines, its desire to continue using such devices for a further nine years in the DMZ. The South Korean government backed the U.S. position, claiming the "unique situation" in the Korea Peninsula as reason for perpetuating the use of land mines in the DMZ.

The South Korean government has announced the existence of four tunnels that it claims have been dug beneath the DMZ from the northern side for purposes of infiltration. The first tunnel, discovered in November 1974, is near P'anmunjom; the second, located in March 1975, is in the middle section of the DMZ; the third, discovered in October 1978, is northeast of P'anmunjom; a fourth was identified in the eastern sector of the DMZ in March 1990. The South Korean government has claimed that electronic sensing equipment has indicated the existence of further excavations beneath the DMZ, and reports emerge from time to time that further tunnels have been discovered. The North Korean government, in rebutting such claims, has described the tunnels as old mine workings.

Despite the tense atmosphere in the zone, partic-ularly around the Joint Security Area at P'anmunjom, the area forms a kind of wildlife reserve, since shooting is prohibited. Deer and Manchurian cranes are found there and pheasants peck unconcernedly around the visitors' area. Civilian activity is not barred. In the southern section of the zone, the village of Taesongdong still exists, though under restrictions, and farmers work the land. Farmers are permitted a larger acreage there than further south. Kijongdong, a village in the northern half, is judged to exist for propaganda purposes only and appears to be uninhabited. It flies a massive flag and broadcasts loudspeaker messages to the soldiers in the South. The value of the DMZ for propaganda is not overlooked by either side. Escorted visitors are permitted to travel through it to the Joint Security Area. On the south side, the tunnel near P'anmunjom is open for visits.

See also: North Korean Use of Terrorism; North-South Boundaries; P'anmunjom.

References: Bolger 1991; History: VI, 1977; Kirkbride 1985, 1994.

DEMOCRATIC PEOPLE'S REPUBLIC OF KOREA (DPRK) (NORTH KOREA)

See Introduction.

DENG HUA (1910–1980)

Deng Hua was a senior member of the Chinese military. He was born in 1910 in Henan Province and joined the Chinese Communist Party in the 1920s. In 1945, he was in Manchuria (Northeast China). From 1949 to 1951, he was commander of the Guangzhou (Canton) city garrison, leading the attack on Hainan Island in April 1950. His association with the 4th Field Army probably led to his assignment to Korea in 1951. He took part in the initial armistice talks at Kaesong in July 1951 and, in October 1951, became one of Peng Dehuai's deputy commanders. Deng was briefly commander of the Chinese People's Volunteers, during September–October 1954, then returned to China. He became a colonel-general in 1955 and then commanded the Shenyang Military Region until November 1959. In May 1960, he became vice-governor of Sichuan Province. This was a downgrading and was probably the result of his links with Peng, disgraced in 1959. Deng disappeared during the

Cultural Revolution and never again achieved prominence before his death in 1980.
Reference: Klein and Clark 1971.

DIPLOMATIC RECOGNITION

With the creation of two separate states on the Korea Peninsula in 1948, it was understandable that they came to compete for international diplomatic recognition. Initially, there was a clear-cut division. The **Union of Soviet Socialist Republics** (USSR) and its allies in Eastern Europe established relations immediately with North Korea, and in 1949 the **People's Republic of China** did so. On the other side, the United States and its allies and supporters recognized South Korea, although few had diplomatic missions in Seoul.

These positions changed little during most of the 1950s. However, as former colonies became independent from about 1957, the two Koreas began a contest for international recognition. In South Korea, the government operated what was known as the Hallstein Doctrine, after a similar policy of the West German government on recognition of East Germany. This meant that South Korea would break off relations with governments that established relations with North Korea and would not establish relations with governments that recognized the North. This worked well for many years. Although North Korea made some gains among newly independent countries, by 1965 it had diplomatic relations with only some 24 countries, whereas South Korea's total was 64. Because of the Hallstein Doctrine, no country recognized both.

In 1972, following the North-South dialogue, the South Korean government announced that it would no longer refuse to have relations with countries that also recognized the North. Chile, which recognized North Korea in June 1972, was the first country to act on this; the South quickly announced that this would not affect South Korean–Chilean relations. With the abolition of the **United Nations Commission for Unification and Rehabilitation of Korea** in 1973, and the statement by South Korean President **Park Chung Hee** that the South would no longer oppose diplomatic relations with the North, a change began, but it was not sudden. As late as March 1973, some 86 countries recognized South Korea only, 47 recognized the North, and 14 recog-

nized both. By March 1974, the numbers were South Korea, 91; North Korea, 63; and both, 32. In December 1976, the figures were South Korea, 94; North Korea, 90; and both, 46.

That was a high point for both North and South Korea. Each had put considerable resources into the pursuit of diplomatic recognition, and the continued effort was expensive and not very rewarding. Still the contest did not disappear. North Korea opened a number of posts linked to international organizations in the 1980s and 1990s as a means of getting around the refusal of some countries to establish relations. A delegation attached to the International Maritime Organization functioned in London from the early 1990s, for example, and there were similar groups in Paris and Rome. From the late 1980s, beginning with Hungary, South Korea steadily expanded its links with the former socialist supporters of North Korea. By then, the effort for the North Koreans in maintaining diplomatic posts was proving difficult as their economy began to falter. From the late 1970s, there were regular reports of North Korean diplomats being caught trafficking in duty-free alcohol, drugs, counterfeit currency, and tobacco to finance their diplomatic posts, which did little to enhance the North's image. By the late 1990s, therefore, the South seemed to have won the diplomatic contest.

See also: Australian Involvement in Korea; Cross-recognition.
References: Hoare 1997; Middleton 1997.

DMZ
See **Demilitarized Zone (DMZ)**.

DPRK
See Introduction.

DULLES, JOHN FOSTER (1888–1959)

John Foster Dulles was a U.S. secretary of state who established a reputation as a formidable negotiator and staunch anti-Communist. Dulles was born in Washington, D.C., and counted two earlier secretaries of state, John Watson Foster and Robert Lansing, among his ancestors. Trained as a lawyer, he also took an early interest in diplomatic affairs and served as legal counsel to the U.S. delegation at the 1919 Peace Conference in Paris. In World War II, he assisted in the drafting of the **United Nations** (UN) charter.

Dulles's connection with Korea began in 1948, when he helped draft the UN General Assembly's resolution of 12 December 1948 on Korea. Appointed a State Department adviser by President **Harry S Truman**, Dulles was given responsibility for drawing up the Japanese Peace Treaty signed at San Francisco in 1951 and that took effect in April 1952. One of the arguments that Dulles used for the speedy conclusion of the treaty was the need for Japan to take on more responsibility for its own defense, as occupation troops were increasingly needed for Korea.

In the course of his negotiations over the Japanese treaty, Dulles visited Korea in June 1950. During his stay, he addressed the National Assembly, describing South Korea as "in the front line of freedom," and visited the **38th parallel**. Ever since, the North Koreans have used these two events, and a picture of Dulles on the 38th parallel, as "proof" of U.S. complicity in the outbreak of the **Korean War**.

Dulles had been a supporter of the Truman administration's approach to the Korean War, but steadily became more critical as time passed.

Appointed secretary of state in the Eisenhower administration in 1952, Dulles showed determination in wanting an end to the war and seems to have considered using nuclear weapons if the **armistice** negotiations failed to produce results. Whatever his intentions, the armistice was concluded in July 1953. Dulles had also to contend with South Korean President **Syngman Rhee**'s opposition to the armistice, and the U.S. Mutual Defense Treaty with the Republic of Korea (South Korea) of October 1953 was one means of reassuring Rhee of continued U.S. support for him.

Dulles continued as U.S. secretary of state until April 1959, dying in May of that year. During the latter part of his career, he adopted an increasingly anti-Communist stand, a position that tended to improve his reputation in South Korea and convince the North Koreans that he had been involved in planning the Korean War and that he, and the United States, were determined enemies.

See also: Paris Conference and Versailles Peace Treaty (1919); United Nations General Assembly Resolutions on Korea.

References: Foot 1985; Kolko and Kolko 1972; Stueck 1995.

EIGHTH ARMY

See United States Forces in the Korean War.

EISENHOWER, DWIGHT DAVID (1890–1969)

Dwight David Eisenhower was president of the United States during the later stages of the **Korean War**. Eisenhower, known as "Ike," was born in Texas in 1890. His distinguished military career began in 1915 and included his role as supreme commander of the Allied Expeditionary Force that invaded France on 6 June 1944 and a period as chief-of-staff from November 1945 to May 1948. In 1950, he was appointed supreme commander of the newly formed North Atlantic Treaty Organization. He retired from the U.S. Army in June 1952 as a five-star general and ran as the Republican Party candidate in the 1952 presidential election and won. Soon after his inauguration, he visited Korea, and thereafter, he and his secretary of state, **John Foster Dulles**, worked hard, even threatening to use nuclear weapons, to bring pressure on the Communist forces to conclude a truce, which was finally achieved in July 1953. Eisenhower died in Washington, D.C., in 1969.

References: Foot 1985; Rees 1964.

EMBARGO

From the outset of the **Korean War**, the United States imposed a trade embargo on North Korea and the **People's Republic of China** (PRC). By the end of 1950, the U.S. government had stopped U.S. companies from supplying oil to North Korea and the PRC, had stopped U.S. ships and aircraft from visiting ports in the PRC, had banned U.S. exports to the PRC, and had seized all PRC assets in the United States. It lobbied in the **United Nations** (UN) and among its allies for an embargo on all exports to North Korea and for a limited embargo on supplies of strategic materials—oil, arms and ammunition, items of transport, and materials for atomic energy—to the PRC. In a UN resolution of 18 May 1951, the United States succeeded in getting the UN General Assembly to pass proposals for selective

economic sanctions against the PRC and continued to press for a full trade embargo. This was never achieved because countries such as Britain were reluctant to provoke China too far, and oil continued to enter the PRC, for instance, through **Hong Kong**.

See also: Blockade of Korean Coasts.

References: Farrar-Hockley 1990; Schnabel 1972; Stueck 1995.

ESPIONAGE

The unresolved state of hostilities between North and South Korea has led the two states to regard each other as a legitimate target for surveillance and subversion. Scalapino and Lee (1972, vol. I: 546–547) suggest that from 1954 the North was training agents for use against the South, to build up Communist cells and rally "progressive forces." South Korean agents, Scalapino and Lee claim, "to be sure" were being sent north for purposes of gathering information.

It is hard to determine the extent of possible spying by South Korean agents in the North. The difficulties of penetrating a tightly controlled society may have encouraged the South to use other tactics, such as **aerial surveillance** of North Korean territory. The North, by contrast, is known to have managed a number of spy networks in the South, using resident South Koreans and agents infiltrated from North Korea (where parallel government, party, and military organizations control such agents). The North Korean vessel sunk on 17 December 1998 by the South Korean navy off the south coast of the Korea Peninsula was "assumed" to have been tasked with picking up an agent in the South or landing agents. South Korean counterintelligence agencies work continually to expose such activities, with varying success. By the time some spies are arrested, they may have been operating over decades. The longest-running spy ring to be uncovered, centered on Ko Young-bok, a former professor of sociology at Seoul National University, was active from 1961 to 1997. Ko is said to have passed the North information on South Korea's nuclear development strategy and on its bargaining position on family reunions. Two North Korean agents detained with him in November 1997 were apparently tasked with recruiting agents, acquiring new South Korean identity cards to be copied for use in further missions, and gathering information about a new productive strain of corn.

The Ko Young-bok case points to some of the basic ambiguities prevailing in the Korea Peninsula. The creation of two ideologically opposed states was not accompanied by a clear-cut separation of ideologies within the population. Before 1948, the South had its share of Communist supporters. Ko, for instance, a southerner, is said to have volunteered in the Korean War for the **North Korean People's Army**, to have been captured by South Korean forces, and to have renounced his Communist allegiance in 1953. His uncle, meanwhile, had gone north during the war to join the **Kim Il Sung** regime. In 1961, Ko was approached by a North Korean agent, to whom he yielded, for whatever reasons. He would seem to be a classic example both of the "sleeping agent"—that is, an agent settled in society, operating under a long-term cover—and of the "false surrenderer." Since 1953, several cases of both types of spy have been uncovered in South Korea. The comparative freedom of movement in South Korea and ease in merging into the background in a society already containing numerous people born in the North facilitate the operations of agents. South Korea is also vulnerable to the attentions of pro–North Korean agents recruited among Korean residents in Japan.

In both North and South Korea, the charge of espionage has been used as a political tool to eliminate opponents to the established regime. In South Korea, under **Syngman Rhee** and **Park Chung Hee**, the leaders of opposition parties were executed on the grounds that they had spied for North Korea; in the North, rivals to Kim Il Sung, such as **Pak Hon-yong**, were branded as spies for U.S. imperialism.

See also: Defections; Infiltration.

References: Bolger 1991; History: VI, 1977; *IHT*, 21 November 1997; *Newsreview*, 22 and 29 November 1997, 26 December 1998; Rees 1970; Scalapino and Lee 1972; Yi 1973.

ETHIOPIAN FORCES IN THE KOREAN WAR

In August 1950, Emperor Haile Selassie committed a volunteer infantry battalion drawn from his Imperial Security Guard to the **United Nations** forces in Korea. Named the Kagnew Battalion after a royal warhorse, the first unit of 931 men reached Pusan on 7 May 1951 and passed under the operational control of the 32nd Regiment of the U.S. 7th Division. The whole battalion rotated after a year's duty, to be replaced successively by the 2nd and 3rd Kagnew Battalions. A total of 3,518 men served in the three units. Casualties were 121 killed and 536 wounded; no Ethiopian prisoners were taken. The last troops left Korea on 3 January 1965.

The three battalions participated in many major engagements of the war, sometimes resorting to hand-to-hand and bayonet fighting. Their skill in patrols and night fighting was acknowledged, and a number of Ethiopian combatants won citations.

Several Ethiopian Red Cross nurses worked in Japan.

See also: Korean War (1950–1953).

References: History: I, 1972 and VI, 1977; Summers 1990; Thomas, Abbott, and Chappell 1986.

FAMILY REUNIONS

The most poignant consequence of the division of Korea in 1945 has probably been the separation of family members in a society for which the continuity of family life is paramount. South Koreans old enough to have experienced the **Korean War** and the years immediately after may eventually mention in conversation a parent, sibling, spouse, or child left in the flight from the North or lost among the crowds of refugees. Many separations were at the time regarded as temporary, and relatives intended to return for those they had left behind. Reunion, however, has been very difficult. Correspondence between South Koreans and ethnic Koreans in Communist countries other than North Korea has been officially permitted since 1973, and visits between South Korea and China are now possible, but direct mail and telephone communications between individuals in the North and South have been severed since 1950, and extremely few meetings have been achieved.

The size of the problem is difficult to assess. The frequently quoted figure of ten million separated relatives is exaggerated. Kim Choong Soon (1988: 35) suggests that the figure is used rhetorically to emphasize that each divided family has become two separate families, one in the North and one in the South. This implies a base figure of five million dispersed family members, which is probably still too high because whole families came south before the Korean War. Much lower figures of 500,000 (*Newsreview*, 1 November 1997) and 403,000 (*Newsreview*, 25 April 1998) are estimates of first-generation divided family members, who by the late 1990s are all elderly. They will have registered with the government or may, if their funds permit, use private agencies, many of which operate through Chinese intermediaries (almost certainly ethnic Korean Chinese) with connections in North Korea. If an agency can arrange a meeting, it is generally at a site in **Northeast China**. Far more frequent are letter exchanges through intermediaries or confirmation, now also provided by the South Korean intelli-

gence services, that a relative is alive or dead. The "success rate" for contacts is very low.

The family reunion issue has inevitably been used as a political tool in relations between North and South. Official discussions between the Red Cross organizations of both sides on family visits have been held intermittently since 1971. In a brief period of détente, seven rounds of talks were held from 1971 to 1973. They resumed only in 1985, and in September of that year 50 individuals from each side were permitted to cross the **Demilitarized Zone** to seek meetings with family members. Only 65 made successful contact. In 1997 and 1998, the South Korean Red Cross proposed the establishment of a center in **P'anmunjom** or even in the North to facilitate family reunion meetings, and a new "Freedom House" to serve such purposes was opened at P'anmunjom in July 1998. The North has made no direct response, but in early 1998 announced plans to set up an Address Inquiry Office to help North Korean citizens anxious to trace relatives at home or abroad. In conjunction with South Korean companies, the North may also be contemplating opening up selected tourist zones in North Korea to South Koreans who once lived there, to allow supervised meetings with family members.

The North's fear is, as ever, of uncontrolled activities. It has also generally sought to set the issue in the context of general reunification or link it to other outstanding problems rather than treat it, as the South has proposed, as one capable of separate negotiation. In Red Cross discussions in 1998 on food and fertilizer aid, the North appeared to be using the issue as a bargaining point. North Korean overtures to Korean Americans, which led to over 700 of the latter being allowed to visit the North in

Scene in 1983 at the area around the Korean Broadcasting System's main building on Yoido, Seoul, where people flocked to display details of missing family members in the hope of locating them. (Seung-yong Uhm, Office of Korean Ministry of Tourism)

1985 and 1986 to meet family members, may have been motivated by a desire to improve relations with the United States and raise foreign currency. The South is now prepared to support attempts by Korean Americans to reopen family links in the North. President **Kim Dae Jung**, speaking in California in June 1998, acknowledged that South Korea had no jurisdiction over overseas Korean organizations, such as a network proposed by the University of South Carolina to facilitate contacts between North Koreans and their relatives in South Korea and foreign countries, and said that the South would not oppose those efforts. Use is also being made of the Internet to solicit information on missing family members.

In the years following the Korean War, the International Committee of the Red Cross endeavored unsuccessfully to organize an exchange of lists of missing people between North and South. In

1956, the South Korean Red Cross ran a unilateral campaign in the South to register information on those who had gone north. The South Korean media, conscious of the publicity value to themselves, but also of their greater reach among the population, have offered their own initiatives. Between 1961 and 1976, the *Hanguk Ilbo* daily newspaper publicized names and details of orphaned and separated family members, but apparently evoked little response. Far more successful was the use of television, which, by the late 1970s, had become widespread in all parts of the South. The state-run Korean Broadcasting System (KBS) had mounted a Red Cross–sponsored radio campaign in the mid-1970s to assist in locating family members. In 1983, it extended this to television; from June to November, KBS carried televised appeals from members of the public who had been separated from their families after coming to the South or in the confusion of fighting. Approximately 109,000 applications to make an appeal were received, of which one-tenth—involving more than 10,000 people—resulted in a family reunion. The campaign was backed up by newspaper lists, computer identification, and the display of applicants' wall posters around the KBS building in **Seoul**.

In 1998, the privately run Munwha Broadcasting Company (MBC) aired a documentary film of a well-known South Korean singer's recent meeting in **Northeast China** with her sister and announced plans to cooperate with private agencies in making and airing film footage of North Koreans identified by people in the South as family members in the hope of eventually achieving meetings. MBC admitted openly that everything depended on North Korean cooperation.

The issues raised by family separation are many and complex. However powerful the claims of family duty, reunion can bring problems if, for instance, a spouse has remarried. Significantly, the greater number of applicants in the KBS campaign were seeking siblings and parents. Yet, even for siblings, the apprehension is shown in a South Korean woman's comment: "How do I know what my response would be to the sister I have never seen, if we were to meet?"

See also: Red Cross North-South Talks; Red Cross Organization; Refugees.

References: Foley (unpublished article); Kim Choong Soon 1988; Macdonald 1996; *Newsreview*, 1 and 15 November 1997, 28 March 1998, 18 and 25 April 1998, 27 June 1998, 11 July 1998, 6 February 1999; *Pyongyang Times*, 28 February 1998; ROK National Red Cross 1977.

FAMINE IN THE NORTH

Although the North Korean government had claimed—before the collapse of one of its main backers, the **Union of Soviet Socialist Republics,** in 1991—that it was self-sufficient in food, this was probably never the case, and even in the best years some grain always had to be imported. Badly hit by floods in 1995, North Korea appealed for international assistance to overcome "temporary difficulties." The country had scarcely recovered from this disaster when it was hit by further flooding in 1996, and again had to appeal for help. In the following two years, drought and tidal waves added to North Korea's problems, forcing the government to admit that it could not feed its people. Help was forthcoming from the World Food Program and other international bodies, as well as from a variety of nongovernmental organizations. These found North Korea a difficult client, but they persisted, and by mid-1998, although there were still areas of great distress, the threat of widespread famine seemed to have lifted.

FIRST COMMONWEALTH DIVISION IN THE KOREAN WAR

Forces from various countries of the British Commonwealth began to arrive in Korea in response to the **United Nations'** call for assistance to the Republic of Korea soon after the outbreak of the **Korean War** in June 1950. For the land forces assembled, this was to lead eventually to the formation of the First Commonwealth Division in July 1951.

The British 27th Brigade, made up of units from the Middlesex Regiment and the Argyll and Sutherland Highlanders, arrived from **Hong Kong** at the end of August 1950 under the command of Brigadier B. A. Coad. In Hong Kong, it had been on

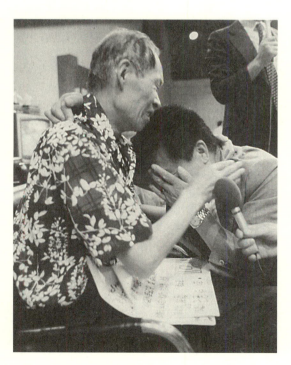

A father and son embrace at the 1983 reunion in Seoul. (Seung-yong Uhm, Office of Korean Ministry of Tourism)

garrison duty, but had also engaged in hill training, in circumstances not unlike those of Korea. After taking part in the last stages of the battle for the **Pusan Perimeter**, the brigade was joined in late September by the Third Battalion of the Royal Australian Regiment, and the 27th Brigade was renamed the 27th Commonwealth Infantry Brigade. This unit was augmented by a New Zealand Field Regiment, and in February 1951, the first Canadian forces joined the brigade. Besides the Commonwealth Brigade, a British 29th Brigade was in Korea from October 1950. Both brigades took part in the advance north during September–November 1950 and in the subsequent retreat south in the "**bug-outs**" that marked the period November 1950–January 1951. In the spring of 1951, these forces played a prominent role in resistance to the **Chinese People's Volunteers**, especially in the fighting along the **Imjin River** and at **Kap'yong**. During this period, the 27th Commonwealth Brigade became the 28th Commonwealth Brigade, following a change of commander and staff. Shortly afterward, in May 1951, when it had become clear that the war would not be over quickly, the Canadian government sent additional troops, who formed the 25th Canadian Infantry Brigade.

Discussions among the Commonwealth governments at the political and military level about forming one combined infantry unit had been under way since the early stages of the war, and by summer 1951, agreement to do this had been reached. Although there had been some degree of Commonwealth cooperation in the past, the First Commonwealth Division, now to be set up, was not only "First" in name but was also the first of its kind. From July 1951, under the command of Major-General **James Cassels**, the various land forces of the Commonwealth in Korea operated under the division. In addition to the Commonwealth forces, the Belgian Battalion was also attached to the division. General Cassels, and the division, came under the authority of the Australian Lieutenant-General Sir Horace Robertson, who was simultaneously commander of the British Commonwealth Occupation Forces Japan, and the British Commonwealth Forces Korea.

The division took part in all the major fighting of the next two years, as the war settled down to relative stalemate. In 1953 at its peak strength, the division numbered some 24,000. Of that number, approximately 14,000 were from Britain; more than 6,000 from Canada; 2,200 from Australia; and approximately 1,400 from New Zealand. More than 1,200 were killed in action, and nearly 5,000 were wounded. Koreans had been used from the early days to provide assistance with transporting goods and supplies, but from late 1952, following the U.S. example, the Commonwealth Division began to use Korean troops for fighting. These **Koreans Attached to the Commonwealth Forces** (KATCOMs) became an important part of the division's resources. The **Indian Army medical team**, the 60th Parachute Field Ambulance Unit, which had served the original British 27th Brigade from November 1950, also served with the First Commonwealth Division after its formation. Other medical teams operating with the division included British and Canadian units. For administration, the division drew heavily on U.S. resources, as well as its own. The Canadians used U.S. rations, for example, whereas most of the other contingents relied on a mixture of U.S. and British rations. The exception was the Indian medical team, which had its own arrangements. For fuel, all units relied on U.S. sources. As well as administrative support in Korea, additional support was provided by the British Commonwealth Forces in Japan. Most leave arrangements involved Japan, although married men who had come from garrison duty in Hong Kong, and whose wives remained there, were allowed to go there for rest and recreation.

The division remained in Korea after the **armistice** in July 1953, but its numbers were steadily reduced until it finally withdrew in 1957. Subsequent historical assessments of its value have varied. To the British and, though perhaps to a lesser extent, to the Commonwealth governments, it was and is seen as a successful example of cooperation and of the willingness of Western countries to show solidarity with the United States against a common enemy. For some South Koreans, it is a reminder that others apart from the United States came to their aid in 1950, but for the majority of South Koreans, the Commonwealth contribution means very little. The same is true for many

Americans, who are scarcely aware of the Commonwealth involvement in Korea. Even those who are aware often think that the Commonwealth contribution was so small compared to that of the United States as hardly to count.

See also: Australian Forces in the Korean War; Belgian Forces in the Korean War; Canadian Forces in the Korean War; New Zealand Forces in the Korean War; United Kingdom and Korea.

References: Barclay 1954; Farrar-Hockley 1990, 1995; Grey 1988; McGibbon 1992, 1996; O'Neill 1981, 1985.

FOREIGN CIVILIAN DETAINEES IN THE KOREAN WAR

As North Korean troops pushed south beginning 25 June 1950, the greater part of the foreign civilian population of Korea fled south or were evacuated. Some chose to remain at their posts, though many had discretion to leave. A few probably had nowhere else to go. Of those who remained, some disappeared, presumably killed; the rest were eventually detained for the greater part of the **Korean War**.

The majority of these civilians were picked up in **Seoul** in the first half of July 1950; others, later in the month. By the end of July, just under seventy foreigners had been gathered in an improvised detention camp outside **P'yongyang**. Their ages ranged from nine months to eighty-two years, for among the detainees, two families—one Turkish and the other Russian, each with young children—had been rounded up. The group comprised eleven nationalities: American, Australian, Austrian, Belgian, British, French, German, Irish, Swiss, Turkish, and Russian. Two-thirds were men and boys; one-third were women and girls. Ten of the group were under the age of twenty. Their professions and hence, for many, their reasons for being in Korea were varied. Diplomats included Vyvyan Holt, minister at the British legation, and two of his staff (one of whom was **George Blake**); Georges Perruche, chargé d'affaires and consul-general at the French legation; and Bishop Patrick Byrne, apostolic delegate to Korea. Catholic priests and nuns from a variety of missions included Monsignor Thomas Quinlan of the Columban Fathers. Protestant missionaries numbered Anglicans, including Bishop Cecil Cooper, head of the Anglican church in Korea; Methodists; and Commissioner **Herbert Lord** of the Salvation

Army. There were two journalists, a doctor, a mining engineer, businessmen, staff of U.S. agencies, a number of dependents, and one or two without any family.

On 5 September 1950, 67 detainees (two had already been removed from the camp), together with seven Korean civilian prisoners and more than 700 U.S. **prisoners of war**, were taken by train from P'yongyang to Manp'o on the western sector of the **Yalu River**, in the far north of the peninsula. From Manp'o, all groups were forced, at the end of October 1950, to march about 100 miles through mountainous country to Chunggangjin, farther up the Yalu. The walk took eight days. For the last stages of the march, transport was made available for the young, the very elderly, the women, and the very sick, but only after a good many deaths, especially among the prisoners of war.

In February 1951, the diplomats and journalists were separated from the other foreign detainees and transported back to Manp'o, which remained their base until March 1953. The main party stayed at Chunggangjin until October 1951, when they were also taken back to Manp'o, but to different quarters. In August 1952, they were moved again. In April 1953, in parallel with the **Little Switch** of sick and wounded prisoners of war, a group of seven men of British or Irish nationality, comprising diplomats, missionaries, and one journalist, were released from captivity via P'yongyang, China, and the Soviet Union. The French group, of similar composition, left next and thereafter the U.S. and other national groups, all by the same route. The Turkish and Russian contingents, as the residual group, were released in March 1954 under the terms of paragraph 59 of the **armistice** agreement of 27 July 1953.

Conditions were difficult for the foreign civilian detainees, especially during the early part of their captivity. They were frequently forced to move, their accommodation was often haphazard and overcrowded, food supplies were erratic and generally insufficient, and sickness and wounds were often left untreated. The light summer clothing they had been wearing when taken had to suffice at first for winter in camps in the extreme north of the Korea Peninsula, where winter temperatures can be very low. Although regular punishments were not administered, rough treatment and banishment to "cold rooms" and solitary confinement might be inflicted, and attempts at political indoctrination were constant. The worst period was the forced march over mountain roads, imposed upon the detainees by an exceptionally severe commandant. Two elderly women died along the route; it is said that they were shot for falling behind. Others succumbed later to illness or privation. In all, some twenty people died in detention. The conditions of captivity and survival rate among the civilian internees, however, were better than those among the prisoners of war.

Throughout their detention, the foreign civilians were under North Korean control. In late 1951, as it became apparent that exchanges of prisoners would feature in armistice negotiations, the Chinese, conscious of the high rate of mortality among prisoners of war held in the North, took charge of camps for all those captured from **United Nations Command** (UNC) forces. This arrangement did not include foreign civilians. Indeed, one of the detainees (Crosbie 1954: 189) reports that the Chinese declined to take responsibility for them, but did agree from August 1952 to supply rations and medical care, while the Koreans were to provide accommodation and guards. Neither the **People's Republic of China** nor North Korea was a signatory to the **Geneva Convention** and thus had no obligation to consider proposals for International Red Cross intervention (though the North Korean foreign minister, shortly after war broke out in June 1950, had stated his government's intention to respect the Convention's stipulations, and China did likewise in July 1952). Communication between the North Korean authorities and the respective governments of those detained had to be effected indirectly through third parties, such as China and the Soviet Union. With Soviet assistance, and in the context of agreement secured through the armistice negotiations at **P'anmunjom** on a Little Switch of sick and wounded prisoners (which took place on 20 April 1953), the foreign civilian detainees were released.

The North Korean government's decision to hold on to them throughout hostilities, instead of ejecting them immediately, is not readily explained. Its professed reason for moving them to the far north was to protect them from UNC bombing. Their removal certainly had the effect of placing them beyond UNC reach. Perhaps the North Korean administration hoped for a while to obtain some bargaining power by keeping them. As it was, it incurred odium and trouble in detaining them, and its efforts to persuade the two journalists (in the case of one man, by using brutal techniques) to broadcast on its behalf failed. It may be that the North Koreans had not expected that foreign civilians might decide to remain in the South or might have been unable to secure evacuation. Philip Deane (1953: 80) records that one of their North Korean commandants observed that capturing them had been "very troublesome." The commandant asked, "Why had we stayed behind to be captured?" The North Koreans had had no policy when they took them, their guard said, but had subsequently developed one: "We were to be treated kindly."

See also: Committee for Assisting the Return of Displaced Civilians; Korean Civilian Prisoners in the Korean War; Press Correspondents in the Korean War; Soviet Role in the Korean War.

References: Blake 1990; Crosbie 1954; Deane 1953; Eden 1960: 25–26; Kim Choong Soon 1988.

40TH PARALLEL
See **38th and Other Parallels.**

FOUR-PARTY TALKS
On 16 April 1996, U.S. President Bill Clinton and South Korean President **Kim Young Sam,** meeting for a summit on the South Korean island of **Cheju,** proposed a four-way meeting between the United States, the **People's Republic of China,** and the two Koreas, in an attempt to bring peace and stability to the Korea Peninsula. The thinking behind the suggestion was not completely new; it derived in part from the idea of **cross-recognition** and also from the successful settlement of the problems over the **North Korean nuclear program,** but there was no indication that the Cheju proposal had been in any way discussed with either China or North Korea before it emerged. The Chinese welcomed it cautiously as a possible way forward. Japan, the European Union, and other Western countries greeted it positively. The North Koreans, however, who were the principal target, displayed little interest. Eventually, they were persuaded to attend a joint U.S.–South Korean briefing in March 1997 in New

York, where they received an explanation of the intentions behind the proposal. Substantive talks were then held in December 1997 and March 1998, but there was little progress, even on setting an agenda. While the United States, China, and South Korea wished to establish subgroups to discuss substantive issues, including confidence-building measures, the North Koreans made it clear that they wanted to negotiate primarily with the United States, in the hope of achieving their long-term aim of a peace treaty. Although the talks have continued, the process looked doomed to failure, despite the U.S. decision to appoint an ambassador-level special envoy to handle Korean affairs. For other countries, progress in the talks was increasingly seen as a measure of North Korean sincerity, and thus their apparent failure became another obstacle in improving relations.

See also: North Korean Proposals on Unification.

FRANKS, OLIVER (1905–1992)

Oliver Franks was British ambassador to Washington during 1948–1952. Franks was born near Birmingham in 1905 and educated at Bristol Grammar School and the University of Oxford. On graduation, he became an Oxford lecturer in philosophy. He was a temporary civil servant during World War II in the Ministry of Supply, where he became acquainted with the minister, Ernest Bevin, later foreign secretary under **Clement Attlee** at the time of the **Korean War**. After World War II, Franks returned to Oxford, but was periodically called back to government until, in February 1948, he was appointed ambassador to Washington. There he established a close relationship with Secretary of State **Dean Acheson**, which was to prove useful during the Korean War. In June and July 1950, Franks encouraged Britain to send ground troops to Korea. Thereafter, his contacts and easy manner helped to smooth over many difficulties in British-U.S. relations during the war. He left Washington in December 1952, and played several important roles in British public life before his death in October 1992.

References: Acheson 1969; Danchev 1993.

FRENCH FORCES IN THE KOREAN WAR

Despite North Atlantic Treaty Organization (NATO) commitments in Germany and the demands of the Indochina War, the French government on 22 July 1950 sent the frigate *La Grandière* to Korean waters and on 24 August 1950 undertook to contribute an infantry battalion of French volunteers to the United Nations force, recruiting among both reservists and men on active duty. The French troops, many with experience of fighting in France's colonial territories, arrived in **Pusan** on 29 November 1950 under the command of Lieutenant-Colonel Ralph Monclar. The battalion, which included a company made up of the South Korean soldiers attached to it, came under the operational command of the 23rd Infantry Regiment of the U.S. 2nd Infantry Division throughout the war. In 1951, it fought at Wonju, Twin Tunnels, and Chipyong-ni in the Wonju area; against the Chinese spring offensive in central Korea; and at the **Punchbowl** and Heartbreak Ridge. During 1952–1953, the battalion saw action along the **38th parallel** at Arrow Head, in the Iron Triangle, and at the **Hook**. On 22 October 1953, the battalion left Korea for Indochina.

At its peak strength, the French Battalion numbered 1,185 soldiers. The whole unit rotated after a year's service, and altogether 3,421 men passed through its ranks. Casualties were high, at 1,277 dead, wounded, or missing in action, and 12 prisoners of war, reflecting fierce fighting conditions that included bayonet charges. The battalion received a number of citations. On arrival in Indochina in November 1953, it was redesignated the Korea Regiment and augmented with other troops to form the Groupement Mobile Nr. 100. The new unit was annihilated in a series of Vietminh ambushes in July 1954.

See also: Bloody and Heartbreak Ridges, Battles of (1951); Hook, the, Battles of (1952–1953); Korean War (1950–1953).

References: Bergot 1983; Blair 1987; History: III, 1974 and VI, 1977; Summers 1990.

GENEVA CONFERENCE (1954)

Article 4 of the **armistice** agreement of 1953 recommended to the two sides that a political conference of interested parties should be held to negotiate the withdrawal of foreign troops from the peninsula and the "peaceful settlement of the Korean question." This led to the convening of a conference in Geneva, Switzerland, from 26 April to 20 June 1954. By the time the conference met, it had also agreed to examine developments in Indochina, which tended to overshadow the consideration of Korea. The participants included the sixteen nations that had contributed troops to the United Nations (UN) side in the **Korean War**, together with the **Union of Soviet Socialist Republics** (USSR), the **People's Republic of**

G

China (PRC), and North Korea. The two Koreas tabled mutually incompatible proposals for reunification of the peninsula, while also demanding the withdrawal of foreign troops. Distracted by the need to consider Indochina, neither the United States on one side nor the USSR and the PRC on the other were willing to put pressure on their respective client states to agree to a compromise. The conference

General view of a session of the Geneva Conference which was held between 26 April and 20 June 1954, to consider the problems of Korea and Indochina. Zhou Enlai, premier and foreign minister of the People's Republic of China, who led the Chinese delegation, is seated in the second row behind the "PROC" sign. Anthony Eden, foreign minister of the United Kingdom, is seated second from the left in the second row. (Urs G. Arni)

therefore ended in mid-June, with no agreement on Korea. Following the breakup of the conference, the sixteen nations that had fought on the UN side reissued the declaration they had first issued on 27 July 1953.

See also: Sixteen-Nation Declaration (1953).

GENEVA CONVENTION (1949)

The 1949 Convention, numbering 143 articles, on the treatment of **prisoners of war** (POWs) was signed on 12 August 1949 at Geneva. It entered into force on 21 October 1950. The 1949 Convention replaced an earlier similar one of 1929. The United States was a signatory to the 1949 Convention, but did not ratify it until 1955. However, on entering the **Korean War** in June 1950, it acknowledged that it would apply the principles of the Convention. Neither China nor North Korea had signed the 1949 Convention, but both agreed, North Korea in July 1950 and China in July 1952, to observe its requirements. In the event, during the Korean War, neither the **United Nations Command** (UNC) nor the Communist command fully honored its stipulations. The Chinese and North Koreans were inclined, according to the prisoners they detained, to denounce the Convention as a "bourgeois" document where it dealt with conditions of imprisonment. The UNC, unable to control activities in many of its prisoner of war compounds, was not always capable of enforcing the standards of treatment required by the Convention.

The biggest area of divergence between the two sides was in the interpretation and implementation of article 118 on the **repatriation of prisoners of war**. This article states: "Prisoners of war shall be released and repatriated without delay after the cessation of active hostilities." The Communist command argued in the **armistice** negotiations, once both sides had agreed to discuss the issue, that all POWs should be returned immediately to the side from which they had been captured. The United States, which represented the UNC at the negotiations, although admitting that article 118 required this, became increasingly reluctant to undertake a straight exchange of prisoners and held out for voluntary or nonforcible repatriation, whereby a prisoner should be able to express a preference for one country of repatriation over another. In the end, the voluntary principle was accepted by the Communists.

Despite lapses, both sides operated within the framework of the Convention for certain purposes, such as the exchange of sick and wounded prisoners in April 1953 in accordance with article 109.

References: Farrar-Hockley 1954; Geneva Convention 1949; Hermes 1966; MacDonald 1986.

GLOSTERS

See **United Kingdom and Korea**.

GLOUCESTERSHIRE REGIMENT

See **United Kingdom and Korea**.

"GOOK"

"Gook" is a term used by Western troops and journalists in the **Korean War** and the **Vietnam War** when speaking of indigenous soldiers and civilians. It has also been applied to Japanese. The British press correspondent René Cutforth (1952: 21–22) maintained that the word was "good Korean," meaning "person'" or "people," and as such should not be found objectionable. The Korean word for "nation" or "state" is indeed *guk*, but it is not certain that this is in fact the origin of the term "gook." The word was borrowed by the French troops fighting in Korea (Bergot 1983: 133 and elsewhere). The French also used the term "Niak," though it is not clear if they applied this to the Koreans or the Chinese or both. Despite René Cutforth's comment, "gook" is generally considered an offensive expression.

References: Bergot 1983; Cutforth 1952.

GRAVES REGISTRATION PERSONNEL

See **Missing in Action (MIA)**.

GREEK FORCES IN THE KOREAN WAR

From December 1950 to October 1955, a volunteer battalion drawn from the regular Greek army and known as the Hellenic Expeditionary Force in Korea served under the **United Nations Command**. Greece also contributed a flight of eight C-47 transport aircraft, the 13th Hellenic Air Force flight.

The Greek battalion contained many veterans of the Greek civil war (1946) between the state and Communist guerrillas. In Korea, it was attached for much of its tour to the U.S. 7th Cavalry Regiment.

From a position north of **Seoul** in December 1950, it moved south, then north again to the **Imjin River** area, and then to positions around the central sector of the **38th parallel**, engaging frequently with Chinese forces, sometimes fighting with bayonets or bare hands. In May 1952, a company from the battalion helped to quell riots among Communist prisoners in the **Koje Island prisoner of war camp**.

In autumn 1953, after the **armistice**, the battalion was augmented to regimental strength and as the Hellenic Regiment was attached to the U.S. 3rd Division, but in March 1955 was reduced to battalion size again and in October 1955 was deactivated. Altogether, 10,184 men passed through the Greek army units. Casualties were 184 dead, 543 wounded, and two captured. The Greeks were respected fighters and received numerous citations.

The Greek transport flight came under the operational command of the U.S. 21st Troop Carrier Squadron. As its first mission, in December 1950, it helped in the airlift of 1,000 wounded men of the U.S. 1st Marine Division encircled at the **Changjin Reservoir** by Chinese troops. A total of 397 men served in the Greek flight. Casualties were 12 dead.

See also: Korean War (1950–1953); United States Forces in the Korean War.

References: Blair 1988; History: III, 1974 and VI, 1977.

GUAM DOCTRINE
See **Nixon Doctrine (1969)**.

HAN RIVER

The Han River flows westerly through the South Korean capital, **Seoul**, to the Yellow Sea. From Seoul it widens into an estuary between North and South; the Military Demarcation Line at this point runs down the middle of the channel. The North's advance on Seoul in the first days of the **Korean War** saw troops and civilians struggling to leave the city, which at that time occupied only the northern bank of the Han, by the few bridges leading south. These bridges were prematurely demolished, leaving many civilians stranded. The river was never a difficult obstacle to cross, yet it acquired symbolic value as a marker by which to judge advance or retreat, and through its associations with the capital.

The Han has two branches that join shortly before Seoul. Its northern branch rises in the Diamond Mountains in North Korea. North Korean plans in 1987 to dam the northern end of this branch caused anxiety in the South, but did not materialize. The southern branch, 298 miles (480 kilometers) long, rises in the **T'aebaek Mountains**.

References: Clark and Grayson 1986; Lautensach 1945/1988.

HAN XIANCHU (1911–1986)

Han Xianchu was a senior member of the Chinese military. Han was born in Henan Province in central China in 1911 (or 1910), and beginning in the 1920s was active with the Chinese Communist forces. After fighting the Japanese, he took part in the occupation of Manchuria (**Northeast China**) and Hainan Island during 1949–1950. In late 1950, he transferred to Korea, and in October 1951 he was the **Chinese People's Volunteers'** (CPV) representative at the **armistice** talks at **P'anmunjom**. He remained in Korea during 1952, as CPV deputy chief-of-staff. On return to China, he joined the National Defense Committee and was made a colonel-general in 1955. From 1960, he was commander of the Fujian Military Region opposite **Taiwan**. Han remained active in army and state roles

during the Cultural Revolution (1966–1976). He died in 1986.

Reference: Klein and Clark 1971.

HEARTBREAK RIDGE, BATTLE OF (1951)

See **Bloody and Heartbreak Ridges, Battles of (1951)**.

HENDERSON, GREGORY (1922–1988)

A U.S. official, and later scholar of Korean art and politics, Gregory Henderson also played a minor role in the controversy over who started the **Korean War**. Henderson was born in 1922. He joined the U.S. Foreign Service, learned Japanese, and in 1948, was posted to **Seoul**. Following the capture of Seoul in June 1950, a memorandum by Henderson recording conversations with South Korean officers in August 1949 fell into North Korean hands. Ever since, it has been used as evidence of South Korea's intention to provoke war with the North.

Henderson's other role was as a critic of South Korean political development, most notably in his book, *Korea: The Politics of the Vortex* (1968). This powerful indictment of the South Korean political system, together with criticisms of **Park Chung Hee** and of U.S. hostility to North Korea and support for Park and **Chun Doo Hwan**, led to Henderson being banned from visiting South Korea for many years. He died in October 1988.

Reference: Henderson 1968.

HIGGINS, MARGUERITE (1920–1966)

From her student days, the U.S. journalist Marguerite Higgins was reporting for the *New York Herald*. As correspondent for the newspaper, she covered the final stages of World War II in Western Europe. From Tokyo, where she was reporting on

East Asia, she was among the first U.S. correspondents to reach **Seoul** in the opening days of the **Korean War**, as the city was falling to the North Korean invaders. She moved south with the retreat from Seoul and witnessed the first engagements between troops of the **United Nations Command** (UNC) and the Communists. She covered the **Inch'on landing** of September 1950 and the evacuation of U.S. Marines from Hungnam after the **Changjin Reservoir** debacle in December 1950. Forthright, courageous, and committed to the U.S. cause, she was eager to expose what she saw as U.S. unreadiness for the war, in the hope that mistakes might be rectified. She also challenged U.S. military presentation of events.

Marguerite Higgins died in 1966 of a disease contracted while on a tour of Southeast and South Asia. *See also:* Press Correspondents in the Korean War. *References:* Higgins 1951; Knightley 1975; Matray 1991.

HISTORIES AND OTHER STUDIES OF THE KOREAN WAR

Official histories have been published for the governments of the United States, Australia, Canada, New Zealand, and the United Kingdom. These accounts draw on official documents and correspondence to contribute to the formal record of the military and diplomatic conduct of the war. The North Korean and South Korean governments have published, in Korean, their own official histories. A six-volume *History of the U.N. Forces in the Korean War*, published in English by the South Korean Ministry of National Defense, details the military and medical contributions of all participant nations under the **United Nations Command**. Several North Korean English-language publications lay out North Korea's record of the war.

Unofficial histories and memoirs commemorate the participation of other nations, such as the Belgians (Crahay 1967) and the French (Bergot 1983). Generals **Matthew Ridgway** (1967) and **Paik Sun-yup** (1992), leading military commanders, have left their accounts of hostilities. From the mid-1970s, U.S. and U.K. official files on the Korean War period and before were being opened up. Standard histories, often drawing on official records, by such authors as Roy Appleman, Clay Blair, Max Hastings, Edwin P. Hoyt, and David Rees, have been written to serve the general English-speaking reader. In the main, they have concentrated on the conduct of the war and especially on U.S. military tactics. At the lower end, they have shaded into fiction, represented by some of James Michener's writing. Studies of particular aspects of the conflict, such as the **armistice** negotiations, medical services, the air and naval war, intelligence operations, and individual campaigns, have filled out the history of hostilities. Personal accounts of soldiering, of life in captivity (Philip Crosbie, S. J. Davies, General **William Dean**, Philip Deane, Anthony Farrar-Hockley), and of press correspondents' experiences (René Cutforth, **Marguerite Higgins**) have added further dimensions to the story.

This traditionalist literature argues that the war was triggered by the North Korean invasion and that the Soviet Union and China played a decisive part in the North Korean decision. Dissent was voiced during the course of the war, however, over the whole UN and South Korean position by such writers as **Isidor Stone**, **Wilfrid Burchett**, and **Alan Winnington**. The traditionalist line was further challenged in the decades after the Korean War in revisionist studies, starting with **Gregory Henderson**'s *Korea: The Politics of the Vortex* (1968), and developed further by academics such as **Bruce Cumings**, Jon Halliday, Gavan McCormack, John Merrill, and Robert Simmons. These scholars focused on the years between liberation in 1945 and war in 1950 to suggest that the conflict's origins lay more in the immense political and social confusion of that period inside Korea than in external Communist collusion with North Korea. They have preferred to see the war as a civil war or a war of national liberation. Their views, often critical of the United States and South Korea, have encountered considerable resistance, particularly from scholars and official organs in South Korea. Nor do they tally with the North Korean official line that the United States and South Korea were alone responsible for launching the initial provocations.

Early accounts from South Korean sources of the war all attributed responsibility for its outbreak to North Korea and its Communist backers. From the mid-1970s, South Korean official documents likewise became accessible to researchers. Kim Hakjoon was among the first to draw on such material.

Despite official sensitivity on the subject, foreign revisionist studies have been published in translation in South Korea, and revisionist interpretations of the causes of the war have circulated freely within South Korean academic circles (and among Japanese scholars). North Korea's presentation of the war, by contrast, in its publications (Foreign Languages Publishing House, n.d., 1950, 1960, 1961, 1977, 1979) has invariably cast the United States and South Korea in the role of aggressors and, apart from a collection of documents captured in Seoul in 1950, has not based itself on archive material.

Other studies in the 1980s and 1990s, notably by Rosemary Foot, Peter Lowe, and William Stueck, have argued the importance of the wider international and diplomatic aspects of the war. Since the mid-1980s, Chinese and Soviet, now Russian, sources, hitherto inaccessible, have been opened up and discussed in published works, allowing a fuller understanding of Chinese and Soviet roles in the conflict. Important contributions in this category are studies by Chen Jian (1994) and by Goncharov, Lewis, and Xue (1993) and the Winter 1995/1996 issue of the Cold War International History Project Bulletin. Assessments (in English) of Chinese-language and Japanese-language studies on the Korean War, by Jun Yasada and Hiroshi Sakurai, respectively, appeared in the first issue of Social Science Japan Journal (April 1998). Traditionalists have welcomed the new material as providing vindication of their views; revisionists have responded by modifying some of their earlier judgments. A recurring assessment of the conflict now is that it started as a civil war, but rapidly acquired an international dimension.

See also: Foreign Civilian Detainees in the Korean War; Literature of the Korean Conflict; Press Correspondents of the Korean War; Prisoners of War; Soviet Role in the Korean War; Television and the Korean War; War Stories and War Films of the Korean War.

References: Appleman 1961 [U.S. official history], 1987, 1990; Bergot 1983; Blair 1987; Brune 1996; Chen 1994; Cold War International History Project Bulletin, Winter 1995/1996; Crahay 19657 Crosbie 1954; Cumings 1981, 1983, 1990, 1992; Cutforth 1952; Davies 1954; Dean 1954; Deane 1953, 1976; Farrar-Hockley 1954, 1990 and 1995 [U.K. official history]; Foot 1985, 1990; Foreign Languages Publishing House [FLPH] n.d., 1950, 1960, 1961, 1977, 1979(a) and (b); Goncharov, Lewis, and Xue 1993; Halliday and Cumings 1988; Hastings 1987; Henderson 1968; Hermes 1966 [U.S. official history]; Higgins 1951; History 1973–1977; Hoare and Pares 1997; Hoyt 1984, 1986, 1990; Kim 1990; Lowe 1988a, 1988b; McCormack 1983; McGibbon 1992 and 1996 [N.Z. official history]; Merrill 1983, 1989; Michener 1953; Millett 1995; Mossman 1990 [U.S. official history]; O'Neill 1981 and 1985 [Australian official history]; Paik 1992; Rees 1964, 1984; Ridgway 1967; Sakurai 1998; Schnabel 1972 [U.S. official history]; Simmons 1975; Stone 1952; Stueck 1981, 1983, 1995; Winnington and Burchett 1953, 1954; Wood 1966 [Canadian official history]; Yasuda 1998.

HODGE, JOHN REED (1893–1963)

John Hodge was a general in the U.S. Army during the **Korean War**. Hodge was born in Golconda, Illinois, in 1893. He became an infantry officer in the U.S. armed forces, serving in France in World War I. For a time thereafter, he taught in a private military academy and then in a variety of army military schools. He served on the General Staff in the years before Pearl Harbor. During World War II in the Pacific, Hodge acquired a reputation as a brave and competent soldier, who got on well with the troops under his command. At the end of the war, as lieutenant-general in command of the XXIV Corps of the 10th Army, he was ordered to move his forces to Korea to accept the Japanese surrender south of the **38th parallel**. He was also to take over from the Japanese the day-to-day running of the southern half of the Korea Peninsula. Hodge had no experience to qualify him for such a task and was to remain effectively without further orders for six months. It was not an auspicious beginning to what was bound to be a difficult task.

On arrival in Korea in September 1945, Hodge and his colleagues seem to have been totally unprepared for the wave of revolutionary enthusiasm that greeted them. Hodge's main initial concern was to preserve law and order, and, making little distinction between the Koreans and the Japanese, apparently regarding both as enemy personnel, at first looked to the Japanese military and police to keep control. Although this policy did not last long, it prejudiced many Koreans against Hodge, as did his policy of suppressing the **People's Committees** and other popular organizations that had emerged following the Japanese surrender.

From relying on the Japanese colonial authorities, Hodge turned to the small group of English-speaking Koreans available. Many of these were from wealthy backgrounds, and many had been seen as collaborators with the Japanese. Lacking trained Korean speakers, however, Hodge believed that he had little choice but to use such people. He and his colleagues felt more at home with those who appeared to be friendly and seemed to believe in Western democracy than with the more radical groups. Despite this, Hodge found it difficult to work with the veteran conservative fighter for independence, **Syngman Rhee**, who returned to Korea in October 1945, and their relationship was generally stormy. At the same time, Hodge's **United States Army Military Government in Korea** tended to be less willing to give responsibility to Koreans than was the case with the Soviet administration in the north and proved incapable of organizing a moderate alternative to Rhee.

It fell to Hodge to represent U.S. interests in the **Joint Commission on Trusteeship**, set up in December 1945. He found it hard to work with the Soviet representatives, whom he did not trust and whose intention, he felt, was ultimately to take over the whole peninsula. When the commission proved unworkable, Hodge was happy to see the issue referred to the **United Nations** in 1947. Hodge left Korea in August 1948, after the emergence of separate regimes on the peninsula. He held a variety of army posts before he retired in 1953. He died ten years later.

References: Cumings 1981, 1990; Matray 1985; Oliver 1954, 1978.

HOME FOR CHRISTMAS (1950)

When British troops first went to France at the outbreak of World War I in August 1914, there was much talk about the war being "over by Christmas." It proved a vain hope, as trench warfare developed and the battle lines solidified across Europe. It is not clear whether U.S. General **Douglas MacArthur** was aware of the 1914 precedent, but in November 1950, he made a similar mistaken prediction. Despite the intervention by the **Chinese People's Volunteers** in October 1950, MacArthur ordered

that Thanksgiving Day (23 November) should be celebrated in style, and on 24 November, issued a communiqué anticipating easy victory. This, he told one of his aides, meant that they could tell the troops that they would be "home for Christmas"; however, Christmas 1950 saw the United Nations troops in headlong retreat in front of Chinese forces, and the war continued until July 1953.

References: Rees 1964; Whitney 1956.

HONG KONG

At the outbreak of the **Korean War**, Hong Kong, on the South China coast, was still a British colony, ceded to Britain by China in a series of nineteenth-century treaties and agreements. During World War II, Britain had been unable to defend the colony, and the Japanese had occupied it from January 1942 to 1945. The establishment of the **People's Republic of China** in October 1949 seemed to bring a new threat to Hong Kong, even though the **People's Liberation Army** stopped at the border. Nevertheless, in June 1950, Britain had a garrison of 30,000 troops, armor, and air support, including a carrier force, in Hong Kong. Some of these forces were directed to Korea in the early stages of the fighting, but generally, Hong Kong played little military role in the war. Neither was it important as a rest and recreation center, as it was to become in the **Vietnam War**. Troops went to Tokyo when on leave. Yet Hong Kong did have a role. Partly because of Hong Kong, Britain, unlike the United States, had recognized the new Chinese government in January 1950, and this placed strains on U.K.-U.S. relations during the Korean War. In particular, the United States argued that Hong Kong was used to avoid the **embargo** imposed on China and North Korea and refused to be convinced by British claims that this was not the case. After the end of the war, Hong Kong became an important trading partner for Britain, and, before the establishment of diplomatic relations between China and South Korea in 1992, it was a useful point of contact between those two countries. Hong Kong reverted to Chinese sovereignty in 1997.

References: Farrar-Hockley 1990, 1995; Welsh 1993.

HONG XUEZHI (1913–)

Hong Xuezhi was a senior member of the Chinese military. He was born in central China in 1913. By the end of the Sino-Japanese War (1937–1945), he was a divisional chief-of-staff in the New Fourth Army. From 1948 to 1950, as deputy commander of an army corps in the 4th Field Army, he played an active role in the Chinese Communist forces' capture of the island of Hainan early in 1950. During 1951, as a member of the **Chinese People's Volunteers**, Hong moved to Korea, where he directed the rear services (logistics) department during 1951–1952. He remained in Korea until September 1954. He then held various state and military posts, and, when ranks were introduced in 1955, became a general. He ceased to be active in 1959, probably because, like other Korean veterans, he was linked with **Peng Dehuai**, who was dismissed in that year. Hong did not reappear until 1977, when he was listed as director of the **People's Liberation Army** Logistics Department. He has been described in Chinese publications as "one of the organizers and commanders of major campaigns in Korea," while the South Korean press has identified him as one of the Korean veterans who advocate close relations between China and North Korea.

References: Klein and Clark 1971; *Who's Who in China* 1989.

HOOK, THE, BATTLES OF (1952–1953)

The Hook is part of a low line of hills situated to the west of the Samich'on River, a tributary of the **Imjin River**, some 20 miles (32 kilometers) to the northeast of **Kaesong**. The Hook, also known as Hill 146, from its highest point, is 4 miles (6 kilometers) to the north of the Imjin and commands the approaches to the river. The two opposing sides in the **Korean War** were in close proximity here, which meant that there was usually some low-level activity, even during quiet periods.

There were also periods of more intense fighting. The area came under heavy Chinese attack in October 1952, when U.S. Marines held it under difficult conditions. Further action followed in November 1952, after the area passed to the **First Commonwealth Division**. The First Battalion of the Black Watch stopped the Chinese in a fierce battle, involving tanks from the Commonwealth Division and hand-to-hand fighting.

The area then was quiet until March 1953. This interval allowed the Commonwealth forces time to construct an elaborate system of trenches, similar to

that used in World War I. These were to be particularly useful when the Hook again came under attack, first in March 1953, when units of the U.S. 2nd Division came under Chinese assault. In further fighting in May and June, Chinese mortar and artillery attacks damaged many of the defense installations. The last bout, also intense, came in July 1953, just before the signing of the **armistice.** In early July, as the armistice negotiations reached their final stages, the British Commonwealth 28th Brigade took over the defense of the Hook from the 29th Brigade. The main units were from the Royal Australian Regiment. The first Chinese attacks drove U.S. Marines from their position to the left of the Australians who were thus left more exposed. This the Chinese tried to exploit, with probing attacks from 15 to 24 July. Then, even though the signature of the armistice was imminent, the Chinese launched what proved to be the last major attack of the war on 24–25 July. The attack failed, but left hundreds of Chinese dead. The Australians suffered two dead and fourteen wounded. Whatever the human cost, the defense of the Hook meant that in the western sector the southern boundary of the **Demilitarized Zone** laid down in the armistice agreement ran well north of the Imjin River. The fighting on the Hook has featured in at least one novel, *L'Hameçon* ("The Hook"), by Vahe Katcha. It was made into a film in 1962.

References: Farrar-Hockley 1990, 1995; Hastings 1987; Hermes 1966; O'Neill 1985.

HUANG HUA (1913–)

Huang Hua was one of the **People's Republic of China**'s most skilled diplomats. Huang was born in central China in 1913. He was active in student politics in the 1930s and met U.S. writer Edgar Snow and his first wife, Helen, who wrote under the pseudonym of Nym Wales. Huang spent the war years in the Communist headquarters of Yan'an, emerging in the late 1940s as an official skilled in dealing with foreigners. After serving as the head of the Shanghai Alien Affairs' Office, he became a counsellor in the Ministry of Foreign Affairs in January 1953. In that role, he was head of the Chinese delegation to the October 1953 negotiations at **P'anmunjom** on a political conference on Korea, as provided for in the July 1953 **armistice** agreement. Huang, who spoke excellent English, proved a tough negotiator, and his tactics led the U.S. team to break off the talks in December 1953.

Huang accompanied **Zhou Enlai**, China's foreign minister and premier, to the 1954 **Geneva Conference** and also acted as press spokesperson for the Chinese delegation. From 1960 to 1971, Huang held a series of ambassadorial appointments and, as ambassador to the United Arab Republic (Egypt) from 1966 to 1971, was the only ambassador to remain at his post during the most intensive phase of the Cultural Revolution. In 1971, he negotiated the beginnings of normalization of China's relations with the United States with U.S. national security adviser Henry Kissinger and from 1971 to 1976 was China's ambassador to the United Nations. During that period, Huang provided much support to North Korea in its campaign for the abolition of the **United Nations Commission for Unification and Rehabilitation of Korea**. He was foreign minister from 1976 to 1982 and a vice-premier from 1982, but in the 1980s, although he continued to hold a number of honorific posts, he was increasingly left behind by the rapid development of China's links with the outside world.

References: Klein and Clark 1971; *Who's Who in China* 1989.

HWANG JANG-YOP (1923–)

Hwang Jang-yop, a high-ranking member of the (North) **Korean Workers' Party** (KWP), and his aide, Kim Duk-hong, defected on 12 February 1997 to the South Korean embassy in Beijing. The two were returning to North Korea via China from an official lecture tour of Japan. By agreement with China, they left Beijing on 18 March 1997 for the Philippines and eventually reached Seoul on 20 April 1997.

Hwang, a secretary of the KWP Central Committee at the time of his defection and a former president of Kim Il Sung University, is to date the highest-placed North Korean to defect. He was related by marriage to **Kim Il Sung**, with whom he was further closely associated through his work in the party secretariat, possibly as Kim's private secretary, and as a theoretician of the *juche* ideology of self-reliance. He was also tutor to Kim's son, **Kim Jong Il**. In explaining his defection, Hwang claimed not to be acting for personal motives but from a sense of frustration that *juche* was no longer meeting the people's needs. He expressed no hostility toward Kim Il Sung, though he had reservations about Kim Jong Il. Hwang urged North Korea to abandon its policy of armed confrontation and expressed his readiness to work with the South toward reunification.

After his arrival in Seoul, Hwang was put under the protection of the Agency for National Security Planning (ANSP), the country's intelligence organization. Though he reportedly brought no documents with him, there was speculation that he might be able to name pro–North Korean agents active in the South. He was installed as head of the Unification Policy Research Institute under the ANSP.

See also: Defections; *Juche;* People's Republic of China Relations with South Korea.

References: Cotton 1998; *Newsreview,* 22 March 1997, 26 April 1997, 25 April 1998; Scalapino and Lee 1972; Suh 1988.

IAEA
See **International Atomic Energy Authority (IAEA).**

IMJIN RIVER, BATTLE OF (1951)

The Imjin River played an important role in the last stages of the war of movement during the **Korean War.** In particular, it was the scene of a major battle in April 1951, when the **Chinese People's Volunteers** (CPV) forces conducted their fifth offensive in an attempt to recapture the South Korean capital, **Seoul.** The Imjin rises near **Wonsan** on the east coast of North Korea and flows into the **Han River** estuary some 157 miles (253 kilometers) to the west. Today, most of the river lies in North Korea, except for the last 30 miles (48 kilometers), which are south of the **Demilitarized Zone.** Following the hasty retreat by forces of the **United Nations Command** (UNC) before the CPV in November and December 1950, the UN line stabilized for a time along the river, but was eventually moved south. By April 1951, however, UNC forces had retaken Seoul, and the area of the Imjin River was held by the British 29th Infantry Brigade. This was an important position, across the traditional invasion routes toward Seoul, although the river itself was hardly an obstacle. The water level was low in April and the river easily forded.

To hold the main part of the UNC front, which was some 7 miles (11 kilometers) wide, the UNC had assigned 650 British soldiers of the First Battalion, the Gloucestershire Regiment (known as "the Glosters"), supported by a mortar troop from the Royal Artillery. These troops commanded the entrance to the valley that takes its name from the village of Solma-ri. To the right of the Glosters was the remainder of the 29th Brigade, made up of the Northumberland Fusiliers, the Royal Ulster Rifles, and the Belgian Capitol Battalion. They were supported by the King's Royal Irish Hussars, with Centurion tanks, the 45th Field Regiment Royal Artillery, and 55 Squadron Royal Engineers.

During the night of 22 April 1951, the Chinese 63rd Army, some 30,000 strong, crossed the Imjin and began an attack across the whole of the British front. The Glosters fought hard, but were steadily forced back to the hills behind the river during the fighting, which continued all night and well into 23 April. A further attack by fresh Chinese troops on 24 April was held, but by the evening of that day, the survivors of the Glosters were concentrated on what was known as Hill 235. The rest of the brigade was ordered to fall back to new positions north of Seoul, which they did with some difficulty. The Glosters were now isolated, with no fire support and rapidly diminishing supplies of ammunition and food. Although they held off more Chinese attacks that night, the outlook was bleak.

On 25 April, the Glosters were advised to try to break out and regain their own lines. They made one last stand and then tried to escape, without much success since the Chinese held the surrounding countryside. The wounded, who had been left on Hill 235 with the chaplain, the medical officer, and various medical staff, were captured. Most of the remainder were picked up by the Chinese and taken into captivity. Although the 29th Brigade had suffered heavy casualties in the battle, it had in turn hit the Chinese hard and delayed their advance by some sixty hours, sufficient for other UN forces to be able to block the advance on **Seoul.** In the fighting, some sixty-three of the Glosters were killed, and nearly 200 were wounded. Most were captured; only five officers and 41 other ranks escaping. Although there was some U.S. criticism of the Glosters' commanding officer, Lieutenant-Colonel J. P. Carne, for his failure to let it be known how dangerous his position had become, Carne was awarded the Victoria Cross, Britain's highest award for gallantry, for his role in the action, and the unit as a whole received a U.S. presidential unit citation.

Since 1957, the site of the Glosters' last stand, Hill 235, known to the British community as Gloster Hill, has been one of the main British Commonwealth commemorative sites in South Korea. An annual ceremony to mark the battle is held on the Sunday nearest 23 April, the feast day of St. George, patron saint of England, and one of the crucial days in the battle. The Gloucester pub on Sloane Street in central London has a sign painted with two heroic actions of the Gloucestershire Regiment; one side shows a soldier and the inscription "Imjin River 1951."

See also: First Commonwealth Division in the Korean War; United Kingdom and Korea.

References: Barclay 1954; Farrar-Hockley 1954, 1990, 1995; Grey 1988.

INCH'ON LANDING (1950)

The city of Inch'on lies some 40 miles (64 kilometers) to the west of the South Korean capital, **Seoul**. Since its opening to foreign trade in the 1880s, when it was generally known as Chemulp'o, it has been the port for the capital. Its importance in this role began in the Japanese period, but a combination of high tides and heavy silting, which created extensive mud flats, limited its development. An elaborate system of locks and other controls, begun in the 1960s, has improved the port's ability to handle larger vessels, but it is still more expensive to land freight at Inch'on than at Pusan in the south of the peninsula, and Inch'on, even today, plays a secondary role as a port.

In September 1950, Inch'on was firmly under North Korean control, having been captured in the great sweep forward following the outbreak of the **Korean War** in June. The range of its tides, with variations up to 30 feet (9 meters), and the hazards of the approach through the mudflats seemed to make it an unlikely target for **United Nations Command (UNC)** forces. But General **Douglas MacArthur**, the UN supreme commander, decided that Inch'on was the place to begin the counterattack. He stuck to this position, despite strong opposition from the U.S. Navy, which would have to get an invading force ashore, and the doubts of the U.S. Joint Chiefs of Staff, the highest U.S. military planning body. To MacArthur, the capture of Inch'on, whatever the problems involved in taking it, would have several advantages. It would open up a front behind enemy lines; make possible the recapture of Seoul, a highly symbolic move; and both relieve pressure on those trapped in the **Pusan Perimeter** and encourage them to begin the breakout from that trap. The attack on Inch'on became known as Operation Chromite. Strong hints were dropped in Tokyo and elsewhere that any UNC landing would be at a more suitable port, possibly on the east coast. Whether these got back to the North Koreans is not clear, but what is certain is that, when Inch'on was attacked, the defense was relatively ineffective.

The landing was planned for 15 September 1950. Because there were few charts available and the U.S. and other naval forces that were to take part in the action had virtually no knowledge of the tides and channels, Japanese naval and coast guard personnel who had known the port in the **Japanese colonial period in Korea (1910–1945)** were recruited to act as guides. It would be many years before their contribution was officially acknowledged, but they provided invaluable information to the attacking force.

Early on the morning of 15 September 1950, and despite hurricane conditions that reduced many of the landing teams to prostrate sea-sickness victims, U.S. and other UN naval units began to bombard Inch'on, concentrating fire on Wolmi-do, a fortified island in the center of the harbor. There was also massive, and largely unopposed, air cover. At 7 A.M., troops from the U.S. X Corps, including the U.S. 1st Marine Division and U.S. 7th Infantry Division, began coming ashore. Many of those who landed on Wolmi-do were trapped there for several hours as the tide receded, but once it returned they were able to push on to the shore. Among those landing were a number of well-known newspaper foreign correspondents, including U.S. correspondent **Marguerite Higgins** and British correspondent **James Cameron**.

Once ashore, the attacking forces met little resistance in Inch'on itself, the enemy having withdrawn to defend Seoul. After two days of fighting, Inch'on was secure, and the U.S. 1st Marine Division, with four battalions of South Korean marines, pressed forward their attack toward Seoul's Kimp'o Airport, then as now, the main entrance by air to the capital. Other forces turned south, heading toward the city of Suwon, and eventually to a reunion with Eighth U.S. Army forces pushing up from Pusan.

By 18 September, Kimp'o Airport was secured

and in use by the U.S. Far Eastern Air Force Combat Cargo Command, while the attack on Seoul continued. Here the UN forces met heavier resistance, and it was not until the end of September that Seoul was finally liberated and, with that, one of the aims of the landing achieved. The **North Korean People's Army**, which had until then proved unstoppable, now began a retreat north, followed by South Korean and UNC forces. Before long, the fateful decision was taken to cross the **38th parallel**, which would introduce a whole new element into the conflict.

Although MacArthur has had his detractors, who point to the relative lack of opposition at Inch'on, it is hard to deny him the credit for conceiving such a daring attack, behind enemy lines and with little real knowledge of what was involved by way of tides and the complexity of the approaches. The South Koreans have no doubt to whom they owe their survival in 1950, and a large statue of him overlooks the beaches where his men came ashore. There is also a museum relating the story of the landing. In 1980, a film extravaganza appeared, entitled *Inch'on*, produced with support from the Reverend **Moon Sun Myung** and his Unification Church. It was a box office failure. There is also an extensive range of literature about the landing.

Although it continued to be important as a staging post, Inch'on played very little further part in the Korean War. Since the war, it has been largely rebuilt.
References: Blair 1988; Edwards 1990; Hastings 1987; Matray 1991.

INDIAN ARMY MEDICAL TEAM IN THE KOREAN WAR

The 60th Parachute Field Ambulance Unit of the Indian Army Medical Corps served from November 1950 in a noncombatant role alongside other Commonwealth troops. In December 1950, the main part of the 346-member unit, commanded by Lieutenant-Colonel A. G. Rangaraj, advanced with the British 27 Infantry Brigade to **P'yongyang**, from where, however, it had to withdraw immediately on 5 December in the general retreat of **United Nations** troops before the Communist counterattack. Rather than destroy their medical supplies, the Indian contingent brought them out on a commandeered train just before the last bridge was demolished.

Thereafter, the main force was principally active in the central sector of the Korea Peninsula, parachuting into the fighting zone when necessary and operating a helicopter ambulance service.

A smaller force commanded by Major N. B. Banerjee was stationed in the southern city of **Taegu**, where it worked in Korean military and civilian hospitals, providing medical and surgical care and outpatient services.

In August 1953, the Indian Parachute Field Ambulance Unit left the Commonwealth Division to support the **Indian Custodial Force** charged with enforcing the provisions of the **Neutral Nations Repatriation Commission**. The unit left Korea in February 1954 when the commission's work was completed.
See also: First Commonwealth Division in the Korean War; Indian Custodial Force.
References: History: II, 1973 and VI, 1977.

INDIAN CUSTODIAL FORCE

The Indian Custodial Force (ICF) was the concrete expression of Indian involvement in working toward settlement of the **Korean War**. In December 1952, the **United Nations** General Assembly voted on a proposal, introduced by the Indian representative, **Krishna Menon**, for a commission to supervise the **repatriation of prisoners of war**. This proposal was later taken up by the Communist side in the **armistice** negotiations and emerged as the **Neutral Nations Repatriation Commission** (NNRC), with Sweden, Switzerland, Czechoslovakia, Poland, and India as members. India chaired the commission, served as umpire, and provided the necessary policing and **Red Cross** services.

The 5,000-member ICF was commanded by General S. S. P. Thorat, under the NNRC chairman, General K. S. Thimayya (1906–1965), and was tasked with maintaining order in the holding areas and supervising the process of screening nonrepatriates. On arrival in Inch'on in September 1953, ICF units had to be helicoptered to the neutral area of the **Demilitarized Zone** because President **Syngman Rhee** refused to allow Indian troops on South Korean soil, such was his suspicion of India's sympathies and his resentment over the armistice and repatriation. South Korean irritation erupted further in violent propaganda against the ICF, leading

India to threaten to withdraw its troops. Both pro- and anti-Communist prisoners of war assaulted their guards and attempted to riot. General Thimayya, although authorized by his government to use force if necessary, declined to. The Indian government followed closely the work of the NNRC and protested against threats to its soldiers. The IFC finished its duties on 23 February 1954, when the NNRC had completed its work.

Red Cross services to the NNRC were provided by members of the 60th Indian Parachute Field Ambulance Unit of the Indian Army Medical Corps, which had served in Korea throughout most of the war.

See also: Indian Army Medical Team in the Korean War
References: Foot 1990; History: II, 1973; MacDonald 1986; Matray 1991.

INDIAN DIPLOMATIC CHANNELS WITH CHINA
See Nehru, Jawaharlal; Panikkar, Kavalam Madhava.

INFILTRATION
North Korean pressure on the territory and population of South Korea has been continuous since the late 1950s. Infiltration by land and sea has been aimed at confronting troops of the United Nations Command (UNC) (both U.S. and South Korean troops) and the South Korean police and army and at intimidating the local population. Naval and air encroachments may sometimes reflect confusion over territorial limits; but the frequent land incursions over the Military Demarcation Line (MDL) can only be assumed to be deliberate. In some instances, agents, saboteurs, or agitators, hoping to get further south, are involved. Some have managed to reach as far as 100 miles (160 kilometers) south of the Demilitarized Zone (DMZ) before being caught. Armed patrols have also penetrated along the length of the MDL into the southern half of the DMZ in violation of the 1953 armistice. Most incursions across the DMZ end in firefights between the military and security personnel of both sides.

Land infiltrations reached a peak in the years 1967–1970. The United States was heavily involved in the Vietnam War, aided by South Korean troops, and in South Korea, President Park Chung Hee had instituted an authoritarian regime. Both these fac-

tors seem to have prompted particularly aggressive policies from North Korea. The year 1968 was especially tense, starting in January with a raid by a North Korean 31-man commando unit tasked with the assassination of President Park. The group almost reached the presidential residence, the Blue House, in Seoul, having earlier crossed the DMZ. The severity of attacks that year was held to justify putting U.S. soldiers serving between the Imjin River and the MDL on "hostile fire zone" pay in April 1968. A UNC report of 4 October 1968 to the United Nations Security Council claimed that 304 "serious incidents" attributed to North Korean infiltrators had been logged in the first eight months of 1968, with considerable loss of life on each side. The volume of infiltrations fell away after 1970, and, between 1983 and 1992, no attempts at North Korean penetration across the DMZ were recorded.

The coasts of South Korea have been the targets of North Korean seaborne commando units. The many islands off the west and south coast have offered shelter to such groups. The straight coastline and short tides of the east coast have necessitated tactics of attempted landings, followed by rapid movement inland. Woo Yong-gak, released in February 1999 after 41 years' imprisonment, had been picked up in 1958 as a seaborne infiltrator on the east coast. The worst episode came during October–November 1968, when a total of 120 North Korean agents landed at eight locations on the east coast between Samch'ok and Uljin in Kangwon Province and headed inland to the T'aebaek Mountains. There they endeavored to set up bases and rally the local people to the Communist cause, in some instances employing force, but were eventually tracked down and killed or captured by South Korean security troops, with some loss of life on the South Korean side. The beaches on the east coast are regularly patrolled, with public access denied for long stretches and a wide strip of sand raked and inspected daily to detect footprints. The frequency of attempted North Korean landings has lessened, but has not ceased. In two separate incidents, in September 1996 and June 1998, a North Korean submarine ran aground or became caught in fishing nets off the east coast of South Korea. Each time, bodies of crew members were found dead in or near the submarine. Others were captured later. On 12

July 1998, the armed body of a North Korean in a diving suit, found dead on an east coast beach, was taken as further proof of North Korean infiltration. North Korean vessels were sighted in South Korean waters on 20 November and 17 December 1998. The second boat, detected off the south coast town of Yosu, was sunk by the South Korean navy and a body recovered.

The seas east and west of the Korea Peninsula have long been patrolled by both North and South Korean naval and security vessels, sometimes on fishery protection duties and at other times on investigative forays. Confrontations between the two sides have occurred, sometimes backed up by military aircraft, and ships have been sunk. U.S. naval vessels have also patrolled these waters. The best-known incident involving the United States was the seizure by North Korea in January 1968 of a U.S. Navy intelligence-gathering ship, the USS *Pueblo*, in what were deemed international waters. Uncertainty over the location at sea of boundary lines and confusion, deliberate or otherwise, over control of offshore islands have been used to explain a number of incidents.

Intrusions into each other's airspace have also occurred, over both the land demarcation and what are claimed as territorial waters. Much airborne activity, by both U.S. and Republic of Korea aircraft, is for the purpose of **aerial surveillance**. Some incursions into North Korean airspace, especially along the DMZ, have been inadvertent as planes or helicopters have strayed off course. North Korean defenses have often shot down the aircraft, but have subsequently returned detained personnel or bodies. On occasion, as in 1969 with an EC-121 of the U.S. Navy, North Korea has brought down what were reconnaissance aircraft.

The frequency of confrontations between North and South at whatever point of contact appears to have diminished in the 1990s, but the capacity for insistent probing of each other's land, maritime, and air defenses doubtless remains.

See also: North Korean Submarine Incidents (1996 and 1998); North Korean Use of Terrorism; North-South Boundaries; United States Navy Reconnaissance Plane EC-121 (1969); *Pueblo,* USS (1968).

References: Bolger 1991; History: VI, 1977; Kirkbride 1994; *Newsreview,* 27 June and 4 July 1998, 26 December 1998.

INTERNATIONAL ATOMIC ENERGY AUTHORITY (IAEA)

Established in 1957 as an independent intergovernmental organization under the **United Nations**, the International Atomic Energy Authority's role has been both to promote the peaceful use of atomic energy and to prevent the spread of nuclear weapons. In this dual role, it has received delegated authority to implement the safeguard provisions of the Nuclear Non-Proliferation Treaty (NPT) of 1962 and a number of related treaties. In regard to the Korea Peninsula, South Korea's nuclear power stations have been under IAEA safeguards since the program began in the 1960s, and South Korea signed the NPT in 1975. A small reactor supplied by the USSR to North Korea was, at Soviet insistence, placed under IAEA control from 1977. As a condition for the supply of further reactors, the USSR requested that North Korea join the NPT, which it did in 1985. However, it was not until 1991 that the North signed a safeguards agreement. It also signed an agreement with South Korea in 1992 on the denuclearization of the peninsula. By then, however, following the revelations during the Gulf War that Iraq had been engaged in a clandestine nuclear program despite IAEA inspections, the IAEA approach to inspections had become much tougher.

The IAEA's insistence that it should be able to establish the full history of the **North Korean nuclear program**, including the possible production of plutonium for weapons purposes, led in 1993 to a North Korean threat to withdraw from the NPT and to cease all cooperation with the IAEA. Although the issue was temporarily defused in 1994 by the U.S.–North Korean Agreed Framework and the subsequent establishment of the **Korean Peninsula Energy Development Organization**, the IAEA remains concerned about the continued lack of transparency in the North's nuclear program and the possibility that North Korea has not relinquished the potential to develop nuclear weapons. Some IAEA safeguards remain in place, and North Korea permits IAEA inspectors access to some of its nuclear facilities. But under the terms of the agreed framework, the full details of the North's nuclear program will not be available to the IAEA until the light-water reactors, which are central to that framework, are almost complete. At the earliest, this is not likely to be before 2005.

See also: Intra-Korean Agreements.

References: Kapur 1995; Mazaar 1995; Oberdorfer 1997; Sigal 1998.

INTERNET

Use of the Internet to exchange messages in South Korea can be risky. In May 1994, Kim Hyong-ryol was found guilty of posting a message on the bulletin board of a computer network in which he disseminated information on a workers' organization deemed a pro–North Korean group. The **National Security Law** (NSL), under which he was charged, makes it an offense to support such "anti-state" organizations. In January 1997, Yun Sok-jin was similarly charged with having contravened the NSL by posting a message that challenged the official line on a North Korean submarine's intrusion into South Korean waters in September 1996. Yun had allegedly asked if the crew on the submarine had really been armed spies and not simply personnel involved in an accident. His message, reprinted without permission in a university newspaper, was spotted there by security police.

North Korea has a short entry on the World Wide Web, but viewing this in South Korea may also lead to legal action against those doing so.

See also: North Korean Submarine Incidents (1996 and 1998).

Reference Amnesty International 1995.

INTRA-KOREAN AGREEMENTS

Although for most of their existence, the two Korean states have barely talked to each other, there have been two occasions when it looked as though a change in the relationship might come about. Following the development of contacts between the United States and the **People's Republic of China** during 1971–1972, the two Koreas began a series of negotiations, first through **Red Cross North-South talks**, and later at government level. These led to the first-ever agreement between the two, when on 4 July 1972 each side issued an identical statement announcing an agreement to end hostilities and to work toward reunification, to be brought about through independent Korean efforts, without outside interference, and by peaceful means; and

national unity would be achieved, transcending all differences. To implement these arrangements, both sides agreed to the establishment of a North-South Coordinating Committee, which began to meet in August 1972. In August 1973, however, the North suspended the dialogue following the kidnapping of **Kim Dae Jung**, and the dialogue was never renewed.

The second attempt was also the result of dramatic changes in the world around the two Koreas. Following the success of President **Roh Tae Woo**'s *Nordpolitik/*Northern Policy, the admission of both Koreas to the **United Nations**, and the collapse of the **Union of Soviet Socialist Republics**, the two Koreas again began talking in 1990, at the level of prime minister. The first set of talks was held in September 1990, and on 13 December 1991 the two sides signed an Agreement on Reconciliation, Nonaggression and Exchanges between the South and the North. This referred to the 4 July 1972 joint statement and repeated many of the sentiments then expressed. This first agreement was followed by others, covering subjects such as joint liaison offices, denuclearization of the Korea Peninsula, and a joint nuclear control commission.

Whatever the intentions of the two sides, the implementation of the agreements quickly fell into difficulties. The North continued to attack the South Korean leadership, including President Roh, who was regularly described as a "traitor" and a "fascist," and a new problem soon emerged over the **North Korean nuclear program**. Although there seemed to be a better prospect of resuming the dialogue following the election of former dissident **Kim Young Sam** as South Korean president in 1992, this proved unfounded. When Kim Young Sam refused to express condolences on the death of the North Korean President, **Kim Il Sung**, in July 1994, the 1991 agreements were effectively dead.

See also: North Korean Proposals on Unification; South Korean Proposals on Reunification; Unofficial Contacts between North and South Koreans.

References: Intra-Korean Agreements 1992; Nahm 1993.

INVASION AND COUNTERINVASION
(1950–1951)

From June to September 1950, according to North Korean claims, their troops occupied more than 90 percent of the South's territory, only to be driven north by forces of the **United Nations Command** (UNC), who in turn occupied most of the northern part of Korea through October and November 1950. Routed by the entry of the **Chinese People's Volunteers** into the war, the UNC withdrew below the **38th parallel** by mid-January 1951, but returned to the parallel, where the line stabilized in early July 1951.

For civilian populations, faced in quick succession by administrations with conflicting aims and ideologies, the first ten months were often the time of greatest torment. From June to December 1950, the Korea Peninsula twice almost came under a single regime, admittedly of two very different persuasions. Of the two sides, the North Koreans set out with the clearest program. Party and propaganda workers followed their troops south to install political structures already developed in the North. **People's Committees**, which had operated in South Korea from 1945 until largely disbanded in 1946, were reestablished, elections for these committees were held, land distribution was effected, and labor and tax systems were overhauled. Many in the South, particularly in Seoul, welcomed the new order. Approximately 50 South Korean National Assemblymen who had remained in the capital extended their support, and 400,000 students and young people, according to North Korean sources, volunteered to fight on the North Korean side. (In practice, many—possibly up to 200,000 (Kim Choong Soon 1988: 32)—were conscripted.) People imprisoned for political offenses were released and encouraged to denounce those who had sentenced them.

The UNC recapture of **Seoul** by the end of September 1950 reversed political control in the South. Forced into retreat, the North Koreans reacted with killings, destruction of property, and **abductions**. The UNC was tasked to occupy the North on behalf of the United Nations, pending national elections, but the South Korean government quickly dispatched police units into the North to impose its authority. Both official and popular retribution against leftists in the North and those who had collaborated with the Communist occupiers in the South led to many arrests and summary executions. Sources speak of "tens" or "hundreds" of thousands killed. The restoration of Communist rule in the North in early 1951 led to similar acts of revenge on those thought to have collaborated with the occupying forces of the South. Massacres of civilians and prisoners of war were perpetrated by both sides. An infamous case was the massacre in February 1951 by South Korean troops of more than 700 inhabitants of a village in Koch'ang in South Kyongsang Province in South Korea, many of them elderly people and children, on suspicion of past collaboration with North Korean occupiers.

The traumas of this period have been explored most intimately in the South from the early 1980s in literature and scholarly research, as the subject of conflicting loyalties, hidden in memory and for long politically unacceptable, has been brought to the surface.

See also: Literature of the Korean Conflict; People's Committees; United Nations Commission for Unification and Rehabilitation of Korea (UNCURK).

References: Halliday and Cumings 1988; Henderson 1968; Kim 1979; Kim Choong Soon 1988; Matray 1991; Tennant 1996; Yoon 1992.

ITALIAN MEDICAL SERVICES IN THE KOREAN WAR

Italy did not contribute any troops to the **United Nations Command** in the **Korean War**, but between November 1951 and January 1955 the Italian Red Cross funded and staffed a hospital in **Seoul**. Italian medical personnel numbered 77. From a capacity of 50 beds, the hospital expanded in February 1953, after a fire had caused rebuilding, to 145 beds. It treated a large number of outpatients, mostly local civilians.

References: History: III, 1974 and VI, 1977.

JAPANESE COLONIAL PERIOD IN KOREA (1910–1945)

From 1910 to 1945, Korea was administered as a colony within the Japanese empire. (Other colonial territories were the island of **Taiwan**, 1895–1945, and the southern half of the island of Sakhalin, off the east coast of Siberia, 1905–1945.) Some have seen the Japanese decision to establish Korea as a protectorate in 1904 and then to annex it in 1910 as the culmination of a process of intervention that had been gathering pace from the 1870s. Others maintain that Japanese actions were not part of a deliberate program, but were taken in response to events. It is, however, clear that, faced by both Chinese and Russian attempts to exert influence in northeast Asia, as well as by predatory Western powers, Japan became increasingly anxious to strengthen its position in the region. It came to view Korea as an essential element in its defenses and later as a key part of its own expansion into mainland Asia. First China (1895) and then Russia (1905) had been defeated by Japan in war. Britain and the United States were prepared to give Japan a free hand in Korea in return for Japanese recognition of their own interests in Asia and the Pacific. There was another angle too. Korea's conservatism irritated Japan, which had committed itself to modernization and encouraged Japan to see its occupation of Korea as a "civilizing" mission.

The effect of Japanese occupation was indeed to introduce Korea to the essential elements of a modern economy, finances, education, and transport. Land tenure was reformed, and the basis of heavy industry was established. The country had its first taste of modern capitalism and of strong, pervasive government. The primary aim of such developments, however, was to make Korea a reliable and productive part of the Japanese empire. A decade of harsh rule was followed by conciliatory policies. As Japan strengthened its military posture, however, increasingly repressive measures after 1930 were intended to make Korea entirely subservient to Japanese needs.

J

The colonial period remains an extremely painful one for Koreans to contemplate, and many are reluctant to discuss it. Although materially it may have helped to ease Korea into the modern age, its impact was distorting and divisive. Among its lasting effects has been a fund of great bitterness toward Japan that still manifests itself in such ways as the demolition in 1996 of the former **Capitol Building in Seoul**, the old seat of the Japanese government-general, and in the feeling in both North and South Korea that Japan should still make reparation for its colonial policies. Perhaps in the hope of comforting national pride and refuting charges of acquiescence in colonial rule, the South Korean authorities between 1945 and 1997 awarded 8,366 citations for bravery in the anti-Japanese struggle, many posthumous, to "independence fighters."

Emotions toward Japan nonetheless remain ambiguous. Some elderly Koreans are still fluent in Japanese. Among foreigners, the Japanese are probably the easiest for Koreans to deal with because both cultures share many attitudes and assumptions. Japan, moreover, has become the most popular tourist destination for South Koreans.

The gravest legacy of Japanese occupation was probably its effect on the Korean opposition. Armed resistance in the years immediately following annexation was soon put down by the Japanese and forced into **Northeast China** and Siberia, from where guerrilla raids were mounted across the northern border into Korea. The spirit of passive resistance burst out in a peaceful uprising on 1 March 1919, when a Declaration of Independence, prepared largely by religious groups, was read out in Seoul. Taken by surprise, the Japanese, after an initial fierce suppression of the uprising, adopted a softer line, particularly in cultural matters. In so doing, they fragmented Korean opposition to their rule. Some of the opposition operated in exile. In April 1919, the **Korean Provisional Government** was founded in Shanghai. For a while, it managed to unite a range of opinion from conservative to socialist and gradualist before splitting into smaller elements. Various **left-wing political factions** formed in China and the Soviet Far East, encouraged by the success of the Communist revolution in Russia. Japan itself, paradoxically, helped to foster radical thinking in the young Koreans studying there through the relatively free atmosphere of its universities. Emigré groups were active in the United States.

Inside Korea, outright resistance was almost impossible because the Japanese colonial administration even after 1919 maintained a high level of covert police surveillance and the use of informers. Nonetheless, leftist attempts were made to organize peasant and labor groups and youth. Student opposition flared briefly in **Kwangju** in 1929. Disillusioned by the failure of the uprising of 1 March 1919 to achieve independence and by the indifference of the Western powers, a number of well-educated Koreans embraced the concept of national regeneration and self-strengthening, in gradual preparation for the day when Korea might become self-governing. They were particularly active in education, the press, and the study of Korean culture and language. At the same time, Korean entrepreneurs were laying the foundations of modern capitalist businesses that in the post-1945 period were to give a boost to the new Republic of Korea.

Such accommodation with the colonial power fairly soon brought charges of collaboration from those who had decided that the way to liberation from Japanese control was through revolutionary struggle. Certainly, some Koreans chose to join the colonial police and the Japanese army; others served in administrative posts or supplied the Japanese with goods, especially as war needs intensified. It was clearly difficult to hold oneself entirely aloof from the colonial authority. Many of those who had been prepared to accommodate themselves to the Japanese continued to hold government and business positions in South Korea after 1945. The issues that this raises, though rarely aired, still cause bitterness among Koreans.

The split between moderates and radicals over questions of independence and nationhood eventually crystallized into a dispute between two ideological concepts of the organization and purpose of society. Such an argument would almost certainly have taken place in the Korea Peninsula, even without the imposition of a colonial framework. China, after all, was going though a similar confrontation in the 1910s to the 1930s between communism and a conservative nationalism. Japanese colonialism, however, had the effect of channeling and constricting the argument, while at the same time sharpening divisions between the various sections of society and introducing painful antagonisms. When, in 1945, Japan was defeated, it was not through Korean endeavor, but through the military victory of the Allied forces. Koreans were left in opposing camps with their differences still unresolved.

See also: Nationalism.
References: Conroy 1960; Duus 1995; Grajdanzev 1944; Nahm 1973; Robinson 1988.

JAPANESE CONTACTS WITH NORTH KOREA

The Korean population in Japan is approximately 650,000 (Ryang 1997), a small element in the total of 5.22 million people of Korean origin estimated by the South Korean Foreign Ministry (annual *White Paper* published August 1997) to be living outside of the Korea Peninsula. Ninety percent of these migrants, or approximately 4.7 million, are settled in four areas: China (especially **Northeast China**), several of the Central Asian republics, North America, and Japan. In the first three, the Korean population has generally been assimilated to the host society and shares its basic political allegiance to either North Korea (in the case of China and the former Soviet Union) or South Korea (in the case of North America). In Japan, however, the Korean minority is divided between supporters of the two.

This division of loyalties emerged soon after the end of World War II in line with developments in Korea. Ch'ongryon, the pro–North Korean grouping, was formed in 1955 from similar earlier organizations. Through a comprehensive system of educational institutions, Ch'ongryon has allowed its supporters to educate their children in step with North Korean criteria. It offers them credit unions and insurance and runs newspapers, publishing houses, and recreational facilities. It has funneled considerable investment into North Korea and, in the absence of official relations between Japan and the North, has served as an unofficial channel of communication between the two countries. The pro–South Korean Mindan, formed in 1946, has been less prominent in promoting its members' interests. Initially, South Korea refused to allow Ch'ongryon members to have any contact with South Koreans and only in 1975 began permitting visits. From the late 1990s, softer policies in South Korea and the gradual impoverishment of the North have worked to defuse some of the tension between North and South, with a consequent weakening of affiliations to their rival support groups in Japan. Membership of Ch'ongryon has been diminishing, and the flow of investments to North Korea is said to have fallen, exacerbated by general economic downturn in Japan.

Korea's relationship with Japan has remained troubled throughout the twentieth century. In 1910, Japan annexed Korea and from the time of World War I absorbed increasing numbers of Koreans as a low-paid labor force, which by the end of World War II had peaked at more than 2 million. Japan also received a smaller number of Korean students, many of whom immersed themselves in left-wing ideologies. Liberation in 1945 led to the widespread repatriation of Koreans from Japan. From 1959, over a period of eight years, a further 100,000 returned to North Korea under national **Red Cross** auspices. Those who remained in Japan were classed first as "aliens," with their legal status long uncertain and obscured by their divided loyalties. After South Korea and Japan normalized relations in 1965, those identifying themselves as overseas nationals of the South were granted permanent residence in Japan. Only gradually did all Korean residents, whichever side they identified with, move to "special permanent resident" status in 1992.

Japan has tried to steer a course between the two states, both of which seek apologies and compensation from it for the earlier period of colonization. Japan's willingness to tolerate Ch'ongryon has contributed to friction with the South, which became particularly acute in 1974 when Mun Se-kwang, a member of the pro–North Korean community in Japan, entered South Korea from Japan with the mission of killing President **Park Chung Hee**. (His assassination attempt in August 1974 succeeded in killing Park's wife.) In an earlier bizarre incident in March 1970, Japanese Red Army members hijacked a Japanese airliner to North Korea. Japan and North Korea have agreed in principle to normalize relations, but working-level discussions held in 1990–1992 and 1997–1998 to prepare for full negotiations have stalled each time on Japanese claims that approximately twenty of their nationals were abducted from Japan in the late 1970s by North Korean agents. North Korea denounces these claims as "groundless." The two sides agreed, however, in August 1997 that on humanitarian grounds approximately 1,800 Japanese women who accompanied their Korean husbands to the North from the 1950s onward should for the first time be allowed to make brief home visits to Japan to renew family contacts. At least two groups have already made such visits.

See also: Japanese Colonial Period in Korea (1910–1945).

References: Macdonald 1996; Ryang 1997; Yi 1973.

JAPANESE INVOLVEMENT IN THE KOREAN WAR

Japan had still not regained its independence at the beginning of the **Korean War**, but the Japanese prime minister, Yoshida Shigeru, welcomed **United Nations** (UN) action and promised on 14 July 1950 that Japan would do what it could to help. The Japanese were involved in several ways. The **United Nations Command** (UNC), under General **Douglas MacArthur**, was established in Tokyo, Japanese firms helped refurbish U.S. equipment for use in Korea, and the use of Japanese as guards on U.S. military installations in Japan freed U.S. troops for Korea. Hospital bases in Japan received UNC casualties from the fighting. Despite denials at the time, Japanese personnel also worked in Korea. Japanese technical expertise about Korean harbors and beaches played an important role in several of the UN landings, notably the **Inch'on landing** in September 1950, when Japanese acted as pilots, and Japanese minesweepers helped clear **Wonsan** harbor in October 1950. In addition, the supply of goods and services for the Korean War provided a major boost to Japan's economic redevelopment.

JOINT COMMISSION ON TRUSTEESHIP

Following the meeting of the foreign ministers of the **Union of Soviet Socialist Republics** (USSR), Britain, and the United States in Moscow in December 1945, at which the **Moscow Agreement** was signed, a joint USSR-U.S. commission on trusteeship was established. It was to consult with political parties and other groups in Korea to bring about the reunification of the **Korea Peninsula**. Formed in January 1946, it was headed on the USSR side by Colonel-General **Terenty Shtykov**, and on the U.S. side by Major-General A. V. Arnold. From the beginning, the commission was unpopular with Koreans. It first met during March–May 1946, but adjourned on 8 May without having reached any agreement. Further meetings were held during June–August 1946 and again during May–August 1947. Thereafter, the commission ceased to function, and, although not formally dissolved, it effectively ended when the U.S. government passed the Korean problem to the **United Nations** in November 1947.
References: Cho 1967; Cumings 1981.

JOINT OBSERVER TEAMS

Ten Joint Observer Teams were authorized in the **armistice** agreement (paragraph 23) to assist the **Military Armistice Commission** (MAC) in the implementation of its duties. Each team was comprised of four to six officers, half nominated by the **United Nations Command**, half by the joint North Korean/Chinese command. Their area of jurisdiction, as for the MAC, was the **Demilitarized Zone** (DMZ) and the **Han River** estuary, where they were to investigate reported violations of the armistice agreement. Such infringements covered unauthorized crossings into enemy territory, unsanctioned entry into the DMZ, and introduction of unauthorized weapons into the DMZ. In practice, the Joint Observer Teams had little effect in deterring such violations of the terms of the armistice.
References: History: VI, 1977; Kirkbride 1994.

JOINT SECURITY AREA
See P'anmunjom.

JOY, CHARLES TURNER (1895–1956)

Charles Turner Joy was born in St. Louis, Missouri, in 1895. He was commissioned in the U.S. Navy in 1916 and served in the Atlantic Fleet during World War I. Various appointments thereafter included a spell as the commander of a U.S. gunboat on the Yangzi River in China. He served both at sea and in Washington during World War II, reaching the rank of rear admiral, and in 1949 became commander of U.S. Naval Forces, Far East.

Joy was still in this post when the **Korean War** began in 1950, and he played an important role in helping to organize the amphibious landings at **Inch'on** and **Wonsan** in September and October 1950, for which he was awarded the U.S. Army's Distinguished Service Order. When the **armistice** negotiations began at **Kaesong** in July 1951, the United Nations (UN) commander, General **Matthew Ridgway**, personally selected Joy as the chief UN negotiator. Joy served in that capacity until May 1952. During this period, he established the pattern that was to mark the negotiations on the UN side. He was determined in his approach, sticking firmly to his points, but avoiding the polemical outbursts often favored by the North Korean/Chinese side. His own inclination was to be unyielding on all points, but he followed his instructions from Washington carefully, avoiding any suggestion that he might disagree with them. As the negotiations dragged on, particularly over the question of **repatriation of prisoners of war**, Joy became increasingly frustrated and eventually asked to be relieved of his post. On his return to the United States, he became superintendent of the U.S. Naval Academy.

Joy remained critical of the conduct both of the war and of the armistice negotiations, especially after **Dwight D. Eisenhower** became president in 1953. In 1955, Joy published an account of the negotiations, *How Communists Negotiate*. This claimed that the only way forward was to adopt a position and stick rigidly to it, and it attacked the Washington policymakers for not allowing him to take a harder line. Joy died a year after its publication. The publication in 1978 of the diaries he kept during the negotiations provided more detail of his views. However, he continued to be respected both for his naval role and for his negotiations, and in 1959, the U.S. Navy named a destroyer after him. It was an alleged North Vietnamese attack on this ship, the USS *Turner Joy*, and on the USS *Maddox* in August

1964 that led to direct U.S. military involvement in Vietnam.

See also: United States Forces in the Korean War.

References: Cagle and Manson 1957; Field 1962; Goodman 1978; Hermes 1966; Joy 1955.

JUCHE

From the mid-1950s, North Korea developed a doctrine of self-reliance and independence. As the dispute between its two chief allies, China and the Soviet Union, sharpened, this evolved into the *juche* doctrine, which has remained the basis of North Korea's official philosophy. *Juche* revolves around two concepts: the people are the masters of their destiny, and they should remain independent of all outside influences. It does not forbid outside links or the acceptance of assistance, but demands that the Korean people should avoid spiritual and psycho-logical dependence, and above all, the traditional Korean practice of *sadaejuui*—looking up to the great—i.e., deferring to China. Although *juche* stresses the centrality of human beings, people achieve this by their subordination to the leader; it thus supported the rule of **Kim Il Sung** and the succession of his son, **Kim Jong Il**. *Juche* has survived as the basis of North Korea's political thought despite the country's actual dependence on outside assistance and the defection to South Korea in 1997 of **Hwang Jang-yop**, widely believed to be the architect of the doctrine.

So intimately is the concept associated with Kim Il Sung that North Korea's official chronology incorporates the term *juche*, taking as its starting point the year of Kim's birth, 1912. Thus, 1998 is expressed as *Juche* 87 (the initial year is counted in).

See also: Sino-Soviet Dispute.

KAESONG

Kaesong, the city that was the capital of the country during the Koryo period (935–1392), lies just below the **38th parallel.** It is some 35 miles (56 kilometers) from **Seoul.** From 1945 to 1950, it was in South Korea and was the first city to be taken by the North Korean forces in the **Korean War.** Because the **Demilitarized Zone** was to the south of it when the war ended in 1953, Kaesong has remained under the jurisdiction of North Korea. When **armistice** negotiations began in the summer of 1951, the **United Nations Command** (UNC) proposed that meetings should be held on a Danish hospital ship off the North Korean port of **Wonsan** but eventually accepted the North Korean–**Chinese People's Volunteers** (CPV) proposal of Kaesong as the site for the first round of talks, even though it was behind the Communist lines. After a preliminary meeting on 8 July 1951, substantive discussions began on 10 July. From the beginning, however, there were problems with Kaesong. Although it was designated a neutral area, the North Korean–CPV side tried both to intimidate UNC officials and to control Western press access. Even after agreement was reached on establishing a neutral zone around the negotiation site, charges of harassment passed between the two sides, and this was eventually one of the factors that led the UNC's chief negotiator, Vice-Admiral **Charles Turner Joy,** to break off the talks on 23 August. When they resumed in October 1951, the UNC insisted that they move to **P'anmunjom,** which was regarded as a more genuinely neutral location, with easy access for both sides.

Kaesong remained the headquarters for the North Korean–CPV negotiating teams while the talks continued at P'anmunjom. As such, it was treated by the UNC as a neutral area, and there was regular contact between it and P'anmunjom. In December 1952, at a difficult moment in the armistice negotiations, and when it was believed that the North Korean–CPV side was using Kaesong to prepare for a major assault, the UNC considered ending Kaesong's immunity and even bombing the

K

area. The moment passed, however, and Kaesong was spared. As a result, it is one of the few North Korean cities to show traces of its historical past, with attractive old houses and traditional inns, as well as temples and royal tombs in the surrounding hills. It is regularly used as a base for those visiting P'anmunjom from the North Korean side. It is also a major center for the production of Korean ginseng, much valued for its medicinal and restorative properties, and remains an important center for North Korean armed forces.

References: Hermes 1966; Joy 1955.

KAP'YONG

In April 1951, Kap'yong, a small town some 30 miles (50 kilometers) to the northeast of the South Korean capital, **Seoul,** was the scene of major fighting involving the 27th British Commonwealth Brigade during the fifth Chinese offensive. Following an attack by the **Chinese People's Volunteers** on 22 April, the South Korean 6th Division began to break up, and the Commonwealth Brigade moved in to support them. Troops involved included the 2nd Battalion Princess Patricia's Canadian Light Infantry, the 3rd Battalion Royal Australian Regiment, and the British 1st Battalion The Middlesex Regiment, supported by the New Zealand artillery and U.S. tanks. They held the position, allowing the South Korean forces to withdraw, and were then able to effect their own withdrawal. In the process, they had broken the advance of an entire Chinese division. Both the Australian and the Canadian forces received a U.S. presidential citation for their part in the battle, and carry "Kap'yong" on their battle honors. Today, Kap'yong is the site of a Commonwealth War

Memorial and of separate Australian and Canadian monuments.

See also: Australian Forces in the Korean War; Canadian Forces in the Korean War; First Commonwealth Division in the Korean War; Imjin River, Battle of (1951); New Zealand Forces in the Korean War.

References: "Canadians in Korea" (World Wide Web site); Grey 1988; O'Neill 1985.

KATCOM

See **Koreans Attached to the Commonwealth Forces (KATCOM).**

KATUSA

See **Korean Augmentation to the United States Army (KATUSA).**

KCIA

See **National Intelligence Service (NIS).**

KCNA

See **Korean Central News Agency (KCNA).**

KEDO

See **Korean Peninsula Energy Development Organization (KEDO).**

KIM CH'AEK (1903–1951)

Kim Ch'aek was an anti-Japanese guerrilla fighter in the 1930s, operating from bases in **Northeast China.** His intimacy with **Kim Il Sung** won him high office after 1945, but he was killed in a U.S. bombing raid in January 1951. He is rare among Kim Il Sung's generation in still being acknowledged. North Korea's main technical university is named after him.

Kim was born in North Hamgyong Province on the Sino-Korean border. Forced after 1941 by Japanese pressure to withdraw into Siberia, where he received military training from the Russians, he returned with the Soviet army to Korea in 1945. In 1946, he was deputy commander in the embryonic **North Korean People's Army** (NKPA), with responsibility for political matters, and from 1948, he was a deputy premier and minister for industry. At the outbreak of the **Korean War,** he belonged to the party Military Affairs Committee and from late 1950 served as front-line commander of the NKPA.

References: Matray 1991; Scalapino and Lee 1972; Suh 1981.

KIM CHI-HA

See **Kim Yong-il (pen name, Kim Chi-ha).**

KIM DAE JUNG (1924–)

A prominent South Korean politician, long known for his opposition to successive presidents from **Syngman Rhee** to **Kim Young Sam,** Kim Dae Jung was elected president in December 1997, at his fourth attempt.

Kim was born in South Cholla Province on 6 January 1924. He graduated from high school in 1943 and became a clerk in a Japanese-owned company in Mokp'o. During the **Korean War,** he was captured by North Korean forces and sentenced to death, but escaped. After several attempts, he entered the National Assembly in 1960, as an opposition member. In 1971, he was the New Democratic Party's candidate against President **Park Chung Hee** in the presidential election, losing by a narrow margin. From then on, he became a bitter critic of Park Chung Hee, alleging in particular that Park used the "threat from the North" to justify repression in South Korea. Park's government regarded him as one of its most dangerous opponents, and during a visit to Japan in 1973, he was kidnapped by agents of the Korean Central Intelligence Agency (KCIA) and brought back to Seoul. Kim claimed that the KCIA intended to kill him, but that he was saved by U.S. intervention.

In the next six years, he remained a stringent critic of Park and was frequently arrested for antigovernment activities. After **Chun Doo Hwan** seized power in 1979, Kim was again arrested. Although in jail, he

President Kim Dae Jung with Sir Timothy Lankester, director of the School of Oriental and African Studies, University of London, after receiving an honorary doctorate from the University in April 1998. (©SOAS)

was accused of responsibility for the **Kwangju** uprising in May 1980 and sentenced to death. Government sources also implied that he was a Communist and sympathetic to North Korea. This last accusation was based on alleged similarities between Kim's proposals on reunification and those from the North. Following U.S. pressure, the sentence was commuted, first to life imprisonment and later to 20 years, and in December 1982 he was allowed to go to the United States for medical treatment. He spent two years studying, speaking, and writing, until he was allowed to return to South Korea in February 1985. In theory, Kim was still banned from politics, but in reality, he was very much involved, with Kim Young Sam, first as an adviser to the Council for Promotion of Democracy and later as a member of the Reunification Democratic Party. He and Kim Young Sam disagreed over the 1987 presidential election. Both stood, allowing **Roh Tae Woo** to win. In the 1992 presidential election, Kim lost again, this time to Kim Young Sam.

Kim announced his retirement from politics and spent some time in Britain. On his return to Seoul in 1993, he resumed his political career, founding the National Council for New Politics. In 1997, he and another veteran political leader, **Kim Jong Pil**, agreed to join forces to fight the presidential election, with Kim Dae Jung as its candidate. The ruling party split, and Kim Dae Jung won by a tiny margin. Despite this, his victory had great symbolic significance because it marked the first time that power had passed out of the hands of the government party since 1948. Although some conservative South Koreans claimed that the North would welcome Kim Dae Jung's election as president, the first reactions from **P'yongyang** were cautious. Kim's first year in office has been taken up with the aftermath of the 1997 economic crisis, as well as with devising a less confrontational approach to North Korea.
References: Kim 1985, 1987(a) and (b).

KIM IL SUNG (1912–1994)
Much mystery surrounds the origins and history of Kim Il Sung, who ruled the Democratic People's Republic of Korea (North Korea) from its foundation in 1948 until his death in July 1994.

He was born in a peasant family near what is now the North Korean capital, **P'yongyang**, in a village called Man'gyondae, on 15 April 1912. His real name was Kim Song-ju. Official North Korean accounts of Kim Il Sung's life that link him through his parents and grandparents to some of the major nationalist and antiforeign events of the last 150 years appear to be pure fantasy.

Kim's parents left Korea for **Northeast China** in 1925, where Kim attended Chinese schools. Although official accounts say that he left home in 1926 to begin his struggle against the Japanese, it is more likely that, after being expelled from school in 1929, he joined one of the Korean anti-Japanese guerrilla bands operating from Northeast China, some of which liaised with groups from the Chinese Communist Party. While later accounts exaggerate his role, he did rise to some prominence and was the subject of special attention by the Japanese police. After 1941, Japanese pressure on the guerrilla groups increased, and Kim retreated into the Soviet Union. There is no clear record of his activities during World War II. In 1945, following the division of Korea, he returned with many of his former guerrilla colleagues and a number of Soviet Koreans, who together helped to establish the administration in the Soviet-run northern part of the peninsula. Kim was not especially chosen for this role; rather, as an able organizer and administrator, he appealed to the Soviet forces. His first official post was that of first secretary of the North Korean Communist Party, later subsumed in the **Korean Workers' Party.** That post he achieved by conciliating or eliminating his rivals. When, with Soviet backing, the Democratic People's Republic of Korea was established on 9 September 1948, following failed U.S.-Soviet attempts at achieving a unified Korean government, Kim became premier.

Kim spent the next two years consolidating his position as supreme leader and in planning to reunify the peninsula. Like most Koreans, he could not accept a permanent partition of a country that had been united for more than 1,000 years, but he could see no prospect of a peaceful union. When he decided to go to war is not clear, but withdrawal of U.S. forces from the South and the victory of the Communists in the Chinese civil war in 1949 were important factors. There was also much tension along the **38th parallel** and regular clashes between the opposing forces. Kim may have thought that, unless he struck first, the South would attack.

North Korean leader Kim Il Sung (right) with Peng Dehuai, commander of the Chinese forces in Korea (the Chinese People's Volunteers), from an undated photo. (Xinhua News Agency)

The assault that began on 25 June 1950 with massive North Korean advances across the parallel was at first a resounding success. By mid-August, the Republic of Korea was reduced to an enclave around **Pusan** in the far south. The North's victory seemed inevitable, but already outside support was being marshaled to aid the South. By September, following the successful landing of **United Nations** (UN) forces at **Inch'on** and a UN–South Korean breakout from **Pusan**, the war was taken to the North. Kim appealed for Soviet and Chinese help. The former was not forthcoming, but as the UN forces reached the **Yalu River**, the Chinese intervened, and Kim's regime was saved. Although the war dragged on until 1953, it ceased to be a war of movement by mid-1951, and Kim would never again have the opportunity to reunify the peninsula.

After 1953, Kim set about reconstruction with determination, proclaiming an increasingly nationalist and self-reliant line, which developed into the *juche* (self-reliance) doctrine—though in reality, North Korea relied on assistance from the Soviet Union, Eastern Europe, and China. Kim also purged potential rivals from the leadership. In economic terms, North Korea pursued a policy of heavy industrialization on the Soviet model and the collectivization of agriculture, similar to but not as sweeping as that in China. The economic gains made in the 1950s and the 1960s were substantial and put the North ahead of the South.

The goal of reunification did not disappear, but it was in the background during the 1950s. In 1960, Kim proposed a "confederated republic of Koryo" in which both Korean political systems would coexist in one state. This remained his unification blueprint until his death, but, while publicizing this scheme and engaging the South in a dialogue during the 1970s, the North also tried to destabilize the South with assassination attempts on its leaders, including the raid on the **Blue House** in 1968 and the bomb attack at **Rangoon** in 1983.

Kim carried out further purges of domestic opponents in the 1960s, and thereafter he was unchallenged. In 1972, under a new Constitution, he became head of state, but remained party secretary. He was now usually referred to as the "Great Leader." The question of a successor concerned him. After several false starts, he selected his eldest son, **Kim Jong Il**. The younger Kim remained in the background until the 1980s and then appeared as the designated successor. Kim Il Sung also worked to maintain a balanced relationship with the Soviet Union and China after their breach of friendship in the late 1950s.

By the 1990s, North Korea was in difficulties. Its economic advance had faltered, and the South had economically surpassed it. North Korea's friends and allies began to trade with, and eventually establish diplomatic relations with, South Korea. Kim Il Sung may have decided that a bargaining chip was to develop nuclear weapons, which led to international pressure to prevent nuclear proliferation.

Kim died, apparently of a heart attack, on 8 July 1994, just before a planned summit meeting with South Korea's President **Kim Young Sam**. Although Kim Jong Il effectively succeeded, he did not at first become either president or party secretary. It was a blighted inheritance, with the industrial economy in decline, continued international concern over nuclear weapons, and devastating floods leading to widespread reports of food shortages.

See also: Carter, James (Jimmy) Earl; Kim Jong Il; North Korean Proposals on Unification; Soviet Occupation of North Korea (1945–1948).

References: Kim 1965; McCormack 1993; Suh 1981, 1988.

KIM JONG IL (1941–)

Kim Jong Il succeeded his father, **Kim Il Sung**, as the leader of the Democratic People's Republic of Korea (North Korea) in July 1994. Although he had long been groomed as the successor, he has taken only one of his father's formal titles as secretary-general of the **Korean Workers' Party** (KWP), and was elected to that post only on 8 October 1997. Until then, his only formal title had been commander-in-chief of the armed forces. In September 1998, after a change to the 1972 Constitution, he was reelected as chairman of the National Defense Commission, a position that was redefined as the highest post. This move left his father, Kim Il Sung, as "president in perpetuity." State ceremonial functions have passed to the chairman of the Supreme People's Assembly, or parliament.

Kim Jong Il was born on 15 February 1941. According to official North Korean accounts, his

A one-won stamp bearing the image of a studious Kim Jong Il.

birth took place in an anti-Japanese guerrilla camp on Mount Paektu, a sacred mountain on the Sino-Korean border. In reality, he was probably born in the Soviet Union, where his father lived from 1941 to 1945. During the **Korean War**, he was sent to **Northeast China** for safety. He was educated at an East German pilot's college and at Kim Il Sung University in **P'yongyang**, graduating in 1963. He then worked in the secretariat of the KWP, eventually becoming his father's secretary and assisting him in the purges Kim Il Sung carried out in 1967. In 1973, he became party secretary in charge of organization and propaganda; from then until he was formally acknowledged as his father's successor in 1980, he was not named but was referred to as "the party center." After October 1980, he was usually described in English as the "Dear Leader," while his father was known as the "Great Leader."

South Korean sources have tended to demonize Kim Jong Il, describing him as a hard-drinking playboy and often attributing to him some of the more aggressive policies followed by North Korea since the 1970s. In fact, not a great deal is known about his role or his abilities, apart from a well-established interest in films and filmmaking. After his father's death, he spent much time with the military, leading to speculation that he is dependent on them for support. He has continued to promote his father's proposals for Korean reunification, and been equally hostile to better relations with South Korea.

References: Kim 1989; McCormack 1993; Oberdorfer 1997; Suh 1988.

KIM JONG PIL (1926–)

Kim Jong Pil is a former South Korean military officer turned politician, who has shown a remarkable talent for survival. He was born in South Ch'ungch'ong Province on 7 January 1926. He attended Seoul National University, but dropped out and joined the Korean Military Academy in 1948. He was linked by marriage to Major-General **Park Chung Hee** and organized the 1961 coup that brought Park to power. Kim set up and was the first head of the Korean Central Intelligence Agency, and also helped found Park's Democratic Republican Party (DRP), of which he was chairman (1964–1968). Kim was prime minister from 1971 to 1975, during the first phase of Park's **Yushin Constitution**. Kim

also played an important role in Park's new policy toward North Korea. After Park's assassination in October 1979, Kim became president of the DRP, but he and his brother were among those purged during 1980–1981 by President **Chun Doo Hwan.**

From 1984 to 1986, Kim lived in the United States, returning to South Korea in 1986 to form the New Democratic Liberal Party, for which he was an unsuccessful presidential candidate in the 1987 elections. Despite this, his political rehabilitation was complete. In a deal with President **Roh Tae Woo** and the opposition political leader, **Kim Young Sam**, Kim joined the ruling Democratic Liberal Party, eventually becoming its chairman in an arrangement that allowed Kim Young Sam to become the party's presidential candidate. However, Kim Young Sam ousted him, and Kim Jong Pil formed the United Liberal Democrats, based in his home province. In 1997, Kim joined the veteran opposition leader—and his own old opponent under Park—**Kim Dae Jung**, in the latter's successful bid for the presidency. His reward was a return to the premiership when Kim Dae Jung assumed office in February 1998.

KIM KU (1876–1949)

Kim, a leading right-wing nationalist, was born in 1876 in Hwanghae Province and soon immersed himself in unrest when, in the early 1890s, he joined the Tonghak movement of protest against foreign influence and modernizing policies. Over the next 25 years, he constantly resisted growing Japanese encroachment on Korea, and, from 1910, Japanese colonial rule, through his activity in irregular military units and protest groups and through acts of violence that included killing a Japanese. He was imprisoned twice.

In 1919, Kim supported the March First Independence uprising, but on its failure fled to China, where he joined the Shanghai-based **Korean Provisional Government** (KPG). He served as head of the KPG's Police Bureau, as minister for internal affairs, and as its premier in 1926. In 1930, he and others founded the **Korean Independence Party**. His tactics for the Korean resistance movement at that time veered toward terrorism—possibly to assure the movement's Chinese hosts of its determination to fight the Japanese—and he was implicated in bomb attacks on Japanese targets in Japan and China. For a while, he had close links with the Chinese Nationalist government, which offered military training to Koreans until Japanese pressure forced it to withdraw the arrangement. Military liaison was renewed when in 1940 the Korean Restoration Army, comprised of non-Communist elements, joined with the Chinese Nationalist army in the war against Japan.

Kim Ku refused any form of collaboration with left-wing elements within a united front and remained a determined supporter of the KPG. When the KPG followed the Chinese Nationalist government in 1940 to Chongqing in western China, Kim became KPG president. After the defeat of Japan in August 1945, he had hoped to return to Korea at the head of the provisional government, but the U.S. military occupying forces insisted that all KPG members return as private individuals and delayed Kim's reentry until 23 November. In his absence, he had been elected minister for internal affairs in the short-lived **Korean People's Republic** and a member of the **Korean Democratic Party** (KDP) on its formation in September 1945. Kim joined in the various political groupings of the postliberation years, but remained violently opposed to attempts to impose solutions from without that might lead to a continuing foreign presence in the peninsula or to its division. In December 1945, he called for demonstrations against proposals for a **Joint Commission on Trusteeship** and attempted a showdown with the U.S. military occupation authorities on the issue. Responsibility for the assassination that same month of the KDP leader, Song Chin-u, who may have been ready to support the trusteeship scheme, has been attributed to him. Kim clashed with **Syngman Rhee** over the holding of elections in the southern half of the peninsula in May 1948 and the establishment of a separate government. That April, Kim attempted with **Kim Kyu-shik** and others to discuss unification with **Kim Il Sung** in **P'yongyang**. In June 1949, having survived an earlier attempt on his life in 1938, he was assassinated by an army officer, possibly with Rhee's knowledge.

See also: Chinese Involvement in Korea (1919–1948).

References: Cumings 1981, 1990; Lee 1963; Nahm 1993; Scalapino and Lee 1972.

KIM KYU-SHIK (1881–1950)

Kim Kyu-shik was a moderate nationalist who worked for much of his life outside of Korea. Kim was born in Kangwon Province. He was a Christian and a protégé of the **Underwood family** and received his college education in the United States. On his return to Korea, he worked as a teacher, but fled the country in 1912 and finally settled in Shanghai in 1918. Early in 1919, he was selected, doubtless partly because of his familiarity with English and Western ways, to represent the Korean Young Men's Association at the **Paris Conference** in France. (Official recognition was denied to Koreans, who were deemed Japanese citizens.) Kim's attempts to present Korean claims failed. While in France, he was appointed foreign minister and then education minister of the **Korean Provisional Government** (KPG), established in Shanghai in April 1919.

From France, Kim moved in September 1919 to chair the Korean Commission set up by **Syngman Rhee** in Washington to lobby the U.S. government, but went back to China in early 1921. He resigned that same year from the KPG in protest at Rhee's domineering attitude toward it. Disillusionment with Western indifference to Korean demands for independence, as manifested again at the Washington Conference (1921–1922), turned Kim, along with other Korean nationalists, toward the newly emerging Bolsheviks, who at that stage were seeking allies in the Russian Far East and were offering support to revolutionary movements. Kim headed the Korean delegation to the First Conference of the Toilers of the Far East, held in Moscow and Petrograd (St. Petersburg) in 1922. Soviet intervention in favor of Korea, however, never materialized, and Kim withdrew back into the Korean nationalist struggle in China. In the early 1930s, he founded the Anti-Japanese United League of Koreans in China and in 1935 joined with Kim Won-bong in setting up the Korean National Revolutionary Party. He was also brought again into the KPG, of which he became a vice-president in 1944 after it had moved to Chongqing in western China.

Kim Kyu-shik returned to Seoul only in December 1945, but in September of that year had been elected, in his absence, as foreign minister of the short-lived **Korean People's Republic**. In 1946, he was brought into discussions for an Interim

Legislative Assembly for the south of the country by the U.S. military occupation, which welcomed him as a well-educated moderate. However, he came to disagree again with Syngman Rhee, this time over Rhee's decision to go for separate elections and a separate government in the South in 1948. Kim still hoped for a solution that would keep the peninsula unbroken, and in April 1948 he made an unsuccessful visit with **Kim Ku** and others to North Korea to discuss unification with **Kim Il Sung**. Kim Kyu-shik returned to the South, but during the early stages of the **Korean War** was abducted by the North Koreans and taken north, where he died.

See also: Chinese Involvement in Korea (1919–1948); Korea Peninsula (1945–1948); Paris Conference and Versailles Peace Treaty (1919); United States Army Military Government in Korea (1945–1948).

References: Cumings 1981, 1990; Lee 1963; Nahm 1993; Scalapino and Lee 1972; Suh 1970.

KIM SONG-JU
See **Kim Il Sung**.

KIM YONG-IL (PEN NAME, KIM CHI-HA) (1941–)

The poet, dramatist, and essayist Kim Chi-ha, by which name he is generally known, was a fierce critic of President **Park Chung Hee**'s regime, which he attacked for its oppression of the poor and promotion of elite groups. In 1972, he was tried for violation of the 1961 Anti-Communist Law, a widely framed piece of legislation that caught those judged to have encouraged anti-state organizations "on foreign Communist lines." Sentenced to death in 1974, he was reprieved in the face of national and international protest. Released briefly during 1974–1975 with a suspended sentence, he was tried again and received a further term of imprisonment, much of it spent in solitary confinement. He was released again in 1980, and publication of his work in South Korea, long thwarted, has since eased. Kim is a Catholic and has been a supporter of radical theology. He has also worked for environmental and human rights causes.

See also: National Security Law.

References: Commission on Theological Concerns of the Christian Conference of Asia 1981; Eckert et al. 1990; Kim 1980; Shaw 1991; *Who's Who in Korean Literature* 1996.

KIM YOUNG SAM (1927–)

Kim Young Sam was president of South Korea from 1993 to 1998, the first elected nonmilitary president since **Syngman Rhee** in 1960. Kim was born on Koje Island in South Kyongsang Province in 1927 and graduated from Seoul National University in 1952. When he became president, some photographs were produced of him in military uniform, but his military service was very short. He worked for the government before entering the National Assembly in 1954 as a member of the ruling Liberal Party. Before long, he switched to the opposition benches, and he was to remain a prominent figure in opposition circles until 1990. In 1971, he lost to **Kim Dae Jung** in the opposition's selection of a presidential candidate, but continued to play a prominent role in opposition politics, becoming leader of the New Democratic Party in 1974. He was expelled from the National Assembly in 1978, at the beginning of the political crisis that eventually led to the death of President **Park Chung Hee** in 1979. Following **Chun Doo Hwan**'s military coup, Kim was arrested in May 1980 and later held under house arrest. In May 1983, he went on a hunger strike for twenty-three days in protest at political oppression. Although technically still banned from political activity, he became a cochair of the Council for Promotion of Democracy on its establishment in 1984 and, like Kim Dae Jung, advisor to the New Korea Democratic Party in 1986. The following year, however, as the presidential election approached, he set up his own party, the Reunification Democratic Party, and ran as its presidential candidate against **Roh Tae Woo** and Kim Dae Jung. He lost, but in February 1990, merged his party with the ruling Democratic Justice Party and the smaller New Democratic Republican Party to form a new government party, the Democratic Liberal Party (DLP). Kim became executive chairman of the DLP and was its successful candidate for the 1992 presidential election.

As president, he began well, with a series of reforming measures. Before long, however, he was faced with the problem of the **North Korean nuclear program** and domestic pressure to reopen inquiries into the 1980 **Kwangju** massacre. In his dealings with the North, Kim Young Sam seemed to lack the interest or skills of his predecessor and to swing between concern and bravado. His refusal to send condolences to the North following the death of **Kim Il Sung** in July 1994, although he had been actively preparing to meet him at a summit meeting, led to much hostile comment from the North and a refusal to reopen direct dialogue with the South. Even though he eventually authorized the trials of Roh and Chun, Kim gained little political benefit because he was felt to have agreed only under pressure. His last months of office were marred by scandal over his son's alleged corruption and tax evasion and his attempts to prevent the election of Kim Dae Jung as his successor.

See also: Intra-Korean Agreements; *Nordpolitik*/Northern Policy.

Reference: Crusader for Democracy 1993; Oberdorfer 1997.

KMAG

See **Korean Military Advisory Group (KMAG).**

KOJE ISLAND PRISONER OF WAR CAMP (1952)

Koje, a mountainous island lying off the southern coast of South Korea, from the end of January 1951 housed the main camp run by the United States on behalf of the **United Nations Command** (UNC) for **prisoners of war** (POWs) captured from the **North Korean People's Army** (NKPA) and the **Chinese People's Volunteers** (CPV). A number of prisoners classified as civilian internees (mainly civilians claiming South Korean residence who had been conscripted into the NKPA) were also held on Koje. The majority of prisoners were male, but some women were also detained.

From the outset, administration of the Koje camp was difficult. The compounds, designed for 12,500 inmates, had to accommodate approximately 170,000 prisoners and were soon crammed. Conditions of detention were poor, and the number of guards, U.S. and South Korean, was insufficient to maintain control. The North Korean POWs in particular were bitterly hostile to the South Korean guards. North Koreans were separated from pro–South Koreans, many of whom had been obliged on capture by the North Koreans to fight for the North, until they were taken prisoner by the UNC. Chinese POWs divided into pro- and anti-Communist elements, the latter often soldiers who during the Chinese civil war (1946–1949) had

fought on the Nationalist side, but had been inducted into the CPV. Leadership within the compounds passed to hard-core groups of political activists from both right and left, who, particularly in the Korean and pro-Nationalist Chinese compounds, intimidated with beatings, "trials," and murder those who opposed them. The compounds, placed close to each other, were separated only by barbed wire. Communication between them and with the surrounding refugees, of whom there were many, and with the villagers was easy. North Korean activists, some of whom may have deliberately courted capture in order to infiltrate the camps, were able to maintain contact with their political headquarters through these other inhabitants of Koje. On the UNC side, shortages of guards, and hesitancy brought on by the possibility that the **armistice** talks at **P'anmunjom** from July 1951 might speedily end hostilities, encouraged a policy of minimal intervention in the running of the compounds.

Trouble flared first in June 1951 when North Korean POWs attempted a mass breakout. Force was used to reimpose order, with ensuing fatalities and injuries. The pattern of rioting and suppression continued, exacerbated by UNC attempts to conduct screening of prisoners and internees during November–December 1951, January–February 1952, and again in April 1952 to ascertain first the status of prisoners and then which country they preferred to be repatriated to. On 7 May 1952, the commander of the camp, General Francis Dodd, was seized by the Communist inmates of compound 76 when he met them at their request to discuss grievances. He was released on 10 May after UNC statements accepting some of the prisoners' demands. The validity of these statements was immediately denied as having been issued under duress. The Chinese POWs were removed to **Cheju Island**, those Korean POWs resisting repatriation were removed to the mainland, pro-Communist and anti-Communist prisoners on Koje were rehoused separately, and the area around the compounds was cleared. Considerable force had to be used to eject some of the Communist prisoners from their old compounds. The resulting deaths were utilized by Communist propaganda as evidence of UNC brutality.

See also: Pongam Island Revolt (1952); Repatriation of Prisoners of War.

References: Halliday and Cumings; Hermes 1966; HMSO Korea No. 1 (1952); MacDonald 1986, 1989.

KOREA PENINSULA (1945–1948)

The three years between liberation from Japan on 15 August 1945 and the formation of separate governments in the North and the South in the late summer of 1948 were crucial in determining the fate of the Korea Peninsula. These years present a confused and sometimes violent picture, as two regimes, each obliged to submit to foreign supervision, struggled to work out a way forward. A unified country was the goal for both, but each side had its own vision of the kind of society it wanted, constructed from the experiences of a quarter-century of colonial rule and exile.

The concept of division was present from the first, when the Allied forces decided that the Japanese surrender in Korea would be taken north of a dividing line, set at the **38th parallel**, by Soviet troops, and south of that line by U.S. forces. The Soviet army arrived first and by 25 August had installed its headquarters in **P'yongyang**, where on 16 September it announced the formation of a military government. U.S. forces did not reach **Seoul** until 8 September. On 11 September, the **United States Army Military Government in Korea** (USAMGIK) started functioning.

Korean political circles, however, had been active from the moment of liberation, and, within a few days of 15 August, preparatory committees for national reconstruction had been set up in Seoul, by Yo Un-hyong, and in the north, by **Cho Man-shik**. Yo Un-hyong's committee led to the establishment of the short-lived **Korean People's Republic** on 6 September, balanced between non-Communist and Communist members. In both north and south, **People's Committees** with a popular representation were forming by early September. The **Korean Communist Party** was revived both north and south. Such initiatives were soon affected by the views and intentions of the two occupying forces. In the north, the Soviet military authorities pressed for equal representation of rightists and leftists in political organizations and started on a gradual centralization of power. In the south, the USAMGIK, headed by General **John Hodge**, was wary of the unfamiliar scene and fearful of Communist influences. It refused to recognize the Korean People's Republic, insisted that members of the **Korean Provisional Government** return as individuals, and looked to Korean conservative circles for advice. The wartime Allies had decided in their discussions on the future of the Pacific region that Korea should be prepared for independence through a period of international trusteeship. Despite the complicating factor of an incipient division of the peninsula, a postwar meeting of the Allies in Moscow in December 1945 produced plans for a U.S.-Soviet **Joint Commission on Trusteeship** for Korea over five years. Initial reaction among Koreans north and south was violently against the scheme; but under Soviet pressure, the Korean Communists swung in favor.

By autumn of 1945, **Kim Il Sung** and **Syngman Rhee** had each returned to the peninsula. Kim, with Soviet backing, set about securing a central position in the political and administrative framework that was evolving in the north along standard Communist lines. A Provisional People's Committee embarked on land reform and nationalization during 1946 and in November of that year held local elections. The situation in the south was always more open and volatile, despite USAMGIK's cautious line. Demonstrations protested against the division of the peninsula as well as against trusteeship. Organizations were set up to promote independence and unification. At the same time, left-wing labor associations and other activist groups were forming, even though the People's Committees were being disbanded under pressure from USAMGIK. In mid-1946, moderate leaders from both right and left tried to negotiate a merger between the two political factions in the south. A more violent challenge to USAMGIK and the new Korean security forces was posed from 1946 by labor strikes and left-inspired riots and guerrilla activities, which particularly affected the southern provinces. (The fear of residual Communist sympathies lying hidden in society has ever since haunted South Korean governments.) Influxes of population, largely from north to south, but also from south to north, during these years added to the general restlessness.

Soviet and U.S. representatives discussed the trusteeship proposals intermittently through

1946–1947, but all the while both north and south were moving toward more elaborate and permanent forms of administration. Syngman Rhee and his supporters had from mid-1946 been advocating a separate government for the south. The creation of an Interim Legislative Assembly in the south in December 1946 was followed by the appointment of a chief civil administrator in February 1947 and during June–August by preparations for a provisional government. These developments were matched in the north by elections in February 1947 to a People's Assembly with legislative powers. The People's Assembly then tasked Kim Il Sung with forming a central People's Committee with administrative authority.

The trusteeship talks finally ended in August 1947, whereupon the United States, in the hope of reviving the concept of a nationwide resolution of the Korean problem, referred it to the United Nations General Assembly (UNGA). On 14 November 1947, an UNGA resolution was passed, calling for elections within each zone, to be monitored by a **United Nations Temporary Commission on Korea** (UNTCOK), and for the withdrawal of U.S. and Soviet troops from the peninsula. Though Rhee saw such elections as a means of securing an acceptable form of government in the south, the north and leftists in the south opposed the resolution, as did several right-wing politicians in the south, such as **Kim Ku** and **Kim Kyu-shik**, for whom national unity was of greater importance. An UNTCOK delegation arrived in the south in January 1948, but was denied access to the north by both the Korean and Soviet authorities. As it became apparent that elections under UN supervision would be held only in the south, considerable anger erupted. On **Cheju Island**, off the south coast of Korea, this dissatisfaction was one of the causes of sporadic guerrilla fighting between April 1948 and April 1949. Kim Ku and Kim Kyu-shik traveled to the north in April 1948 for political talks, ultimately unsuccessful, on unification. The elections themselves in May were boycotted by leftists and rightists who favored attempts at negotiation with the north.

Following the May 1948 elections in the south, a National Assembly was brought into being, which on 1 July designated the south as the Republic of Korea and on 20 July elected Rhee as its first president. USAMGIK was terminated and the new republic was formally established on 15 August 1948. The north quickly responded with the election of delegates to a Supreme People's Assembly on 28 August and the declaration of the establishment of the Democratic People's Republic of Korea on 9 September 1948.

The creation of two separate states on the peninsula effectively closed off any further chance of dialogue. During the next two years, U.S. and Soviet troops withdrew from South and North Korea, leaving only military advisors. Although pockets of Communist-inspired guerrilla fighting in the south were gradually eliminated, the antagonism between the two states continued to explode in June 1950.

See also: Soviet Occupation of North Korea (1945–1948); United Nations General Assembly Resolutions on Korea; Yosu-Sunch'on Rebellion (1948).

References: Cumings 1981, 1983, 1990; Henderson 1968; Merrill 1983, 1989; Yi 1973.

KOREAGATE (1977)

Highlighted in the **Nixon Doctrine** outlined by President Nixon in July 1969, the shift in U.S. policy toward encouraging its allies to take on a greater share of the burden of maintaining security was badly received in South Korea, especially when the United States proposed, in March 1970, a cut of one division in the strength of the U.S. military forces stationed in the South. At once, a campaign was planned, sanctioned by President **Park Chung Hee**, to influence U.S. opinion against further cuts in troop levels and in the budget for military modernization of the **South Korean armed forces**. A further campaign, starting in 1974, was aimed at softening the bad impression caused in the United States by Park's harsh enforcement of his **Yushin Constitution** of 1972 and infringements of human rights in South Korea.

The target was the U.S. Congress and the American public. Lobbying and campaigning were carried out through three main channels: the Korean Central Intelligence Agency (KCIA), the Unification Church of the Reverend **Moon Sun Myung**, and an individual, Park Tong-sun. Moon and Park Tong-sun had their own interests also in mind when they undertook lobbying. A number of U.S. congressmen were said to have taken bribes—

some, to further their own careers; others, to help the anti-Communist cause. The Koreagate scandal broke in October 1976 and led to five official hearings during 1977–1978, directed mainly against congressmen. Even though Park Tong-sun testified in exchange for immunity from prosecution, no convictions resulted from his testimony. Moon was summoned to appear for questioning, but left the United States. The KCIA could not be investigated. The affair overshadowed U.S.–South Korean relations for some time.

References: Boettcher 1980; Moon 1997.

KOREAN AIR FLIGHT KA858 BOMBING (1987)

On 29 November 1987, as it flew over the Andaman Sea toward Burma, Korean Air flight KA858 to Seoul from the Middle East was destroyed by a bomb on board. All 115 crew and passengers were killed. A Korean man and woman who had disembarked at a fueling stop in the Gulf came immediately under suspicion. Faced with capture, both attempted suicide. The man succeeded in killing himself, but the woman, Kim Hyon-hui, was seized and taken to South Korea, where she admitted under interrogation to being a member of a North Korean special task force. Sentenced to death, she was eventually amnestied and has since married, written an account of her role in the disaster, and lectured against communism.

Kim has been identified as an agent of the Korean Workers' Party Liaison Department, an organization said to have considerable responsibility for supervising North Korea's unconventional warfare. The bombing of flight KA858 has generally been explained as an attempt to discourage participation in the 1988 Seoul Summer Olympics.

See also: Abductions; Bomb and Other Attacks; North Korean Use of Terrorism.

References: Bermudez 1988; Bolger 1991; Macdonald 1996.

KOREAN AIR LINES FLIGHT KE007 DISASTER (1983)

In the early hours of 1 September 1983, as it passed over the southern tip of Sakhalin Island, flight KE007, a Korean Air Lines Boeing 747, was shot down in Soviet airspace by two missiles fired from a Soviet SU-15 fighter. The aircraft exploded in mid-air and fell into the sea west of Sakhalin, killing all 269 crew and passengers on board. Sakhalin lies off the east coast of Siberia and is Russian (formerly Soviet) territory.

KE007 was on a journey from Anchorage to Seoul that should have taken it down a heavily used route parallel with, but well away from, the eastern seaboard of Siberia. When it was shot down, it was some 365 miles off course. The Soviet decision to attack the aircraft was apparently discussed at the highest level but only among the military command. The Soviet authorities subsequently claimed that KE007's pilots had been flying without navigation lights, had refused to respond to Soviet radio signals, and had ignored tracer shells fired to attract their attention, leaving Soviet air defenses with no clear indication that they were dealing with a civilian aircraft. The aircraft's flight, moreover, was taking it over highly sensitive coastal radar defenses.

The disaster aroused widespread revulsion and condemnation of the then Soviet Union. It immediately became an issue between the United States and the Soviet Union, both still locked in Cold War rivalry and countermeasures. The United States pointed to Soviet barbarity; the Soviet Union claimed that the aircraft had been engaged in surveillance. The east Siberian seaboard, housing the Soviet Pacific defenses, was known to be under constant probing from U.S. electronic devices. A U.S. RC-135 military reconnaissance aircraft had been detected in the vicinity of the KE007 at one point. It is not known if the aircraft's flight data recorder and cockpit voice recorder were ever retrieved from the sea, despite extensive searching. Evasive and incomplete statements from both the Soviet and U.S. sides did nothing to clarify the situation. Japanese air traffic control, which had recorded some of the aircraft's movements, was unable to contribute anything decisive; the South Koreans could offer nothing.

Speculation over the reasons for KE007's erroneous flight path ranges from pure accident—the pilots had inadvertently put the aircraft on autopilot mode selection instead of switching to the inertial navigation system—to deliberate diversion to allow it to undertake some kind of surveillance or, by its intrusion, to force Soviet radar defenses to expose themselves. Other suggestions have been that the pilots took a shorter, but more dangerous, route to save fuel or that deliberate Soviet electronic interference with the aircraft's navigation equipment caused it to stray. Korean Air Lines changed their name in 1984 to Korean Air. Russia, as the successor state to the Soviet Union, has declined to assume any guilt for the incident and in 1993 concluded at the end of an investigation that the disaster was the result of "a series of blunders and mistakes" by the aircraft's pilots. The mystery remains.

See also: Soviet/Russian Relations with South Korea.
Reference: Johnson 1986.

KOREAN AUGMENTATION TO THE UNITED STATES ARMY (KATUSA)

Koreans were recruited from the early days of the **Korean War** into the U.S. ground forces, severely depleted in resisting the initial North Korean onslaught. On 15 August 1950, Lieutenant-General **Walton Walker**, commanding the U.S. Eighth Army, was instructed to incorporate 100 Koreans into each company and battery of his troops. This augmentation of U.S. military manpower, to a total of 1,000–3,000 per division, was to proceed in parallel with reorganization of the South Korean army. Pay, administration, and discipline of the Korean recruits remained the responsibility of the South Korean military, but the men received U.S. rations and equipment and a short period of training.

Most of the KATUSAs, as they became known, were taken into the infantry and cavalry. At first, a buddy system was tried, whereby a U.S. soldier was to befriend and help instruct a Korean recruit, but difficulties of language and cultural differences made such an arrangement problematic. The preferred structure was to place the Korean soldiers in separate squads and platoons under a U.S. or Korean officer. Doubts about the reliability and military skills of the Korean augmentation were voiced at first, but from late 1950 their value came to be recognized as their assignments shifted from menial support tasks to those of drivers and mechanics and then to serving as patrol scouts and guards and in intelligence work. By July 1951, there were 12,718 KATUSAs attached to U.S. units; and by 1952, the **United Nations Command** (UNC) was beginning to replace front-line troops with veteran KATUSAs. In July of that year, the figure of 2,500 Korean recruits per division was approved. By the end of the war in July 1953, the number of KATUSAs stood at 23,922.

Elite divisions of the U.S. armed forces, such as the Marine Corps, refused to accept inexperienced Korean recruits and instead incorporated the 1st Regiment of the Korean Marine Corps into their ranks under their own advisers as the 4th Infantry Regiment of the 1st Marine Division. The **French forces in the Korean War** similarly formed the Korean soldiers attached to them into a separate company within their battalion (following the pattern favored by the French army for its non-French troops). The Belgians allowed some of the Koreans assigned to them by the Korean Service Corps as support personnel to assume a fighting role within their units. The Netherlands and Commonwealth forces also accepted Korean recruits.

The Korean troops attached to the UNC forces, by relieving the latter of routine and menial tasks, clearly aided their combat effectiveness and in time supported them in a military and intelligence capacity. In some instances, the relationship between UNC units and the Koreans augmenting them was good; elsewhere it might be difficult. The underlying problem was one of trust. Nonetheless, the U.S. Army in Korea has maintained the KATUSA system and still allocates approximately 2,500 posts to selected Korean recruits in the infantry division that constitutes the main U.S. ground combat force in Korea.

See also: Koreans Attached to the Commonwealth Forces (KATCOM); United States Forces in the Korean War.
References: Crahay 1967; MacDonald 1996; Matray 1991; Millett 1995; Summers 1990; Thomas, Abbott, and Chappell 1986.

KOREAN CENTRAL INTELLIGENCE AGENCY (KCIA)

See **National Intelligence Service (NIS)**.

KOREAN CENTRAL NEWS AGENCY (KCNA)

The (North) Korean Central News Agency (KCNA) was established in 1946, during the period of the **Soviet occupation of North Korea (1945–1948)**. It was closely modeled on the Soviet news agency TASS and on the Chinese Communist **New China News Agency** (now better known by its Chinese name, Xinhua). As an agency, KCNA has always been under direct central government control. It is the sole official distribution point for both domestic and foreign news, producing daily bulletins that form the basis of most newspaper and radio news coverage in North Korea. It clearly monitors other news agencies' output on a regular basis and replays stories that are favorable to North Korea and hostile to the South. It is frequently used to make statements on North Korean policy or to reply to observations about North Korea. Some commentators believe that a KCNA statement carries less authority than a government statement, but it is hard to tell if this is really the case.

KOREAN CIVILIAN PRISONERS IN THE KOREAN WAR

The largest single group of Korean civilian prisoners in the **Korean War** were the civilian internees, estimated at approximately 37,000, who in December 1951 were reclassified from the general body of **prisoners of war** (POWs) captured by the **United Nations Command** (UNC). By that time, the U.S. military authorities, acting for the UNC, held approximately 170,000 men and women in their prison camps. Of these, 132,000 were categorized as POWs. Those classified as civilian internees were civilians claiming South Korean resident status who had been forced to join the **North Korean People's Army** or who, as innocent bystanders, had been swept up in the fighting. A further number were refugees from North Korea who had collaborated with the UNC. Those wishing to remain in South Korea were rehoused on the mainland, and in the summer and autumn of 1952, the majority were released back into civil society in South Korea. Those refusing release remained interned and formed part of the exchanges of prisoners between the UNC and the North Korean/Chinese commands in spring and autumn of 1953. In the first exchange of sick and wounded, in April 1953, 446 civilian internees, of whom three were women, were handed over from the UNC side. In the August–September exchange of that year, 8,899 civilian internees, including 23 children, transferred to the North.

More shadowy is the fate of other groups of Korean civilians who endured captivity. As the North Koreans advanced south in the summer of 1950, they seized individuals and groups, including politicians, scholars, and writers, possibly as hostages, and took them north on their retreat dur-

ing September–October 1950. As many as 84,000–85,000 may have traveled north. Some undoubtedly went voluntarily, but it is impossible to know how many may have gone of their free will. Many, such as the nationalist leader **Kim Kyu-shik**, were never heard of again or, like An Chae-hong, another nationalist leader, survived for a while. Some were forced to join the captives' journeys north. One such group was that of seven "South Korean politicians" attached to the party of foreign civilians taken north in September 1950. The journalist Philip Deane (1953) named them all and described six of them as members of the "South Korean Parliament," in which one of them had held office as minister of the interior. A number of members of the National Assembly are known to have remained behind in **Seoul** when the North Koreans took the city; possibly some of them formed this group of "politicians." For a while, such men may have been allowed to participate in a united front of non-Communist groups within the North Korean political system, but eventually would have been eliminated as being too suspect. Other Korean civilians, identified as political prisoners, were kept in North Korean police centers in the utmost subjugation. Captain, now General Anthony Farrar-Hockley (1954) described a period of incarceration in 1951 with such detainees.

Groups of civilians were similarly rounded up in South Korea on suspicion of being Communists or collaborators with the enemy. Their treatment was equally harsh. The lack of supervision over their guards and the casual way in which many of the prisoners were put to death were the subject of angry comment by Western **press correspondents** and heightened doubts among them and some UNC soldiers over the purpose of participation in the Korean War.

See also: Foreign Civilian Detainees in the Korean War.

References: Cameron 1967; Cutforth 1952; Deane 1953; Farrar-Hockley 1954; Hermes 1966; Kim Choong Soon 1988; Matray 1991; Scalapino and Lee, Pt. I, 1972.

KOREAN COMMUNIST PARTY (KCP)

The formal history of the Korean Communist Party (KCP) is meager, from its Soviet beginnings in 1918 to the failed attempts between 1925 and 1931 to launch the party within Korea, then from its revival in 1945 to its eventual merging with the North and South Korean Workers' Parties in 1946. The Korean Communist movement, by contrast, has shown considerable vigor, diversity, and indeed tenacity, if the continued existence of the North Korean regime is considered.

Korean communism was launched outside of the peninsula in 1918 when Nam Man-ch'on, an expatriate, established a Korean section of the Russian Communist Party in Irkutsk in Siberia, and Yi Tong-hwi, likewise an expatriate, founded the Korean Socialist Party in Khabarovsk in the maritime region. In 1919, Yi took his party to Shanghai to join the recently established **Korean Provisional Government**, and reorganized it as the Korean Communist Party. The Irkutsk and Shanghai groups soon challenged each other and even came into armed conflict because both were competing for members and for funds and support from the Comintern, the international arm of the Soviet party organization. Moreover, they suspected each other's motives. The Irkutsk party, incorporating many Russian-born Korean settlers, saw itself as part of the international Communist movement. Yi Tong-hwi's Shanghai group was activated by nationalist feeling as much as by Communist theory and sought Soviet support primarily for the struggle against Japan.

From the early 1920s, attempts were made to set up inside Korea a Communist organization, supported by small left-wing groups, some of them composed of returned students inspired by their contacts in Japan with Japanese Marxist-Leninists. In 1925, the first official Korean Communist Party was established in **Seoul**, but soon disintegrated under Japanese pressure. Five further attempts to revive it during the years 1926–1931 also failed. From 1927 to 1931, the Communist movement in Korea, following Comintern directives, formed a united front with Korean nationalists, but withdrew in 1931 when the Comintern turned against collaboration with "bourgeois" elements. Thereafter, no formal Communist organization existed in Korea. Local activists worked with youth groups and regional peasants' and workers' groups. The northeast of the peninsula was an especially militant area. Branches of the KCP set up in China, Manchuria, and Japan eventually joined the Chinese or Japanese Communist parties.

In 1945, such activists as had survived the Japanese occupation reemerged with strong anti-Japanese credentials to resurrect the KCP. Despite early squabbling, a unified KCP was created in September 1945 under the chairmanship of **Pak Hon-yong**. Although the party's headquarters were sited in Seoul, a Northern Branch Bureau of the KCP, established in October 1945, began to issue party membership certificates for the North, and the focus of KCP initiative began to swing toward **P'yongyang**. After initial hostility, the KCP's decision in January 1946 to accept the proposal for a **Joint Commission on Trusteeship** for Korea that resulted from the **Moscow Agreement** of December 1945 considerably weakened popular support in the South for the party. In November 1946, the KCP in the South merged with the New People's Party to form the South Korean Workers' Party.

See also: Left-Wing Political Factions; Nationalism; Soviet Involvement in Korea (1917–1945).

References: Robinson 1988; Scalapino and Lee 1972; Suh 1970, 1981.

KOREAN DEMOCRATIC PARTY (KDP)

Two parties known in English by the name Korean Democratic Party (KDP) emerged in late 1945 in the northern and southern halves of Korea. (Their Korean names differ slightly, reflecting the political divergence between them.) In the North, the moderate nationalist leader **Cho Man-shik**, aspiring to a nationwide organization, set up a Korean Democratic Party in November 1945. For a while, this enjoyed even more support, especially among the educated, than the rival **Korean Communist Party**, and by the end of 1945 had a membership of 500,000. However, it immediately started losing influence after Cho Man-shik disappeared from public life in January 1946 following a confrontation with the occupying Soviet forces in North Korea over the proposed **Joint Commission on Trusteeship**, which Cho would not tolerate. His supporters fled south, where they tried to revive the party, but it appears to have dissolved. In the North, the party's name survived, but the organization itself was swallowed up in the push for a united front that would ostensibly allow the Communists to claim a multi-party system, while retaining full political control. After extensive reorganization, individuals, often from religious backgrounds, could, from the end of 1951, describe themselves as members of the northern Korean Democratic Party, but it had no formal structure. It still exists as a political entity in North Korea, but with no power and no mass organization.

In the southern part of the country, Song Chin-u, a past president and editor-in-chief of the leading newspaper *Donga Ilbo*, together with two other right-wing colleagues, formed a Korean Democratic Party in September 1945. Its membership, drawn largely from the landowning and business sections of society, was conservative in outlook, and the party was denounced by leftists as a reactionary group sheltering former collaborators with the Japanese colonial administration. Certainly, members of the southern KDP cooperated closely with the U.S. military administration in the autumn of 1945. Song Chin-u, cofounder of the party, supported the December 1945 proposals for trusteeship. Probably because of his views on trusteeship, he was assassinated at the end of December 1945 by an extreme rightist. In December 1947, another cofounder of the party, Chang Tok-su, was also assassinated. By 1948, the Korean Democratic Party formed the main opposition to President **Syngman Rhee**'s political supporters. From February 1949, when it merged with other right-wing parties, it lost its separate identity, but lived on in name in a string of subsequent political parties that generally incorporated the term "Democratic" in their title.

It is unclear if any formal link ever existed between the northern and southern Korean Democratic Parties.

See also: Korea Peninsula (1945–1948).
References: Nahm 1993; Scalapino and Lee, Pt. II, 1972.

KOREAN INDEPENDENCE PARTY

The right-wing Korean Independence Party (KIP) dated its origins to 1930, when two separate groups emerged in Shanghai and in Jilin Province in **Northeast China** (then known as Manchuria). Both groups bore the name of Korean Independence Party. The Jilin branch withdrew in 1933 into other parts of China and for a while liaised with Shanghai members until it re-formed itself in 1934 in Manchuria as a separate party.

The KIP came to be associated principally with **Kim Ku**, one of its cofounders in Shanghai, and was

intended to support the **Korean Provisional Government** (KPG). The party had terrorist overtones. Between 1933 and 1940, it was in abeyance, but revived in 1940 in Chongqing under Kim Ku's leadership, again in support of the KPG, which Kim also headed. The KIP returned to Korea in 1945 with Kim, but on his assassination in June 1949 it dissolved again. An attempt to resurrect it in 1963 was unsuccessful.

See also: Chinese Involvement in Korea (1919–1948).
References: Lee 1963; Nahm 1993.

KOREAN MEMBERSHIP OF THE UNITED NATIONS

For understandable reasons, the two Korean states have had very different attitudes toward the **United Nations** (UN) for most of their existence. For the Republic of Korea (South Korea), its very inception seemed to come from the UN after the U.S. decision in 1947 to hand over the Korean problem to the UN General Assembly for a solution. In the **Korean War** (1950–1953), it was forces answering the UN call for assistance that saved the South. For the Democratic People's Republic of Korea (North Korea), on the other hand, the UN was its opponent in the same war, and the UN flag has continued to fly over military institutions in South Korea apparently dedicated to the overthrow of the North.

At the same time, almost from the beginning of their existence, both Koreas have sought, or allowed others to seek on their behalf, membership in the United Nations. Both applied in January 1949. The North's application, which was sponsored by the **Union of Soviet Socialist Republics** (USSR), was not even put on the table, whereas the South Korean application was vetoed. A further South Korean attempt in 1955 also failed (as did a parallel application by the Republic of Vietnam). In 1957, another South Korean application was put forward. The USSR proposed an amendment to allow both Koreas in, but both the original motion and the amendment were rejected. In 1958, a similar approach also failed. In 1961, the South again applied, but the application was not considered. Yet, from its earliest days, South Korea enjoyed observer status at several UN organizations.

From 1961 until the mid-1970s, the issue was not raised. North Korea, having formulated a reunification proposal in 1960, began to argue that the admission of the two Koreas would only serve to continue the division between them. South Korea still called for its admission to the UN, but argued that the North did not qualify. The situation seemed to change in the 1970s following the 1972 joint communiqué between the two Koreas and the dissolution of the **United Nations Commission for Unification and Rehabilitation of Korea** in 1973. At that point, North Korea began to seek observer status at UN bodies. But when South Korea tried to raise the issue of UN membership twice in 1975, North Korea remained hostile.

The issue was not brought up again until the late 1980s. Then, as part of the policy of *Nordpolitik/* **Northern Policy**, the South Korean president, **Roh Tae Woo**, announced that South Korea would seek admission to the UN. It would be better, he said, if both Koreas entered together; if that did not happen, then the South would pursue a separate application. By then, neither the USSR nor the **People's Republic of China** was prepared to back North Korea's opposition to joint entry, and on 17 September 1991, both Koreas joined the United Nations. To the end, the North argued that this was a divisive move, and that it was joining only under protest.

See also: Diplomatic Recognition; United Nations Command (UNC); United Nations Commission on Korea (UNCOK); United Nations General Assembly Resolutions on Korea; United Nations Security Council Resolutions on Korea; United Nations Temporary Commission on Korea (UNTCOK).
References: Hoare 1997; Middleton 1997.

KOREAN MILITARY ACADEMY (KMA)
See **Role of the Military in North and South Korea.**

KOREAN MILITARY ADVISORY GROUP (KMAG)
The Korean Military Advisory Group (KMAG) was formally established on 1 July 1949, following the withdrawal of U.S. forces from Korea, to train an army for the Republic of Korea. A team of U.S. officers and men had been in Korea since 1946 working on a similar mission, but from 1949, KMAG's numbers increased to some 500. It concentrated on infantry training, partly because its commander, Brigadier-General William Roberts, though an armored warfare veteran, thought that tanks were not suitable for Korea. The training program was hampered by small numbers, by lack of equipment and facilities, and by most of its members not understanding Korean. However, by the time the **Korean War** began in June 1950, the KMAG had achieved some success. In the war, it became a subordinate unit of the U.S. Eighth Army, but continued its training role, still suffering from lack of numbers.

See also: South Korean Armed Forces; United States Forces in the Korean War.
References: Matray 1991; Noble 1975; Sawyer and Hermes 1962.

KOREAN NATIONALIST PARTY
The English name "Nationalist Party" has been given to at least three political organizations whose names in Korean all differ slightly, thereby indicating their different allegiances and histories. The first Korean Nationalist Party (KNP) was founded in 1936 in China by the exiled **Korean Provisional Government** (KPG) as a counterweight to the united front tactics of left-wing sections of the Korean opposition active in China. The right-wing leader **Kim Ku** headed the party's board of trustees. This first KNP lasted until April 1940, when it merged with two others to form a new **Korean Independence Party**.

After liberation, An Chae-hong, a moderate nationalist, formed a new KNP in September 1945, but the party lost support when he became civil administrator of the South Korean Interim Government in July 1947. A more right-wing KNP emerged in November 1949 to represent supporters of President **Syngman Rhee**. Its chief rival was the Democratic Nationalist Party, itself formed in February 1949 from a merger between the **Korean Democratic Party** and other political groups. This third KNP survived until 1952, when it was taken into Rhee's Liberal Party.
References: Lee 1963; Nahm 1993.

KOREAN PENINSULA ENERGY DEVELOPMENT ORGANIZATION (KEDO)
Following the 1994 agreement between North Korea and the United States that effectively froze the **North Korean nuclear program**, the Korean Peninsula

Energy Development Organization (KEDO) was established in March 1995 by the governments of Japan, South Korea, and the United States. A number of other governments subsequently also joined the organization. The main purposes of KEDO are to provide for the financing and supply of 1,000-megawatt light-water reactors to North Korea; to provide interim energy resources in the period before these reactors can begin to supply electricity; and to carry out any other measures that will help the objectives of the Agreed Framework. KEDO began work at Kumho in North Korea in July 1997. As well as offering a solution to the nuclear problem, KEDO has led to the first private mail and telephone exchanges between North and South Korea since the **Korean War**.

KOREAN PEOPLE'S REPUBLIC (1945)

The short-lived Korean People's Republic (KPR) was inaugurated on 6 September 1945 on the initiative of Yo Un-hyong (Lyuh Woon-hyung), a nationalist with former close links to the left, who had remained in Korea imprisoned by the Japanese. As surrender approached on 15 August 1945, the Japanese administration invited him to assist in a handover of power. Two days later, Yo announced the formation of a Committee for the Preparation of Korean Independence; and three weeks later, the creation of the KPR on a platform of national independence and social reform and on a broad political base that would exclude only collaborationists. Its leadership, some of which was still abroad, was balanced between Communist and non-Communist elements. The KPR was supported both north and south by a network of local **People's Committees** and enjoyed some popularity.

The imminent arrival of U.S. occupying forces in the south prompted the speedy formation of the KPR. The U.S. military administration, however, was suspicious of the new organization from the outset and, persuaded that it was largely under Communist domination, quickly rejected its claims to legality and insisted that it function only as a political party. Yo Un-hyong capitulated and on 22 October 1945 dissolved the KPR. He went on to form the People's Party, elements of which eventually merged into the South Korean Workers' Party. On 12 December 1945, General **John Hodge** declared the activities of the KPR unlawful. Yo himself was assassinated in July 1947 by a right-wing nationalist.

See also: Korea Peninsula (1945–1948); United States Army Military Government in Korea (1945–1948).
References: Cumings 1981; Henderson 1968; Nahm 1993.

KOREAN PROVISIONAL GOVERNMENT (1919–1945)

Under the impact of the March First 1919 uprising against Japanese colonial rule, Korean independence fighters fleeing abroad set up a provisional government in exile to continue the struggle. Shanghai, on the east coast of China, was chosen for its good communications and relative nearness to Korea, and the provisional government installed itself in April 1919 in the French concession of the city, where it could enjoy comparative protection from Japanese harassment. By autumn 1919, approximately 700 Koreans had arrived in Shanghai. "Governments" also existed temporarily in Vladivostok in Siberia and in Seoul itself, but Shanghai remained the headquarters. Later, as the Nationalist Chinese government retreated into the interior of China in the face of chaotic conditions and then the Japanese advance, the Korean Provisional Government (KPG) followed it, first to Nanjing (1932), and then eventually to Chongqing (1940), where it remained until 1945.

The KPG had by September 1919 elected a president, **Syngman Rhee**, who was living in the United States; a prime minister, the socialist Yi Tong-hwi; and a cabinet. The KPG ran a newspaper, *Independence News*, and engaged in diplomatic lobbying in Paris and New York. During the first two years, a degree of consensus was maintained between the differing elements represented in the provisional government, but from 1921, disagreements surfaced, exacerbated by Western indifference to the fate of Korea. Yi Tong-hwi and other officeholders resigned. Thereafter, the KPG drifted for a number of years, though still claiming a central role in the Nationalist movement. Many Nationalists, indeed, regarded it as a continuation of the March First movement. It was, however, split between three different programs and suffered the accompanying clashes between personalities. One section, headed by Rhee, favored diplomatic lobbying in Western capitals to obtain foreign backing. Another group of socialists, led by Yi Tong-hwi, urged liaising with the

Soviet Union to carry out armed attacks on Japanese businesses and institutions. Yet a third lot of supporters preferred the gradualist approach of self-education and nation building. Differences of view on policy and tactics were made worse by problems over financing the KPG and access to funds. China's vast scale made it difficult to keep control over disparate groups, and it was never easy to maintain contact with the scene inside Korea.

In the end, the Korean freedom movement in China broke into two broad sections: the conservatives and moderates who preferred a policy of diplomatic agitation and publicity for Korea's plight; and the Communists and socialists who wanted direct action against Japanese targets. The latter were critical of the KPG and distanced themselves from it. In the clash between Chinese Communists and Nationalists, the KPG drew close to the Nationalists. It succeeded in hanging on and, after war was declared between China and Japan in 1937, received support from Korean Nationalists in North America and Hawaii. In 1943, it was reorganized with the right-wing nationalist **Kim Ku** as president and **Kim Kyu-shik** as his deputy. Ironically, liberation from Japan in August 1945 did not bring the fulfillment the KPG had hoped for. The U.S. forces occupying the southern half of the peninsula after the Japanese surrender refused to recognize it and insisted that its members return to Korea as private individuals. It never made the transformation from provisional to actual government.

See also: Chinese Involvement in Korea (1919–1948); Japanese Colonial Period in Korea (1910–1945); Nationalism.

References: Lee 1963; Lone and McCormack 1993; Robinson 1988; Yang 1994.

KOREAN WAR (1950–1953)

War came to Korea at 4 A.M. on Sunday, 25 June 1950, when North Korean artillery opened up along the line of the **38th parallel**. The initial artillery attack was followed by an armored advance, which met little resistance. Within three days, the North Korean armies had swept aside demoralized South Korean forces and were in **Seoul**. The North Korean advance continued down the peninsula, the South Korean government fleeing before it, first to **Taejon**, then to **Taegu**, and finally to the port of **Pusan**.

Meanwhile, the United States, which in 1949 had declared that Korea lay outside its area of defense interests, now decided that the North Korean attack represented a Communist challenge to the "free world" and could not be ignored. The United States immediately sent troops to try to shore up the South Korean resistance, but without success. The United States also mobilized the **United Nations Security Council,** in the absence of the Soviet Union, to agree to a series of resolutions between 25 June and 7 July 1950. These called for an end to hostilities and the withdrawal of North Korean forces, recommended that the member states of the **United Nations** (UN) should furnish assistance to South Korea, and established a Unified Command, under a U.S.-designated commander, to resist the North Korean forces. U.S. President **Harry S Truman** appointed the Supreme Allied Commander in Japan, General **Douglas MacArthur,** as the head of the Unified Command, while sixteen nations—Australia, Belgium, Canada, Colombia, Ethiopia, France, Greece, Luxembourg, the Netherlands, New Zealand, the Philippines, South Africa, Thailand, Turkey, the United Kingdom, and the United States—supplied contingents to serve under him. Denmark, India, Italy, Norway, and Sweden sent medical assistance.

By early September 1950, North Korean forces had occupied most of the peninsula, although their supply lines were very extended, and in many parts of the country their forces were thinly spread. The South Korean government held onto the area around Pusan, known as the Pusan Perimeter. The tide of war turned against North Korea when General MacArthur launched Operation Chromite against the port of **Inch'on** in early September 1950. Using Japanese naval personnel to guide his forces through the sandbanks, on 15 September 1950 MacArthur achieved a major victory. Inch'on was taken, and Seoul was soon recaptured. Meanwhile, UN forces began a breakout from the Pusan Perimeter and drove the North Korean forces back up toward the 38th parallel.

Soon, North Korean troops were fleeing north in disarray. UN forces, with the South Koreans in the lead, pursued them. MacArthur urged that there should be no stopping at the 38th parallel, a position endorsed by a further UN Security Council resolution on 7 October 1950. The North Korean capital, **P'yongyang**, fell on 19 October, and the UN forces pushed on to the **Yalu River**. North Korea had virtually ceased to exist as a functioning state. There was much talk of the end of the war and being "**home for Christmas.**"

The Yalu marks the border with China, where Communist forces had established the **People's Republic of China** one year previously. The Chinese had not opposed the North Korean plan to attack the South, perhaps believing **Kim Il Sung's** assurances that his forces would easily overcome South Korean opposition or thinking that the Soviet leader **Joseph Stalin** would make sure that North Korea survived. When the UN moved into North Korea, however, the Chinese became concerned, and they began to hint that, unless the non-Korean forces stopped advancing, they would intervene. The warnings were discounted, as were initial contacts with small groups of troops from the **Chinese People's Volunteers**. When massive Chinese forces were thrown at the UN troops at the end of October 1950, however, it was no longer possible to ignore the Chinese. MacArthur panicked, and the UN forces began to retreat south.

Soon the retreat became a headlong rout, known as the "**bug-out.**" The Chinese swept across the 38th parallel, and on 4 January 1951, they took Seoul. The UN forces regrouped south of Wonju, 100 miles (161 kilometers) south of Seoul, and from there launched a counterattack in February 1951. Now extended supply lines hampered the Chinese forces, who were steadily forced back. Seoul was retaken on 15 March, and UN forces again crossed the 38th parallel in April. This time there was no desire to push further north, and the war settled down to a stalemate. The Chinese launched a major attack south in April. This led to the battles of **Imjin River** and **Kap'yong**. Although the Chinese forces inflicted heavy casualties, they failed to penetrate the UN lines. On the UN side, April 1951 saw the dismissal of General MacArthur, who was replaced by General **Matthew Ridgway**.

The war now became one of attrition, similar to World War I trench warfare. Following a Soviet initiative, supported by the Chinese, that talks for a cease-fire should begin, the United Nations responded positively, and talks began on 10 July 1951 at **Kaesong**, once in the South but now behind North Korean lines. Talks at Kaesong were suspended in August after alleged Chinese and North Korean violations of the area's neutrality; they resumed on 25 October 1951 at a new venue, **P'anmunjom**.

The truce negotiations dragged on until the summer of 1953, with intermittent fighting, sometimes heavy, continuing at the same time. After much discussion, sick and wounded **prisoners of war** were exchanged between 20 April and 3 May 1953 in Operation **Little Switch**. At the same time, diplomats and other civilian detainees held in North Korea since 1950 were released via the Soviet Union. In an attempt to sabotage the truce negotiations, South Korean President **Syngman Rhee** released some 27,000 anti-Communist prisoners of war on 18 June. Despite this and the continued fighting along the front almost to the last minute, an **armistice** was finally signed at 10 A.M. Korean time on 27 July 1953 and became effective at 10 P.M. The Korean War was over.

The cost of the war was enormous. Killed, wounded, and missing amounted to some four million, of which three million were Koreans. Many more Koreans saw their families broken up by the war; most remain divided with no news. Large numbers of **refugees** had moved up and down the peninsula as the fighting waxed and waned. Physical damage was equally horrendous; vast areas of the peninsula had been heavily bombed or damaged by the movement of armies. Economically, both North and South Korea had lost most of the gains made since liberation in 1945 and were left heavily dependent on outside support. Politically too there had been a price to pay. In the North, **Kim Il Sung** was able to consolidate his hold on power and create a dictatorship. In the South, the war had both reinforced Syngman Rhee's autocratic tendencies and paved the way for nearly three decades of military dominance.

See also: North Korean People's Army (NKPA); Peng Dehuai; South Korean Armed Forces; United Nations Security Council Resolutions on Korea; United States Forces in the Korean War.

References: Halliday and Cummings 1988; Hoyt 1985; Koh 1993; Rees 1964; Whelan 1990.

KOREAN WORKERS' PARTY (KWP)

The Korean Workers' Party (KWP) was formed in June 1949 when the North Korean Workers' Party (NKWP) absorbed the South Korean Workers' Party (SKWP). **Kim Il Sung** was elected chairman of the unified party and **Pak Hon-yong**, first vice-chairman. The NKWP itself represented the merging in August 1946 of the Northern Branch of the **Korean Communist Party** (KCP) with a section of the **New People's Party** (NPP). A similar fusing of the KCP with the NPP and the People's Party in the south in November 1946 produced the SKWP. The SKWP remained active in the south, organizing guerrilla raids and other forms of disruption. Only when its registration was canceled in October 1949 as part of a general drive by the South Korean government against left-wing parties and organizations, and two of its leaders were arrested in March 1950, was it finally eliminated.

The consolidated KWP came to be dominated by Kim Il Sung, whose power base it was. From 1966 until his death he occupied its highest post of general secretary, a position his son now holds. The KWP is a pyramid of party cells supporting local committees and the Central Committee, which is elected by the party congress. True control rests with the Central Committee's Politburo and its Standing Committee.
See also: Left-Wing Political Factions.
References: Merrill 1983; Scalapino and Lee 1972; Suh 1981; Yang 1994; Yi 1973.

KOREANS ATTACHED TO THE COMMONWEALTH FORCES (KATCOM)

In October 1952, 1,000 Korean recruits were attached to the **First Commonwealth Division** under the **United Nations Command** (UNC), at a rate of two per infantry section. They performed duties—driving, maintenance work, and patrol—similar to duties assigned to the **Korean Augmentation to the United States Army** (KATUSA), Korean soldiers incorporated into the U.S. ground forces. The KATCOMs were issued with the relevant uniforms and could be promoted to the rank of noncommissioned officer. Their pay and administration, however, were handled by the South Korean military authorities. (The Belgian Battalion had a similar arrangement.) Relations between the KATCOMs and the units that they were attached to varied great-

One of the first 200 Koreans attached to the Commonwealth Forces (KATCOMs) to join Commonwealth troops receives an item of equipment from a member of the Duke of Wellington's Regiment. (Imperial War Museum BF 11015)

ly, but some remember with apparent affection breakfast porridge and tea with British troops.

Both KATUSAs and KATCOMs counted among them many young Korean men who went on to hold important posts in South Korean politics and society.
See also: Belgian Forces in the Korean War.
References: Forty 1982; Thomas, Abbott, and Chappell 1986.

KWANGJU

Kwangju is the capital city of South Cholla Province in the southwest of South Korea. It has featured prominently twice in the history of twentieth-century Korea. During the Japanese colonial period, Kwangju was regarded as a center of student leftist anti-Japanese agitation. During October–November 1929, this erupted into fighting between Japanese and Korean students, and this fighting led to nationwide demonstrations against the Japanese. The protesters demanded educational reforms, the end of police interference in schools, and the release of those arrested during what was known as the "Kwangju incident." In the end, many students were imprisoned or expelled from their schools.

Kwangju's reputation as a center of leftist activity revived after 1945. The city, along with the rest of Cholla, suffered much discrimination under President **Park Chung Hee**. The ensuing resentment came to a head in 1980 in the confused period after

Park's assassination in 1979. The increasingly dominant role of the military under **Chun Doo Hwan** had led to the extension of martial law and the arrest of a number of leading politicians, including **Kim Dae Jung**, who was born in South Cholla. Large-scale demonstrations in Seoul in May 1980 against these developments were followed in Kwangju by violent protests, including attacks on the police and public buildings. To suppress the protests in Kwangju, Chun dispatched paratroop Special Warfare Commandos, who were trained to handle North Korean infiltrators. Although these forces used much brutality, they were unable to recapture Kwangju. Instead, they withdrew to the outskirts, sealing Kwangju off from the rest of the country from 22 May. On 27 May, regular army units, together with some special forces in regular uniforms, attacked the city at 3 A.M. and succeeded in restoring order, but at cost of life. Official figures gave the total number of dead as 170. This was revised in 1985 to 240, but it is widely believed that many more died, though perhaps not as many as the 2,000 claimed by some of the student groups involved.

The events in Kwangju cast a shadow over Chun's presidency, and North Korea used them regularly in propaganda as evidence of Chun's authoritarian rule. As political controls relaxed in South Korea, demands to reopen the matter grew. There were also claims that the United States was involved in the massacre because no attempt had been made to stop Chun from withdrawing the troops sent to Kwangju from the joint U.S.–Republic of Korea command. A Ministry of National Defense inquiry in 1985 was unsatisfactory, and the National Assembly conducted a further inquiry in 1988 after Chun had left office. This led Chun's successor, President **Roh Tae Woo**, to apologize for Kwangju and to reclassify the Kwangju uprising as a stage in the development of democracy. Later, when both Roh and Chun were under investigation during 1995–1996, Kwangju again featured in the charges against them. In Chun's case, it was one of the reasons why he was sentenced to death (later commuted). Kim Dae Jung's election as president in December 1997 may remove Kwangju from the political agenda.

Reference: Clark 1988.

KWP
See **Korean Workers' Party.**

LEE BUM SUK (1) (1900–1972)

A Korean freedom fighter in China and later a politician in independent South Korea, Lee Bum Suk (Yi Pom-sok) was born in **Seoul** in 1900. In 1915, he went to China, where he graduated from the Yunnan Military Academy in 1919 and then engaged in anti-Japanese guerrilla activities in **Northeast China.** Later he served as an instructor to **Chiang Kai-shek**'s forces at the Loyang Military Academy and as an officer in the Guomindang (Nationalist) forces. During World War II, he held senior staff positions in the Korean Restoration Army. He returned to Seoul after liberation, and was the chief organizer of the Racial Youth Corps, a nominally nonpolitical patriotic youth group designed to train men for a future South Korean army. However, Lee had visited Germany in 1933 and was known for his admiration for Adolf Hitler, an admiration reflected in the Youth Corps, with its vision of racially pure, patriotic, and anti-Communist activists.

In 1948, Lee became the first prime minister and concurrently defense minister of the new Republic of Korea under President **Syngman Rhee.** Rhee forced Lee to disband the Racial Youth Corps, though some of its members and ideas lived on in the Taehan Youth Corps, founded in 1949. Lee lost both ministerial posts early in 1950, but was recalled to help at the outbreak of the **Korean War**, first as an unofficial adviser and later as the vice-chairman, and effective organizer, of Rhee's Liberal Party. For a brief period in 1952, Lee was home minister, in which role he used the police to coerce the National Assembly into accepting Rhee's proposal for a presidential system in place of the existing cabinet system. Lee was dismissed and blamed for the tough measures that had been taken against Rhee's opponents. He made two unsuccessful attempts, in 1952 and 1954, to be elected vice-president. During the Second Republic (1960–1961), he was a member of the Upper House, but never again held an official position before his death in 1972.

References: Cumings 1981; Matray 1991; Nahm 1993.

L

LEE BUM SUK (2) (1922–1983)

Lee Bum Suk (Yi Pom-sok) was foreign minister of South Korea from May 1982 until he was killed in the **Rangoon bombing** of October 1983. Lee was born in **P'yongyang**, graduated in 1936 from Posung College, the forerunner of Korea University, and subsequently studied at the University of Maryland and George Washington University in Washington, D.C. He served during the **Korean War** and later joined the South Korean ministry of foreign affairs, holding senior posts before becoming a vice-president of the (South) Korean National Red Cross. In this role, he was the senior South Korean delegate to the **Red Cross North-South talks** from 1972 to 1976. He was ambassador to India from 1976 until appointed minister of national unification in 1980. Because of North Korea's hostility to President **Chun Doo Hwan**, Lee was able to achieve little in this post. He was a popular foreign minister, partly because of his excellent English.

LEE HU RAK (1924–)

Lee Hu Rak was born in **Pusan** in 1924. He served as a noncommissioned officer in the Japanese army and later attended the (South) Korean Military Academy. From 1963 to 1970, he was secretary-general to President **Park Chung Hee** and therefore in a very powerful advisory position. In 1970, he was briefly ambassador to Tokyo and later the same year became head of the Korean Central Intelligence Agency (KCIA). In that capacity, he visited North Korea twice in 1972 and met with **Kim Il Sung** as part of Park's attempt to begin a dialogue with the North. The following year, Lee was blamed for the KCIA's kidnapping of the opposition leader **Kim Dae Jung** and for the agency's excessive use of violence against

Park's opponents. Lee resigned for health reasons, but reappeared in 1978 as an independent member of the National Assembly. Following **Chun Doo Hwan**'s takeover in 1980, Lee was arrested for embezzlement and banned from politics.
Reference: Oberdorfer 1997.

LEFT-WING POLITICAL FACTIONS

Kim Il Sung's unassailable control of state and party in the Democratic Republic of North Korea for the thirty years before his death was achieved in part through the neutralizing of political rivals and the sidelining of the factions they were associated with. By the early 1960s, Kim had succeeded in establishing himself and those he trusted at the center of the political apparatus in North Korea.

Four main groups, all with varying backgrounds and experiences, are generally identified among the Communist activists who reemerged in Korea after the defeat of Japan in August 1945 or entered the country at that time. Within the peninsula, the "old" Communists who had survived Japanese occupation immediately revived the **Korean Communist Party** (KCP) under **Pak Hon-yong**. In the north, the Soviet forces entering Korea to accept the Japanese surrender in the area above the **38th parallel** brought with them a number of Russian-born Koreans to assist with interpreting and administration. This second group, whose education and political training placed them in the Soviet orbit, constituted the Russian, or Soviet, faction. For a while they formed a larger faction with members of Kim Il Sung's circle, with whom they shared some background. Kim and his comrades, who during the 1930s had launched guerrilla attacks on the Japanese from their bases in **Northeast China**, probably retreated into the Soviet Union during the years 1941–1945. This third group was known as the Kapsan faction, from the Kapsan Mountains in South Hamgyong Province of northeastern Korea, where they carried out some of their raids.

The Yan'an (Yenan) faction constituted the fourth group. These activists were associated with the Chinese Communists, the other backers of the Korean Communist revolution. Their leaders were **Mu Chong** and Kim Tu-bong. By 1941, Mu had come to head the Korean Volunteer Force in China, later renamed the Korean Volunteer Army. This group operated out of Yan'an, the headquarters of the Chinese Communist Party in the north-central province of Shaanxi from 1936 to 1947, and also along the front line of the Japanese attack in north China, where they set up the North China Korean Independence League in 1942.

In the period following the Japanese surrender, the KCP, with headquarters in **Seoul**, was initially stronger in the south of the country. Its chairman, Pak Hon-yong, favored a single Communist party for the whole of the peninsula, but by the end of 1945, his "domestic" faction found itself facing a virtually independent northern branch. The Yan'an group had returned to Korea, but its impact on the political scene was weakened when the Korean Volunteer Army, its military wing, was disarmed and disbanded by the occupying Soviet forces when it tried to enter Korea in the autumn of 1945. Early in 1946, the **New People's Party** (NPP), led by Kim Tu-bong, was formed in Korea from the old North China Korean Independence League, with branches both north and south. The NPP was prepared to make common cause with the KCP in both halves of the country, and thus by the end of 1946, two single left-wing parties had emerged in Korea, the South Korean Workers' Party (SKWP) and the North Korean Workers' Party (NKWP). All the time, as a Communist regime was being fostered in the north of the country, the focus of leftist power was gravitating to the north and falling increasingly under the influence of Kim Il Sung and the Soviet-Kapsan group. Pak Hon-yong saw his membership decline as left-wing activists moved north. He himself, threatened with arrest by the U.S. occupying forces, joined them at the end of 1946. His organization degenerated into an increasingly fugitive guerrilla-type movement as a conservative form of government emerged in the south.

In reorganizing and institutionalizing the Communist movement in the north, Kim Il Sung had initially to balance political appointments between his Soviet-Kapsan group, the Yan'an group, and Pak's domestic faction. By March 1948, however, Kim felt able to mount an open attack on the domestic group. With the formalization during August–September 1948 of the division of the Korea Peninsula into two states, the southern element in the Communist movement found that its base had virtually disappeared. In mid-1949, the formation of the **Korean Workers' Party (KWP)** through the merging of the SKWP and the NKWP signaled the end of an independent party in the south.

The **Korean War** provided opportunities to Kim to oust his rivals. Mu Chong, commander of the Second Army Corps of the **North Korean People's Army**, was removed from his post in December 1950 on grounds of incompetence and disobedience of orders. The stalemate in hostilities and the unsatisfactory outcome of the war were blamed on Pak Hon-yong and his "factionalists." Charges of treason and spying were brought against the latter in August 1953, followed by death sentences. Pak himself was held until the end of 1955, when he faced similar charges and accusations of power gathering and likewise was sentenced to death. In April 1955, a party warning on factionalism had been directed at the Soviet and Yan'an groups.

Kim Il Sung's absence abroad in the summer of 1956 encouraged the emergence of a broad coalition against him. At a meeting of the KWP Central Committee in August after his return, he denounced his opponents, who included members of the two factions. This time, Soviet and Chinese leaders intervened with Kim in support of those purged and they were reinstated; but the removal or sidelining of those judged unreliable continued throughout the decade and beyond. By the late 1950s, those left-wing groups active in the pre-1945 era had been virtually eliminated, with the exception of Kim Il Sung's own circle of intimates.

Various reasons have been suggested for Kim's success in gaining the upper hand in confrontations with his rivals. Soviet backing was undoubtedly crucial. Scalapino and Lee (1972: 230) argue that Kim was the Soviet choice at a time when the Russians had power to enforce their wishes. Yang (1994) suggests that Kim and the Soviet occupying forces saw mutual advantage in working together and, moreover, that the domestic and Yan'an factions both arrived too late in North Korea—after Kim had consolidated a power base. Much lay probably in Kim's own capability for careful and ruthless maneuvering.

References: Scalapino and Lee 1972; Suh 1970, 1981; Yang 1994.

LI KENONG (1898–1962)

Li Kenong was a prominent Chinese intelligence and security official. Li was born in Anhui Province in 1898. A member of the Chinese Communist Party from the 1920s and active in the Shanghai underground Communist movement, he later became a close associate of **Zhou Enlai**. Following the establishment of the **People's Republic of China** and Zhou's appointment as foreign minister, Li became one of the vice–foreign ministers. In that role, he accompanied Zhou to the 1954 **Geneva Conference**, and for a time was left in charge of the Chinese delegation. He held a variety of appointments thereafter, but in 1957 suffered a physical fall, from which he never recovered. He died in 1962.
Reference: Klein and Clark 1971.

LI KWON-MU (1910–1970)

In 1950, at the outbreak of the **Korean War**, Li Kwon-mu was a major-general in the **North Korean People's Army** (NKPA). He trained in the **Union of Soviet Socialist Republics** and served as a lieutenant in the Red Army during World War II. He also fought with the Chinese Communist 8th Route Army against the Japanese. Following the establishment of the Democratic People's Republic of Korea in September 1948, he was appointed chief-of-staff of the North Korean army. As the war began, Li's 4th Division swept south and captured the South Korean capital, **Seoul**, within three days, an event still highly regarded in North Korean accounts of the war. In October 1950, he became commander of II Corps. After the war he was commander-in-chief of the NKPA, becoming chief-of-staff again from 1958 to 1960.
Reference: Matray 1991.

LI TIANYOU (1905–1970)

Li Tianyou took part in the Chinese Communist Party's Long March in the 1930s and played a prominent role in the fighting against the Japanese in World War II and against the Chinese Nationalists during the 1946–1949 civil war. In the autumn of 1950, he was commander of the 13th Army Group, made up of the 38th, 39th, 40th, and 42nd armies, which assembled at Shenyang in preparation for an expected intervention in Korea. Later, the 50th and 60th armies joined his group, which began to move into Korea in mid-October 1950. General Li commanded the troops on the western side of the peninsula, while **Song Shilun** was in charge on the eastern side. After his command in Korea, his career is obscure.

See also: Chinese People's Volunteers; Peng Dehuai; People's Liberation Army (PLA).

LINGUISTIC DIFFERENCES BETWEEN NORTH AND SOUTH

Since the mid-fifteenth century, Korean has had its own alphabet and script, both devised to give the spoken word a more accurate written form. Until then, Chinese characters had been used to write Korean, although the two languages are very differently structured. Characters continued in favor, nonetheless, especially among the educated. Attempts were first made around the beginning of the twentieth century to exclude characters, seen as marks of foreign culture, from written Korean. In 1933, a group of scholars, pursuing language reform as one way of strengthening Korean culture against Japanese influences, produced the first standard spelling of Korean. In 1945, Korea regained cultural and linguistic autonomy.

The separate governments of North and South after 1948 both claim Korean and in particular its written form, *han'gul,* as a unique national asset, but have evolved different philosophies and policies toward the language. In the North, **Kim Il Sung** from 1966 promoted the development of a "cultured language" (*munhwa o*), based on the Korean spoken around **P'yongyang**, as a challenge to the tradition of a "standard language" (*pyojun o*), based on the speech of **Seoul**. His aims were to defend the purity of Korean, which he claimed the South had allowed to degenerate, and to build a language that would help to mold the new Communist society he sought. The approved norm for this language was to be that of the ordinary people. Loanwords were targeted, especially the many borrowings from Chinese, to be replaced by pure Korean expressions. New concepts required new words, established words acquired new meanings, and words expressing discredited ideas were discarded. Dialectal forms became standard elements.

One result of such changes was that misunderstandings and confusion arose at the first North-

South talks in P'yongyang in 1972. The extent of linguistic divergence that was revealed disturbed those from the South, where language was not seen as a tool to implement government policies and where neologisms and foreign borrowings—by the mid-1990s estimated to include more than 10,000 English loanwords—were constantly absorbed.

The South Korean reaction was to accuse the North of a deliberate policy of deviation; yet North and South have followed roughly similar policies over such issues as spelling reform and Chinese characters in written Korean. After pushing for the complete exclusion of characters from official material and school textbooks, the South settled in 1972 for the retention of 1,800 basic characters, to be taught to older school students and used in newspapers. The North banned characters altogether in 1949, but from 1968 has likewise allowed a few to be taught to older students. On spelling reform, neither society has so far been willing to move far from the base provided by the 1933 orthography in the direction of simplification or the addition of new letters. Kim Il Sung himself warned against radical changes as too divisive. Noticeable differences between practice in North and South are in the direction of writing (always horizontal in the North and either vertical or horizontal in the South); in the continuation of the use of Chinese characters in the South; in minor areas of phonetics and word formation; in alphabetical word order; and in slightly varying ways of romanizing *han'gul,* that is, expressing the sounds of the language using the Roman or Latin alphabet.

References: King 1997; Kumatani 1990; Lee 1990; Sohn 1997.

LITERATURE OF THE KOREAN CONFLICT

Korean responses to the often painful history of the peninsula in the twentieth century have frequently been made through literature. The experiences of Japanese colonialism, occupation by foreign powers, civil war, territorial division, rapid industrialization, and authoritarian leadership have been mined, though in very different ways, by writers both North and South for the subject matter of poetry, novels, and short stories. The latter is a genre in which modern Korean writers have excelled. Their general taste for literary realism, allied to frequently oblique and restrained comment, produces work of great power through which, as Pihl, Fulton, and Fulton (1993) have suggested, South Korean writers at least have helped to "socialize" their readers into the harsh realities of the nation's modern history.

In parallel with the political divergences of the mid-1920s, left-right divisions also marked the literary scene in the 1920s and 1930s. Leftist writers, banded into the Korean Artists Proletarian Federation (KAPF), demanded that literature should serve socialist purposes and clashed with those who pursued "pure literature" or who wrote in a moderate realist style. These divisions erupted again after liberation in 1945 and eventually led to the physical relocation of writers between North and South as political antagonism hardened into two separate regimes. It has been estimated that by the early 1950s more than 100 writers, about one-third of the Korean literary establishment, had moved from the South to the North, a far greater number than those migrating southward. Increasing pressure from both the U.S. military government and the right-wing administration in South Korea during 1945–1948 sent left-wing writers north in two waves. Some of those remaining in the South after 1948 made an ideological "conversion," but as North Korean troops retreated north in late 1950, having earlier overrun most of the peninsula, some of these "converts" moved north voluntarily with them. Other, right-wing, writers, such as Yi Kwang-su, were taken north forcibly and subsequently disappeared. At the same time, disaffected writers in the North took advantage of the fluid military situation to come south. Official curbs on expression in the South meant that discussion of these migrating writers and publication of their work in South Korea were very circumscribed until 1988, when all major restrictions were finally lifted.

South Korea

The desire to regain a national identity and to reclaim both language and culture from the recent colonial past was strong after liberation in 1945, but did not lead to prolific writing. Political rivalries distorted the cultural scene, further confused by the demands imposed by two differing occupying forces. This period of upheaval was reflected in novels by Ch'ae Man-shik (1902–1950) (*Mister Pang* [1946], set during the U.S. military occupation) and Hwang Sun-won (1915–) (*The Descendants of Cain* [1954], based on Hwang's experiences of land reform in the Soviet-administered North).

The **Korean War** (1950–1953) produced no domestic genre of "war stories" as that category is understood in the West. Kim Chong-un (1974) has suggested that perception of the war as a civil war discouraged its treatment in terms of military heroism. Certainly, the moral and social dilemmas that confronted many Koreans, obliged to make difficult choices and to accept loss and division, made simple tales of soldiering inappropriate. Instead, to make observations about the war and its effects on human beings, writers such as Hwang Sun-won, Chang Yong-hak (1921–), and Son U-hwi (1922–) examine their characters' behavior in extreme situations. Time and again, the war is characterized as irrational and absurd.

The writing of the immediate postwar period is marked by a sense of dislocation and frustration that matched the chaotic conditions of the time (*A Blank Map* [1956] by So Ki-won [1930–]), yet also by an insistence on greater individual freedom of decision (*Kapitan Ri* [1962] by Chon Kwang-yong [1919–1988]). The mood was further sharpened by experimentation with Western existentialist thinking, of which *The Square* (1961) by Choi In-hoon (Ch'oe In-hun [1936–]), on the theme of conflicting ideologies, bears the imprint.

From the late 1960s, as issues of political legitimacy, rapid industrialization, and social change demanded the attention of writers, the war lost its immediacy. Instead, a "literature of division" emerged that by the 1980s was exploring the complexities of the Korean conflict, encouraged by a relaxation of prohibitions on discussion of the causes and effects of that conflict. Stories of great poignancy (*Land of Exile* [1981] by Cho Chong-nae; *My Father's Land* [1984] by Im Chol-u [1954–]) reveal situations where political and personal realities are entwined, often with tragic consequences. The crucial period of confrontation and dilemma was clearly from June 1950 to January 1951, during the most active part of the war, when opposing forces demanded conflicting loyalty from the people they had overrun and dealt mercilessly with recalcitrants.

Two Korean authors who have written mainly in English on the Korean conflict are Richard Kim (1931–) and Peter Hyun (1928–). Kim's *The Martyred* (1969), set in **P'yongyang** in the crucial period of the early months of the war, deals with issues of conscience and trust. Hyun's *Darkness at Dawn: A North Korean Diary* (1981) recounts the author's visit to his native province in the North.

North Korea

Official guidelines on the purposes of art and literature were soon established in North Korea after 1945 under the influence of the occupying Soviet administration, and by early 1946 writers and artists had been organized under the North Korean Federation of Literature and Art (NKFLA). The cultural scene, in parallel with the political scene, quickly split into factions around individuals, whose maneuvering continued until **Kim Il Sung's** final purges of the early 1960s. Kim himself gave two important talks on art and literature in May 1946 and June 1951 and continued to concern himself with cultural affairs. The glorification of his achievements had already emerged by the late 1940s as a literary theme, but intensified only after the mid-1960s.

NKFLA members followed North Korean troops on their advance south in June 1950 to report on the fighting and to conduct propaganda in areas controlled by the North. The intention was not just to seize territory but also to install new political and cultural systems. Some writers served in the regular forces, and a number were lost in the fighting. By July 1950, NKFLA reports were appearing in the **P'yongyang** press. These contributions and the novels that began to be published presented the enemy, whether military or civilian, in the starkest terms, as monsters whose bestiality and cruelty merited retribution (*U.S. Embassy*, by Yi T'ae-jun). Other writers, such as Han So-rya (1900–?1970), underlined the spontaneous spirit of young North Korean fighters (*Soldier's Farewell* [1951], *Taedonggang* [1952], and *Liberation Tower* [1953], the latter two both set in P'yongyang during its occupation by United Nations forces in late 1950). Another of Han's targets was the U.S. missionary community in Korea (*Jackals* [1951], *Love* [1960]). The same crude distinction persisted in later fiction set in the South,

where the villains are consistently South Korean or U.S. officials and military.

Writers in North Korea, however, have, in their way, as suggested by Brian Myers (1994), responded faithfully to the requirements laid upon them to indicate the chosen way forward and to delineate the boundaries of their society. The greatest flaw in their writing is that, as Marshall Pihl (1993) puts it, under the pressure of party control, it is "less a reflection of social reality than a statement of social ideals."

See also: Histories and Other Studies of the Korean War; War Stories and War Films of the Korean War.

References: Choi 1961; Hyun 1981; Kim R 1969; Kim Chong-un 1974; Myers 1994; *Nineteen Contemporary Korean Novelists* 1985; Pihl 1993; Pihl, Fulton, and Fulton 1993; Tennant 1996.

LITTLE SWITCH (1953)

Despite the suspension of the **armistice** talks from 8 October 1952 to 26 April 1953, discussions continued at liaison-officer level between the two negotiating parties, the **United Nations Command** (UNC) and the North Korea/Chinese side, particularly on the question of an exchange of sick and wounded **prisoners of war** (POWs). Possibly as a reflection of the softening Communist position following the death of **Joseph Stalin** in March 1953, agreement was reached on the repatriation of these POWs. The document of 11 April 1953, signed by Major-General Lee Sang-cho for the Communist side and by Rear Admiral J. C. Daniel for the UNC, provided for a prisoner exchange through the truce site of **P'anmunjom** under the appropriate article (109) of the 1949 **Geneva Convention**.

The operation, known as Little Switch, lasted from 20 April to 3 May. In all, 5,194 North Korean POWs were released by the UNC; this number included 18 women POWs; 446 Korean civilian internees (of whom three were women) and 1,030 Chinese POWs were also handed over. The North Korean/Chinese side released 684 UNC prisoners, of whom 471 were Koreans returning to the South and 149 were U.S. POWs (all figures from Hermes 1966). Little Switch was also the occasion for the release in small groups of many of the **foreign civilian detainees** who had been held in camps in the far north of the peninsula since September 1950. These detainees were repatriated via China and the **Union of Soviet Socialist Republics.**

On their way to the holding post at Munsan and then to P'anmunjom, a number of the North Korean and Chinese POWs threw away the rations that they had been given by the UNC or spoiled their new clothing as a gesture of defiance either to emphasize their contempt, to demonstrate that they had been badly treated, or possibly to persuade their compatriots that they had not capitulated to the enemy.

See also: Big Switch (1953).

References: Hermes 1966; History: VI, 1977.

LORD, HERBERT ARTHUR (1889–1971)

Commissioner Herbert Lord of the Salvation Army, held on 2 July 1950 after North Korean troops had occupied **Seoul**, became a spokesperson and interpreter for the other **foreign civilian detainees.** His fluent knowledge of Korean came from nearly thirty years of missionary work in the peninsula. As territorial commander for Korea in 1947, Lord headed the Salvation Army organization in the country and refused to leave in face of the North Korean invasion. The officials in charge of foreign detainees and accompanying **prisoners of war** chose him to interpret for both groups as they were moved north, and he often acted as intermediary between his fellow prisoners and their captors. In this exposed position, he sometimes found himself interceding with a pistol to his head. He was released on 9 April 1953 and returned to his native Britain via Moscow in company with six other Western detainees.

References: Crosbie 1954; Deane 1953; Kenyon 1966.

LUXEMBOURG FORCES IN THE KOREAN WAR

See **Belgian Forces in the Korean War.**

MAC

See **Military Armistice Commission (MAC).**

MACARTHUR, DOUGLAS (1880–1964)

Douglas MacArthur, general of the army from 1944 and commander-in-chief of the U.S. forces in the Far East at the end of World War II, was appointed supreme commander for the Allied powers in Japan in 1945 after the Japanese surrender. Following the outbreak of the **Korean War** on 25 June 1950 and the formation of the unified **United Nations Command** (UNC) in Korea, U.S. President **Harry S Truman** appointed MacArthur to the additional post of commander of the United Nations' forces on 8 July 1950. On 14 July 1950, South Korean president **Syngman Rhee** gave MacArthur operational command of South Korean forces as well. In this dual role, MacArthur planned and executed

General Douglas MacArthur, commander of the United Nations Command, in conversation with General Matthew Ridgway, then commander of the U.S. Eighth Army, 3 April 1951. MacArthur was dismissed by President Harry Truman on 11 April 1951, and was succeeded as UNC commander by Ridgway. (MacArthur Memorial Foundation Library)

M

Operation Chromite, the massive sea and land attack at **Inch'on** on 15 September 1950. This broke the North Korean advance into South Korea, cut the North Korean forces in two, and allowed a counterattack to begin. By 1 October 1950, MacArthur had achieved the original purpose of the UN intervention, with the restoration of the status quo of 25 June. The UN forces did not stop at the **38th parallel**, however. With South Korean troops in the lead, they swept across the parallel, and, meeting little or no resistance from the North Koreans, continued north. Flushed with success, MacArthur discounted hints from the **People's Republic of China** that the Chinese would intervene if the advance continued, and the United Nations' forces pressed on. Even when they began to encounter Chinese troops in October, MacArthur remained optimistic. As late as 24 November 1950, he was promising that Korea would be reunified and that the troops would be "**home for Christmas.**" The following day, Chinese units intervened in force, and the UN forces fell back in disarray.

MacArthur now panicked. He demanded to be allowed to blockade the Chinese coastline and to bomb military positions across the **Yalu River** in China's northeastern provinces. This was refused, and the refusal remained a grievance with MacArthur until he died. Meanwhile, General **Matthew Ridgway** was given battlefield command in Korea and stopped the UN forces' retreat. In Washington, the idea of reunifying the peninsula was abandoned in favor of containing communism at the 38th parallel. Although MacArthur did not publicly oppose this change of policy, he made it clear that it was not to his liking. Increasing concern in Washington at what was seen as his insubordination came to a head in April 1951, when a letter to a U.S. congressman from MacArthur advocating the use in Korea of Chinese Nationalist forces from Taiwan was read out loud in Congress. MacArthur was relieved of his command on 11 April 1951, and Ridgway took over.

MacArthur returned to the United States for the first time since before the United States became involved in the war in the Pacific. A hero's welcome awaited him, but his popularity did not last. He appeared before the joint U.S. Senate Foreign Affairs and Armed Service Committee in May 1951, but made relatively little impact. From then until his death in 1964, he gradually faded from public view, although from time to time, he continued to criticize those, such as the British, whom he held responsible for limiting his actions in Korea. He is still remembered with affection in South Korea as the man who saved the country in 1950. Since the mid-1980s, a statue of MacArthur holding binoculars has stood in Inch'on on Radio Hill, now renamed Freedom Hill, one of the highest points in the town.
See also: Chinese People's Volunteers; Inch'on Landing (1950).
References: MacArthur 1964; Perret 1966.

MAGRIN-VERMEREY, CHARLES (1892–1964)
General Charles Magrin-Vermerey, better known by his nom de guerre of Ralph Monclar, the name he assumed in the early 1940s, commanded the French Battalion during the Korean War from November 1950 to December 1952. In his late fifties by the time of the Korean War, and scarred by earlier war wounds, Monclar accepted a lower grading (to lieutenant colonel from general) to take up this command. During his tour of duty, the French forces were engaged in fierce fighting in the central sector of Korea.

Monclar fought in both world wars. In 1940, he commanded the 13th demi-brigade of the Foreign Legion at Narvik (Norway), and then went on to serve in Eritrea (northern Ethiopia). When he signed up in 1950, he was an inspector in the Foreign Legion. Among many seasoned soldiers in Korea, Monclar stood out for his appearance (black beret, steel-rimmed spectacles, and walking stick to ease his limp) and for his courage and closeness to his men.

See also: French Forces in the Korean War.
References: Bergot 1983; Blair 1987; Crahay 1967; History: III, 1974 and VI, 1977.

MANCHURIA
See Northeast China.

MAO ZEDONG (1893–1976)
Mao Zedong was born in China's Henan Province in 1893. A founder-member of the Chinese Communist Party (CCP), he had become its leader by the mid-1930s. After fighting the Japanese in World War II, Mao and the CCP began a civil war against Chiang Kai-shek and by 1949 had succeeded in driving Chiang and his followers to Taiwan. After some twenty years of sporadic fighting, Mao may have wished for a period in which to consolidate the new People's Republic of China (PRC), but the Korean War changed that. When the United Nations Command took the war across the 38th parallel in September 1950, Mao sent the Chinese People's Volunteers, including his eldest son, Mao Anying, who was killed, to protect China's frontiers and to prevent the defeat of the Democratic People's Republic of Korea (DPRK). Mao continued to support the DPRK after the war, waiving debt repayments and providing economic assistance.
References: Chen 1994; Goncharov, Lewis, and Xue 1994.

MARSHALL, GEORGE CATLETT (1880–1959)
George C. Marshall, a U.S. soldier and diplomat, was secretary of defense during the early part of the Korean War. He was born in Uniontown, Pennsylvania, in December 1880. He joined the U.S. Army in 1902 and served in France in World War I. From September 1939 to November 1945, he was U.S. Army chief-of-staff, becoming general of the army in 1944. During 1945–1946, he was U.S. President Harry S Truman's envoy to China, and on retirement in 1947, he became secretary of state. In that role, he devised the Marshall Plan for European economic recovery and was responsible for bringing the Korean question before the United Nations General Assembly in September 1947, leading to the resolution of 14 November 1947. Marshall became secretary of defense in September 1950 and held the post for a year. Although he was supportive of General Douglas MacArthur, Marshall saw the need

for a political settlement of the Korean War and accepted Truman's dismissal of MacArthur in April 1951. Marshall died in Washington, D.C., in 1959.

See also: United Nations General Assembly Resolutions on Korea.

MARTIAL LAW

Martial law has been available since 1946 in the South as a means of dealing with political crises. A railway strike of September 1946 appears to have provoked the first recourse to martial law, when troops of the occupying U.S. military administration were sent to restore order. Martial law was imposed in July 1950 throughout South Korea under the impact of the North's invasion; in April 1960, following student riots against President **Syngman Rhee**; in the following year by the new president, **Park Chung Hee**; in 1972, as Park introduced his **Yushin Constitution**; and again after his assassination in 1979. President **Chun Doo Hwan** declared full martial law in May 1980, extending it to the offshore island of **Cheju**. Angry popular response to Chun's move was largely responsible for provoking the **Kwangju** uprising in the same month. The Constitution of 1987 provides for the application of martial law in certain circumstances, but it has not been invoked since 1980.

M*A*S*H* (FILM AND TELEVISION SERIES)

The inspiration for both the film and the television series of *M*A*S*H* was the 8055 Mobile Army Surgical Hospital (MASH), one of many serving **United Nations** troops in the **Korean War**. The fictitious *M*A*S*H* unit was numbered 4077.

The film, produced in 1970 for 20th Century Fox by Ingo Preminger, directed by Robert Altman, with screenplay by Ring Lardner, Jr., and music by Johnny Mandel, was based on a 1968 novel by Richard Hooker, the pen name of Dr. Richard Hornberger (1924–1997), who had served in the 8055 MASH. The producer of the 1972–1983 CBS television series, for which 251 episodes were made, was Gene Reynolds; the scriptwriter was Larry Gelbart. Though set in the Korean War, Korean characters are few and were often played by non-Korean actors. The early years of *M*A*S*H*'s popularity were dominated by the Vietnam War, and the tone of both film and series reflects the preoccupations of that era. Although Western audiences enjoy the action and characterization, many Koreans dislike *M*A*S*H* for what they see as its trivializing presentation of Koreans and the Korean War.

See also: Mobile Army Surgical Hospital (MASH); War Stories and War Films of the Korean War.

MEMORIALS AND MUSEUMS TO THE KOREAN CONFLICT

The northern part of the Republic of Korea (ROK) is dotted with a large number of **Korean War** memorials; they are particularly numerous in and around **Seoul** and in the area between Seoul and the **Demilitarized Zone** (DMZ), the scene of extensive fighting. All sixteen of the countries that sent combat troops to serve under the **United Nations Command** (UNC) have single or joint memorials, often in places where they were heavily engaged. Individual units are also commemorated. Some monuments were erected by individual contingents or countries or by groups of countries; a joint Commonwealth memorial, for instance, was dedicated in 1967. Between 1974 and 1976, the South Korean Ministry of National Defense undertook the construction of memorials to those allies, including the United States, not yet commemorated by monuments and of a joint memorial to those countries that had dispatched medical support units. In 1977, a memorial was dedicated to the eighteen **press correspondents** killed while covering the fighting.

The construction of a permanent memorial and museum dedicated to South Korean troops was much delayed, funding being one of the factors. Only in 1994, three decades after first being mooted, was the War Memorial opened in Seoul, on the site of the former ROK Army headquarters, replacing an earlier private museum on Yoido Island in the **Han River**. Its purpose is comprehensive: to record all the wars from earliest times in which Koreans have fought, both within and without the country. Nationalist armed movements against the Japanese colonialists are commemorated; similar Communist activities are ignored. The Korean War of 1950–1953 forms one section in the display. Another room marks South Korean participation in the **Vietnam War** and in UN peacekeeping missions. Sections dedicated to the various branches of the ROK armed services, to military equipment, and to the South

Korean defense industries stress South Korea's preparedness for combat (by comparison with its poor level of readiness in 1950) and do not conceal that South Korea considers the principal threat to come still from the North, which is perceived as maintaining a constant high state of war preparedness.

The War Memorial also contains archives and a library centered in a research institute. It is flanked by galleries where tablets record the names of the 160,000 killed since 1946 in conflicts involving South Korean troops—the Korean and Vietnam wars—and the names of policemen who died on duty. (Many of the latter were killed in anti-guerrilla operations in the south of the peninsula during 1945–1950.) The National Cemetery, also in Seoul, contains the graves of many South Korean war dead. (From 1954 to 1965 it was designated the Armed Forces Cemetery.) War dead from the UNC forces are buried or commemorated at the **United Nations Cemetery (Pusan)**, established in January 1951.

Within South Korea, a number of sites, such as the site of **Koje Island prisoner of war camp**, remain as reminders of episodes in the Korean War or as evidence of the continuing unresolved tension between North and South. The armistice site of **P'anmunjom**, north of Seoul and approached by Freedom Bridge, is much visited by tourists who can also descend into the Third Tunnel, discovered in 1978 and allegedly dug to allow North Korean troops to pass under the DMZ into the South. Two "unification" observatories, Kosong at the eastern end of the DMZ and Odusan at the western end, permit viewers in the South to gaze into the North.

The Democratic People's Republic of Korea commemorates its war dead at the Revolutionary Martyrs' Cemetery just outside **P'yongyang** and in the Monument to Victory in the Fatherland Liberation War (as the Korean War is termed in the North). The latter is a group of stone monuments and massive figures sculpted in bronze, completed in 1993, and occupying a large area in central P'yongyang. A museum of the war was also opened in the capital in 1953 and rebuilt in 1974. It devotes much space to the North's initially successful occupation of the South. The **Chinese People's Volunteers**, who fought in large numbers on the North Korean side, are commemorated at various cemeteries and monuments in P'yongyang and other regions of North Korea; at the Friendship Tower in P'yongyang, dedicated in 1959 to Sino-Korean friendship; and at many memorials within China, chiefly in the northeast. The principal monument is at Shenyang, the capital of Liaoning Province.

Outside of the Korea Peninsula, the most striking national memorial is undoubtedly the Korean War Veterans Memorial, created in the center of Washington, D.C., in commemoration of U.S. troops, whose casualties mounted to 54,246 dead and 8,177 missing. A group of nineteen figures, slightly larger than life and sculpted in stainless steel, represent a foot patrol in winter clothing advancing across open country. Figures and faces copied from photographs held in the National Archives and etched on a polished granite wall flanking the sculptures record the many support personnel who also served in the war. A Pool of Remembrance completes the memorial, which was dedicated on 27 July 1995.

Troops from other national contingents are commemorated in their homelands, as at the Australian War Memorial in Canberra, at St. Paul's

Monument to Victory in the Fatherland Liberation War, P'yongyang. (Victorious Fatherland Liberation War Museum)

U.S. Korean War monument in Washington, D.C. (Korean War Veterans Memorial)

Cathedral in London (U.K. troops are further remembered in the Anglican cathedral in Seoul), and at a site near the Pont Marie in Paris. Archival material on the Korean War, including photographs, is held in such centers as the National Archives, Washington, D.C., and the Imperial War Museum, London.

Memorials and archives, together with national veterans associations, provide a focus for survivors of the Korean War and a continuing reminder of past military commitments to the UNC. The political reasoning that prompted the military contribution of so many countries in the first place may be expressed publicly in terms of "service of the United Nations" or "defense of the free world," even if privately a range of more complex and particular reasons prevailed, such as the desire to placate a powerful ally or to preempt wider hostilities. For the two Korean states, their principal memorials allow them to present their competing interpretations of the significance of the war and the **armistice**. The North Korean leaders do not consider that their state was defeated; rather, they were able to rid it of foreign intervention and develop it along self-sufficient lines. Their country's patriotism and readiness for self-sacrifice remain untarnished. The South Korean position is that, even before the Korean War, the South was actively holding the Communists at bay and that it is determined to maintain invulnerability against the North and moreover to stand by allies in their own conflicts elsewhere in the world.

References: Highsmith and Landphair 1995; History: VI, 1977; *The Victorious Fatherland Liberation War Museum* 1979; War Memorial Service (n.d.).

MENON, V. K. KRISHNA (1896–1974)

The Indian diplomat Krishna Menon was born into a large and wealthy family and studied at the University of Madras and the London School of Economics. While in London, he also qualified as a barrister. During these years, he became friendly with India's future prime minister, **Jawaharlal Nehru**. After India's independence in 1947, Menon was high commissioner in London. In 1952, he headed India's **United Nations** delegation, playing a significant role in developing India's nonaligned foreign policy. This was partly achieved by attacks on U.S. foreign policy, which led many Americans to view him with suspicion. Despite this, however, he played an important role in encouraging the truce talks at **P'anmunjom** and in finding a formula that, much modified, provided a basis for settling the **prisoners of war** issue. Menon later served as India's minister of defense and in the Indian parliament, but after Nehru's death in 1964, he ceased to have much influence. He died in 1974.

References: Dockrill 1989; MacDonald 1986; Matray 1991.

MIA
See **Missing in Action (MIA)**.

MILITARY ARMISTICE COMMISSION (MAC)
The Military Armistice Commission (MAC) has had the task of supervising the implementation of the **armistice** agreement signed on 27 July 1953 between the **United Nations Command** (UNC) and the joint North Korean/Chinese forces to end the **Korean War**. The armistice did not bring about a permanent peace, but nonetheless yielded a minimal agreement that has kept North and South Korea from resuming outright warfare. The MAC, attended by both sides, has provided a mechanism for discussing infringements of the armistice within the **Demilitarized Zone** and the **Han River** estuary, its area of jurisdiction.

The MAC, located at **P'anmunjom**, was constituted with five senior officers from each side, of whom three on each side were to hold the rank of general. It is a joint organization with no chairman and is supported by a secretariat and ten **Joint Observer Teams**. The two sides sit facing each other across a table, down the length of which runs a cord designating the Military Demarcation Line dividing North from South. In the past, the two sides have striven to outrival each other in the size and height of their respective flags. Daily meetings, as required by the armistice agreement, are maintained by duty officers. Less frequent plenary sessions have been

General Officers' meeting of the Military Armistice Commission, 23 June 1998. Note the cord running the length of the table, which marks the line of the boundary between the North and South. This passes through the middle of the MAC hut. Because this is not a full session, no flags are displayed. (Brigadier Colin Parr, Defence Attaché, British Embassy, Seoul)

The United Nations Command team at a 1988 MAC meeting. Note the boundary cord and the North Korean flag in the lower right-hand side of the photo, displayed at a full session. (Brigadier Colin Parr, Defence Attaché, British Embassy, Seoul)

held on demand from either side and used to air grievances and conduct propaganda. As a result of the **ax murders** incident in August 1976, a supplementary agreement was drawn up in September 1976 to change the layout of the MAC headquarters areas.

Until February 1991, the UNC permanent delegation to the MAC was led by a senior U.S. officer, flanked by two South Korean generals and two other officers representing British Commonwealth forces and one of the other UNC countries in rotation. In March 1991, the UNC designated a South Korean general as their senior member. The North Korean/Chinese side refused to accept this appointment, which would have placed their senior member, a North Korean officer, opposite a senior South Korean officer, and suspended attendance at plenary MAC meetings. Lower-level secretariat meetings continued.

The North Korean objection was based on their contention that the armistice agreement had nothing to do with the South Koreans, whose president in 1953, **Syngman Rhee**, had rejected the whole

concept of an armistice and had only consented to it under U.S. pressure. The North Koreans have argued further that the armistice agreement should be replaced by a peace treaty between themselves and the United States, who they consider to have been their true opponent in the Korean War. In 1991, they charged the United States with violating the agreement by attempting to appoint a South Korean general as senior member. In April 1994, they withdrew from the MAC, replacing their representatives in August of that year by a Korean People's Army P'anmunjom Mission. They also persuaded the Chinese to withdraw their representatives from the MAC, which they did in December 1994. Both North Korea and China have called for a new mechanism to ensure peace on the Korea Peninsula. The **four-party talks**, initiated in December 1997, may have taken pressure off the MAC, for long the only meeting point between the two sides. At all events, the UNC and North Korea agreed in June 1998 to resume high-level military talks, on condition that a U.S. general head the UNC team.

MILITARY EQUIPMENT USED IN THE KOREAN WAR

Because the **Korean War** (1950–1953) began so soon after the end of World War II in 1945, it is not surprising that much of the military equipment in use on both sides during the war dated from the 1939–1945 period. In fact, much of the technology, especially in the case of small arms, was even older.

Weapons

Among the troops under the **United Nations Command** (UNC), the South Korean forces were equipped with U.S. pistols and rifles that, despite modifications during World War II, generally dated from World War I. This was so with most of the U.S. forces, for whom the standard weapon was the Browning automatic rifle (BAR). Although these weapons were of World War II vintage, the basic technology dated from 1917–1918. U.S. light machine guns were generally of World War II make, but by 1950 the technology was at least twenty years old. For the British Commonwealth forces, the standard infantry weapon was the Mark 4 Lee Enfield rifle, also dating to World War I, as did the .455 Webley pistol. The main British Commonwealth machine gun was the World War I–vintage Vickers, supplemented by the World War II–vintage, Czech-designed Bren light machine gun.

Even older fighting techniques occasionally surfaced in Korea. The **Turkish forces**, for example, used bayonets in January 1951. Although this was seen as a good morale booster, and there were UN exhortations to use bayonets, the practice did not catch on. Most of the small arms in use with the North Korean troops in 1950 were Soviet-made World War II–vintage weapons, where again the technology was much older. When the **Chinese People's Volunteers** intervened, they still generally relied on a mixture of Japanese and U.S. captured weapons from the just concluded Chinese civil war, together with copies of Soviet-made weapons, which were becoming increasingly standard in the **People's Liberation Army**. The most common machine gun with both the Chinese and North Korean forces was the 7.62-mm Soviet-made PPSH-41, with a round magazine, which became

This helicopter, in an unidentified location and situation, is typical of those used extensively in the Korean War for ferrying supplies or evacuating medical casualties. (Imperial War Museum BF 156)

widely known among the UN forces as the "burp gun" from its characteristic sound when fired.

Other weapons and equipment were also often of World War II vintage. The North Koreans deployed Soviet-built T-34 tanks, which were one of the best World War II tanks, with high velocity and great maneuverability. Their firepower and ease of use meant that North Korean forces were able to dominate the early stages of the fighting from June 1950. When the United States intervened, U.S. forces at first deployed light M.24 Chaffee reconnaissance tanks, but these proved no match for the tanks used by the North Koreans. When, however, the United States deployed M.46 Pattons, and the United Kingdom sent Cromwell and Centurion tanks, all of which had proved themselves in World War II, the North Korean armor proved insufficient, and from late summer 1950 it ceased to be a threat. As far as heavy guns were concerned, here too the UN forces dominated the fighting in all but the earliest days of the war. In addition to heavy and light howitzers, the UN side was also able to deploy antiaircraft guns as artillery because North Korean and Chinese aircraft were unable to fly over UN-held territory from late 1950. Rockets, which were in general very inaccurate, were used as artillery.

Naval Equipment

In naval terms, the Korean War saw little in the way of new developments from World War II. Most of the ships in use were from that period, often hastily brought out of mothballs because of the urgent needs of June 1950. The UN side quickly established naval superiority, with a mixture of aircraft carriers and other ships, against which the North Korean/Chinese side could do little. The one exception was in mining, at which the North Koreans proved very skillful.

New Developments

Some new developments in military equipment emerged during the Korean War, at least on the UN side. Napalm, developed in World War II from World War I flamethrowers, now became an effective bombing ingredient, which proved especially useful against tanks and dug-in troops. Recoilless rifles, useless against tanks, were deployed successfully as antipersonnel weapons. Among the U.S.

forces, experimental use of armored vests began in 1951 and was widespread by the summer of 1952. But it was in the air that the major changes took place during the Korean War.

Airpower

Although jet fighters were in use by the end of World War II, it was in Korea that they came into their own. Propeller aircraft were still in use, especially as bombers, but the jet was clearly superior and, in the case of fighter aircraft, quickly came to dominate on both sides. In November 1950, the North Korean/Chinese side began to use the Soviet-made MiG-15, with its characteristic swept-back wings. MiG-15s proved very effective against the UN forces' main fighter aircraft, the propeller-driven F-51 and the jet F-80, but were outmatched by the F-86 Sabre jets introduced from early 1951 onward. These latter quickly established control over most of the Korea Peninsula, MiG patrols eventually being limited to an area over the northeast of Korea, the "MiG corridor," from where the predominantly Chinese and Soviet pilots could escape across the **Yalu River**. Other jet aircraft in use in Korea included the British Meteor-8, flown by the Royal Australian Air Force.

Korea also saw the development of the helicopter as an important military aircraft. Invented before World War II, it was only after the end of that conflict that the potential of the helicopter was realized. In Korea, where they were extensively used by the UNC, helicopters provided valuable means of transport for both equipment and personnel. They were widely used for medical evacuation.

Although the provisions of the **armistice** agreement of 27 July 1953 banned the introduction of new weapons into the Korea Peninsula, in practice both sides began to introduce new weapons soon after the armistice was signed.

See also: Inch'on Landing (1950); *M*A*S*H** (Film and Television Series); Mobile Army Surgical Hospital (MASH); Wonsan.
References: Macksey 1993; Peacock 1991; Summers 1990.

MISSING IN ACTION (MIA)

In any war, certain numbers of soldiers have not been accounted for when the fighting comes to an end. There are many reasons for this. In modern warfare, high explosives can cause damage that leaves bodies unrecognizable or that leaves nothing that can be identified. In a war of movement, such as the early stages of the **Korean War**, those killed are buried as they fall, and it is not always possible afterward to trace these makeshift graves, especially if they lie behind enemy lines. It is also difficult to keep track of **prisoners of war** (POWs), particularly, as again happened in Korea, if they are frequently moved about and if inadequate or no records were kept of their movements. The **armistice** agreement of 27 July 1953 made provision for graves registration personnel from each side to enter the territory of the other side to recover the bodies of deceased soldiers and POWs where grave were actually found, but little seems to have been achieved by this arrangement.

There is no total figure for all those missing in action (MIA) from the **United Nations Command** (UNC) in Korea. Many disappeared in circumstances where it was impossible to say what happened to them. Some 8,000 MIAs are unaccounted for on the U.S. side, although most are presumed dead. Many thousands of South Korean soldiers are listed as missing, and a small handful of other UN troops and a few civilians also fall into this category. In addition, more than 2,000 UNC soldiers were known to have been alive at some stage in North Korean or Chinese prisoner of war camps and were not repatriated at the end of the war. Hope that at least some of the Westerners missing might still be alive has been raised from time to time by alleged sightings of white people otherwise unaccounted for in China, North Korea, and even the former Soviet Union, but there has been no authenticated case so far.

In 1954, the North Koreans returned the remains of just over 4,000 U.S. service personnel found in the North. For many years, the issue of the remaining MIAs was raised regularly at meetings of the **Military Armistice Commission**, but the North Korean/Chinese side always denied any knowledge of those missing. However, more substantive direct discussion on the issue took place between the United States and North Korea in 1987, and in May 1990 the North Koreans returned the remains of five U.S. soldiers. Thereafter, the North Koreans began to return U.S. remains on a regular basis. In 1991, the United States and North Korea agreed to set up a joint committee to organize searches. A further agreement between the North Korean army and the UNC followed in 1993, and in 1995 formal talks at governmental level were held in Hawaii. This led to the signing of an agreement in May 1996 on the establishment of joint excavation teams. These began work in July 1996 and have continued ever since. In a further agreement, in May 1997, the United States agreed to pay North Korean expenses resulting from the searches. Although there have been some problems resulting in temporary delays, on the whole, the agreements have worked well. Since 1990, the remains of more than 300 U.S. soldiers and one British soldier have been found and handed over. In addition, although there is no systematic searching in South Korea, occasionally the remains of North Korean or Chinese soldiers have come to light and have been returned.

References: The People's Korea; Summers 1990.

MOBILE ARMY SURGICAL HOSPITAL (MASH)

Mobile Army Surgical Hospitals, consisting of transportable tented accommodations that followed the line of fighting in the **Korean War**, provided the first point where major surgery could be performed in the chain of medical evacuation from the front. Casualties brought in from the clearing stations underwent emergency operations, then, when stabilized, were transported, often by helicopter, to rear hospitals. The average MASH had about 100 personnel, at least one operating theater, and up to 60 beds.

The mobile hospitals were part of the U.S. military contingent to the Korean War. NorMASH, administered initially by the Norwegian Red Cross, was incorporated in late 1951 into the U.S. Army medical services. MASH units continued to serve U.S. military personnel stationed in Korea since 1953, and the final unit, the 43rd, closed in mid-1997 as part of a program of replacing all remaining MASH with smaller, faster units. The 8055 MASH provided the inspiration for the film and television series *M*A*S*H*.

See also: Danish Involvement in the Korean War; Indian Army Medical Team in the Korean War; Italian Medical Services in the Korean War; *M*A*S*H* (Film and Television Series); Norwegian

Involvement in the Korean War; Swedish Involvement in the Korean War.
References: Cowdery 1987; Forty 1982; Summers 1990.

MONCLAR, RALPH
See **Magrin-Vermerey, Charles.**

MOON SUN MYUNG (1920–)
The Reverend Moon Sun Myung founded his charismatic Unification Church in **Pusan** in 1954 and sent his first overseas missionary in 1959 to the United States. In the 1970s, his church moved its headquarters to the United States and expanded into business and cultural activities. Moon's strong anti-Communist line has made him tolerated in Korea, especially under **Park Chung Hee,** but acceptance there and elsewhere has been tinged with doubt over recruiting methods and alleged financial irregularities. The Unification Church was implicated in the 1977 **Koreagate** scandal over lobbying tactics in the U.S. Congress.

Moon was born in what is now North Korea into a Christian family. At 16, he claimed, he received a divine mission to reform the Christian church. His first proselytizing activities around **P'yongyang** led to imprisonment by the Communist authorities in 1945. He was released by **United Nations** troops in 1950 as they moved north, and he fled to the South. In November 1991, he returned to North Korea on a visit.
References: Grayson 1989; Howard, Pares, and English 1996.

MOSCOW AGREEMENT (1945)
From 16 to 26 December 1945, the foreign ministers of the United States, the United Kingdom, and the **Union of Soviet Socialist Republics (USSR)** met in Moscow to discuss problems remaining unresolved from Allied wartime negotiations. On Korea, they agreed that there should be a provisional democratic government; that in order to bring this into existence a joint U.S.-USSR commission should be established, formed of representatives of the two occupation forces, which would set up a Korean provisional government in consultation with democratic parties and social organizations; and that the United States, China, the United Kingdom, and the Soviet Union should exercise a five-year trusteeship.

No sooner had the agreement been released on 28 December 1945 than it was denounced both north and south of the **38th parallel.** The U.S.-USSR **Joint Commission on Trusteeship** was formed in January 1946, but met only three times before, in September 1947, the United States referred the Korean question to the **United Nations,** and the Joint Commission ceased to function. The Moscow Agreement had by then virtually ceased to operate.
References: Cumings 1981; Nahm 1993.

MU CHONG (1905–ca. 1951)
Mu Chong was a Korean Communist active in China from the mid-1920s until his return to Korea in 1945. His Chinese name was Wu Ding. Mu Chong was born in North Hamgyong Province and moved to north China, where he studied at Henan Military Academy. Thereafter, he largely followed a military career, specializing in artillery warfare, first in the Chinese Nationalist army and then later with the Chinese Communist forces. In 1925 or 1926, he joined the Chinese Communist Party (CCP) in Shanghai. He is said to have participated in the Chinese Communists' Jiangxi Soviet Republic in southeast China and to have undertaken the Long March (1934–1935) with them from Jiangxi to Shaanxi Province in the north. By 1939, he was organizing a Korean military unit in northern China to fight alongside Chinese forces against the Japanese. In 1942, he took a leading role in the creation of the North China Korean Independence League (which later formed the basis of the **New People's Party**) and went on to command the Korean Volunteer Army (KVA). The Chinese Communist leadership, then based at Yan'an (Yenan) in Shaanxi, regarded Mu as a key figure among Korean revolutionaries.

In 1945, Mu returned to Korea, held office in the Northern Branch Bureau of the **Korean Communist Party,** and subsequently became a member of the Central Committee of the North Korean Workers' Party. His career did not prosper, however. He had been deprived of his independent military backing when the Soviet occupying forces disarmed members of the KVA as they tried to cross the Sino-Korean border in the autumn of 1945. He held various posts in the fledgling **North Korean People's Army** (NKPA) and in July 1946 was placed in charge of the artillery corps. When the **Korean War** broke out, Mu headed the 2nd Army Corps. He was tasked with defending **P'yongyang**, but fell back in October 1950 before the **United Nations Command** surge north and retreated into **Northeast China** to regroup his forces. For this he was purged at a December 1950 meeting of the party's Central Committee on charges of incompetence, disobedience of orders, and even, apparently, the unwarranted killing of a subordinate. He was stripped of his post and rank and relegated to lowly work. It is thought he died shortly afterward of illness. The Yan'an faction, with which he was associated, eventually lost all political strength.

See also: Chinese Involvement in Korea (1919–1948); Left-Wing Political Factions.

References: Nahm 1991; Scalapino and Lee 1972; Suh 1970, 1988; Yang 1994.

MUCCIO, JOHN JOSEPH (1900–1989)

John Joseph Muccio was the first U.S. ambassador to the Republic of Korea. Muccio was born in Italy in 1900. His parents emigrated to the United States when he was a child, and he was brought up in Providence, Rhode Island. He joined the foreign service in 1923 and served in a variety of posts, mainly in China and Latin America. In 1948, he was appointed the U.S. president's special envoy to Korea following the establishment of the Republic of Korea and became ambassador in 1949 after the United States extended full recognition to the new government. He was sympathetic to Koreans and appears to have had a good relationship with the South Korean president, **Syngman Rhee**, even though Muccio was aware of criticism of Rhee's style of government. According to Harold Noble, a member of his staff, Muccio preferred to solve problems by indirect means rather than by confrontation. Muccio was in Seoul when the **Korean War** began in June 1950. He supervised the evacuation of U.S. citizens and encouraged other foreigners to leave, but stayed with the South Korean government, following it south to **Taejon, Taegu**, and ultimately to **Pusan**. During this period, he played an important part in encouraging Rhee in very difficult circumstances.

Following the **Inch'on landing** in September 1950, Muccio returned to Seoul with the South Korean government, but was again forced to go south in January 1951 after Chinese intervention and the **United Nations Command** retreat. He remained U.S. ambassador until August 1952, trying to persuade an increasingly obstinate Rhee that there would be no second attempt at a military solution to the division of Korea, and that a negotiated settlement was the only likely end of the war. After leaving Korea, Muccio served as the U.S. delegate to the United Nations Trusteeship Council (1952–1954), as envoy extraordinary to Iceland (1954–1956), and as ambassador to Guatemala (1959–1961). He retired in 1961 and died in 1989.

Reference: Noble 1975.

MUTUAL DEFENSE TREATY (1953)

See **United States Mutual Defense Treaty with South Korea (1953)**.

NAEWOE NEWS AGENCY

The Naewoe (Home and Abroad) News Agency is a South Korean government-affiliated organization, established in the mid-1970s. Its task is to publish information and analysis about North Korea from a South Korean perspective, which it does in books and in journals such as the monthly *Vantage Point: Developments in North Korea*. Since 1996, it has also been available on the World Wide Web. Its products have become less propagandist since the late 1980s and are often a useful source of information on North Korea. Since January 1999, it has been merged with the **Yonhap News Agency**, but its Naewoe imprint continues in use.

NAKTONG RIVER

The Naktong River and its tributaries make up the chief river system of the southeastern part of the Korea Peninsula and form the second largest river system in South Korea. The Naktong rises in the **T'aebaek Mountains**. The main river flows south, entering the sea by a series of outlets west of **Pusan**. Following the outbreak of the **Korean War** in June 1950 and the retreat south of the South Korean forces, the Naktong became one of the defining lines of the **Pusan Perimeter** as these forces began to regroup and U.S. and other military contingents arrived under **United Nations** (UN) auspices. In August 1950, North Korean troops tried to cross the Naktong, which became the scene of a major battle. They were repulsed and, although they made a further attempt in September 1950, their lines were now too extended and they could not sustain the attack. Following the **Inch'on landing** on 8 September, UN forces broke out from the Pusan Perimeter, crossed the Naktong, and went north.
References: Appleman 1961; Bartz 1972.

NAM IL (1913–1976)

Nam Il was a soldier and negotiator of Soviet Korean background. He served as chief-of-staff of the **North Korean People's Army** (NKPA) during the **Korean War**, and then headed the North Korean/Chinese

N

delegation to the **armistice** talks that took place at **Kaesong**, then **P'anmunjom**, between July 1951 and July 1953. As minister of foreign affairs, he led the North Korean delegation during April–June 1954 at the **Geneva Conference**, which was convened in part to find a political resolution of the Korean problem. The tough line on reunification he put forward on that occasion long formed the standard North Korean response on the issue.

Nam was born in 1913 in Russia of parents who had emigrated from the northeastern province of North Hamgyong. In addition to Korean, he spoke Russian and Chinese. He trained at Smolensk Military Academy in western Russia, served as a captain in the Soviet army, and was said to have fought at Stalingrad. He returned to Korea with the Soviet army in 1945 and soon threw in his lot with **Kim Il Sung**. His constant loyalty to Kim enabled him to survive where other Soviet Koreans were eased out or returned to the Soviet Union. He held a number of posts: vice-premier (1957–1976), minister of foreign affairs (1953–1959), chairman of the State Construction Commission (1960–1962), and chairman of the Light Industry Commission (1972–1976).
References: Matray 1991; Scalapino and Lee 1972; Suh 1981.

NAMP'O

Namp'o, a west coast city at the mouth of the Taedong River, was formerly known as Chinnamp'o and developed rapidly after it was opened to foreign trade in 1897. It is the port for **P'yongyang**, now the capital of North Korea and some 30 miles (50 kilometers) inland. In December 1950, Namp'o was the scene of a major evacuation of **United Nations** troops retreating before the **Chinese People's Volunteers**. Canadian, Australian, and U.S. naval ships played a major part in the evacuation. For the Royal Canadian Navy, it was their major engagement of the **Korean War**. During the evacuation, heavy damage was inflicted on the enemy's shore installations.

Since the end of the Korean War, Namp'o has developed as a market center for the surrounding area and as a major industrial city. It is the site of the West Sea Barrage, which has cut off the Taedong River from the sea and provides water for industrial and domestic use. Namp'o has become a major tourist destination for visitors to North Korea and is often combined with visits to **Kaesong** and the **Demilitarized Zone**.

See also: Canadian Forces in the Korean War.

NATIONAL INTELLIGENCE SERVICE (NIS)

The forerunner of the National Intelligence Service, the (South) Korean Central Intelligence Agency (KCIA), dates from June 1961. **Kim Jong Pil**, one of the architects of **Park Chung Hee's** military coup, was its first head. Modeled on the U.S. **Central Intelligence Agency**, the KCIA was charged primarily with gathering and assessing information about North Korea. On the domestic side, it used the "threat from the North" to bolster Park's autocratic rule. Its officials also played a prominent role in the North-South dialogue in the 1970s. Among the KCIA's most notorious activities were the kidnapping and attempted murder of the opposition leader **Kim Dae Jung** in 1973. It suffered an eclipse when its director killed President Park in 1979, but it reemerged in 1980 as the Agency for National Security Planning and under that name was active under Presidents **Chun Doo Hwan**, **Roh Tae Woo**, and **Kim Young Sam**. On becoming president in 1998, Kim Dae Jung promised far-reaching reforms of the organization, and in January 1999, it changed its name to the National Intelligence Service.

NATIONAL SECURITY LAW

National Security Law (NSL) is a name that applies to a series of laws operative in South Korea and amended seven times between the introduction of the first law in 1948 and the most recent amendment in 1991. The rationale has at all times been the need to counter Communist subversion from the North in whatever manifestation. Interpretation of what constitutes a threat has always been determined by the government in power and the security services. The law has a wide sweep, in terms both of the range of offenses it lists and of the sections of society it targets. Among its chief aims are official control of all contacts between South and North; prevention of espionage; suppression of anti-state organizations, activities, and utterances, however defined, that might be construed as giving comfort to the North; and suppression of activities deemed to disturb national and social harmony. Even the expression of ideas similar to those of the North Korean government has been targeted by the law; as a consequence, the study of Marxist and leftist texts was for long hazardous in South Korea.

The first NSL was enacted by the National Assembly in November 1948 in the aftermath of the **Yosu-Sunch'on rebellion** and riots the previous month, for which Communists were held responsible. President **Syngman Rhee** was quick to use the law against his political opponents, even turning it against members of the National Assembly during 1949–1950. The successive regimes of Chang Myon and **Park Chung Hee** produced amendments to the NSL, all directed against any expression of support for the North. In an additional piece of legislation, the Anti-Communist Law of 1961 (rescinded in 1980), Park defined North Korea and all socialist states as "enemy states"; in 1971 gave himself wide-ranging powers of emergency in a set of Special Measures for Safeguarding National Security; and in 1975, in Emergency Decree No. 9, made it an offense to criticize the president and the decree itself.

The NSL remains in force as of 1999, with North Korea still classed among "anti-state organizations." The NSL is used to control student, teacher, and worker dissent and the activities of left-wing groups, and in the late 1980s it was directed in particular against those making unauthorized visits to North Korea. Some aspects of the law have been modified, such as provisions for the continuing surveillance of those released after serving prison sentences for violating the NSL. Revision of the law has been discussed, but no radical changes yet enacted. Since 1990, North Korea has called for the abolition of the NSL and has intensified its pressure since the inauguration of **Kim Dae Jung** as president in 1998, pointing to the mistreatment Kim suffered earlier for his contravention of the law. In February 1999, Kim Dae Jung promised that the law would be modified.

References: Amnesty International 1990, 1995; Cumings 1997; Eckert et al. 1990; Macdonald 1996; Park 1993; Shaw 1993.

NATIONALISM

Nationalism has been defined as "a consciousness, on the part of individuals or groups, of membership in a nation, or a desire to forward the strength, liberty, or prosperity of a nation" (Lee 1965: ix). Nationalism is both a modern and a modernizing force. Its first stirrings in Korea more than a century ago helped to drive forward the reform movement of the 1880s and 1890s and partly filled the gap left by the collapse of the monarchy and the decline in a strict Confucian order. The desire to preserve national integrity and resist foreign encroachment, which later turned to domination, took the practical form of establishing armed guerrilla groups. These were forced out of the Korea Peninsula into China and Russia, from where some of them eventually returned to help set up the North Korean regime after World War II.

Nationalist ideals are a potent element in rival claims by the North Korean and South Korean regimes to legitimacy and leadership in the Korea Peninsula. The two share a common goal of a unified, powerful, autonomous state, but have a separate understanding of how that state should be organized.

The development of the two regimes over the past 50 years, characterized by differing political and economic systems, shows how North and South each interprets its idea of nationhood; but the basic split between the two ideas goes back to the colonial period (1910–1945). Once it became clear that the Declaration of Independence of 1 March 1919 was going to have no significant effect on Korea's colonial status, Korean resistance to Japanese occupation moved in opposing directions. Within Korea, what has been termed "cultural nationalism" emerged, with the aim of regenerating the Korean people culturally and morally in preparation for eventual nationhood. The danger here was of compromising too much with the Japanese administration. Some Koreans went so far as to suggest amalgamation with Japan. In 1924, the *Donga Ilbo* newspaper denounced them as "national traitors." Some of the Korean nationalists abroad, particularly in the United States, concentrated on lobbying Western powers and on fundraising. In outlook they were generally conservative. Other Koreans abroad looked to the newly formed Soviet Union and the Bolshevik movement for inspiration and support.

It was extremely difficult for any kind of leadership to emerge within Korea, such was the efficacy of Japanese control. During the colonial period, many leaders of both left and right chose to conduct their activities outside of Korea. The nationalist movement was scattered over Korea, the Soviet Union, China, and the United States and was continually weakened by factionalism. The only cause around which the various groups inside Korea could and sometimes did unite was that of self-determination and opposition to Japanese rule. Such joint action rarely lasted long. The Soviet leadership of the Communist movement was used by non-Communist nationalists as evidence of foreign control over Korean Communists. The latter charged other nationalists with being "bourgeois reactionaries" and feared being ideologically contaminated by them.

The combination of nationalism and communism was a powerful one, and many Koreans were drawn into the Communist movement via support for the nationalist cause. Others became Communists out of the conviction that the goal of Korean self-determination could best be achieved through that channel. For many native Korean Communists, the line between participation in international communism and devotion to Korean independence was blurred. In the early 1920s, they were ready to assist the new Soviet government in its struggle against its enemies in Siberia in return for Soviet support for Korea's liberation. Other Korean Communists who had become "Russianized" through their families' settlement over several generations in Siberia were committed to the international Communist movement under Soviet direction. Such differing outlooks thus created a point of division among the pre-1948 **left-wing political factions**.

By the end of the **Korean War** (1953), **Kim Il Sung** had outmaneuvered fellow Communist leaders to wrest power for himself and his intimates in North Korea. The course he set was resolutely socialist, but just as important was the principle of independence from both of his large Communist neighbors, China and the Soviet Union. His philosophy of *juche* (self-reliance) was developed from the mid-1950s as the incarnation of a particular form of nationalism, and his admirers have presented him as a patriot as much as a Communist leader. Kim Il Sung himself was quick to denounce leaders in the South for compromising their nationalist principles to U.S. interests.

South Korea has become in the decades since 1948 an economically powerful country, moving slowly toward political liberalization. Pride in its growing strength and influence manifests itself in an emphatically expressed patriotism, though such shows of national confidence are aimed as much at the former colonial power, Japan, as at North Korea. Reflecting the themes of the "cultural nationalism" of the 1920s and 1930s, a movement has gathered momentum since the early 1960s to promote aspects of traditional culture such as crafts and folk customs, including the creation of new festivals and customs.

One tradition that North and South lay equal claim to is the Tan'gun legend of national foundation. This relays the story of Tan'gun, son of the heavenly king Hwanung and a bear turned woman, who founded the first Korean kingdom. The interpretation of historical and archaeological evidence is a further area where the rival claims of the two states to a kind of moral leadership is intermittently played out.

See also: Japanese Colonial Period in Korea (1910–1945); Korean Communist Party (KCP).

References: Lee 1965; Robinson 1988; Scalapino and Lee 1972; Shin 1990.

NCNA

See **New China News Agency**.

NEHRU, JAWAHARLAL (1889–1964)

Jawaharlal Nehru was prime minister of India from 1947 until his death in 1964. Nehru came from a wealthy family and was educated as a lawyer. From 1919, he was active in the Indian independence movement, playing an important role in the 1947 independence negotiations with Britain. When the **Korean War** began in June 1950, Nehru's government supported **United Nations** intervention. Nehru then moved toward a more neutral position, as mediator between the two sides. India sent an **Indian Army medical team** to Korea, but not fighting troops. India also acted as a channel of communication: the Chinese premier, **Zhou Enlai**, passed messages to the Indian ambassador in Beijing, which Nehru's government passed on to London and Washington. The messages were discounted and the Chinese intervened in the fighting. An Indian proposal led to the settlement of the **prisoners of war** (POW) issue, and thus to the signing of the **armistice** agreement in 1953. From September 1953 to February 1954, the **Indian Custodial Force** helped to implement the armistice arrangements for POWs. Thereafter, Nehru appears to have taken little further interest in Korea.

See also: Non-Aligned Movement; Panikkar, Kavalam Madhava; Rau, Sir Benegal Narsing; Repatriation of Prisoners of War.

References: Hermes 1966; Matray 1991; Stueck 1995.

NEPOTISM

To many, one of the most curious aspects of the North Korean regime has been the succession of the leadership from **Kim Il Sung** to his son, **Kim Jong Il**. The term "Communist dynasty" has been applied. It is an exceptional example of nepotism, but the reasoning behind the older Kim's decision may not necessarily be so strange to other Koreans. The tradition of looking within one's family for loyal supporters whose reliability can be counted on is well established in Korean society. Conversely, members of a family are entitled to expect assistance in furthering their interests from the most powerful people in that family.

Within a family, the link between father and son or sons is regarded as the predominant relationship, but is one that does not preclude other members from calling for assistance. Such support is regarded as customary family duty and is sometimes carried spectacularly into the public sphere, as in North Korea, when a successful man's family rises with him as he is elevated in the political or social scene. The reverse is often true; if he falls, his family may suffer with him.

Despite general distaste for the practice, politicians in South Korea continue to place family members in positions of influence. President **Chun Doo Hwan** put a brother in charge of the important New Community rural movement and promoted the interests of his wife's family. The second son of former president **Kim Young Sam** was disgraced for using his influence in securing political appointments, despite offering as justification his duty toward his father. The destabilizing effects of such family involvement, together with the sometimes intensely personal tone of politics, have contributed toward the often unsettled political scene in South Korea.

NETHERLANDS FORCES IN THE KOREAN WAR

On 14 July 1950, the government of the Netherlands announced it would place a volunteer force under the **United Nations Command** (UNC) in Korea, and on 23 November 1950 the Netherlands Infantry Battalion, together with several nurses, arrived in **Pusan**. The battalion, at 636 men, was understrength because the Dutch army had been depleted by recent fighting in Indonesia. A Dutch naval destroyer, HNLMS *Evertsen*, was deployed immediately from Indonesia and arrived in July 1950.

The Netherlands Battalion was attached to the 38th Infantry Regiment of the U.S. 2nd Division. It experienced tough enemy opposition in the January 1951 fighting around Wonju. In the battle of Hoengsong (11–13 February 1951), the battalion lost an estimated 100 men, including its commander, den Ouden, killed when Chinese soldiers, disguised as South Korean troops, infiltrated the Dutch ranks and then opened fire. In April 1951, the Dutch fought against the Chinese spring offensive in the Kumhwa area in central Korea, enduring a 24-hour hunger march without food. The following year, the battalion was active in the Iron Triangle along the **38th parallel** and also assisted during April–July 1952 in suppressing riots at the **Koje Island prisoner of war camp**. The battalion remained in Korea until 1 October 1954.

A total of 3,972 men passed through the Netherlands Battalion. Casualties were 120 dead, 645 wounded, and three repatriated.

The HNLMS *Evertsen* was the first of a total of three destroyers and three frigates of the Dutch navy that rotated under the UNC naval command from 19 July 1950 to 24 January 1955 in Korean waters. The *Evertsen* provided cover to the **Inch'on landing** in September 1950. It and succeeding Dutch naval ships carried out patrols; bombardment of coastal targets; troop support; and escort, antiaircraft, and blockading duties in the seas west and east of the Korea Peninsula. A total of 1,350 personnel served in the Dutch naval contingent.

See also: Korean War (1950–1953).
References: Blair 1987; History: III, 1974 and VI, 1977; Thomas, Abbott, and Chappell 1986.

NEUTRAL NATIONS INSPECTION TEAMS

Twenty inspection teams were permitted initially under the terms of the **armistice** agreement of 27 July 1953 setting up the **Neutral Nations Supervisory Commission** (NNSC), the members of which were Sweden, Switzerland, Czechoslovakia, and Poland. Each team was comprised of at least four military officers, half of them appointed by Sweden and Switzerland and half by Czechoslovakia and Poland. Ten of these teams were divided among five South Korean "ports of entry"—Inch'on, **Taegu**, Pusan, Kangnung, and Kunsan—and five in North Korea—**Shinuiju**, Ch'ongjin, Hungnam, Manp'o, and Sinanju. They were there to supervise for the NNSC the armistice provisions on the introduction and movement of troops and weapons in each half of the peninsula and to investigate infringements of the arrangements. Their task was not easy because both sides ignored the armistice provisions. In 1955, following South Korean government pressure, the teams at Taegu and Kangnung were withdrawn and those at Inch'on, Pusan, and Kunsan were reduced in size.

NEUTRAL NATIONS REPATRIATION COMMISSION

The Neutral Nations Repatriation Commission (NNRC) became effective through the **armistice** document of 27 July 1953, which stipulated in paragraph 51(b) that after 60 days "each side shall release all those remaining prisoners of war, who are not directly repatriated, from its military control and from its custody and hand them over to the Neutral Nations Repatriation Commission for disposition."

An annex signed on 8 June 1953 by the two senior delegates to the armistice negotiations, General **Nam Il** and Lieutenant General William K. Harrison, detailed the commission's terms of reference.

The purpose of the NNRC was to allow those **prisoners of war** (POWs) who had declined repatriation to hear explanations from representatives of their own countries on the choices before them and to decide where they wanted to go. During the 90 days allocated for explanation, the NNRC was to hold the POWs within the **Demilitarized Zone** (DMZ) in areas north and south of the Military Demarcation Line and was to decide on applications for repatriation. Prisoners still declining repatriation would have their cases referred to the political conference recommended in the armistice agreement. If, at the end of a total of 120 days, such POWs had still not decided, they would be released to civilian status and assisted by the NNRC to go to neutral countries. Its job once completed, the commission would disband.

The NNRC member nations were Sweden, Switzerland, Czechoslovakia, Poland, and India. India was nominated as the chair, executive agent, and umpire of the commission, and India alone provided operating personnel and an armed detachment—the **Indian Custodial Force**—and Red Cross representatives. The commission had its headquarters near **P'anmunjom**. Its chairman was General K. S. Thimayya of the Indian Army.

The NNRC's task was arduous and its achievements incomplete. President **Syngman Rhee** suspected India of favoring Communist interests and refused to allow Indian troops on South Korean soil. (The NNRC operated in the neutral territory of the DMZ.) The political activists who had dominated the **United Nations Command** (UNC) POW camps before the armistice, particularly the anti-Communist activists, continued to coerce their fellow detainees throughout the period of explanation. The United States was anxious that the principle of nonforcible repatriation, which it had upheld from 1951, should be vindicated as proof of the numbers who would choose "freedom," and it greatly feared Communist persuasion. Through their role as UNC observers, U.S. personnel schooled Korean and Chinese nonrepatriates for the interviews. Indian attempts to reduce some of the outside pressures on prisoners irritated the United States. The Communists were angered at UNC-imposed delays and at the way non-Communist POWs succeeded in forcing the NNRC to agree that prisoners who had received explanations should not subsequently be segregated from those who had not. They retaliated by also hindering the explanation process. Some POWs refused to attend for explanations. The political conference, moreover, never materialized, leaving the commission facing the need to consider the next step.

In the end, only approximately 15 percent of the 22,600 nonrepatriates delivered to the NNRC received individual explanations; the rest either refused to attend or opted for mass explanations. On 22 January 1954, the NNRC restored the outstanding 21,600–21,800 nonrepatriates to civilian status, returned them to their original detaining side, and dissolved itself a month later, on 22 February 1954.

See also: Repatriation of Prisoners of War.

References: Foot 1990; Hermes 1966; History: II, 1973 and VI, 1977; MacDonald 1986.

NEUTRAL NATIONS SUPERVISORY COMMISSION

The concept of a body comprised of neutral nations—that is, nations that had not participated in the **Korean War**—to supervise the implementation of the **armistice** in both North and South Korean territory was raised at an early point in the armistice negotiations. Over the period December 1951 to April 1952, the choice of states acceptable to both the **United Nations Command** (UNC) and the North Korean/Chinese commands was whittled down to four: Sweden and Switzerland (both committed to international policies of neutrality) for the UNC, and Czechoslovakia and Poland for the Communist side. The armistice, signed on 27 July 1953, incorporated detailed instructions on the composition and operation of the Neutral Nations Supervisory Commission (NNSC). While the **Military Armistice Commission** (MAC) was to supervise implementation of the armistice inside the **Demilitarized Zone,** the task of the NNSC's four senior officers was to ensure that the provisions of the armistice relating to the movement of troops, weapons, and military equipment into and out of the two halves of the peninsula were respected. They were to be assisted initially by twenty **Neutral Nations Inspection Teams**, of which half were to be stationed at ten approved ports of entry, five in the North and five in the South. The NNSC had its headquarters at **P'anmunjom**.

From the outset, the commission's work was difficult. Both sides ignored the restrictions on the movement of troops and equipment. **Syngman Rhee**, president of South Korea at the time of the armistice signing, did not tolerate the concept of "neutral" nations and withheld cooperation. In March 1955, the South Korean National Assembly, claiming the right of "national self-defense," urged the government to expel the NNSC from South Korean territory. The government reacted in August 1955 with complaints to the UNC that the Czech and Polish members of the NNSC were obstructing the commission's operations in North Korea and were engaged in espionage in the South and demanded that the NNSC withdraw from South Korean territory. In September, as a compromise, the commission's organizational strength and the scope of its activities in South Korea were reduced. The following year, the UNC suspended NNSC inspections on its side until North Korea agreed to honor relevant provisions of the armistice. In the end, the two sets of neutral nations operated only on "their" side of the armistice line.

The political changes in Europe in the late 1980s and consequent ousting of Communist regimes in Czechoslovakia and Poland led North Korea to question the reliability of the Communist-appointed neutral nations. The split in Czechoslovakia provided them with an opportunity to get rid of that delegation in 1992 because they refused to accept the proposal of the two new nations (Czech Republic and Slovakia) that the Czech Republic succeed Czechoslovakia on the NNSC. In April 1994, North Korea announced its intention to withdraw from the MAC and to end the NNSC's role. The Poles continued under increasing pressure from North Korea until in February 1995 the North withheld all guards, support staff, and facilities from the Polish delegation, obliging it to withdraw from P'anmunjom. UNC and international protests had no effect on the North Korean decisions. The Swedish and Swiss delegations continue to meet on the south side of the border, and the four members

of the NNSC, arguing that the commission has not been formally dissolved, are said to meet together on occasion in third countries.

References: Hermes 1966; History: VI, 1977; Yi 1973.

NEW CHINA NEWS AGENCY

The New China News Agency (NCNA) was established in 1929 as the press outlet of the Chinese Communist Party (CCP). Widely known until the late 1970s in the Wade-Giles transliteration as Hsinhua News Agency, it is now better recognized in its *pinyin* transliteration as the Xinhua News Agency; both *Hsinhua* and *Xinhua* mean "New China." During World War II, the NCNA developed an overseas broadcasting capability and established its first overseas branches. After the CCP victory in the Chinese civil war and the establishment of the **People's Republic of China** in 1949, it became the official Chinese agency, headquartered in Beijing and with numerous domestic and overseas offices. It played an important role in the **Korean War** as a source of information on North Korea and, probably more vitally, as a means of communicating the North Korean–**Chinese People's Volunteers'** position on negotiations, exchanges of prisoners, and other matters, when there was no direct contact between the **United Nations Command** and the North Korean–Chinese side. After 1953, it continued to report on North Korea and to relay **Korean Central News Agency** broadcasts to the rest of the world. From 1992 onward, however, following the establishment of diplomatic relations between the People's Republic of China and South Korea, this coverage has been somewhat reduced.

NEW PEOPLE'S PARTY

The New People's Party (NPP) (sometimes called the New Democratic Party) represented the Yan'an (Yenan) faction of Korean Communists. These were left-wing exiles active in China who had received backing from the Chinese Communists and who were based at Yan'an in the central-northern province of Shaanxi. Under the leadership of **Mu Chong** and Kim Tu-bong, they set up the North China Korean Independence League and formed a Korean Volunteer Army. On liberation in August 1945, they returned to Korea, where, in early 1946, they established the NPP both north and south. The northern branch was popular with radicals and intellectuals, and by mid-1946 had a membership of 90,000. Under Soviet pressure, however, the NPP proposed a merger with **Kim Il Sung's** (North) **Korean Communist Party**, and in August 1946 the two organizations joined to form the (North) **Korean Workers' Party** (KWP). Initially, Kim kept a balance between the various political factions, and Kim Tu-bong was chairman of the first two congresses (1946 and 1948) of the northern KWP, but by 1956 had been downgraded and was disgraced in 1958.

The southern branch of the NPP, together with the People's Party, likewise merged with the (South) Korean Communist Party to form the (South) Korean Workers' Party in November 1946. In 1949, the northern and southern parties joined up into the **Korean Workers' Party**, based thereafter in North Korea.

See also: Korean Workers' Party; Left-Wing Political Factions.

References: Scalapino and Lee 1972; Suh 1981, 1988; Yang 1994.

NEW ZEALAND FORCES IN THE KOREAN WAR

New Zealand responded quickly to the **United Nations'** call for support following the outbreak of the **Korean War** in June 1950. The New Zealand government joined the international condemnation of the North Korean attack, which it viewed as evidence of the expansionist policies of the **Union of Soviet Socialist Republics.** Once it was clear that British forces would be sent to aid South Korea, the government also pledged that New Zealand would provide military support. At first, New Zealand, again following the British example, expected to supply only naval forces. Two frigates, HMNZS *Pukaki* and *Tutira*, left for Korean waters on 3 July 1950. They, and their successors, joined the U.S. Navy's Far Eastern Command and were mainly employed in operations off the west coast of North Korea, including blockading and coastal raiding. A total of some 1,350 men of the Royal New Zealand Navy, about half its total strength, served in Korea.

When it became apparent that the Korean conflict would not be settled quickly, New Zealand also agreed to send ground forces. Because the New Zealand army was only 3,000 strong and was essentially a training force, the government launched a special recruitment campaign to raise the 1,000 men needed for what was to be known as Kayforce (for "Korea force"). Nearly 6,000 responded. The first troops left New Zealand in early December 1950 and were in action in late January 1951. The main group was from the 16th Field Artillery and was equipped with 25-pounder guns. They fought initially as part of the British Commonwealth Brigade and then, from July 1951, with the **First Commonwealth Division**. The New Zealand gunners took part in the battle of **Kap'yong** in April 1951. Like other artillery units, they played an important role in the static war from the summer of 1951 until the **armistice** in July 1953. New Zealand troops remained in Korea until July 1957. A small contingent stayed on as part of the British Commonwealth Liaison Mission to the **United Nations Command**.

In the period during and after the war, 22 New Zealanders were killed or died of wounds and another 24 were killed accidentally. At least 79 were wounded, and one was captured. The New Zealand monument is near Kap'yong. Although the war itself made little direct impact on New Zealand society, involvement in Korea was an important stage in the country's move away from dependence on Britain toward a more independent international role. It saw an increase in links with the United States, symbolized by the signing of the Australia, New Zealand, and United States Treaty (the ANZUS Treaty) in September 1951.

See also: Australian Forces in the Korean War; Koreans Attached to the Commonwealth Forces (KATCOM).

References: History: II, 1973; McGibbon 1992, 1996.

NIXON DOCTRINE (1969)

By the late 1960s, the United States, seemingly permanently trapped in the **Vietnam War**, was anxious to limit its worldwide military commitments. Speaking at Guam in 1969, U.S. President Richard Milhous Nixon (1913–1994) set out guidelines for what became known as the Nixon Doctrine. Essentially, this stated that, although the United States would continue to be concerned with the security of its friends and allies, the latter should shoulder an increasing share of the burden themselves. In the case of the Republic of Korea, this meant a reduction in U.S. forces in South Korea and the assumption by South Korean forces of a bigger role in the country's security. The Nixon Doctrine, together with the improvement of U.S. relations slightly later with the **People's Republic of China,** was one of the factors that led the two Koreas to begin talking to each other in the early 1970s, for it was a reminder that the U.S. commitment to support South Korea was closely linked with the United States' wider Asian policy. Although in subsequent years, Nixon's successors have regularly reaffirmed U.S. support for South Korea, especially during the crisis over North Korean nuclear developments between 1991 and 1994, the original proclamation of the Nixon Doctrine, and the proposed U.S. troop reductions under President **Jimmy Carter,** have left a degree of doubt in the minds of many South Koreans about how strong that commitment really would be if it clashed with other U.S. interests.

See also: Koreagate (1977); North Korean Nuclear Program; Park Chung Hee; Red Cross North-South Talks.

References: Kim 1996; Nam 1986; Pollack and Cha 1995.

NKPA

See **North Korean People's Army (NKPA).**

NO TAE-U

See **Roh Tae Woo.**

NON-ALIGNED MOVEMENT

The Non-Aligned Movement (NAM) was a reaction to the Cold War between the West and the Communist bloc. The movement sprang from a meeting in 1961 of 25 states in Belgrade, the capital of former Yugoslavia, itself committed to independence from Soviet control. The movement thereafter met regularly as it sought a middle course between powerful and antagonistic groups of nations. The NAM was popular with countries newly achieving independence from colonial rule and eventually expanded to include 108 states and liberation movements. North Korea was an active supporter during the 1960s (its *juche* policies preached self-reliance and independence) and in 1975 was elected a full member of the NAM. The North Korean Constitution explicitly bases foreign policy on the

"five principles of peaceful coexistence" supported by the NAM. South Korea, by contrast, has been seen as too closely identified with the United States to join the movement. By 1992, however, when the NAM met in Bandung in Indonesia, it was clear that the ending of the Cold War had weakened former alliances and entrenched positions, and the reasons behind nonalignment had largely lost their strength.
References: Kim 1979; Macdonald 1996.

NORDPOLITIK/NORTHERN POLICY

Nordpolitik, or "Northern Policy," was the name given to President **Roh Tae Woo's** moves in the late 1980s to improve South Korea's relations with the **People's Republic of China** (PRC), Eastern Europe, and the **Union of Soviet Socialist Republics** (USSR), as a means of ending confrontation with North Korea. The term had been in use since 1971 and derived from one used to describe similar policies pursued by West Germany in the early 1970s. Then, the West German leader, Willy Brandt, redirected his country's formal attitude toward East Germany and the USSR from a policy of total hostility toward one of improved relations and acceptance of the existence of East Germany. This became known as the *Ostpolitik,* or "Eastern Policy."

The term *Nordpolitik* appears to have first been used by a U.S. State Department official in 1971, who suggested the need for new South Korean policies toward the North and its allies to replace the total hostility that had been the official line since the time of President **Syngman Rhee.** As U.S. relations improved, first with the USSR and then the PRC, South Korean President **Park Chung Hee** came to accept the idea. South Korea began a new approach, first in the **Red Cross North-South talks** and then with full-scale North-South talks in 1972. In June 1973, the government announced that it would seek better relations with the PRC and the USSR and would no longer break off diplomatic relations with countries that recognized North Korea. *Nordpolitik* had effectively begun. There was little response at first. A few South Koreans were able to make private visits to the USSR in the 1970s and to the PRC from about 1981. Some trade was carried out, mainly through third countries, but there was nothing like the gains West Germany had made from its change of policy.

The pace of contacts speeded up in the 1980s, despite occasional setbacks. The South Korean foreign minister, **Lee Bum Suk (2)**, used the term *Nordpolitik* during 1983 to describe attempts to improve relations with the PRC and the USSR, although in such a way as to indicate continued hostility toward North Korea. Meanwhile, South Korean economic growth attracted interest in a number of Eastern European Communist countries. Hungary went a step further, establishing a trade office in South Korea in March 1988. The rise to power of Mikhail Gorbachev had led to major changes in Soviet foreign policy. In the PRC, economic reforms were altering attitudes to the outside world.

In his election pledges in 1987, Roh Tae Woo promised that *Nordpolitik* would be at the center of his foreign policy. He defined the policy as helping to achieve Korean unification through encouraging the North to expand its international contacts, while the South would pursue trade and other links with all countries. The decision by most Communist countries to attend the 1988 **Seoul** Olympic Games, despite opposition from North Korea, was a major breakthrough. In February 1989, Hungary decided to establish diplomatic relations with South Korea; other Eastern European countries soon followed. Roh and Gorbachev met in San Francisco in June 1990, and diplomatic relations were established that September. In 1991, the USSR and the PRC ceased to oppose South Korean entry to the **United Nations**, and both Koreas joined.

When South Korea and the PRC established diplomatic relations on 24 August 1992, *Nordpolitik* could be said to have run its course. It had not achieved the original purpose of improved North-South relations, but it had succeeded fully in its other aim, of establishing links with North Korea's international friends and supporters.

See also: Cross-recognition; Intra-Korean Agreements; Korean Air Lines Flight KE007 Disaster (1983); Korean Membership of the United Nations; Nixon Doctrine (1969); People's Republic of China Relations with North Korea; People's Republic of China Relations with South Korea; Soviet/Russian Relations with North Korea; Soviet/Russian Relations with South Korea.

References: Abramowitz, 1971; Cotton 1993; Kim 1991; Nahm 1993.

NORTH KOREA
See Introduction.

NORTH KOREAN NUCLEAR PROGRAM

North Korea began a program in the 1950s to develop nuclear power for civilian purposes, with assistance from the Soviet Union. Such a program made sense because the fuel resources of the Korea Peninsula are limited, but there are indigenous supplies of uranium and graphite, both required for nuclear plants, in the North. North Koreans received Soviet training, and the Soviet Union provided an experimental reactor in 1965, which was built at Yongbyon. At Soviet insistence, it was registered with the **International Atomic Energy Authority** (IAEA) in 1977 and was subject to IAEA inspection. In 1985, again at Soviet insistence, North Korea joined the Nuclear Non-Proliferation Treaty (NPT), though it refused to sign the required safeguards agreement or to submit a full list of nuclear facilities to the IAEA until 1992. After a South Korean declaration that there were no nuclear weapons in South Korea, the two Koreas signed a non-nuclear declaration in December 1991.

By then, satellite photography indicated the presence of more facilities than the Soviet reactor at Yongbyon; this was confirmed by the list supplied by the North Koreans to the IAEA. Part of the facilities, described as a radiochemical laboratory, appeared to be a reprocessing plant for spent nuclear fuel, which would allow the extraction of plutonium, required for the making of nuclear weapons. When the IAEA insisted on inspecting this and all other nuclear facilities, North Korea announced in March 1993 that it was withdrawing from the NPT. There was considerable international concern, led by the United States, at the implications for the whole non-proliferation system, and much pressure was put on North Korea, including the threat of **United Nations** sanctions, not to pull out. The North Koreans eventually agreed to suspend their withdrawal, and, following the visit of former U.S. President **Jimmy Carter** to North Korea in June 1994, negotiations began that led to an agreement in October 1994 between the United States and North Korea for the supply of less dangerous light-water reactors to North Korea. These were to be provided by the **Korean Peninsula Economic Development**

Organization (KEDO), established in 1995. A groundbreaking ceremony for the reactors took place in 1997, with South Korea supplying the reactors and most of the staff for the work.

The issue of whether or not North Korea had been working on a nuclear weapons program remains unresolved, but the 1994 agreement stipulates that the IAEA will not investigate it further until after the completion of the light-water reactor project in 2003.

References: Mazaar 1995; Oberdorfer 1997; Sigal 1998.

NORTH KOREAN PEOPLE'S ARMY (NKPA)

The North Korean People's Army (*Inmingun* in Korean) traces its origins to the guerrilla groups that fought the Japanese in **Northeast China** and in Korea from the late 1930s to 1945. After the end of World War II, and as the **Union of Soviet Socialist Republics** (USSR) occupied the northern part of Korea, the Soviet authorities began to turn these guerrilla groups into a modern army. The main emphasis was on the creation of infantry units, but there were also naval and air units. The army formally came into existence in February 1948 and grew rapidly thereafter. By the time of the proclamation of the Democratic People's Republic of Korea in September 1948, North Korea had a well-organized and efficient army.

Its efficiency was further increased by the efforts, beginning in December 1948, of a Soviet military advisory group, headed by the Soviet ambassador and former head of the Soviet occupation forces, **Terenty Fomich Shtykov**. During 1949, as the Chinese civil war drew to a close, and especially after the proclamation of the **People's Republic of China** in October 1949, ethnic Koreans who had been fighting with the Chinese Communists were released for recruitment into the North Korean People's Army. They joined a number of Soviet Koreans who were already there. Both groups had considerable fighting experience, either in the just-ended Chinese civil war or in World War II.

At the outbreak of the **Korean War** in June 1950, the North Korean People's Army was some 135,000 strong, in contrast to the Republic of Korea's armed forces, which were then approximately 98,000. The commander-in-chief was 38-year-old Marshal (also Premier) **Kim Il Sung**, and his deputy was Marshal

Ch'oe Yong-gon. Both had fought in China and then with the Soviet forces against the Japanese. The chief-of-staff was **Nam Il**. The North Korean forces had eight full divisions, each including an artillery regiment, together with two half-strength divisions, two separate regiments, an armored brigade with 120–150 Soviet-made T-34 tanks, and five border Constabulary brigades. According to some South Korean accounts, the border Constabulary was directly trained by Soviet military advisers and its members were particularly ideologically committed. All these forces were organized into two corps. In addition, the North Korean air force had between 110 and 180 Soviet aircraft (estimates vary), all World War II–vintage fighter and attack bombers, whereas the navy had a few patrol boats, suitable only for coastal operation.

In June 1950, this army swept all before it. Cities such as **Kaesong** and **Uijongbu** were captured within hours of the first moves across the **38th parallel**. Within three days, the South Korean capital, **Seoul**, had fallen to the 4th Division, led by Major-General **Li Kwon-mu**. After a brief pause to recuperate, the advance continued on the west side of the peninsula, forcing the South Korean government under President **Syngman Rhee** to retreat ever further to the south, until it reached **Pusan**. From there, there was nowhere else to go. A strong boost to North Korean morale was the ease with which their forces dealt with the first U.S. intervention. When the North Koreans met Task Force Smith at Osan near Suwon early in July 1950, they swept it aside, leading some to see the North Koreans as invincible. In the meantime, other North Korean army units, aided by special forces that had landed behind South Korean lines, pushed down the east coast.

The North Korean advance was stopped at the **Pusan Perimeter**. At that stage, the North Korean army structure remained intact. Losses in the fighting were more than made up for by recruitment, sometimes, but not always, forced among South Koreans, and North Korean brigades became divisions as more soldiers poured in. However, once halted at the Pusan Perimeter, the North Koreans, instead of concentrating their forces, engaged in piecemeal attacks. Despite many individual acts of bravery, the perimeter remained a barrier. Extended supply lines also began to cause difficulties for the

North Korean forces. Once the U.S. Far Eastern Air Force was able to deploy aircraft to Korea, the North Korean air force was quickly eliminated as a fighting power.

North Korean difficulties increased following the **Inch'on landing** in September 1950. The gamble by the **United Nations** (UN) commander, General **Douglas MacArthur,** of landing behind enemy lines paid off. North Korean forces retreated before the UN advance, and the North Korean troops in the South found themselves forced back when General **Walton Walker** broke out of the Pusan Perimeter. By late September 1950, the North Korean army was reduced to about 38,000 men trying to escape back in disorderly fashion across the 38th parallel, but leaving large numbers behind as guerrillas to harass South Korean troops.

Following the intervention of the **Chinese People's Volunteers** in October 1950, which saved North Korea from a total UN takeover, the North Korean army had time to recuperate and rebuild. By mid-spring 1951, North Korean forces were again in operation, albeit now alongside Chinese forces. By July 1951, when the war began to settle down to its long, static phase, North Korean troops had reformed, and 211,000 men were organized into seven corps and three divisions. In July 1953, on the eve of the signing of the **armistice,** North Koreans under arms numbered 260,000.

Following the armistice, North Korea continued to maintain a large army and to develop other aspects of its military capability. By the late 1980s, it was regularly claimed by South Korean and U.S. sources that North Korea had a million men under arms. Even though North Korea has announced from time to time, beginning in 1987, that it is releasing military personnel for civilian work such as road construction and assistance to farmers, the numbers in the military are still high. Defense expenditure has also been high, although figures published in 1997 showed that the South Korean military budget at some $14.4 billion was more than twice that of North Korea at $5.2 billion. In addition to regular forces, North Korea maintains a group of special forces, whose roles appear to include espionage and infiltration of the South. Since 1992, General **Kim Jong Il** has been commander-in-chief of the North Korean forces.

See also: Demilitarized Zone (DMZ); Military Armistice Commission (MAC); Naktong River; North Korean Use of Terrorism; Ongjin Peninsula; P'anmunjom; *Pueblo,* USS (1968); Pusan and the Pusan Perimeter; Role of the Military in North and South Korea; Soviet Role in the Korean War.
References: Hermes 1966; Kim 1973; Matray 1991; Summers 1990.

NORTH KOREAN PROPOSALS ON UNIFICATION

From the time of the establishment of separate regimes in Korea in 1945, both have developed plans for the reunification of the peninsula. Both Koreas rejected the idea of a perpetual division: Koreans, they argued, have historically belonged to one state, and they should belong to one state again. However, Korea was divided not only physically, but also on ideological lines, a fact that has always complicated the reunification issue.

From 1948 onward, the government of North Korea, like that in the South, claimed to be the only legitimate government of Korea and sought the allegiance of all Koreans. Its first formal statement on unification was a proposal from the Democratic Front for the Attainment of the Unification of the Fatherland, on 30 June 1949, two days after the front was established in **P'yongyang.** The front called for the withdrawal of foreign forces in order to allow the Korean people to settle their own future; simultaneous elections North and South to elect one legislature for the whole country, which should adopt a Constitution based on that of North Korea; the ending of persecution of democratic parties in the South and the exclusion from the election process of those who had carried this out; and the merger of the armed forces of the two sides. Unsurprisingly, these terms were rejected in the South. They were repeated, slightly modified, on 3 June 1950.

Three weeks later, on 25 June 1950, the North sought to achieve unification by force. When the **Korean War** ended in 1953, the attempt had failed, and the division between the two Koreas was more rigid. For most of the 1950s, domestic concerns preoccupied the two Koreas, although the idea of eventual reunification did not go away. For North Korea, the war had made things worse because the United States was now established as the political and military guardian of South Korea. The North demanded the removal of U.S. forces to allow Koreans to settle their affairs themselves, but it was not an appeal that found much favor in the South. For its part, the North realized that it could not enforce its wishes on the South and so accepted that there would be a time gap while it built up its strength.

By 1960, when the North's postwar economic rehabilitation program had outstripped the South's, the North was ready with new suggestions. On 14 August 1960, the North Korean premier, **Kim Il Sung**, proposed a North-South Confederation. This proposal, regularly repackaged, remains the basis of the North Korean position on reunification to this day. Kim argued that, although the two Koreas should continue to function separately in domestic terms, internationally there should be one Korean state. This state would be free of all foreign links, would enter the **United Nations** and related organizations as one entity, and would be neutral and non-aligned. Only genuine "democratic" organizations and people could take part, however.

The proposal was further refined on 10 October 1980, when the combined state was given the title Democratic Confederal Republic of Koryo. It was again presented on 6 April 1993, essentially unchanged, as Kim Il Sung's 10-Point Program for the Great Unity of the Whole Nation for the Reunification of the Country and remains the official policy of North Korea on the question of reunification.

See also: Cross-recognition; Diplomatic Recognition; Intra-Korean Agreements; Joint Commission on Trusteeship; Moscow Agreement (1945); Pro-unification Activities; Red Cross North-South Talks; Rhee, Syngman; South Korean Proposals on Unification.

References: Eberstadt 1995; Gills 1996; Kim 1992; Kwak, Kim, and Kim 1984; "Selected Reunification Policy of DPRK" (World Wide Web site); Whan 1994.

NORTH KOREAN SUBMARINE INCIDENTS (1996 AND 1998)

In September 1996, a submarine with a crew of more than twenty North Korean personnel ran aground on a reef off the east coast town of Kangnung. Eleven bodies were discovered on the

The South Korean navy takes a North Korean submarine that had become caught in fishing nets in tow on 22 June 1998. (AP/Ahn Young-joon)

beach, all shot, one crew member was captured, and the remaining men went on the run until almost all were killed by South Korean soldiers. The South claimed this as attempted infiltration. The North insisted that the submarine had developed engine trouble and had drifted into South Korean waters; asked for the return of the submarine, bodies, and captured crewman; and on 29 December 1996 apologized for the intrusion. The following day, the cremated remains of twenty-four North Korean commandos killed in the aftermath of the intrusion were returned to the North at **P'anmunjom**.

A further intrusion by a North Korean submarine into South Korean waters off the east coast in late June 1998 was handled more coolly by the South Korean authorities. The submarine became caught in fishing nets on 22 June, was taken in tow by naval ships, sank, and was refloated three days later. The North Korean crew of nine appeared all to have committed suicide. Their bodies were likewise returned to the North. The North tacitly admitted

South Korean soldiers inspect a North Korean submarine that ran aground on 18 September 1996 off the coast of South Korea near Kangnung. (AP/Ahn Young-joon)

on 30 June that its submarine had been on an infiltration mission.
See also: Infiltration; North Korean Use of Terrorism.
References: Newsreview, 27 June and 4 July 1998.

NORTH KOREAN USE OF TERRORISM

The **armistice** signed on 27 July 1953 between the **United Nations Command** (UNC) and the North Korean and Chinese army commands ended formal hostilities in the **Korean War**. Over the following decades, however, North Korea maintained a campaign of harassment of South Korean targets, in apparent continuation of its leaders' guerrilla techniques during the anti-Japanese struggles of the 1930s and early 1940s and of the irregular fighting in the South immediately after liberation. North Korea's aims can only be conjectured: defiance of the South Korean government and armed forces and of the U.S. military command in South Korea; the wish to discourage South Korean military adventurism; intimidation of the South Korean population, coupled with a desire to rally that same population's support for Communist aims; and promotion of a state of vigilance among its own armed forces and people. What is clear is that its aggressiveness has contributed to the prolongation of tension on the Korea Peninsula. The timing and volume of some incidents would seem to be related to South Korean policies, such as South Korean participation between 1965 and 1973 in the **Vietnam War** (the years 1967–1970 were particularly marked by sustained attempts at infiltration and harassment), or to a particular achievement, such as **Seoul's** success in securing the 1988 Summer Olympics. The South in turn has used the threat from the North to justify the imposition of **curfews and civil defense measures,** of **censorship** and restrictions on mass gatherings and demonstrations, and the perpetuation of a **National Security Law**.

It is difficult to check the veracity of every report of North Korean terrorism. UNC charges brought through **Military Armistice Commission** meetings are probably accurate, but are almost always rejected by the North Korean side. Many of the reports of the North's infiltration of South Korean territory and of North Korean spying come from South Korean authorized sources and cannot easily be verified. Attacks on South Korean targets outside of the peninsula are not acknowledged by North Korea, though generally are proved to be its work. At the same time, North Korea has usually released both U.S. and South Korean military personnel, such as pilots shot down over the **Demilitarized Zone,** as well as a certain number of civilians taken in **aircraft hijackings** or of fishermen abducted from disputed waters.

The range of North Korean terrorist tactics has been considerable: abduction of both individuals and groups of people; aircraft hijackings; assassination attempts on South Korean leaders; bomb attacks inside and outside of South Korea; and infiltration of agents by land and sea for purposes of spying or agitation. South Korea has from time to time charged some of its own nationals with spying for North Korea. Interceptions of North Korean armed personnel and encounters between UNC/South Korean and North Korean naval vessels and military aircraft have been common. North Korean terrorist operations are said to be entrusted to special units of the **North Korean People's Army,** supported by a network of intelligence agencies. They resist capture, if necessary with use of arms, and if apprehended, often attempt suicide. South Korea on its side maintains military and police antiterrorist troops, backed up by a Combat Reserve Corps, formed in 1975.

Only in the 1990s has North Korean belligerence showed signs of diminishing; and in December 1996, the North apologized for the intrusion of a submarine into South Korean waters two months earlier.

See also: Abductions; Assassinations and Attempted Assassinations; Bomb and Other Attacks; Espionage; Infiltration.

References: Bolger 1991; History: VI, 1977; Kirkbride 1994.

NORTH-SOUTH BOUNDARIES

The division of the Korea Peninsula into two states has created a highly sensitive set of boundaries. On land, the Military Demarcation Line (MDL) running down the middle of the **Demilitarized Zone** (DMZ) is fairly clearly defined, though not sufficiently well to prevent villagers living in the DMZ from sometimes straying over it, as happened as late as October 1997. At sea, however, the MDL is far less easily traced. Confusion over the exact course of the maritime boundary between North and South,

doubtless real enough on both sides, but sometimes probably deliberate, has led to frequent confrontations between South Korean fishing boats and North Korean patrols, who may seize both men and vessels on the grounds that they have intruded into North Korean territorial waters. South Korean naval ships on fishery protection duties may also find themselves confronted by North Korean patrols. South Korea's position is that its boats are in international waters. Both North and South assert a territorial waters limit of 12 miles, but both also claim some form of jurisdiction beyond this, such as North Korea's "military sea boundary," announced in August 1977, which increases the scope for conflicting claims. North Korea's justification for its seizure of the **USS** *Pueblo* in January 1968 was that the ship, an electronic-surveillance vessel, had intruded into its waters for the purposes of espionage.

Particularly sensitive zones are those around five groups of islands off the west coast of the peninsula that were specified in the 1953 **armistice** agreement as coming under control of the **United Nations Command** (UNC). In 1973, North Korea challenged this interpretation, arguing that the agreement ceded to it the coastal waters surrounding these islands, but the UNC rejected its claim. Though the possibility of continuing confrontations at sea remains high, the volume of such incidents has diminished in recent years.

The difficulty of demarcating the airspace between the two states presents a similar scope for confusion and overflying, whether deliberate or unintentional. The air corridors along the DMZ and airspaces over the waters to east and west of the peninsula have been the scenes of military aerial confrontations that have led to aircraft being shot down. The disputed airspace is often above waters claimed by the North as territorial seas and by the South as international waters.

See also: Abductions; Aerial Surveillance; Infiltration.

References: History: VI, 1977; Park 1983.

NORTHEAST CHINA

The area of China immediately to the north of the Korea Peninsula has long been geographically and historically important for Korea, representing as it does the principal land route into and out of the peninsula. The region, known in Chinese as *dongbei* (literally, "eastnorth"), comprises the three provinces of Liaoning, Jilin, and Heilongjiang. The name Manchuria, employed for much of the twentieth century but now dropped from official usage, derives from the name of the Manchu people, early inhabitants of the area who in the mid-seventeenth century subdued China and formed the last Chinese dynasty, the Qing. In 1931, Japan extended its control of northeast Asia from Korea to Manchuria, and in 1932 created a puppet state (known in Chinese as Manzhouguo) separate from China. This came to an end in 1945, with the defeat of Japan.

Koreans started to emigrate into the northeast provinces of China in the 1860s, even though at the time emigration was forbidden. However, famine and poverty drove many farmers in the northern provinces of Korea across the borders. In 1881, China opened up its northeast to them, and Korean settlements quickly grew in number, especially in the area of Jilin Province immediately to the north of the Tumen River, which forms the northeast section of the boundary between China and Korea. This area, still heavily Korean, is home to about 40 percent of the Korean national minority community in China. Known formerly as Jiandao (Chientao), it is now called the Yanbian Korean Autonomous Prefecture and enjoys a measure of self-administration. Over one million Koreans (though with Chinese nationality) live in Jilin Province.

The presence of settled Korean communities in the northeast of China made the region a natural place of refuge for Korean guerrilla fighters through much of the **Japanese colonial period** (1910–1945). Armed resistance from within Korea in the first decade of the twentieth century to ever-increasing Japanese encroachment in the peninsula diminished after 1910 as the Japanese extended their control over the country. Some fighters fled into Northeast China and launched raids back across the border into Korea.

The success of the 1917 October Revolution in Russia introduced new influences into the region, as Marxist-Leninist doctrines spread and the new Soviet government looked for allies against its enemies in the extreme east of Asia. Communist teaching took a quick hold among sections of the Korean resistance movement, much of it of peasant

origin, strengthening already existing nationalist sentiment. From 1920, the Chinese northeast sheltered groups of Koreans active in the anti-Japanese struggle, many of them operating as Communist guerrilla units, though often split against each other. Jiandao was a particularly strong anti-Japanese base. From 1925, however, such activities came under threat as the Japanese authorities in Korea put pressure on the Chinese administration of the northeast provinces to curb what they regarded as Korean subversion. In September 1931, Japan seized control of the whole of Manchuria. Korean guerrilla units joined up for a while with the 2nd Army of the Chinese-led Northeastern People's Revolutionary Army, which was active along the Russian and Korean borders of Manchuria, but the 2nd Army itself was routed by the Japanese, and Korean armed resistance in Jiandao was effectively crushed by 1936. Korean guerrilla groups, among them one led by **Kim Il Sung**, were forced in 1941 to retreat into Siberia. The Korean civilian population of Northeast China, meanwhile, grew rapidly as Japan at first encouraged, then after 1937 compelled, Korean labor to move into the region to serve its war effort. At the time of the Japanese defeat in 1945, more than two million Koreans were living in the northeastern provinces, and it is not uncommon to meet middle-aged Koreans who were born in erstwhile Manchuria.

Postwar repatriation back to Korea reduced the numbers in Northeast China, but a strong nucleus remained, estimated at 1.2 million. Detachments of Chinese-trained, armed Koreans, who had operated as the Korean Volunteer Army alongside Chinese Communist forces against the Japanese, moved into the area after the defeat of Japan to assist the Communists in their struggle with the Chinese Nationalists. A number of them were eventually permitted to enter North Korea to support the new regime there. With the outbreak of the **Korean War** in 1950, Chinese Koreans from the northeast joined the **North Korean People's Army** or the **Chinese People's Volunteers**.

During the war, the Chinese northeast provided a secure hinterland for North Korea. In October 1950, North Korean troops fleeing before the **United Nations** (UN) push north were able to retire into

China and the Soviet Union, and the government temporarily made its capital in **Shinuiju**, right on the Sino-Korean border. However, the presence of non-Korean UN forces at the border (in November 1950 they reached the **Yalu River**, which forms a long stretch of the western frontier between China and Korea) was instrumental in bringing the Chinese on the North Korean side into the fighting. Many of China's heavy industries were (and still are) located in the northeast. The threat to them from hostile action added to Chinese anxiety. The region provided a route for the transport of war supplies to the North and a base for Chinese airborne action over the Korea Peninsula.

The Chinese northeast continues to be important for North Korea. For many years, the principal rail routes into and out of the country, leading through the region, have linked it with the rail systems of the rest of China and of the Russian Far East. Now, with Chinese recognition of both North and South Korea, the Korean minority areas in Jilin Province, free to engage commercially with South Korea, are opening up more and more to South Korean influence. Not all of this is in trade. South Korean Christian churches have been established. A missionary from one of them was reportedly abducted from the Yanbian region into North Korea in 1995, and North Korea complains of the activities of South Korean agents along the Chinese side of the Sino-Korean border. Though details are rarely available, it seems clear, moreover, that the border is being breached by a growing number of defectors from the North, who pass initially through Northeast China on their way out of the peninsula. Also, a few reunions between separated North-South family members have taken place in the area. Cross-border trade in foodstuffs has grown rapidly since the onset of severe food shortages in North Korea since 1995.

See also: Chinese Involvement in Korea (1919–1948); People's Republic of China Relations with North Korea.

References: Hoare and Pares 1988; Howard, Pares, and English 1996; Kim 1988; Lee 1963; Scalapino and Lee 1972; Suh and Shultz 1990.

NORWEGIAN INVOLVEMENT IN THE KOREAN WAR

Norway did not contribute troops to the **United Nations Command** in the **Korean War**, but sent a mobile surgical hospital, known as NorMASH. The unit arrived in June 1951 and stayed in Korea until November 1954. Initially administered by the Norwegian Red Cross, it was supported by the U.S. Army medical services from November 1951. The personnel, numbering 105, remained Norwegian. The 200-bed hospital with operating theater provided inpatient and outpatient services to soldiers and civilians, largely in the Tongduch'on area north of Seoul.

Norway also played a role in diplomatic maneuvers to end hostilities.

See also: Mobile Army Surgical Hospital (MASH).

References: Forty 1982; History: III, 1974 and VI, 1977.

OFFICIAL TELEPHONE LINKS BETWEEN NORTH AND SOUTH

Despite long-standing policies of hostility between North and South Korea, telephone links do allow direct official communication between the two. In August 1972, when agreement was reached during the first full-scale **Red Cross** talks to discuss divided families, twenty direct telephone lines were installed between **P'yongyang** and **Seoul** via **P'anmunjom**. The number rose to twenty-six, but, as of October 1997, only five were in operation. Since August 1997, a direct telephone link has operated between the **Korean Peninsula Energy Development Organization** in Kumho (in North Korea) and Seoul. In November 1997, a further direct telephone line was opened between air traffic control towers in both North and South for the exchange of flight information. The month before, in aviation talks in Bangkok, the two states had agreed to open their Flight Information Regions to each other's airlines from April 1998. North Korea hopes to benefit from the payment of overflight fees; South Korean airlines expect to be able to reduce flying times. Other international airlines are also benefiting from the freedom to overfly North Korean territory and thereby cut flight times.
Reference: History: VI, 1977.

OLYMPIC GAMES
See **Seoul.**

ONGJIN PENINSULA

The Ongjin Peninsula lies just south of the city of Haeju. Both are now in North Korea, but from 1945 to 1950, Ongjin, which is south of the **38th parallel**, was in South Korea. Ongjin was effectively isolated from the rest of South Korean territory and could be supplied and reinforced only by air and sea. It was the scene of much fighting between North and South border forces during 1948–1950 and was probably the first part of South Korea to be attacked on 25 June 1950 at the beginning of the **Korean War**. Exaggerated early South Korean press reports that troops on the Ongjin Peninsula had fought back and captured Haeju have been used by the North Koreans and others to argue that the South began the war, but most evidence does not bear out this interpretation. By 26 June 1950, the South Korean forces on the peninsula had all been evacuated by sea or air, and the peninsula passed to North Korean control.
References: Halliday and Cumings 1998; Merrill 1989.

PAIK SUN-YUP (1920–)

Paik Sun-yup (Paek Son-yop), a prominent member of the South Korean military during the **Korean War** and after, was appointed South Korea's first four-star general at the age of 33. Paik was born on 23 November 1920. He was educated at the Manzhouguo Military Academy, and during World War II he served as a junior officer in the Japanese army. After 1945, he joined the newly formed Constabulary and then the South Korean army. In June 1950, when the Korean War began, he was the commander of the 1st Division, one of the four South Korean divisions on duty on the **38th parallel**. Although many of his forces were on leave and he had only recently returned from a training course, the division fought well, retreating across the **Han River** only after the fall of **Seoul** on 28 June. The division quickly re-formed and, when the **United Nations** forces took the war north during September–October 1950, the 1st Division was in the vanguard, taking the North Korean capital, **P'yongyang**, on 19 October 1950.

Paik's next major role was as representative of South Korea at the **armistice** negotiations from July to October 1951. He then became commander of Task Force Paik, made up of the South Korean 8th and Capital Divisions and of police. Task Force Paik conducted Operation Ratkiller against guerrilla forces in the southwest between December 1951 and March–April 1952. The operation was deemed to be a success, but it has frequently been claimed that Paik conducted it with great brutality. In 1952, President **Syngman Rhee** appointed him chief-of-staff, a post Paik held until 1954. He was again chief-of-staff from 1957 to 1959, and in 1959 was appointed chairman of the South Korean chiefs-of-staff. However, he soon resigned from the post under pressure from younger officers who carried out an anticorruption campaign in the army. Under President **Park Chung Hee**, he held a number of ambassadorial posts and later was a prominent businessman.

Paik is widely credited with turning the South Korean forces, defeated easily in June 1950, into the successful fighting force that played a major part in the later stages of the Korean War. His autobiography, *From Pusan to Panmunjom*, published in English in 1992, is an interesting account of the war from a Korean soldier's perspective, although it avoids discussing controversial issues such as the question of atrocities.

Reference: Paik 1992.

PAK HON-YONG (1900–1955)

An early Communist activist, Pak Hon-yong played a major role in the establishment of the first **Korean Communist Party** (KCP) in 1925 and reemerged in 1945 as its leader. He eventually joined **Kim Il Sung** in the North with his "domestic" group of Korean Communists, but fell out of favor with Kim and was executed in 1955.

Pak Hon-yong was born in 1900 in South Ch'ungch'ong Province. After study in **Seoul** and Tokyo, where he was much influenced by Japanese socialists, he arrived in 1921 in Shanghai, where he launched into activities in support of the Irkutsk faction of Korean Communists. In 1922, he attempted to enter Korea, but was arrested at the border and imprisoned by the Japanese colonial authorities.

On his release, Pak joined the Tuesday Society, one of several left-wing activist groups in Korea, and in April 1925 participated in the founding of the first KCP and the creation of the Korean Communist Youth League. When the KCP collapsed in November 1925, Pak was again arrested and imprisoned by the Japanese. On release in 1928, he fled to the Soviet Union, but eventually returned to Shanghai to resume Communist activities. Arrested in Shanghai in 1933, he was sent back to Korea and remained imprisoned until 1939. Thereafter, he appears to have eluded Japanese surveillance by undertaking menial work in the south of the country.

Immediately on liberation, Pak returned to Seoul to revive the KCP and in September 1945 was accepted both north and south as chairman of a single party. The gathering strength of a Soviet-supported Communist administration in the North, however, increasingly undermined his influence, and the installation of a U.S. military administration in the South that turned to moderate Korean elements for advice left little space for the KCP. The party's and Pak's acceptance in January 1946 of the Soviet line in favor of the **Joint Commission on Trusteeship** cost them support. As KCP members increasingly moved north, Pak's power base dwindled. In September 1946, a warrant was issued for his arrest, and by the end of the year, he had fled north.

Kim Il Sung initially accepted Pak and his domestic faction. When the Democratic People's Republic of Korea was established in September 1948, Pak was appointed a vice-premier and minister of foreign affairs. In 1949, he was named a vice-chairman of the **Korean Workers' Party** (KWP), and at the outset of the **Korean War** in June 1950 he was a member of the KWP's Military Affairs Committee. Some reports suggest that he promised Kim Il Sung the support of many southern Communist activists if the North were to invade the South. The failure of the North's campaign was used by Kim to break Pak and his faction on charges of treason and spying. Members of his group were tried and executed in August 1953, a month after the **armistice**. Pak himself was held from February 1953 to December 1955, when he was tried on the same charges and the additional one of having sought to seize power and was sentenced to death.

See also: Left-Wing Political Factions; Underwood Family (1885–).

References: Matray 1991; Scalapino and Lee 1972; Suh 1967, 1970, 1981; Yang 1994.

PANIKKAR, KAVALAM MADHAVA (1895–1963)

Sardar Kavalam Madhava Panikkar was Indian ambassador to the **People's Republic of China** (PRC) at the time of the outbreak of the **Korean War** in June 1950. With the reputation of being a supporter of

pan-Asian policies, he became ambassador soon after India established diplomatic relations with the PRC and quickly established a good relationship with the Chinese premier, **Zhou Enlai**. At the beginning of the war, Panikkar thought that the Chinese were not interested in Korea, but when the **United Nations** forces crossed the **38th parallel**, Zhou used Panikkar to pass on increasing Chinese concern. The messages that the Indian government communicated to London and Washington were ignored. Even when Panikkar was summoned by Zhou to receive a late-night warning on 3 October 1950, this too was discounted at senior levels in the U.S. administration. After the **Chinese People's Volunteers** intervened in force in October 1950, Panikkar's role diminished, and he left Beijing in 1952.

P'ANMUNJOM

P'anmunjom lies toward the western end of the **Demilitarized Zone** (DMZ), and is approximately 25 miles (40 kilometers) north of the South Korean capital, **Seoul**. An earlier village was destroyed during the **Korean War**, but the site was selected in late 1951 as the second meeting place for the **armistice** talks between the **United Nations Command** (UNC) and the North Korean/Chinese command. Its position, halfway between the UNC command at Munsan, and the Communist command headquarters at **Kaesong**, made it acceptable to both sides. (The first site for the talks, Kaesong, was judged not to be sufficiently neutral.) Armistice discussions were held intermittently at P'anmunjom from 25 October 1951 until the armistice was signed there on 27 July 1953. Exchanges of **prisoners of war** took place through P'anmunjom in April 1953 and again from August to September of that year. The armistice document designated P'anmunjom as the site for both the **Military Armistice Commission** (MAC) and the **Neutral Nations Supervisory Commission** (NNSC) and for other temporary bodies.

P'anmunjom is thus the symbol of the division of Korea. For years it was also the only regular meeting point between North and South. (The two sides have met occasionally in the North Korean capital, **P'yongyang**, and in Seoul and now participate in discussions in other world centers.) The significance of the site far outweighs its modest appearance. It is

Aerial view of P'anmunjom taken at the time it was serving as the site for armistice talks (1951–1953). Tents provided much of the accommodation. (Xinhua News Agency)

the customary exchange point for bodies of soldiers killed in the Korean War that have since been unearthed, as well as the returning point for the crews of shot-down aircraft. The crew of the USS *Pueblo* came back through P'anmunjom in December 1968 after nearly a year's captivity in the North. President **Jimmy Carter** entered North Korea through P'anmunjom in June 1994 on his way to visit **Kim Il Sung**.

The area is strictly known as the Joint Security Area (JSA), covers a roughly circular ground some 2,600 feet by 1,970 feet (800 meters by 600 meters) in dimension, and is bisected by the Military Demarcation Line, which runs straight through the building constructed for direct talks. The JSA also houses the offices of the MAC and the NNSC, visitor reception areas, and offices for other organizations such as the Red Cross. In July 1998, a new Freedom House, replacing an older structure, opened on the UNC side to facilitate family reunion meetings, should these become possible.

Until September 1976, military and civilian personnel could move freely throughout the JSA, in recognition of its neutral status. The constant proximity to each other of soldiers from the two opposing sides led on occasion to scuffles and attacks. These culminated in the killing of two U.S. officers in August 1976 by North Korean security personnel in the **ax murders**. Thereafter, the movement of soldiers and police inside the JSA was restricted to the section controlled by each side, and the demarcation between the two zones was made clearer. (The new arrangements were embodied in a supplementary agreement of 6 September 1976 to the armistice agreement.) Toward the end of 1998, rumors surfaced of unauthorized contacts between North and South Korean security personnel within the JSA. Gunfire was exchanged for the first time in the JSA in November 1984, when a Russian translator attached to the Soviet embassy in P'yongyang took the opportunity of a visit to P'anmunjom to make a dash to the UNC sector. Approximately six defectors from Communist or former Communist countries have fled to the South through the JSA since 1959.

They have included two North Koreans: a journalist and, in February 1998, a soldier.

Such dramatic incidents should not overshadow the important role P'anmunjom has played over the past quarter-century in facilitating initial contacts between the two Koreas. Meetings initiated in 1971 at P'anmunjom between the **Red Cross** organizations of both sides on **family reunions** led to parallel political discussions from 1971 to 1973, held alternately in Seoul and P'yongyang. A decade later, meetings in 1984 on economic issues and between parliamentarians were held first at the site, even if they continued elsewhere. In the 1990s, P'anmunjom no longer has the same unique role as a point of contact, but is still the only land crossing between the North and the South, as witnessed in the transfer of two consignments, each of 501 head of cattle, from the South in June and October 1998 through P'anmunjom, a gift from the industrialist **Chung Ju-yung** to the North.

See also: Defections.

References: History: I, 1972; Kirkbride 1994; Macdonald 1996; *Newsreview*, 7 February 1998.

PARIS CONFERENCE AND VERSAILLES PEACE TREATY (1919)

Koreans responded positively to the Fourteen Points proclaimed by U.S. President Woodrow Wilson in January 1918. They thought that this declaration of the principles for ending World War I and settling peace provided an opportunity for self-determination for colonial peoples. The opening of the Peace Conference in Paris on 18 January 1919 reinforced these hopes, which were further intensified in an outburst of strong nationalist feelings following the death of the Korean Emperor Kojong on 22 January 1919. Kojong's funeral, planned for 3 March 1919, was the occasion for the peaceful demonstrations known as **Samil** ("Three-one," or March First), which were brutally put down by the Japanese. Two Korean exiles in the United States, **Syngman Rhee** and Henry Chung, tried to go to the conference, but were prevented because they did not have the correct documents. Despite this, at least one other group of Korean exiles, in Shanghai, decided to send a delegation and chose **Kim Kyu-shik** to present the Korean plea for self-determination. Although Kim reached Paris in May 1919, he failed to get a formal

hearing, and the Versailles Treaty took no account of the Korean case. This refusal still rankles among Koreans in both halves of the peninsula.

Reference: Lee 1965.

PARK CHUNG HEE (1917–1979)

Park Chung Hee, a former president of South Korea, was born in North Kyongsang Province in 1917, the son of a poor farmer. He attended Taegu Normal School and in 1937 became a primary school teacher. Soon afterward, however, he moved to the Japanese puppet state of Manzhouguo in **Northeast China** and enrolled in the Manzhouguo Military Academy. Later he attended the Japanese Military Academy, graduating as a second lieutenant in 1944. He returned to Korea in 1945, completed a short course at the new Military Academy established by the U.S. occupation forces, and became a captain in the new Korean Constabulary in 1946. Following the outbreak of the **Korean War**, Park joined the new Republic of Korea (ROK) army. By 1953, he was a brigadier general and became a major general in 1958. By 1960, he was engaged in planning a coup, which was postponed following the April 1960 student uprising and the overthrow of

Park Chung Hee, President of South Korea. (Korean Cultural and Information Service)

Syngman Rhee. However, in May 1961, the military plotters, citing a mixture of political and military problems, relaunched their plan and seized power. There was little resistance. President **Yun Po-sun**, though unhappy about both the domestic unrest and the military coup, nevertheless remained in office long enough to give the appearance of legality to the military moves. Having seized power, neither Park nor his military colleagues had a particular program to implement, apart from banning all political activity and purging those deemed to be too greedy. When Yun resigned in 1962, Park, who had been the chairman of the Supreme Council for National Reconstruction from May 1961, became acting president. The following year, he retired from the army with the rank of lieutenant general and was elected president of the Third Republic.

Park was reelected president in 1967, 1971, 1972, and 1978, becoming steadily more autocratic in the process. He had no particular policies in mind except to develop a strong economy for protection against the North. To this end, he introduced a series of five-year plans, which by the mid-1970s were beginning to transform South Korea from a backward and poor country into one of the leaders of the developing world. Through the *saemaul*, or new community movement, he ensured that the rural population gained some benefit from industrial expansion.

The rapid economic development was not achieved without cost. Much emphasis was placed on the "threat from the North" to justify restrictions on labor rights and civil liberties. Park worked hard to ensure U.S. support for South Korea, including committing ROK forces to the **Vietnam War**. Following the opening of contacts between the United States and China in the early 1970s, however, and while remaining staunchly anti-Communist, he began a dialogue with North Korea that ultimately ended in mutual name-calling. At the same time, he used the alleged danger that such contacts posed to South Korea to introduce in 1972 the new and more restrictive **Yushin Constitution**, designed to allow him to remain president for as long as he wished.

After 1972, Park grew steadily more aloof and suspicious, and increasingly so after the assassination of his wife in 1974. At the same time, domestic and international concern was growing at the steady increase in authoritarianism and the repressive role of institutions such as the Korean Central Intelligence Agency (KCIA). Student and worker demonstrations became commonplace, as did the use of riot police and tear gas to suppress them. Faced with widespread protests in the summer of 1979, the government reacted by expelling the opposition leader **Kim Young Sam** from the National Assembly and declaring martial law in the southern city of **Pusan**. A split then developed between those, such as the head of the KCIA, Kim Jae-kyu, who favored a compromise, and others, including Park, who preferred further repression. At this point, Park accepted a dinner invitation at a KCIA restaurant on 26 October 1979. A quarrel developed and Kim Jae-kyu shot and killed the president, thus setting in motion the events that brought General **Chun Doo Hwan** to power.

Park was widely seen as personally incorruptible, and many believed that, for all his authoritarian ways, he acted with the best interests of the country at heart. As South Korea has faced economic difficulties since 1997, there have been those who have expressed nostalgia for what are seen as the economic certainties of Park's regime. But although real economic gains were made under Park, he left a much more dubious political legacy, which has affected the South Korean political process long after his death.

See also: Assassinations and Attempted Assassinations.
References: Nam 1989; Park 1979; Sohn 1991.

PARK TONG-SUN (1935–)
See **Koreagate** (1977).

PENG DEHUAI (ca. 1897–1974)
Peng Dehuai commanded the **Chinese People's Volunteers** (CPV) in the **Korean War** from their intervention in October 1950 until the signing of the **armistice** in July 1953. Peng was born to a peasant family in Xiangtan County, Hunan Province, around the beginning of the twentieth century. (Dates for his birth vary from 1897 to 1902.) At thirteen, he left home to become a soldier and later trained at the Hunan Military Academy, emerging as an officer in the Chinese Nationalist (Guomindang) forces. Around 1928, he joined up with the

Communist leaders, **Mao Zedong** and Zhu De, and became a member of the Chinese Communist Party (CCP) because, it has been reported, he was dissatisfied with the Nationalists' lack of interest in the needs of the peasants. For the next twenty years, Peng was engaged in constant fighting against **Chiang Kai-shek**'s Chinese Nationalists in the civil wars or against the Japanese after the beginning of the Sino-Japanese War in 1937. From then until 1954, Peng, as deputy commander-in-chief, was the second-highest-ranking officer in the CCP military organization. He was also involved in more political activities, as a member of the controlling Politburo of the CCP from 1945, and was regarded as close to Mao.

It is sometimes claimed that, when the Chinese party and government decided to act in Korea, Mao first selected Lin Biao, commander of the 4th Field Army, to head the forces to be sent, and some argue that Lin did serve in Korea, at least in the early stages. Most evidence, however, indicates that, if Lin was selected, he declined, and Mao turned to Peng

who accepted without quarreling. Peng's headquarters were at Shenyang in **Northeast China**, and it was from there that he began to move troops into Korea in October 1950. He followed soon afterward, and, because of the collapse of the North Koreans in the face of the **United Nations Command** (UNC) advance, became the effective leader of the North Korean–CPV forces. Peng was always careful, however, to defer to the North Korean premier and head of the armed forces, Marshal **Kim Il Sung**, thus preserving a good working relationship with his ally.

It seems to have been Peng who devised what became the characteristic strategy of the CPV. An attack in force, using large numbers of troops, would be aimed at a weak section of the enemy's front and would inflict heavy casualties. Then the Chinese forces would break off contact before their next attack, rather than pursuing the enemy to the kill. There was nothing ill-disciplined about these attacks. The CPV operated as army units, with clear objectives. Although they were sometimes described by the UNC as "hordes," with the implication that

Peng Dehuai, commander of the Chinese People's Volunteers in Korea, chats with a CPV soldier. (AP/Wide World Photos)

these were primitive troops using primitive tactics, this was not the case.

Peng's problems came from the long supply lines and lack of equipment of his forces. His troops' supplies came, not by trucks and air support like those of the UN side, but on the backs of laborers toiling over the mountains. Although the CPV managed on much smaller rations than the UN forces, they still needed new ammunition and fresh supplies of food. Attacks could therefore be sustained only for a relatively short period and then had to be broken off to allow the troops to recover. Once the UNC stopped retreating and began to fight back in the spring of 1951, Peng could not maintain the momentum of 1950, and the war became a stalemate. He pursued this with firmness, just as he had the fast-moving campaigns of 1950–1951, determined to hold as much territory as possible when the **armistice** came into force. Peng also used the period between the failure of the last Chinese offensive in spring 1951 and the 1953 armistice to help re-create the **North Korean People's Army**, which had been almost wiped out after the UNC forces carried out the **Inch'on landing** and the breakout from the **Pusan Perimeter** in September 1950. Peng signed the armistice agreement in July 1953 on behalf of the CPV and left Korea soon afterward, having received a series of North Korean decorations and honors for the part he had played in preserving North Korea.

Peng returned to China to a hero's welcome in August 1953. He became first vice-chairman of the CCP's Central Military Commission and then minister of national defense in 1954. When military ranks were introduced in the **People's Liberation Army** (PLA) in 1955, Peng became a marshal. His long military experience convinced him that China needed a more professional army, skilled in modern techniques rather than sustained by ideology, and he used his position as minister to begin work on this. In August 1959, however, when China faced famine following Mao Zedong's introduction of people's communes and the Great Leap Forward, Peng criticized Mao's policies at a meeting of the CCP Central Committee held at Lushan. He was heavily attacked and in September 1959 lost his post as minister of defense to Lin Biao. Lin, with Mao's support, reversed some of the military reforms that Peng had favored, and the PLA again became dominated by

ideological rather than professional military thinking. Peng continued to appear in minor posts until the outbreak of the Cultural Revolution in 1966. In December 1966, he was "arrested" by young Red Guards and subjected to public humiliation. He died in 1974, still in disgrace, but was rehabilitated in 1978.

Peng was perhaps more a determined than an imaginative military commander, and his forces sustained heavy casualties. But he made the best of relatively few resources and was respected as personally brave in both his military and political roles.

See also: Invasion and Counterinvasion (1950–1951); People's Republic of China (PRC).

References: Gittings 1967; Klein and Clark 1971; Matray 1991; Peng 1984.

PEOPLE'S COMMITTEES

Release from Japanese colonial oppression and the expectation of independence and self-rule created a surge of enthusiastic political activity among Koreans throughout the peninsula. A Committee for the Preparation of Korean Independence (CPKI) was announced in **Seoul** on 17 August 1945, two days after liberation. Branches of the new committee formed immediately both north and south. With the establishment of the short-lived **Korean People's Republic** on 6 September 1950 from the CPKI, these branches evolved into People's Committees in support of the new body, extending from provincial level down through major cities to county and village level. The People's Committees reflected a range of political interests in their composition from conservatives to left-wingers and developed formal structures to deal with day-to-day administration of local needs. High among the priorities of many committees were land reform and the expropriation of former Japanese landowners. The committees were frequently supported by newly emerging mass organizations. The product of mass enthusiasm operating in local conditions, they varied in their duration and effectiveness and followed no prescribed pattern, at least in the southern half of the country.

The People's Committees did not consciously evolve as Communist groups. However, an influx of political prisoners released after liberation and the return home of radical students demobilized from the Japanese army swelled the left-wing element in the committees. The strong organizational skills of local Communist cells also helped to bring Communists to the fore. The People's Committees in the southern half of Korea were consequently viewed with distrust by the incoming U.S. military occupation forces and the **United States Army Military Government in Korea** (USAMGIK), which suspected them of being under Soviet direction. USAMGIK and right-wing Korean groups therefore set about eliminating the People's Committees, without necessarily replacing them by alternative local forms of government, and by the end of 1946, almost all committees had been disbanded. A few held on in remote parts of the South. The committee on **Cheju Island** in particular persisted until 1949. For a few months in 1950, during the North Korean occupation of the South from late June to late September, People's Committees were revived by the North Koreans, but disappeared after the South regained control.

In the northern half of Korea, the People's Committees soon came under Soviet pressure to admit equal numbers of Communist representatives. The **P'yongyang** committee had started as a branch of the CPKI under the leadership of the moderate nationalist **Cho Man-shik**, but by early February 1946, Cho had been ousted, and the whole system of People's Committees was evolving into a formal Communist apparatus.

See also: Invasion and Counterinvasion (1950–1951); Korea Peninsula (1945–1948).
References: Cumings 1981; Henderson 1968; Yang 1994.

PEOPLE'S LIBERATION ARMY (PLA)
The armed forces of the **People's Republic of China** (PRC), the People's Liberation Army (PLA), is an all-service organization, with a PLA navy and a PLA air force in addition to the land forces. Officially, the PLA did not take part in the **Korean War** from 1950 to 1953, but the **Chinese People's Volunteers** (CPV), who did, were virtually all drawn from the PLA. The CPV forces were organized on PLA lines and commanded by the PLA deputy commander-in-chief, **Peng Dehuai**. By calling its forces volunteers, the PRC hoped to avoid a direct confrontation with the United States and thus limit the conflict to Korea.

The PLA dates its origins to the 1 August 1927 uprising in Nanchang, Jiangxi Province, and the "autumn harvest" uprising on the Hunan-Jiangxi border on 9 September 1927. Until 1947, the Communist forces were known as the Red Army. Thereafter, they became the PLA. The Korean War created strong personal ties between the PLA and the **North Korean People's Army**. These links still exist, but are now less strong as the generation that fought together disappears from the political scene.
See also: Military Armistice Commission (MAC); People's Republic of China Relations with North Korea.
References: Chinese Academy of Social Science 1989; Gittings 1967.

PEOPLE'S REPUBLIC OF CHINA (PRC)
On 1 October 1949, the Chinese Communist leader, **Mao Zedong**, proclaimed the establishment of the People's Republic of China (PRC) from the Tiananmen (Gate of Heavenly Peace) in Beijing. Although pockets of resistance remained in various parts of the country, and neither Tibet nor **Taiwan** had been incorporated into what was now known as "New China," the civil wars that had been a feature of China since 1911 were at an end. For North Korea, formed just a year before, the establishment of the PRC provided another international ally and released many Koreans who had been fighting with the **People's Liberation Army** for service with its own newly established army. The PRC saved North Korea from destruction during the **Korean War** and provided much postwar reconstruction aid. In 1961, it signed a defense treaty with North Korea, and, although relations were occasionally strained during China's Cultural Revolution (1966–1976), they improved thereafter. Following the collapse of the **Union of Soviet Socialist Republics** in 1991, the PRC became the main supplier of aid to North Korea.
See also: Chinese People's Volunteers; Embargo; Nehru, Jawaharlal; New China News Agency; Northeast China; Panikkar, Kavalam Madhava; Peng Dehuai.
References: Koh 1969; Matray 1991; Sanford 1990.

PEOPLE'S REPUBLIC OF CHINA RELATIONS WITH NORTH KOREA
Communist China in the late 1940s seemed a natural ally for the North Korean state newly established in September 1948. Korean Communists during the **Japanese colonial period in Korea** had found sanctuary in the Chinese Communist–occupied areas,

and the Chinese Communist leadership had supported political and armed groups of Korean resistance fighters in northern China during the war against Japan (1937–1945) and had taken Korean soldiers into its armies fighting the Nationalist Chinese in **Northeast China** after the end of that war. The Chinese Communists, however, achieved political power only in 1949, when the **People's Republic of China** (PRC) was established on 1 October. From 1945 to 1948, the northern half of Korea was administered by a Soviet army of occupation, which introduced the North Koreans to Soviet political and economic models. The Chinese and North Korean Communists nonetheless recognized each other's new governments and by August 1950 had exchanged ambassadors.

The PRC had foreknowledge in 1950 of North Korea's hopes to unify the peninsula by force, though it is unlikely it urged the North down such a path, well aware that conflict in Korea might have adverse repercussions for itself. At the same time, it started to make tentative preparations by regrouping its forces in the northeast. China may have hoped that the **Korean War**, which broke out on 25 June 1950, would be a wholly Korean affair or could be contained within the peninsula; but when troops of the **United Nations Command**, led by U.S. forces, advanced as far as the **Yalu River**, the frontier between China and North Korea, China believed that its interests were threatened and committed the **Chinese People's Volunteers** on the North Korean side. It also publicly supported the North, negotiated with the Soviet Union for more support for the Chinese war effort, and in 1952 promised postwar aid to North Korea. The PRC played an important diplomatic role, together with the Soviet Union, in finally securing the compromises that made an **armistice** possible in 1953. There is little doubt that China saved North Korea.

After the war, Chinese troops remained in the North until 1958. They assisted in the economic rehabilitation of the country, but also may have been intended, by the PRC, to act as a restraint on any North Korean thoughts of launching a new invasion of the South. Indeed, China has generally warned the North against such military adventures. It was prepared, however, to sign a mutual defense treaty with North Korea in 1961, in balance with one agreed on between North Korea and the Soviet Union.

From the late 1950s until the early 1990s, the PRC, in its dealings with North Korea, was locked in a triangular relationship with the Soviet Union and the North, as the North Korean leader **Kim Il Sung** pursued a policy of independence in domestic and foreign affairs. This encouraged him to indulge in a certain amount of playing his two main allies against each other, particularly during the **Sino-Soviet dispute**, which dragged on from the late 1950s into the 1980s, and during China's Cultural Revolution (1966–1976), when even Kim himself came under criticism as a revisionist. Kim's commitment to *juche* principles of self-reliance led him to downplay the extent of foreign aid and the "friendship" prices in trade that North Korea benefited from at the hands of both the Soviet Union and the PRC. North Korea's greatest needs were for loan credits, new weapons technology, nuclear power technology, and help in developing heavy industry and the country's infrastructure. The Soviet Union was for long able to provide a greater share of such goods, including nuclear technology, than the PRC could. By the late 1980s, however, as the Soviet Union embarked on economic and political reforms, and in 1991 finally collapsed, the support it had been giving North Korea was increasingly replaced by demands for repayment of loans and for trade at market prices. The PRC, which had been liberalizing its economy since the late 1970s, likewise took a sterner line with the North. Nonetheless, with North Korea's economy shrinking and its people facing food shortages, it is now China that appears ready to continue supplying it with loans, food, and oil.

The PRC, indeed, may judge that it is not in its interests to see North Korea destabilized. It now has a flourishing relationship with South Korea, after a period of rapprochement followed by the establishment of diplomatic relations between the two countries in 1992, but may welcome a buffer state between itself and a country still so committed to U.S. military support. China's vision is now much wider than North Korea's. In 1971, it was already seeking a normal relationship with the United States and by 1978 had entered into diplomatic relations with the United States, had signed a peace accord with its former enemy Japan, and had abrogated the Sino-Soviet friendship treaty. Regional security in east Asia is now an important issue for China, and the Korea Peninsula is viewed in that light.

See also: North Korean Nuclear Program; People's Republic of China Relations with South Korea; Soviet/Russian Relations with North Korea; Zhou Enlai.

References: Hoare 1997; Hwang 1993; Kim 1981; Kwak, Patterson, and Olsen 1983.

PEOPLE'S REPUBLIC OF CHINA RELATIONS WITH SOUTH KOREA

From the moment of the establishment of the **People's Republic of China** (PRC) on 1 October 1949, the Republic of Korea (ROK) (South Korea), itself only a year old, viewed its new neighbor with suspicion. This was partly the traditional Korean fear of a strong government in China because such governments had in the past often taken an active interest in Korean affairs; but it was made worse by the fact that the PRC was a Communist state. Given their respective ideological stands, it was not surprising that the two sides had no dealings with each other until their armed forces met on the battlefield from late October 1950 onward. After the end of the **Korean War** in July 1953, the South Koreans continued to regard the PRC as an enemy, a view confirmed by the PRC's behavior at the 1954 **Geneva Conference.** Only when South Korean President **Park Chung Hee** announced in 1973 that South Korea would no longer oppose links with "nonhostile" Communist states did low-level contacts between the ROK and the PRC begin. At first, such contacts were very limited. Substantive links were largely confined to sporting groups, together with the occasional cultural visit. Trade links were also established, but these were restricted by the Chinese in the mid-1980s because of alleged South Korean trade relations with Cambodia and North Vietnam. Perhaps more significant in the longer term was the PRC's willingness to let ethnic Chinese-Koreans from the Korean autonomous areas in **Northeast China** visit South Korea, a practice that began in the early 1980s.

By the end of the 1980s, PRC–South Korean trade was developing to mutual satisfaction. Growing evidence of this was to be seen in Chinese cities, where South Korean goods were freely on sale, and South Korean companies seemed to find little difficulty in advertising their products. A further clear sign of the PRC's willingness to develop links with South Korea

came in 1986, when PRC athletes attended the Asian Games held in the South Korean capital, **Seoul.** Two years later, the Chinese attended the 1988 Seoul Olympics. The North Koreans were unhappy at these developments, but their protests were ignored. Finally, in 1992, the PRC and South Korea established diplomatic relations at ambassadorial level. North Korea remained unhappy but was powerless to prevent this development. Since then, relations have been marked by a high degree of cordiality, frequent diplomatic exchanges, and good trade relations.

See also: Hwang Jang-yop; *Nordpolitik*/Northern Policy; People's Republic of China Relations with North Korea.

Reference: Lee 1996; Sanford 1990.

PHILIPPINES FORCES IN THE KOREAN WAR

On 19 September 1950, a medium Sherman tank company and the 10th Battalion Combat Team (BCT) (Motorized) of the Philippines armed forces joined the **United Nations Command** in Korea. The 10th Battalion was succeeded by four others before the last one returned in May 1955. These units were attached largely on support duties to various divisions of the U.S. ground forces and also briefly to British and Canadian brigades.

After helping to clear Communist guerrillas in southern Korea, the 10th BCT participated in action against the fifth Chinese offensive, launched in April 1951 in the **Imjin River** area. Their tanks attempted unsuccessfully to relieve the besieged British "Glosters" battalion. Thereafter, Filipino troops were active in the central sector of Korea, and various citations were won.

A total of 7,420 men served with the Filipino units. Casualties were 112 dead, 299 wounded, 16 missing in action, and 41 prisoners of war, who were all repatriated.

See also: Korean War (1950–1953); United Kingdom and Korea; United States Forces in the Korean War.

References: History: I, 1972 and VI, 1977; Summers 1990; Thomas, Abbott, and Chappell 1986.

PLA

See **People's Liberation Army (PLA).**

POLAND

See **Neutral Nations Supervisory Commission.**

POLITICAL PRISONERS

The concept of political offense flows from the continuing struggle for legitimacy and authority between North and South Korea and the determination of both regimes to maintain the cooperation of their citizens.

South Korean publications detail an elaborate system of political class divisions within North Korean society, based often on family background or affiliation during the period of Japanese colonization and the **Korean War** and therefore embedded in the formation and history of the North Korean state. This system is said to radiate from a core around the leader and his family out through a large group comprising almost half the population to a rejected class of "national enemies." North Korea does not reveal much about these classifications to outsiders; however, such categorization of the population into reliable and unreliable elements has also been the policy with its two main Communist allies, the former Soviet Union and China. Of greatest significance has been **Kim Il Sung**'s demand for loyalty to himself and his family, such loyalty becoming the touchstone of political acceptability.

The North Korean security system is known to be extensive. It carries out rigorous investigation of those suspected of being a threat to the state and the political order and may have them sentenced to long or indefinite terms in prison camps under harsh conditions. Those eventually released remain under surveillance. In spring 1995, an Amnesty International delegation was told that only 240 political prisoners were held, but defectors' reports suggest that numbers are far greater. Early in 1999, South Korean sources, quoting international organizations, gave an estimate of 200,000 political prisoners detained in about ten camps in North Korea.

Until President-elect **Kim Dae Jung** undertook in February 1998 to seek the eventual release of the South's "prisoners of conscience," said to number approximately 650, successive South Korean governments had denied the existence of political prisoners. Those imprisoned under succeeding versions of the **National Security Law** were charged with aiding the North or with disrupting national and social harmony. Amnesties in late 1987 and early 1988 sanctioned the release of many detained, some since the late 1960s, for acts of political dis-

sent, but left approximately 200 still imprisoned. Those released may be subject to surveillance under the 1989 Social Surveillance Law.

In a special category are a small group of "unconverted prisoners," generally former North Korean soldiers captured during the Korean War, often when isolated in guerrilla bases in the South. Other prisoners were later caught as spies or charged with pro-Communist activities. Their refusal to admit to or renounce their Communist allegiance has earned them long prison sentences, sometimes broken by short periods of freedom. Many were finally released in amnesties between 1988 and 1995, but remain under surveillance. One of them, Ri In Mo, was repatriated in March 1993 following North-South negotiations, and since then the North has pressed for the return of others. Kim Dae Jung's government in July 1998 announced an end to the policy of "conversion" as a prerequisite for release, but insisted in its place on a pledge to abide by the law. An amnesty of 7,700 people in August 1998 from varying types of sentences did not include 17 long-term Communist prisoners who refused to give such a pledge. These 17, however, were released in February 1999 without having to pledge acceptance of the law, as part of an amnesty of around 8,000 offenders. Among the 17 was Woo Yong-gak, an "unconverted prisoner," who spent 41 years in jail.

Organizations agitating for the return of political prisoners to their respective homelands are now actively using the media, including the **Internet**, to push their cause. A small international gathering was held in Paris in June 1998 to campaign for the repatriation of three former prisoners to North Korea. North Korea, commenting on 23 February 1999 on the South Korean government's release of the 17 long-term Communist prisoners, called for their return to their native places, but South Korea has rejected an "unconditional return" and may press in exchange for the release by North Korea of South Korean **prisoners of war** it is still thought to hold.

References: Amnesty International 1989, 1995; *Newsreview*, 7 February 1998, 11 July 1998, 1 August 1998, 6 February 1999; *Pyongyang Times*, 6 and 27 December 1997; Ri 1997; Scalapino and Lee 1972; *White Paper* 1997.

PONGAM ISLAND REVOLT (1952)

Pongam Island, a small island not far from Koje Island, housed 9,000 civilian internees (prisoners claiming South Korean residence who had been captured by North Korean troops, impressed into the North Korean army, then taken prisoner by forces of the **United Nations Command** [UNC]) during the **Korean War**. Some had been transferred there in February 1952 after rioting in the **Koje Island prisoner of war camp**. The internees' increasing defiance of their South Korean guards and the U.S. administrators of the camp culminated in revolt in December 1952, when approximately 3,600 inmates refused orders to cease military drill. The guards opened fire, killing more than 85 prisoners and seriously injuring 113. Both the Communists and the International Committee of the Red Cross protested to the UNC over the severity of the measures taken to restore order.

See also: Prisoners of War.
Reference: Hermes 1966.

PORK CHOP HILL, BATTLES OF (1951–1953)

Pork Chop Hill was the name given to one of the many hills in the east-central part of Korea, some 70 miles (113 kilometers) from Seoul, which saw sporadic fighting during the long **armistice** negotiations from July 1951 to July 1953. It was linked to "Old Baldy," another hill, where **Chinese People's Volunteers** attacked Thai forces in November 1952. During March–April 1953, it was the scene of heavy fighting involving Colombian and U.S. forces. To avoid excessive casualties, the U.S. Eighth Army commander, General **Maxwell Taylor**, abandoned Old Baldy, although the U.S. 7th Division held Pork Chop Hill. On 11 July 1953, following another Chinese attack, Taylor ordered a withdrawal from Pork Chop Hill. The armistice, signed on 27 July, left the hill partly in the **Demilitarized Zone** and partly in North Korea. The dilemma of "fighting while talking" and holding hills of little military value has been examined in novels, and in at least one film, *Pork Chop Hill*, starring Gregory Peck, which appeared in 1959.

See also: Bloody and Heartbreak Ridges, Battles of (1951); Colombian Forces in the Korean War.
References: Hermes 1966; Marshall 1956.

POTSDAM CONFERENCE (1945)

Following the defeat of Germany in May 1945, U.S. President **Harry S Truman**, British Prime Minister **Winston Churchill** (later replaced by **Clement Attlee**), and Soviet Premier **Joseph Stalin** met in the Berlin suburb of Potsdam in July 1945 to discuss Allied policy toward Germany and the prosecution of the war against Japan. On 26 July they issued the Potsdam Declaration. This reaffirmed that the terms of the Cairo Declaration, agreed on at the 1943 **Cairo Conference**, "shall be carried out" and repeated the call for the unconditional surrender of Japan (which did not accept defeat until 15 August 1945).

PRC

See **People's Republic of China (PRC)**.

PRESS CORRESPONDENTS IN THE KOREAN WAR

The North Korean invasion of South Korea on 25 June 1950 brought an immediate response from the Western media. The small foreign press corps already in **Seoul** was swiftly joined by four U.S. press correspondents who had been assigned to Tokyo to cover developments in U.S.-occupied Japan and the Pacific region. They arrived in Seoul on 27 June in time to flee south from the city as it fell to the North Koreans. They and other correspondents joining them accompanied the retreating South Korean government and witnessed the first encounters between North Korean troops and the newly arrived U.S. contingents forming the spearhead of the **United Nations** (UN) resistance to the North Koreans.

By August 1950, 270 correspondents from nineteen countries were in South Korea and distinguished by their green shoulder flashes. The U.S. press formed the biggest single group, but British, Australian, and French correspondents, among others, were in evidence. The majority of correspondents were reporting for newspapers and for news agencies such as Reuters, Associated Press (AP), and United Press. Only a few represented radio and television services, such as the British Broadcasting Corporation (BBC) and the Columbia Broadcasting System (CBS), or film news services, such as Pathé. Television news was then in its infancy. The U.S. magazine *Life* and the British *Picture Post* (now

Two Western press correspondents, Alfred van Sprang from Holland (second from left) and Allain de Prelle from Belgium (fourth from left), interview Ms. Chang (center), who served as an interpreter at the armistice talks at Kaesong, 18 July 1951. (Imperial War Museum MH 31945)

defunct) sent photographers. Most of the press corps reported on events as they happened, but a small group of front-line correspondents accompanied UN detachments as they engaged with the enemy. Many of them went armed. Some of these front-line correspondents became casualties. Eighteen were killed in the course of the war; approximately half of these were said to have perished through "friendly" bombing. Some were wounded. At least three correspondents were captured by the North Koreans: Frank Noel, an AP photographer, who was detained in a **prisoner of war** camp; and Philip Deane, correspondent for the London *Observer*, and Maurice Chanteloup, the Seoul correspondent for Agence France Presse, both of whom were held with other **foreign civilian detainees** in the far north of the peninsula. Both men were invited to cooperate in broadcasting on behalf of their captors, and Deane was subjected to interrogation and torture.

The first year of the Korean War and particular-

ly the first six months saw the greatest action. Consequently, there was much to report. Communications out of Korea were often poor, with stories having to be routed via Tokyo. Chinese intervention, which had become apparent by the end of November 1950, suggested, however, that the fighting might be prolonged, and by mid-1951, when stalemate set in, many correspondents appear to have moved on from Korea. The opening of **armistice** talks on 10 July 1951 brought new interest, but the negotiations dragged on for a further two years. During that period and, indeed, throughout the various stages of the war, the **United Nations Command** (UNC) was at dispute with sections of the press corps in Korea. Military provision of facilities for correspondents, as at the **Inch'on landing**, was regarded as poor. Censorship was a more enduring problem.

Some of the accounts sent back to the United States of the first engagements between North Korean and U.S. forces spoke of a chaotic situation and demoralized U.S. soldiers. Subsequent reports expressed disquiet or even disgust over South Korean police behavior and the treatment of prisoners. In the first months of the war, a voluntary code of reporting was in operation that initially demanded protection of military secrecy and then forbade criticism of UNC commanders or of UNC conduct on the battlefield. In the absence of censorship, but also of military briefings, correspondents had to draw on their own evidence. The frankness of some reporting angered the UNC, particularly its supreme commander, General **Douglas MacArthur**, who threatened to suspend offenders. (MacArthur himself preferred to deal with a few selected journalists and was ready to use chosen press channels during 1950–1951 to promulgate his own points of view.) Eventually, in December 1950, correspondents were placed under full military censorship and in January 1951 under military jurisdiction, with its implication of sanctions against reporters who did not support the UNC effort.

The handling of the press at sessions of the armistice negotiations, held first at **Kaesong** (10 July–22 August 1951), then at **P'anmunjom** (25 October 1951–27 July 1953), brought its difficulties. The third session, scheduled for 12 July, was delayed by Communist objections over the presence of UNC correspondents. They were thereafter allowed to attend, but were not permitted in the conference room and were required to accept official UNC briefings on the progress of the talks. They attempted to circumvent this restriction by briefing themselves through talking to the two Western journalists attached to the North Korean/Chinese side, **Wilfrid Burchett** and **Alan Winnington**, who claimed to have fuller access to the Communist negotiators. In February 1952, General **Matthew Ridgway** tried unsuccessfully to break such fraternization. Eventually the UNC side improved the extent of its briefing.

On a wider scale, journalists critical of UNC decisions and of South Korean conduct found that their reports were not always used. Frustrated by such restrictions and sometimes disturbed by the incoherence and cruelty of what they had seen, several of them, such as **Marguerite Higgins** (*New York Herald Tribune*), Reginald Thompson (London *Daily Telegraph*), and René Cutforth (BBC),

described their experiences and reactions in books published in 1951 and 1952 that provide some of the most vivid accounts of the fighting and its effects on combatants. Edward R. Murrow (CBS) and **James Cameron** (*Picture Post*) wrote later of their experiences.

Not so much is known in the West about Communist reporting of the Korean War. Journalists and writers followed the North Korean troops south after 25 June to report on the establishment of what was to be a new regime and to support propaganda efforts. The **New China News Agency** reported to its Chinese readers and listeners. Correspondents from the **Union of Soviet Socialist Republics** and from Communist bloc countries such as Hungary and Poland also contributed reports, particularly on such issues as **bacteriological warfare**.

The memorial to the eighteen UNC correspondents killed in the course of the war was dedicated in April 1977 at Munsan, from which point many journalists had traveled regularly by train to sessions of the armistice negotiations.

See also: Stone, Isidor Feinstein; Television and the Korean War.

References: Cameron 1967, 1974; Cutforth 1952; Deane 1953, 1976; Halliday and Cumings 1988; Hermes 1966; Higgins 1951; Knightley 1982; Schnabel 1972; Stone 1952; Thompson 1951, Winnington 1986.

PRINCESS PATRICIA'S CANADIAN LIGHT INFANTRY

See **Canadian Forces in the Korean War.**

PRISONERS OF WAR

Neither side appears to have made provision for the large numbers of prisoners captured in the early months of fighting. The North, aiming at a quick pacification of the South when it launched its initial attack in June 1950, had not anticipated the speed of the **United Nations** (UN) response and did not expect to have to cope with non-Korean belligerents. The rapidity of the **United Nations Command** (UNC) counterattack after the **Inch'on landing** and the breakout from the **Pusan Perimeter** in September 1950 left many North Korean troops stranded in the South. Some joined up with guerrilla groups; others were captured. The entry of the

Chinese People's Volunteers (CPV) into the war during October–November 1950 on the North Korean side added to the volume of potential prisoners. From September 1950, the United States had assumed control of all prisoners on behalf of the UNC. By the beginning of 1951, the U.S. military had responsibility for a total of 137,000 prisoners of war (POWs), housed initially in the **Pusan** area, but from January 1951 mainly housed on **Koje Island**, off the southeast coast of Korea. The North Koreans generally dealt with those South Koreans they captured by absorbing them into their own armed forces or by releasing them after "reeducation." They moved their non-Korean prisoners, fewer in number, who included military and civilian detainees, together with some South Koreans, to camps in the far north of the peninsula.

The issue of release of prisoners was first raised in December 1951 in the **armistice** talks and led to an agreement to exchange information and lists of names. The UNC had by then reclassified its detainees into POWs, numbering approximately 132,000, and civilian internees, approximately 37,000 in number. Among the POWs were many Chinese and North Korean soldiers, but also men claiming South Korean residence. The latter comprised civilian volunteers in the **North Korean People's Army** (NKPA), members of the South Korean army drafted on capture into the NKPA, and other stray South Korean troops. The group classified as civilian internees included South Korean civilians conscripted into the NKPA and those termed "innocent bystanders." By January 1952, the two sides had agreed to exchange POWs, but straightaway diverged on the basis on which **repatriation of prisoners** should take place. The North Koreans and Chinese favored the immediate release and repatriation of prisoners in an "all-for-all" exchange, basing themselves on article 118 of the **Geneva Convention** of 1949. The United States, although initially acknowledging the intention of this article, quickly came to prefer the principle of voluntary or nonforcible repatriation on a "one-for-one" basis. In April 1952, in an attempt to move things forward, the UNC proposed that all its detainees should be screened to ascertain their choice of country of repatriation; the Communist side gave tacit acceptance. However, the results—of 170,000 POWs and civilian internees, only some 70,000 had indicated that they would consent to be repatriated to the Communist side—were unacceptable to the North Koreans and Chinese, and discussions stalled. The United States put pressure on the Communists through heavy bombing raids on the North and even hinted at the use of atomic weapons. Eventually, by March 1953, both sides had agreed to the formation of a **neutral nations commission** to arrange the eventual disposal of those declining repatriation. The exchange of sick and injured prisoners and civilian internees, 6,670 from UNC camps and 684 from North Korean/Chinese camps, was achieved in Operation **Little Switch** in April 1953. On 8 June 1953, a joint agreement on the repatriation of POWs was arrived at ahead of the conclusion of the armistice. President **Syngman Rhee** of South Korea, angered by the prospect of Korean POWs being traded in repatriation exchanges, organized the release on 18 June 1953, with the connivance of South Korean guards, of 25,000–27,000 Korean detainees who had declared against repatriation. Despite this rebuff, the agreement of 8 June 1953 and the signing of the armistice went ahead, and in Operation **Big Switch,** between 5 August and 6 September 1953, 75,823 POWs and civilian internees from the UNC camps and 12,773 POWs from North Korean camps, all of whom had accepted repatriation, were exchanged through **P'anmunjom**.

Conditions in the UNC Camps

The situation in the UNC camps, in particular those on Koje Island, soon became tense. The compounds were crowded, food and medical attention were poor, and the U.S. and South Korean guards, stretched to capacity, were often brutal. By the end of December 1951, 6,600 prisoners in UNC hands had died. The Koje compounds became political flash points, largely beyond the control of UNC administrators, as both sides, right and left, carried on their struggle through their fellow detainees. North Korean party members were even said to have allowed themselves to be captured in order to infiltrate the camps. The ideological struggle between communism and the "free world", moreover, involved two Koreas and two Chinas (MacDonald 1986: 138). The CPV had incorporated large numbers of soldiers who, in the Chinese civil war (1946–1949), had fought for the Nationalist government. To implement their educational and training programs in the Chinese POW camps, the UNC administration recruited Chinese personnel from Taiwan, some of whom were probably sent as political agitators in the Nationalist cause. Korean and Chinese political activists of both right and left formed tight cores of resistance, in particular on the issues of screening and repatriation, and used violence to the point of murder to coerce fellow prisoners into following their lead. Despite confinement, camp leaders were able to communicate with their respective headquarters: the North Koreans through a network of refugees and guerrilla fighters, the pro–Nationalist Chinese through their instructors, and the pro–South Korean camps through contacts with the South Korean government.

Such tensions formed the background to the negotiations on POW exchanges at the armistice talks. Problems in the UNC camps culminated in riots in the Koje Island prisoner of war camp in May 1952, when the camp commandant, General Dodd, was held hostage for several days by camp inmates. The fatalities among POWs incurred in subduing the protest were seized upon by Communist propaganda as evidence of UNC brutality.

Conditions in the North Korean/Chinese Camps
The first UNC prisoners generally suffered most as they were sent north in the autumn and winter of 1950–1951 by their North Korean captors, sometimes just ahead of the UNC advance into the North, and most deaths occurred during that period. North Korean handling of UNC POWs was haphazard and often brutal. During April–May 1951, the Chinese took over the running of camps. Prisoners were separated by race, nationality, and rank and exposed to harsh and restrictive living conditions and persistent ideological reeducation and self-criticism sessions. The Chinese in particular aimed to secure confessions of UNC guilt as warmongers and in alleged bacteriological warfare. Recalcitrants and escapees were punished with interrogation, torture, solitary confinement, and loss of privileges. UNC bombing raids added to the hazards. Of a total of approximately 7,140 U.S. prisoners taken, approximately 2,700 died. Losses

among other UNC contingents were less. The trials of camp life have been described by several former prisoners (Davies 1954; Farrar-Hockley 1954; Pelser and Pelser 1984).

Atrocities were recorded against POWs of both sides. Kim Chong-won, a South Korean army officer with a reputation for brutality, had 50 North Korean POWs beheaded in August 1950. Approximately 100 U.S. prisoners held outside P'yongyang were shot by the North Koreans in reprisal as UNC troops advanced on the city in mid-October 1950.

In late 1998, information began to emerge in South Korea on the continued survival of South Korean POWs in North Korean camps. Defectors arriving in the South from North Korea are said to have confirmed the existence of such prisoners. The South Korean ministry of defense in February 1999 estimated their number at 233. There is speculation in the South that the government may seek to negotiate with the North for an exchange of these POWs for recently released "unconverted" prisoners.

See also: Burchett, Wilfrid; Foreign Civilian Detainees in the Korean War; Korean Civilian Prisoners in the Korean War; Political Prisoners; Pongam Island Revolt (1952); Winnington, Alan.

References: Davies 1954; Farrar-Hockley 1954; Foot 1990; Halliday and Cumings 1988; Hermes 1966; MacDonald 1986; Matray 1991; Pelser and Pelser 1984.

PROPAGANDA WARFARE

Modern techniques of propaganda were developed in the Korean War on the United Nations Command (UNC) side from those deployed in World War II psychological warfare. From the outset, the UNC made use of leaflets, loudspeakers (often mounted on aircraft or brought up close to combat areas), and radio broadcasts to offer reassurance of support, to cast doubt in enemy soldiers' minds over their leaders' honesty and competence, and to encourage enemy troops to surrender. Both soldiers and civilians were targeted, and leaflets and broadcasts were also deployed against guerrilla fighters in the Chiri Mountains. The North Korean/Chinese command made leaflet drops and skillfully exploited the prisoners of war (POW) issue to highlight bad conditions in the UNC camps. They broadcast radio confessions from captured

UNC soldiers and dropped leaflets allegedly signed by such POWs.

In the post–Korean War era, more indirect and sustained efforts have been required, although leaflet drops from balloons have continued over "enemy" territory. (North Korean slogans and photographs of **Kim Il Sung** and later **Kim Jong Il** have regularly been picked up in **Seoul**.) In both North and South Korea, these activities form only a small part of a massive propaganda effort, directed primarily at the citizens of the rival state, but also intended to reinforce loyalty within each state to the government and to rally international support. The tone of this propaganda war has at times been crude and abusive, with the South denouncing the North as a brutal and illegal regime and the North describing the South as a puppet of the United States trampling on popular rights.

In the North, propaganda in the sense of disseminating doctrine has been an essential tool for the ruling **Korean Workers' Party**. Press, radio, television, and educational and cultural activities are all under party control and are required to promote acceptable material and reject unsuitable subject matter to the point, it is claimed, that all radio and television sets are fixed to receive domestic channels only. In the first two decades after the Korean War, economic and industrial advances in the North meant that it had achievements of which to boast. The world Communist movement took a sympathetic view of North Korea's successes, and for a while the North's propaganda effort paid off in terms of a thriving society at home and of a measure of international prestige. A clandestine "South Korea Liberation Radio," apparently based in North Korea, began broadcasting in March 1967 with the aim of provoking antigovernment sentiment in South Korea. In recent years, however, political rigidity, economic failure, and the collapse of international Communist support have left the North stranded and its propaganda output increasingly unconvincing.

Under the authoritarian regimes of South Korean Presidents **Park Chung Hee** and **Chun Doo Hwan**, fear of North Korean attack and subversion was strong (understandably so, in view of the North's attempts at infiltration and assassination). Official views on the need for vigilance against the Communist threat led to crude denunciations of the North Korean regime, even in government-sponsored publications. South Korea's propaganda efforts have become less strident in recent years as the economy has, at least until recently, flourished and the country has grown in international stature, by contrast with the North's isolation. Pressure on the North still continues, nonetheless: in March 1997, Radio Free Asia, a U.S. government–sponsored radio station directed largely toward Asia, started broadcasting in Korean to the North. In South Korea, however, under President **Kim Dae Jung**'s "sunshine" policy of overtures to the North, anti-North propaganda has become more nuanced.
Reference: Pease 1992.

PROSTITUTION
See **United States Military Presence in South Korea since 1953.**

PRO-UNIFICATION ACTIVITIES
Frustration at the lack of progress in official discussions on reunification prompted South Korean dissident groups in the late 1980s to propose alternative approaches. In the course of 1989, members of left-wing movements endeavored to organize pan-national conferences with participation from North and South or to attend meetings to which they had been invited by the North. On several occasions, they marched on **P'anmunjom** in the **Demilitarized Zone** (DMZ) with the intention of making contact with North Korean colleagues. Such actions were in contravention of the South Korean **National Security Law**, which forbids unauthorized contact with the North, and the marchers were turned back short of the DMZ. Individual South Koreans have also from 1988 made unauthorized visits to North Korea in support of reunification.
See also: Unofficial Contacts between North and South Koreans.
References: Amnesty International 1989; Macdonald 1996.

PUEBLO, USS (1968)
On 23 January 1968, the USS *Pueblo*, a U.S. information-gathering ship equipped to receive North Korean electronic and radio signals, was seized off the east coast of North Korea by North Korean patrol boats, assisted by fighter aircraft, and taken to

the northern port of **Wonsan**. When the ship attempted to escape, the North Koreans opened fire, killing one of the crew of eighty-three and wounding three others. The surviving eighty-two (who included two civilian hydrographers) under their captain, Commander Lloyd Bucher, were detained until 23 December 1968. Confessions were obtained from them, and they appear to have been subjected to some mistreatment. Large-scale U.S. naval and air strength was deployed at the time, but no ground forces were mobilized. The crew was finally released only after lengthy negotiations in the **Military Armistice Commission** at **P'anmunjom** and the signing of a U.S. apology (immediately repudiated by the U.S. side) for the ship's intrusion into North Korean waters for the purposes of espionage. The North had claimed that the *Pueblo* was inside its 12-mile territorial waters limit; the United States asserted that the ship was in international waters.

The incident took its place in an escalation of North Korean aggression against the South and the United States—it followed the North Korean commando raid of 20 January 1968 on the **Blue House**—and against the background of the North Vietnamese Tet Offensive of 30–31 January 1968 against South Vietnamese and U.S. forces in the **Vietnam War**.

The *Pueblo* itself was never returned to the United States, but was kept on display in Wonsan harbor.

See also: North-South Boundaries.
References: Bermudez 1998; Bolger 1991; Bucher 1970.

PUNCHBOWL

The Punchbowl was the name given during the **Korean War** to a circular valley, probably in origin a volcanic crater, some 20 miles (32 kilometers) northeast of the Hwachon Reservoir, which supplied hydroelectric power and drinking water for the South Korean capital, **Seoul**. In 1951, it was held by North Korean forces, who could observe and fire upon **United Nations Command** (UNC) forces to the south. UNC forces mounted attacks on it and eventually succeeded in clearing it of North Korean forces.

The Punchbowl lay to the west of **Bloody and Heartbreak Ridges** and was closely associated with the fighting there. It remained in UNC hands until the end of hostilities in 1953, when it became part of the demarcation line laid down in the **armistice** agreement.

References: Hermes 1966; Summers 1990.

PUSAN AND THE PUSAN PERIMETER

Pusan is the second largest city and the largest port in South Korea, with a population in the mid-1990s of just under four million. It sits at the head of a deep and sheltered bay at the mouth of the **Naktong River**. Pusan has long been a center of foreign trade. From the seventeenth century onward, it was the site of a Japanese trading post and was one of the first treaty ports opened to trade in the nineteenth century. In the **Japanese colonial period in Korea**, it developed as a modern port with links to Japan and China and as a major rail terminus.

At the end of World War II, many repatriated Koreans settled first in Pusan. After the beginning of the **Korean War** in June 1950, its population was further swelled by refugees from the fighting. From 18 August 1950 to 15 August 1953—broken only by a brief period (27 October 1950–4 January 1951) when President **Syngman Rhee** returned to **Seoul** to reclaim the temporarily liberated **Capitol Building**—it was the temporary capital of South Korea and the seat of the South Korean government. It was also, from 1 August to 16 September 1950, the center of the area known as the Pusan Perimeter, or the Naktong Perimeter. This perimeter marked the furthermost advance south of the North Korean forces and was the scene of heavy fighting until the **United Nations** (UN) forces broke out, following the **Inch'on landing**, and began to advance north on 16 September 1950.

For the remainder of the war, Pusan was the main port for supplies and reinforcements. On its then southeastern outskirts, but now absorbed by the growing city, is the **United Nations Cemetery**, which was established during the Korean War and where many of those who died fighting for the UN cause are buried. The cemetery is still managed by representatives of the sixteen UN nations who sent forces to Korea.

See also: Taegu.
References: Field 1962; Hoyt 1984; Pusan History Compilation Committee 1993.

P'yongyang in the aftermath of U.S. bombing raids during the Korean War. (AP/Wide World Photos)

P'YONGYANG

P'yongyang has been the capital of the Democratic People's Republic of Korea (North Korea) since 1948. At the end of the twentieth century, it is the principal city of North Korea, with a population estimated at some two million. It is a city with long historical links, stretching back to the mythical origins of the Korean people. From A.D. 427 to 668, it was the capital of the kingdom of Koguryo, one of the three kingdoms within the Korea Peninsula until Silla overcame it in 668. Thereafter, its importance declined until the Choson period (1392–1910), when it was designated the Western Capital. It was on the Taedong River at P'yongyang in 1866 that the U.S. merchant ship *General Sherman* was trapped and burnt by Koreans in the first U.S.-Korean clash. It was the scene of heavy fighting during the Sino-Japanese war (1894–1895). In the **Japanese colonial period in Korea** (1910–1945), it was a major

center of opposition to Japanese rule and also a center for Christianity.

In 1945, it became both the de facto capital of the Soviet-controlled northern zone of Korea and the temporary capital of North Korea. It suffered badly in the **Korean War**, because of heavy fighting during the **United Nations** forces' advance in September 1950 (they captured the city on 19 October 1950) and their retreat south in December 1950. It was also heavily bombed all through the war, so that there was little left standing in 1953. After the war, it was rebuilt in monumental style with tall buildings and wide boulevards. Many monuments to the revolutionary exploits of **Kim Il Sung** have been erected in the city, including the Tower of the *Juche* Idea, the Arch of Triumph, and the Chollima (Thousand League Horse) Statue. Kim's birthplace at Man'gyongdae, some 7.5 miles (12 kilometers) from the center of P'yongyang, is a place of pilgrimage, as is his tomb at the former Mansu Palace, now the

Panoramic view of the center of modern P'yongyang. (Xinhua News Agency)

Mansu Mausoleum. North Koreans present P'yongyang as testimony to the benevolent leadership of Kim and of his son, **Kim Jong Il.** Outsiders tend to describe it as a tribute to both leaders' monomania.

Reference: Pang and Hwang 1991, 1997.

RAJIN-SONBONG DEVELOPMENT ZONE

The Rajin-Sonbong Development Zone, an area of 240 square miles (621 square kilometers) around the northeastern port of Rajin (or Najin), on the Korean side of the Tumen River that forms North Korea's borders with China and Russia, was established in the early 1990s as the site of a free trade zone. It has enjoyed only modest success, with a limited amount of investment, mainly from overseas Koreans. The North Korean project lies within two much larger ones, for a Tumen River economic zone, itself to be within a wider Tumen River area development program. This vast scheme has been sponsored by the United Nations Development Program. China, North Korea, South Korea, and Mongolia were involved from the start; Russia joined in later, but Japan, whose role would be that of investor, has not committed itself. Development costs have been projected at $30 billion over 15–20 years. North Korean anxieties over too easy access to its territory led it to suggest development of three separate zones within the region. Reservations over the high cost of the project and rival plans from China and Russia have added to the doubts, and the scheme has stalled.

Rajin, lying on the Soviet–North Korean border, was an important aerial target during the **Korean War.**

See also: Aerial Bombing; People's Republic of China Relations with North Korea; Soviet/Russian Relations with North Korea.
Reference: Marton, McGee, and Paterson 1995.

RANGOON BOMBING (1983)

On 9 October 1983, seventeen high-ranking officials of the South Korean government, including **Lee Bum Suk (2),** the minister of foreign affairs, were killed in a bomb explosion at the Aung San Mausoleum in Rangoon. The officials were accompanying President **Chun Doo Hwan** on a state visit to Burma. Chun himself escaped attack when the South Korean ambassador's car was mistaken for the president's and the explosive device detonated prematurely, killing those already assembled.

R

The capture of two North Koreans in Rangoon (a third was killed in a shoot-out with the Burmese police) confirmed the attempt on Chun's life as the work of North Korean agents. The three-member team, identified as members of the **North Korean People's Army,** had been brought to Rangoon in a North Korean freighter. They had been sheltered in a North Korean diplomatic house, from where they had planted devices at the mausoleum that they detonated on 9 October by remote control. The two surviving agents were tried by the Burmese authorities and sentenced to death.

The attack at a national monument caused outrage to the Burmese, who broke off diplomatic relations with North Korea and withdrew recognition from that state.
See also: North Korean Use of Terrorism.

RAR
See **Australian Forces in the Korean War.**

RAU, SIR BENEGAL NARSING (1887–1953)

The Indian lawyer and diplomat Sir Benegal Rau was born in 1887 in what is now Karnataka. After studying law at Madras University and the University of Cambridge, he joined the Indian Civil Service and achieved distinction as a lawyer. As a member of the Indian delegation to the **United Nations,** he was president of the Security Council in June 1950, when the **Korean War** broke out. He called the council into emergency session and supported the initial Security Council resolution of 25 June 1950 on Korea. Thereafter, he attempted both as Security Council president and subsequently as a member of the Korean War Cease-fire Committee to restrain the **United**

Nations Command's wish to take the war north of the **38th parallel**. Later, he tried to persuade the **Chinese People's Volunteers** not to cross the parallel. From 1952 until his death in November 1953, he was a judge of the Permanent Court of International Justice at the Hague.

RED CROSS NORTH-SOUTH TALKS

Red Cross organizations have functioned in the Democratic People's Republic of Korea (North Korea) and in the Republic of Korea (South Korea) since the earliest days of their existence. Although both have in theory been independent nongovernmental bodies, in practice in North Korea, where no organizations are independent of the party-government structure, the Red Cross has been effectively part of the government machine. The South Korean Red Cross has generally enjoyed more independence, although it too has been used to further state aims.

In 1971, following the emergence of the **Nixon Doctrine** and the improvement of relations between the **People's Republic of China** and the United States, the two Koreas began a series of talks under Red Cross auspices. The original suggestion that there should be Red Cross talks appears to have come from the South Korean side, but it was eagerly taken up by the North Korean Red Cross. In reality, both organizations were working on behalf of their respective governments. The talks were officially about arranging for reunions of divided families, but they quickly became a front for more political talks. There were four meetings in 1972, held alternately in the South Korean capital, **Seoul**, and the North Korean capital, **P'yongyang**.

As long as the parallel political dialogue, which began in 1972, was going well, so did the Red Cross talks. Once the political talks began to run into problems, so did the Red Cross talks. Only three full-scale meetings were held in 1973, then the North broke off the talks, ostensibly in protest at the alleged kidnapping in Japan of the South Korean opposition leader, **Kim Dae Jung**, by the (South) Korean Central Intelligence Agency (KCIA). Since the head of the South Korean side of the North-South Coordinating Committee was **Lee Hu Rak**, who the year before had been head of the KCIA

negotiators who had gone to P'yongyang, the North Korean position was not altogether without logic. Red Cross links were not broken entirely and continued in a series of "working-level meetings" until March 1978, though without any result. The North then broke off contact.

Attempts to revive the Red Cross contacts were not successful until 1985. Then, following North Korea's offer of flood relief goods, links between the two Red Cross societies were reopened. This led to the first-ever **family reunions** between North and South in September 1985. Again, however, the contacts fizzled out. Under South Korean President **Roh Tae Woo** there were suggestions from 1988 onward that Red Cross talks might be resumed, and the South Koreans made sure that the South Korean Red Cross was staffed at its highest levels by people with close government links. The North Koreans proved unwilling to cooperate. Since the mid-1990s, however, North Korea's food problems have led to new contacts between the two Red Cross organizations, and the South Korean Red Cross has arranged for the supply of food and fertilizers to North Korea.

See also: Red Cross Organization.
References: Koo and Han 1985; *Korea Annual*; Macdonald 1996.

RED CROSS ORGANIZATION

In common with many states, both North and South Korea have their national Red Cross societies, which are affiliated with the International Federation of the Red Cross and Red Crescent. The two Korean societies, in their dealings with each other, have acted generally within the framework of their respective governments' policies. In 1971, they took the lead in initiating cross-border talks, in the first instance to discuss families separated during the **Korean War**, and have since then remained in intermittent contact with each other. Their most recent negotiations, since the mid-1990s, have involved the supply of food and fertilizer to the North through the South Korean Red Cross. The South Korean society also participated in campaigns in the mid-1950s to register details on family members who had gone north and then in the mid-1970s and early 1980s to locate family members separated in the South. In November 1998, the head of the International Federation visited both North and

South Korea to discuss, among other topics, the issue of divided families.

The International Committee of the Red Cross (ICRC), founded in 1863 and based in Geneva, operates in time of war as an intermediary between opposing sides in locating **prisoners of war** (POWs) and in securing delivery of mail and other necessities to them. During the Korean War, the ICRC, though mistrusted by the North Koreans and Chinese, helped in the exchange of lists of POWs and, where it could, monitored conditions in the POW camps run by the **United Nations Command** and the North Korean/Chinese command.

The Red Cross movement grew out of the work of a Swiss humanitarian, Jean-Henri Dunant, who organized emergency relief for the wounded at the Battle of Solferino (northern Italy) in 1859. The first national societies appeared in 1864, in which year the movement in its first multilateral document drew up the first Geneva agreement on the care of those wounded in war.

See also: Family Reunions; Red Cross North-South Talks.
References: Encyclopedia Britannica. 1997; Segal 1993.

RED CROSS TALKS ON FAMILY REUNIONS
See **Family Reunions.**

REFUGEES
Official and unofficial accounts of the **Korean War** return repeatedly to the wretched spectacle of refugees uprooted as the fighting moved through the Korea Peninsula. Some of the most memorable photographs of the war show long columns of Koreans, dressed in their customary white cotton clothing, pushing their belongings on handcarts or struggling across country because they were often kept off the roads by military traffic. **United Nations Command** (UNC) soldiers had ambivalent feelings about them. Concern, especially for the many orphaned children, led to troops' befriending and feeding them when they could. At the same time, refugees were suspected of harboring North Korean infiltrators or of mounting surprise attacks on UNC soldiers. They were a fluid, constant element in the war. Their presence was generally not welcomed. They impeded military movement; might be used as cover by guerrilla fighters; imposed demands for food, shelter, and medical aid; and, more intangibly, must have seemed an image of despair and failure.

The wartime refugees followed an earlier wave of migrants south. Between 1945 and 1950, many people, especially those who felt themselves targeted by the new leftist regime in the North—landowners, Christians, intellectuals—or young men evading the draft, had come to the South, often in family groups. The often-quoted figure of 3.5 million is almost certainly too high, and estimates of 460,000–760,000 for these migrants seem more probable. Like those who came later, these refugees settled predominantly in the northern parts of South Korea or in the cities of **Seoul**, **Pusan**, and Inch'on.

Those uprooted by the Korean War in general moved from north to south. The North Korean initial invasion in June 1950 pushed many people, including the South Korean government, eventually to the southeast corner of the peninsula around **Pusan**. The UNC counterattack took the fighting momentarily to the far north; then the North Korean and Chinese armies recovered the terrain down to the **38th parallel**. The second big flight south came during November–December 1950 as UNC forces started to retreat before the new Communist advance. Many left **P'yongyang**; others from the northeast attempted to leave via east coast ports such as Hungnam and **Wonsan**. The South Korean position has always been that all these refugees were fleeing Communist rule. For some, especially those who feared reprisal on religious, political, or economic grounds, that was doubtless so, especially after the reestablishment of the Communist administration in the North. Others, however, probably left to escape the fierce UNC **aerial bombing** of North Korea. Fear of the Chinese may have been another factor.

Exact numbers are difficult to establish. Figures for refugees from the North range from one million to half that number—between 452,000 and 646,000. The lower figures seem more likely. The number of those moving from the South to the North has been put at 286,000, probably comprised in the main of conscripts, civilian detainees, and prisoners of war. The North would insist that many of these people left voluntarily in support of communism. Some of those accompanying the North Koreans in their retreat north in autumn 1950 may have done so

Refugees on the move, date and location unknown. (Imperial War Museum BF 166)

willingly. The term "refugee" is sufficiently imprecise to allow many interpretations.

See also: Family Reunions; Invasion and Counterinvasion (1950–1951).

References: Halliday and Cumings 1988; Kim 1988; Kwon 1977.

REPATRIATION OF PRISONERS OF WAR

Repatriation was the most contentious issue of the **armistice** negotiations that took place between July 1951 and July 1953 to end the **Korean War**. Although the **United Nations Command** (UNC) on one side and the North Korean/Chinese forces on the other had agreed in January 1952 to exchange prisoners, they immediately differed on the basis of repatriation. Neither China nor North Korea had signed the 1949 **Geneva Convention**, the international agreement governing the treatment of **prisoners of war** (POWs), but North Korea had signified its willingness in July 1950 to observe its requirements, and China gave a similar undertaking in July 1952. The United States, a signatory to the Convention, had not ratified it by June 1950, but likewise accepted its rec-

ommendations on POWs. Article 118 of the Convention called for the release and repatriation of prisoners of war "without delay after the cessation of hostilities." Initially, both the United States, which represented the UNC in the armistice talks, and the Communists accepted the principle of the return of all POWs to their respective sides. The Communists continued to insist on this until a late stage in the talks, arguing that a prisoner's army, not his place of residence, should determine his repatriation. The United States, however, moved by distaste for the ideology and practices of communism, fairly quickly came to favor the principle of voluntary, later nonforcible, repatriation, whereby a prisoner indicated the country he or she wished to be repatriated to. The North Korean/Chinese side maintained that voluntary repatriation conflicted with the intentions of article 118.

The problem was compounded by the presence among the UNC prisoners of war of two groups: those claiming South Korean residence, who had been captured by the North Koreans, impressed into the North Korean army, then recaptured by UNC forces; and members of the **Chinese People's Volunteers** (CPV) who had fought in the Nationalist armies during the Chinese civil war (1946–1949) and had been drafted after 1949 into the Communist Chinese forces. On top of the 132,000 detainees classified as prisoners of war were a further 37,000 accepted by both sides as civilian internees.

The choice for Korean POWs under voluntary repatriation was between North and South Korea; for the Chinese POWs, between the **People's Republic of China** and **Taiwan**. Such alternatives were repugnant to the North Korean/Chinese side. However, in April 1952, the Communists, encouraged by UNC estimates that, of the total of 132,000 POWs, approximately 116,000 might be willing to be exchanged, tacitly accepted a UNC proposal that UNC POWs and civilian internees be screened to determine their preferences for repatriation. The process was only partially successful. Intimidation in many of the UNC prison compounds, dominated by rightist and leftist political activists, distorted the validity of some of the screening. Seven North Korean pro-Communist compounds at **Koje Island prisoner of war camp** refused violently to cooperate. Nonetheless, the figures presented on 19 April 1952 to the North Korean/Chinese side indicated that, of a total of 170,000 POWs and civilian internees, only 70,000 had opted for repatriation. The Communists refused to accept this figure, so far short of the earlier estimate of 116,000. Rioting at the UNC prison camps during the spring and summer of 1952 and suspension of the armistice talks on 8 October 1952 further stalled discussions on repatriation.

On 17 November 1952, India presented a proposal to the United Nations General Assembly for a commission to supervise repatriation and to be composed of two UNC and two Communist nations, with an umpire. The commission's task would be to ensure that all prisoners understood their rights and that any still declining repatriation would be referred to the political conference proposed in the armistice agreement. Prisoners would be brought to the **Demilitarized Zone** around **P'anmunjom**. The Communist response, which included the Soviet Union, was wholly negative. Only in March 1953 did China, followed by North Korea, accept the idea. From then on, the process of repatriation acquired momentum.

In Operation **Little Switch**, sick and wounded POWs from both sides were exchanged between 20 and 26 April 1953. On 7 May, the North Korean/Chinese side proposed the formation of a **Neutral Nations Repatriation Commission** (NNRC) and nominated Sweden, Switzerland, Czechoslovakia, Poland, and India as members. The UNC eventually accepted this development of the earlier Indian proposal, with its implication that the Communist side had resigned itself to the concept of voluntary repatriation. Discussion focused on the treatment of those Koreans who had refused repatriation, on the time scale and scope of the process of explanation to prisoners of the choices before them, and on the final disposition of those declining repatriation.

The first issue was resolved dramatically when President **Syngman Rhee** on 18 June 1953 ordered the release of 25,000–27,000 Korean detainees who had declined repatriation; they were eventually inducted into the South Korean army. Arrangements for the NNRC and for the disposition of nonrepatriates were agreed to by both sides on 8 June 1953: the only armed force permitted to assist the NNRC was to be provided by India; the period for explanation was set at 90 days; and those still declining repatriation at the end of that time should be helped to move to a neutral nation. In Operation **Big Switch**, between 5 August and 6 September 1953, those accepting immediate repatriation were exchanged: 70,183 North Korean POWs and civilian internees and 5,640 Chinese POWs were released back into Communist hands; a total of 12,773 UNC POWs were returned to the UNC. (These and the following figures for POW repatriation are taken from Hermes 1966.) From 23 September to 23 December 1953, the process of interviewing nonrepatriates took place at P'anmunjom. Twenty-one U.S. soldiers and one British soldier (many of whom later returned home) and 325 Koreans from the UNC side chose to remain with the Communists; of the 22,604 nonrepatriates held by the UNC, a total of 628 returned to Communist hands, but 14,235 Chinese and 7,604 Koreans still declined repatriation. Early in 1954, the Chinese were sent to **Taiwan**, and the Koreans were released into the hands of the South Korean authorities. A total of eighty-six Chinese and Koreans elected to go to India.

Repatriation seems to have brought mixed comfort to those released. U.S. POWs, numbering just under 3,600, became the objects of much soul-searching in U.S. society on their return amid suspicions of collaboration with the enemy and fears that they had gone "soft." Some were court-martialed for misconduct. Those Chinese sent to Taiwan were generally retained in the Nationalist Chinese armed forces; the Korean nonrepatriates apparently underwent "reeducation." Communist Chinese–returned POWs, it seems, never regained the trust of the authorities, and returned North Korean POWs may have likewise suffered by being placed politically in the "unstable" class of society.

The South Korean writer, Choi In-hoon, who was much influenced by Western existentialist thought, used the central character of his novel *The Square* (1961) to comment on the futility of ideological doctrines and the bizarre nature of the conflict. The central character was a Korean who had defected from the South to the North, had been captured by the UNC, and had chosen finally to go to India.

See also: Committee for Assisting the Return of Displaced Civilians; Committee for Repatriation of Prisoners of War; Indian Custodial Force; Korean Civilian Prisoners in the Korean War; Neutral Nations Repatriation Commission.

References: Foot 1990; Halliday and Cumings 1988; Hermes 1966; MacDonald 1986; *White Paper on Human Rights in North Korea* 1997.

REPUBLIC OF KOREA (ROK) (SOUTH KOREA)
See Introduction.

REUNIFICATION
See **North Korean Proposals on Unification; South Korean Proposals on Unification**.

RHEE, SYNGMAN (1875–1965)
Syngman Rhee (Yi Song-man) was the first president of the Republic of Korea. Rhee was born at P'yongsan in Hwanghae Province (now in North Korea) into an aristocratic family that had links with the royal family. His family moved to **Seoul** while he was still a child, and Rhee was educated first in the Chinese classics and later at a missionary school. During this period, he became a Methodist and

remained so throughout his life. He was a founding member of the modernizing Independence Club, established in 1896, and in 1898 was sentenced to life imprisonment for his alleged part in a plot to overthrow the monarchy and found a republic. On his release in 1904, he went to the United States. There he studied at Princeton University, where Woodrow Wilson was president, and gained a Ph.D. in 1910. He returned briefly to Korea, by then under Japanese colonial rule, was arrested, and was forced to leave in 1912.

For the next 33 years he spent most of his time in Hawaii or the mainland United States. In 1919, he was selected by the Korean government in exile in Shanghai as president, a post he held until ousted by **Kim Ku** in 1931. Rhee spent his time trying to gather support for Korean independence, rather than taking an active part in the provisional government, and in the process, he became the best-known Korean in the United States, famed for his anti-Japanese sentiments. He therefore seemed a natural choice as a political leader when Korea was liberated in 1945. Through a mixture of adroit political maneuvering, police support, political assassinations, and U.S. support, he became the first president of the Republic of Korea in August 1948. He held the post, with much constitutional juggling, in further elections in 1952, 1956, and 1960. He was bitterly disappointed at the division of the peninsula in 1945 and firmly anti-Communist, but lack of resources prevented him from trying to reunify the peninsula on his terms.

The outbreak of the **Korean War** in 1950 caught him by surprise, and he fled with his government first to **Taejon**, then to **Taegu**, and finally to **Pusan**. He welcomed the **United Nations'** (UN's) intervention and pressed hard for the war to be extended across the **38th parallel** after the **Inch'on landing** in September 1950. After the Chinese intervention led to the eventual opening of **armistice** negotiations in July 1951, Rhee expressed his opposition, demanding that the UN forces should continue the war until the Communists were defeated. In the meantime, he used the war as a justification for continued domestic political repression. As the armistice talks neared their end in the summer of 1953, Rhee released some 27,000 **prisoners of war** who did not wish to be repatriated to North Korea, a move

President Syngman Rhee (left) in conversation with General John Coulter and General Clovis Byers of the U.S. Army, 22 August 1951. (Imperial War Museum MH 32041)

which was designed to end the negotiations. After the end of the war, he continued to demand that he be allowed to move against the North, but the United States made sure that he did not have the means to reopen the conflict, and Rhee had to content himself with organizing anti-Communist associations with like-minded leaders such as **Chiang Kai-shek** in Taiwan. He also remained firmly anti-Japanese.

Rhee's rule became steadily more autocratic after the war, yet at the same time he grew out of touch with political and social developments within South Korea. In 1960, following massive vote-rigging in the presidential elections, there was widespread student unrest, brutally suppressed by the police. The unrest spread to other groups, including university teachers, and Rhee was eventually persuaded to resign. He returned to Hawaii, where he died in 1965. After his death, his Austrian widow, whom he had married in 1934 and who was a staunch defender of her husband's reputation and policies, returned to Seoul, where she lived until her death in 1992. Rhee's body was later brought back to South Korea and reburied

in the National Cemetery in tribute to his long struggle for an independent Korea.

See also: Korean Provisional Government (1919–1945).
References: Oliver 1954, 1978.

RIDGWAY, MATTHEW BUNKER (1895–1993)

Matthew Bunker Ridgway was born in Fort Monroe, Virginia, in 1895 and graduated from the U.S. Military Academy in 1917. Before World War II, he held a range of staff appointments before commanding various field operations in that war. By 1945, he was a lieutenant general and was deputy supreme allied commander in the Mediterranean during 1945–1946.

Following the death of General **Walton H. Walker** in a traffic accident in December 1950, Ridgway, then in the Pentagon, succeeded him as commander of the U.S. Eighth Army in Korea. On arriving in the country, he decided that the **United Nations** (UN) forces should abandon the South Korean capital, **Seoul**, but should regroup on the **Han River** and then counterattack. To do this, Ridgway introduced what was known as the "meat grinder" strategy, designed to inflict maximum casualties on the **Chinese People's Volunteers**, who by this stage were bearing the brunt of the fighting on the Communist side. The policy was successful. Seoul was retaken on 14 March 1951, and UN forces pushed on to the region of the **38th parallel**, where the **Korean War** had began in June 1950. Ridgway resisted pressure from the UN commander-in-chief, General **Douglas MacArthur**, to push north, and the battle line was stabilized around the 38th parallel until the July 1953 **armistice**. In the meantime, following U.S. President **Harry S Truman**'s decision to recall MacArthur in April 1951, Ridgway became commander-in-chief of the **United Nations Command**, a post he held until May 1952. In that capacity, he continued to keep to a cautious approach, resisting any attempt to push the war back into North Korea. He favored the armistice negotiations, which began in July 1951, but found the Communist negotiating tactics frustrating and tended to be inflexible in his instructions to the UN negotiators.

In May 1952, Ridgway succeeded General **Dwight D. Eisenhower** as supreme commander of the Allied forces in Europe. He retired from active service in June 1955. In his later years, his experiences in Korea made him critical of U.S. involvement in Vietnam, and he constantly recommended U.S. disengagement from that conflict. He wrote a memoir, *Soldier*, published in 1956, and a more detailed and personal account of the Korean War, which appeared in 1967. General Ridgway died in 1993.

References: Ridgway 1956, 1967.

ROH TAE WOO (1932–)

Roh Tae Woo (No Tae-u) was president of South Korea from 1988 to 1993. He was born in the village of Talsong, near **Taegu,** in North Kyongsang Province in 1932, the son of a minor local official. Roh attended local schools and then joined the army. In 1951, he transferred from the military police to the Korean Military Academy, graduating, together with **Chun Doo Hwan**, in 1955. He attended a U.S. Special Warfare School in North Carolina in 1959 and graduated from the South Korean Army War College in 1968. He then served with the South Korean forces fighting in the **Vietnam War.**

After his return from Vietnam, he was promoted to brigadier general and in 1974 became comman-

der of the Airborne Special Warfare Brigade, a post he held until early 1979, when he was named commander of the 9th Infantry Division and, later in the year, head of the Capital Security Command. He played an important part in the coup d'état that brought Chun Doo Hwan to power in December 1979. Following the coup, Roh succeeded Chun as commander of the Defense Security Command in August 1980.

In July 1981, Roh was appointed full general and retired from the army to become minister of state for political and security affairs. From then on, he was widely seen as Chun's choice as successor. In March 1982, Roh became minister for sport, an important position because of the 1988 **Seoul** Olympics, and minister for home affairs the following month. In July 1983, he was appointed president of the Seoul Olympic Organizing Committee, a post he held until 1986.

Further signs of his role as Chun's successor included his election to the National Assembly and as president of the ruling Democratic Justice Party (DJP) in 1985. In June 1987, Chun announced that Roh would be the DJP candidate for the presidential elections. This decision led to widespread demonstrations that included many of the middle class as well as students. The protests ended only when Roh announced on 29 June that he would not stand unless a series of reforms were introduced. These included direct election of the president and an amnesty for the veteran opposition leader, **Kim Dae Jung**. Chun reluctantly accepted these proposals, and Roh became president of the DJP in August 1987.

In the December 1987 presidential election, the opposition vote was split between **Kim Dae Jung** and **Kim Young Sam**, and Roh won by two million votes, with 36.6 percent of the vote. His presidency was notable for the successful Seoul Olympics in the summer of 1988 and for his policy (*Nordpolitik*/**Northern Policy**) and achievements in establishing relations with Communist countries. The same policy also led to a series of agreements with North Korea during 1991–1992, but these remained largely unimplemented by the time he left office in early 1993 and were increasingly overshadowed by concern about the **North Korean nuclear program**. His domestic policies, which saw a more liberal approach in some areas such as press freedom, were generally deemed to have failed to redress the injustices of the past. In 1990, he concluded an alliance with Kim Young Sam that brought that veteran opposition leader into the government party and secured him election as president in 1992.

After he left office, Roh, like Chun, found himself under constant attack from those who wished to reopen the question of responsibility for the 1980 **Kwangju** massacre. In 1993, former General Chung Sung-hwa, who had been imprisoned after the 1979 coup, brought a case of mutiny to the courts against both men. The prosecution accepted that the 1979 incident was a mutiny, but declined to take action because of the passage of time. Popular protest continued, and in December 1995 the two were arrested on charges of bribery and corruption, to which charges of treason and mutiny were soon added. Both men were convicted in 1996, with Roh sentenced to 22½ years' imprisonment and fined. The prison sentence was later reduced on appeal to 17 years. Following the 1997 presidential election, President Kim Young Sam, with the approval of the incoming president, Kim Dae Jung, released both from prison, though the heavy fines still stood.

References: Bedeski 1992; Cotton 1993; Oberdorfer 1997; Roh 1990; Sigur 1992.

ROK

See **Introduction.**

ROLE OF THE MILITARY IN NORTH AND SOUTH KOREA

Civil government by the ruler and his advisers was for centuries the tradition in Korea, though sometimes undermined by powerful soldiers. Of the two orders of officers, civil and military, the former were always held in greater esteem. The predominance between 1961 and 1992 of the military, or, more exactly, of military attitudes and priorities in South Korea, thus cuts across earlier concepts of government.

Japan's wartime militarization incorporated Koreans—President **Park Chung Hee** among them—into the Japanese forces. To the Japanese tradition was added that of another powerful modern army, that of the United States, after the **United States Army Military Government in Korea** was installed in the southern half of Korea in 1945. As part of a U.S. undertaking to improve training in the South Korean army, the Korean Military Academy (KMA) was formed and by 1946 had produced its second class of graduates. They numbered Park and Kim Jae-kyu, the man who was to shoot and kill Park in 1979. The pattern of close relations between friends and classmates, a recurring principle in Korean society, was repeated notably in the intimate links between Presidents **Chun Doo Hwan** and **Roh Tae Woo**, both graduates of the eleventh grade of the KMA.

The South Korean military emerged from the **Korean War** considerably better trained and equipped than they had entered it, largely because of U.S. help. Dissatisfaction with the failings of civilian government had prompted the military in 1960 to plot against President **Syngman Rhee**. In 1961, following the student-led overthrow of Rhee and a period of increasingly unsettled experimentation with democratic norms, the army, led by Park Chung Hee and **Kim Jong Pil**, took charge. They established a style of government, perpetuated after 1979 by Chun Doo Hwan in another coup, that emphasized economic strength but tight, sometimes brutal, political control as the means of countering the perceived threat from the North. These were not military regimes; Park, Chun, Roh, and their followers in turn resigned their military posts. Nonetheless, the charges that finally discredited Chun and Roh during 1995–1996 included the military charge of mutiny.

In North Korea, in accordance with a basic tenet of Communist organization, the military has functioned as an integral part of a society where all elements and activities, in principle and generally in practice, have been guided by the Communist Party apparatus. Controlling this apparatus and indeed the whole scene was **Kim Il Sung**. His experience of war was primarily as a guerrilla fighter, and his closest loyalties remained with his fellow partisans, but he understood the need for a regular and modernized army. Soviet assistance helped him to achieve this. The country's economic difficulties since 1995 have led increasingly to food shortages, but rumors that the military has claimed the first share of scarce resources have not been altogether substantiated. It is noticeable, though, that photographs of **Kim Jong Il** frequently show him in military company; it may be that he prefers the society of this conservative section of North Korean society.

References: Cumings 1997; Eckert et al. 1990; Macdonald 1996.

ROOSEVELT, FRANKLIN DELANO (1882–1945)

Franklin Delano Roosevelt was four times president of the United States, from 1933 until his death in 1945. Roosevelt's interest in Korea was limited, but by March 1943, he had decided that Korea would need a period of trusteeship before it could expect independence. This idea was developed further at the **Cairo Conference**, held in November 1943 in Cairo, Egypt, with British Prime Minister **Winston Churchill** and Chinese leader **Chiang Kai-shek**. At Roosevelt's prompting, the conference participants issued the Cairo Declaration on 1 December 1943, detailing Allied war aims against Japan. These included unconditional surrender and the relinquishing of all territory acquired by Japan since 1875. The declaration added that the "great powers, mindful of the enslavement of the Korean people, are determined that in due course Korea shall become free and independent." These conditions were reaffirmed at the **Potsdam Conference** in 1945. By then, Roosevelt had died and had been succeeded by **Harry S Truman** as U.S. president.

ROYAL AUSTRALIAN REGIMENT

See **Australian Forces in the Korean War.**

RUSK, DAVID DEAN (1909–1994)

Secretary of state of the United States and an academic, Dean Rusk (he never used his first name) was born in Georgia in 1909. After studying at Davidson College, North Carolina, he was a Rhodes scholar at St John's College, Oxford. He then taught political science at Mills College in California from 1934 to 1940, becoming dean of the faculty in 1938. In World War II, he reached the rank of colonel and served in the China-Burma-India theater under General Joseph Stilwell and as a member of the Planning and Operations Staff of the General Staff. In that capacity he helped to choose the **38th parallel** as the division line for the surrender of Japanese troops in Korea in 1945. This decision was to lead to the emergence of two separate Korean states.

In 1947, Rusk joined the U.S. State Department, and was assistant secretary of state for Far Eastern affairs at the outbreak of the **Korean War**. He was therefore very much involved in the U.S. decision to intervene in Korea and pushed hard for U.S. participation to be under **United Nations** auspices. He favored the attempt to unify the peninsula after the **Inch'on landing** in September 1950 and took some of the blame for the failure of that policy, but he opposed General **Douglas MacArthur**'s wish to extend the fighting into China. Rusk left office in 1953 and worked for the Rockefeller Foundation, but returned to government as secretary of state under both Presidents John F. Kennedy and Lyndon Baines Johnson from 1961 to 1969.

Rusk remained staunchly anti-Communist, seeing the **Vietnam War** as a further example of Communist aggression, and opposed recognition of the **People's Republic of China**. After his second retirement from public life in 1969, he became professor of law at the University of Georgia, a post he held until 1984.

References: Cohen 1980; Rusk 1991; Schoenbaum 1988.

SAMIL (MARCH FIRST) MOVEMENT (1919)

The penultimate ruler of independent Korea, Emperor Kojong, who had been deposed by the Japanese in 1907, died on 22 January 1919. The days before his funeral, planned for 3 March 1919, were the occasion for the peaceful demonstrations known as Samil ("Three-one" or "March First"). Inspired by U.S. President Woodrow Wilson's "Fourteen Points," and with great hopes for the **Paris Conference**, Koreans throughout the country demonstrated in favor of the Declaration of Independence that was read out in Seoul's Pagoda Park on 1 March 1919. The Japanese response was swift and brutal. From 1 March until 30 April 1919, Japanese statistics show almost 30,000 arrests. Many were killed and many tortured, until the Japanese government, alarmed by hostile international reaction, switched to a more conciliatory role. Today, for those in the Republic of Korea, the Samil movement is the first battle in the struggle that would lead to freedom after 1945. In the Democratic People's Republic of Korea, the same movement is regarded as showing the limits of a non-Communist–led uprising.

See also: Paris Conference and Versailles Peace Treaty (1919).

References: Ku 1985; Lee 1965; McKenzie 1929/1975.

SASEBO NAVAL BASE

The Sasebo Naval Base is situated on the western side of the Japanese island of Kyushu, 33 miles (53 kilometers) from Nagasaki. Until the end of World War II, it was an important center for the Japanese Imperial Navy. With the defeat of Japan in 1945, it became an equally important center for the U.S. Navy. Although theoretically subordinate to the base at Yokuska near Tokyo, its proximity to Korea—156 miles (251 kilometers) away—meant that it soon became more important as both a naval base and a military transit center for troops of the **United Nations Command** en route to Korea.

See also: Japanese Involvement in the Korean War; United States Forces in the Korean War.

S

SEOUL

Situated on the **Han River**, at about the midpoint of the western side of the Korea Peninsula, some 20 miles (32 kilometers) from the port of Inch'on, Seoul was the capital of unified Korea from 1392 until the end of World War II. During that period, it became the political, cultural, and social heart of the country. In the **Japanese colonial period in Korea (1910–1945)**, it developed into a major economic and transport center and was transformed into a modern city, with paved streets, department stores, and new government buildings. So important was Seoul that the decision to draw the line for the Japanese surrender at the **38th parallel** was partly based on the wish to have the capital in the U.S. zone. After the establishment of separate states in 1948, Seoul became the capital of South Korea. At the outbreak of the **Korean War**, the city's population was about a million and a half.

On 25 June 1950, Seoul was a prime target for the North Korean forces, who swept down the western coastal plain and captured the city on 28 June. The North Koreans held Seoul until September, and they introduced political and social reforms similar to those already in place in the North. Despite some brutality, on the whole the occupation period did not see a reign of terror. Following the **Inch'on landing**, Seoul was retaken during 26–28 September 1950 and was formally handed back to President **Syngman Rhee** by General **Douglas MacArthur** in a ceremony in the **Capitol Building** on 29 September. However, the city had suffered much damage during the North Korean retreat, and the government for the most part continued to function in the southern city of **Pusan** for the rest of 1950.

U.S. Marines take cover in shell craters dotting Seoul's streets as they pursue the last of the North Korean forces, 1 October 1950. (UPI/Corbis-Bettmann)

Aerial view of the center of modern Seoul. (Official U.S. Navy Photograph)

Plans to restore Seoul as the capital were thwarted by the intervention of the **Chinese People's Volunteers** in October 1950 and the **United Nations** (UN) retreat. Seoul fell to the Chinese on 4 January 1951, after being set on fire by UN troops. It was recaptured by UN forces in March 1951 and remained in UN hands for the rest of the war. The fighting took a heavy toll on the city, although many of the major buildings survived. The population fell to about 200,000 (from a figure of over 1 million in 1946). Because the front line was only 35–40 miles (56–64 kilometers) away, Seoul was deemed unsafe for the South Korean government until well after the 27 July 1953 **armistice**. Only by the end of 1953 had the government and diplomatic corps moved back to the city.

Seoul recovered, but it was not until President **Park Chung Hee** introduced his economic reforms in the 1960s that major changes began to take place. By the 1980s, when Seoul hosted the 1986 Asian Games and the 1988 Olympic Games, the city's population was some ten million, and Seoul had expanded well beyond its old boundaries. Its vulnerability to North Korean attack for many years inhibited development to the north of the city. Since the late 1980s, however, these concerns appear to have lessened, and Seoul's suburbs now reach as far north as **Uijongbu**.

See also: Invasion and Counterinvasion (1950–1951).
References: Clark and Grayson 1986; Riley and Schramm 1951/1973.

SHINUIJU

Shinuiju lies in the extreme northwest corner of Korea, almost at the mouth of the **Yalu River** where it flows into the Yellow Sea. The Yalu here forms the boundary between North Korea and the **People's Republic of China**. Shinuiju is thus a frontier town and an important railway crossing and route into the peninsula. For several weeks from 19 October 1950, it served as the temporary capital of North Korea when the government was forced to retreat to the border in face of the drive north by troops of the **United Nations Command** (UNC). The UNC was soon pushed south again, and the capital was re-established at **P'yongyang** on 6 December 1950.

Five years earlier, in November 1945, students in Shinuiju had rioted against Soviet occupation forces and North Korean Communists active in the area, one of the few known instances of public protest in the North against the occupying Soviet authorities. The students were suppressed, with resulting deaths and injuries.

SHTYKOV, TERENTY FOMICH (1907–1964)

Terenty Fomich Shtykov was born in Vitebsk Province in the **Union of Soviet Socialist Republics** (USSR) in 1907. At 18, he worked in Leningrad (now Saint Petersburg), where he became active in the Communist youth movement, later joining the Soviet Communist Party. He was active politically in Leningrad in the years before 1941, but he survived the purges that marked the late 1930s. During World War II he was a political commissar with the Red Army, and by 1945 he was a colonel general, stationed in the Maritime Province adjoining China and Korea. In August 1945, his unit, the 28th Military Army (or Corps), was instructed to enter North Korea to assist in accepting the Japanese surrender. Following the establishment of the North Korean Provisional **People's Committee** in 1946, under **Kim Il Sung**, who had served with Shtykov during World War II, the latter became the Soviet adviser to the new administration. He and his colleagues are generally credited with being more politically sensitive in their handling of the Koreans in the north of the peninsula than the U.S. forces under General **John Hodge** were in the south. Shtykov also became the chief Soviet representative to the U.S.-USSR **Joint Commission on Trusteeship,** established by the December 1945 **Moscow Agreement,** at its meetings in 1946 and 1947, where he proved to be a tough opponent.

Following the foundation of the Democratic People's Republic of Korea in 1948, Shtykov became the first Soviet ambassador but also remained in charge of all the Soviet advisers. Documents available from the Soviet archives now reveal that he played an important role in the lead-up to the **Korean War**, as the principal Soviet military adviser, and in encouraging the North Koreans to attempt to settle the question of unification by force. Once the war had begun, the same material indicates that he continued to play a leading role both as adviser and as a channel of communication between Kim Il Sung and the Soviet leader, **Joseph Stalin**. He returned to Moscow in early 1951, but did not emerge in a new role until 1954, when he appeared as the Communist Party secretary in Novgorod Province, a post he held until 1956. From 1956 until 1961, he reverted to his wartime role as political commissar to the Maritime Province military district based in Vladivostok. In 1961, he became chairman of the government of the Russian Republic, and, later, chairman of the Communist Party control commission for the same republic, a post he held until his death in 1964.

See also: Soviet Occupation of North Korea (1945–1948); Soviet Role in the Korean War; Soviet/Russian Relations with North Korea; Union of Soviet Socialist Republics.

References: Cold War International History Project Bulletin 1995/1996; Cumings 1981, 1990; Matray 1985, 1991.

SINO-SOVIET DISPUTE

Although they were formally good after the establishment of the **People's Republic of China** (PRC) in 1949, relations between the PRC and the **Union of Soviet Socialist Republics** (USSR) were rarely as close as they appeared on the surface. **Joseph Stalin** and **Mao Zedong** were suspicious of each other's motives, and during the **Korean War**, the Chinese tended to believe that the USSR was less than wholehearted in its support for the Communist side. The resulting tension was one factor leading to the breakdown of the Sino-Soviet relationship in the late 1950s. Others included the different economic development of the two countries and the private, later public, de-Stalinization program carried out in the Soviet Union under Nikita Khrushchev after 1956. The North Korean leader **Kim Il Sung** had doubts about de-Stalinization, but the dispute allowed him some degree of maneuverability between his two large neighbors, which he was able to exploit to North Korea's economic and military advantage until the quarrel petered out in the 1980s.

See also: Mao Zedong; Stalin, Joseph.

References: Cumings 1997; Gittings 1968.

SIXTEEN-NATION DECLARATION (1953)

After the signing of an **armistice** on 27 July 1953, the sixteen states that had contributed combatants to the **Korean War** under the **United Nations Command** issued a statement in Washington, likewise dated 27 July. They expressed their support for the armistice agreement, affirmed their determination to carry out its terms, and promised to support **United Nations** (UN) efforts to bring about an equitable settlement in Korea, with the aim of achieving "a united, independent and democratic Korea." They undertook to unite again to resist any renewal of armed attack in defiance of UN principles, but they warned that the consequences of such a breach of the armistice might render it impossible to confine hostilities to Korea.

In any event, unity has still to be reached; at the same time, the situation has never deteriorated to the point of provoking renewed outside intervention. In the absence of any settlement on Korea at the 1954 **Geneva Conference**, the sixteen nations reissued their earlier declaration.

See also: Armistice; Geneva Conference (1954).

References: History: VI, 1977.

SOLMA-RI

See **United Kingdom and Korea**.

SONG SHILUN (1907–1995)

By October 1950, when he led the Chinese 9th Army Group of the **Chinese People's Volunteers** (CPV) into Korea, Song Shilun was a veteran soldier of the **People's Liberation Army** (PLA). Song, who was born in Liling, Hunan Province, in 1907, attended the Huangpu Military Academy and joined the Chinese Communist Party in about 1927. In 1949, he was commander of the Shanghai garrison and a member of the East China Military and Administrative Committee, a post he held while in Korea. His task in October 1950, on the instructions of **Mao Zedong**, was to stop the U.S. Marine Corps's advance up the east coast. To do this, he had 150,000 men in twelve divisions. Song's forces met the marines at the **Changjin Reservoir**. Although they stopped the advance and the marines retreated, the Chinese forces suffered heavy losses from the fighting and the extreme weather. Song remained in Korea as deputy commander of the CPV until 1952. On his return to China, he became president of the PLA's Higher Infantry School. In 1955, he was made a colonel general, and from 1952 to 1985, he was vice-president and then president of the Military Academy, as well as holding other state and party posts.

See also: Changjin Reservoir (1950); People's Liberation Army (PLA).

References: "The Chinese Failure at Chosin" (World Wide Web site); Klein and Clark 1971; *Who's Who in China* 1989.

SOUTH AFRICAN FORCES IN THE KOREAN WAR

From November 1950 to July 1953, the 2nd Squadron of the South African Air Force, known as the "Flying Cheetahs," served in the **Korean War** as part of the 18th Fighter-Bomber Wing of the U.S. Fifth Air Force, flying first F-51D Mustang propeller aircraft, then, from January 1953, F-86F Sabre jet fighters.

In November 1950 the 2nd Squadron flew in close support of the **United Nations Command** ground forces' advance to the **Yalu River**. Thereafter it fell back before the North's counterattack to a southern base at Chinhae. After the front stabilized in mid-1951 it carried out reconnaissance and bombing raids from forward bases on northern targets such as airfields, hydroelectric plants, supply dumps, weapons depots, and communication links, engaging at times with enemy MiG fighters. The squadron left Korea in July 1953.

A total of 826 men served in the squadron; casualties were 34 killed or missing. Nine prisoners were repatriated.

See also: Korean War (1950–1953); United States Forces in the Korean War.

References: History: VI, 1977; Moore and Bagshaw 1991; "Second Squadron SAAF (Flying Cheetahs) in Korea" (World Wide Web site).

SOUTH KOREA

See Introduction.

SOUTH KOREAN ARMED FORCES

When the **Korean War** broke out on 25 June 1950, the military forces of the Republic of Korea (South Korea) proved no match for the Soviet armed and trained army of the Democratic People's Republic of Korea (North Korea). Although North Korea claimed in 1950, and continues to claim to this day, that it was the South Korean forces that began the conflict, those forces were singularly ill-prepared for such action.

The South Korean armed forces traced their origins to eight "Constabulary regiments" formed in June 1946 during the period of the **United States Army Military Government in Korea**. These regiments were to act in support of the national police and were trained by U.S. military units. After the establishment of the Republic of Korea in August 1948, the Constabulary became the basis of a national army. Many of its officers had been noncommissioned officers or junior officers with the Imperial Japanese forces in World War II. As U.S. forces gradually withdrew from South Korea in the following twelve months, training and support functions passed from regular U.S. Army units to the **Korean Military Advisory Group** (KMAG). Although they were spread out very thinly among South Korean units, KMAG officers had strong views about the needs of the South Korean armed forces. In particular, they argued that the Koreans had no need of tanks, since these would be of little use in the mountains of Korea. They also believed that South Korean forces would be a match for the **North Korean People's Army** in any likely conflict on the peninsula.

The reality proved different. On the eve of the outbreak of the Korean War, South Korean forces were officially divided into eight divisions. Most were understrength and all were ill-equipped. Their weapons were mostly of ex-U.S. World War II vintage, and the units lacked heavy artillery and effective antitank weapons. They also had virtually no tanks. The only armor available was a small number of armored cars. The Capital Division still had a horse cavalry unit. Although total numbers were between 95,000 and 115,000, about a third of these were administrative units, not combat troops. When the war began, four divisions were strung out west to east along the **38th parallel**, while the remainder were deployed throughout the southern half of the peninsula. In the far south, some units had been engaged in antiguerrilla activities, but otherwise, most had little or no experience of combat. In addition, there was a small South Korean navy, mostly equipped for coastal patrols, and a fledgling air force. The latter had no combat aircraft, although it had requested them from the United States. Its inventory was made up of a number of light liaison airplanes and some trainers. All were obsolete.

The North Korean advance on 25 June 1950 broke this army, and although there were some attempts to stand and fight, most South Korean units collapsed before the North's onslaught and fled south. Many eventually reached the **Pusan perimeter.** There they were reorganized and regrouped and were turned again into a fighting force. During the fighting around the perimeter in August 1950, the South Korean I and II Corps, made up of five divisions, held the right sector of the line, while the U.S. Eighth Army and the British 27th Brigade held the left. Following the September 1950 **Inch'on landing,** South Korean forces joined the **United Nations Command** in the outbreak from the **Naktong River** and the pursuit of the now-demoralized North Korean forces first to **Seoul,** then across the 38th parallel, and on into the North. By 26 October 1950, the South Korean 6th Division, part of II Corps, had reached the **Yalu River,** the traditional border with China.

Although there was now a widespread expectation that the war would soon be over, the intervention by the **Chinese People's Volunteers** in November 1950 not only halted the **United Nations** (UN) advance but soon saw the UN forces in retreat, first to the North Korean capital, **P'yongyang,** then south to Seoul. South Korean forces were particularly badly hit by the Chinese, and by early 1951, they were again in danger of disintegration. However, the retreat stopped south of Seoul, and gradually the South Korean units were reorganized and once again turned into a fighting force. When the spring 1951 Chinese offensive was stopped at the battle of the **Imjin River** and **armistice** negotiations began that summer, South Korean forces, like those of the UN, moved into a more or less static war, which was to last until the signature of the armistice agreement on 27 July 1953. Although neither side gained much ground during this period, the fighting was often intense, with heavy losses on both sides, and South Korean forces suffered many casualties.

By July 1953, the tiny South Korean army of 1950 had grown into a capable fighting force of some 590,000, well equipped and organized into 16 battle-hardened divisions. The navy too had expanded and

had played an important role in blockade work throughout the war. The South Korean air force, scarcely a factor in 1950, had begun to take shape as a true fighting arm, equipped with F-51 Mustang fighters and flying with other UN units. South Korean officers had proved themselves, like their men, capable of tough combat and tough decisions in difficult conditions.

Following the Korean War, the South Korean army grew and developed. At the time of the military coup in 1961, it was probably the main modernizing force in the country, in which young men—there were few if any young women in the army at that stage—could expect a bright future. It saw action during the **Vietnam War,** in which two future presidents, **Chun Doo Hwan** and **Roh Tae Woo,** both served. In recent years, South Korean forces have gradually taken over more and more of the duty of patrolling along the **Demilitarized Zone,** so that by 1999, virtually all the line had come under their command. Today, the South Korean armed forces are made up of a series of highly professional units, equipped with good modern equipment, often Korean made.

See also: Combined Forces Command (Republic of Korea–United States); Home for Christmas (1950); Invasion and Counterinvasion (1950–1951); Korean Augmentation to the United States Army (KATUSA); Koreans Attached to the Commonwealth Forces (KATCOM); Paik Sun-yup; Role of the Military in North and South Korea; Task Forces.

References: History: II, 1973; Matray 1991; Paik 1992; Savada and Shaw 1992; Summers 1990.

SOUTH KOREAN NUCLEAR PROGRAM

South Korea has suffered from a lack of energy sources since the division of the peninsula in 1945 cut it off from supplies of electricity from the north. The lack became more acute after President **Park Chung Hee** began his program of massive industrialization in the 1960s. Then in 1973, the worldwide oil crisis showed up the South's vulnerability to fluctuations in oil supplies. It was understandable, therefore, that South Korea should look to nuclear power as a solution to its energy needs, and that it began to build nuclear power stations in the late 1960s. The first plant started operating in July 1978, and the program has expanded ever since. By 1995, eight light-water reactors were in operation, producing about 11 percent of the country's energy needs. All operated under **International Atomic Energy Authority** safeguards.

This civilian nuclear energy program soon led to speculation that there might also be a South Korean nuclear weapons program. Nuclear weapons were already present in South Korea. During the 1950–1953 **Korean War,** the United States had hinted that it might use such weapons. Later, although it was not formally admitted, the U.S. forces in South Korea were equipped with nuclear weapons. This "nuclear umbrella" operated well enough until the late 1960s. Then came the announcement of the **Nixon Doctrine** and some U.S. troop withdrawals. Signs of improved relations between the United States and both the **Union of Soviet Socialist Republics** and the **People's Republic of China** added to South Korean concern and led President Park to think that the nuclear umbrella was no longer reliable. From 1971 onward, Park's government began work to develop a South Korean nuclear weapons capability, even though South Korea had signed the Nuclear Non-Proliferation Treaty (NPT) in 1968. The South made no open admission of such capability, but there were widespread suspicions. To stop the spread of nuclear weapons, the United States urged third countries not to supply further nuclear technology to South Korea. It also halted troop withdrawals and renewed the nuclear guarantee. These measures worked, and South Korea ratified the NPT in 1975.

When U.S. President **Jimmy Carter** decided to withdraw all American troops from Korea in 1977, Park reopened the nuclear program. Again, pressure was applied by the United States, the troop withdrawals stopped, and the Koreans suspended their activity. It appears to have remained suspended since then. In 1991, the United States decided to withdraw tactical nuclear weapons worldwide. Soon after, South Korean President **Roh Tae Woo** announced there were no longer any nuclear weapons in South Korea. At the end of the year, the two Koreas undertook not to possess or develop nuclear weapons.

The nuclear issue has not disappeared, however. Some in South Korea argue that, if North Korea is developing nuclear weapons, then the South should do the same. During the 1993–1994 North Korean nuclear crisis, the South Korean media drew attention to South Korean nuclear weapons–related research in the 1970s, while some opposition members of parliament argued that South Korea should develop its own nuclear reprocessing facilities to produce plutonium, an essential requirement for nuclear weapons. The government has kept quiet.

See also: Korean Peninsula Energy Development Organization (KEDO); North Korean Nuclear Program; United States Relations with North Korea; United States Relations with South Korea.

References: Hayes 1991; Oberdorfer 1997; Sigal 1998; Summers 1990.

SOUTH KOREAN PROPOSALS ON UNIFICATION

Although there has been much rhetoric over the years since the division of the peninsula in 1945 and calls from both sides for the reunification of Korea, it is not always easy to pin down precise proposals. With the establishment of separate regimes in 1948, the issue became more complex. As far as the South Korean government under President **Syngman Rhee** was concerned, their government, established under the auspices of the **United Nations** (UN), after UN-supervised elections, was the only legitimate government on the **Korea Peninsula.** Unification, therefore, was a matter of the South taking over North Korea, thus recovering territory that was illegally occupied by what was described as an "anti-state regime." The pre–**Korean War** Rhee government made no approaches to North Korea, since to do so would imply that there was a legitimate government in the northern half of the peninsula.

The outbreak of the Korean War led the South Korean government to argue that the peninsula should be reunified by force. With the crossing of the **38th parallel** in September 1950, this seemed a distinct possibility until the intervention by the **Chinese People's Volunteers** in October 1950 pushed the South Korean and **United Nations Command** forces out of North Korea. Although the South Korean government continued to advocate reunification by force, neither the United Nations nor South Korea's main supporter, the United States, was willing to try this again. Reunification by force remained the South Korean position after the end of the Korean War in 1953, and the South Korean government continued to refuse to recognize North Korea. Without support from the United States, however, there was no way in which the South Korean government could achieve its aims.

There was no formal change in the South Korean position during the brief interlude between Rhee and **Park Chung Hee**, and under Park, the South Korean government continued to view North Korea as an illegitimate interloper. At the same time, however, Park concentrated on the economic and industrial development of the South, and the question of reunification was generally regarded as a less pressing issue than it had been under Rhee.

North-South contacts between 1971 and 1973 seemed to provide a degree of common ground, with each side appearing to accept the other's existence and agreeing that reunification was a domestic concern; but these contacts fizzled out in mutual recriminations. After Park's assassination in 1979, unification appeared high on the agenda of the student and other demonstrators who demanded a new approach to the North, but such views were stamped out following General **Chun Doo Hwan**'s military coup and accession to the presidency.

Under Chun, there was little new in the way of a North Korean policy. Chun's successor, **Roh Tae Woo**, who came to power in very different circumstances, encouraged some fresh thinking in the late 1980s. By then, however, German reunification raised the issue of a North Korean collapse, and the South Koreans began to think in terms of reunification by absorption of the North. A number of schemes were suggested to make this more or less palatable to the North, but all were rejected. Since 1997, the new government of President **Kim Dae Jung** has stressed that it wishes only to see a peaceful reunification of the peninsula, but clearly North Korea still retains suspicions of South Korean intentions.

See also: Geneva Conference (1954); Korean Membership of the United Nations; National Security Law; North Korean Proposals on Unification; Pro-unification Activities.

References: Kim 1976; Kim 1992; Koo and Han 1985; Kwak, Kim, and Kim 1984; Kwak, Patterson, and Olsen 1983; National Unification Board 1989.

SOVIET DEFENSE TREATY WITH NORTH KOREA (1961)

In 1961, the Democratic People's Republic of Korea (North Korea) signed treaties of "Friendship, Cooperation and Mutual Assistance" with the **Union of Soviet Socialist Republics** (USSR) and the **People's Republic of China** (PRC). Both treaties provide military guarantees to North Korea if it is attacked. Of the two, the Soviet treaty was the more important. Without spelling out details, it provided North Korea with a nuclear umbrella to balance that provided by the United States to the Republic of Korea. Since 1958, the United States had hinted that it had nuclear weapons in South Korea to compensate for the rundown in **United Nations Command** forces. When the North Korean leader **Kim Il Sung** visited Moscow in 1984, the two sides reaffirmed that the treaty was still effective, but since the collapse of the Soviet Union in 1991, the treaty's status has been in doubt. Russia says that it intends to renegotiate the treaty, but the North Koreans have argued that if the treaty is revoked, they might need to reconsider their attitude toward "certain types of weapons"—presumably a threat to develop a nuclear capability. Negotiations to replace the 1961 treaty have so far (February 1999) not been successful.

See also: North Korean Nuclear Program; Soviet/Russian Relations with North Korea.

References: Chung 1978; Kim 1986; Koh 1969.

SOVIET INVOLVEMENT IN KOREA (1917–1945)

The doctrines inspiring the 1917 October Revolution in Russia found a ready reception among Koreans settled in Siberia and the Russian Maritime Region. Many were of peasant origin. Some had emigrated for economic reasons, others to escape Japanese colonial rule after 1910. Those settled for several generations often had Russian citizenship, a policy continued by the new Soviet Union after its formation in 1922. A body of "Russianized" Koreans thus existed by the 1910s–1920s.

Given their experiences, the Koreans were among the first in East Asia to collaborate with the Bolsheviks, and the first Korean Communist groups were formed, in 1918, in Irkutsk (Siberia) and

Khabarovsk (Maritime Region). Both Bolsheviks and Koreans sought allies in the region, the Bolsheviks against invasion by White Russians, Japanese, and Western forces, the Koreans against their Japanese colonial masters. The Comintern, the Soviet international front organization created in 1919, supported the Korean Communist movement financially and indicated policy directions it should follow. It also sought to impose a degree of unity and discipline.

Rivalry soon broke out between the two main groups, the Irkutsk and the Shanghai factions. (Yi Tong-hwi, founder of the Khabarovsk group, took his party to Shanghai in 1919.) They split basically over organization and motives: the Irkutsk faction, containing many "Russian" Koreans, was prepared to function as one element in the international Communist movement; the Shanghai faction was ready to use Communist activism as a means of achieving Korean independence. In the Alekseyevsk incident of June 1921 in Siberia, the two groups actually fought each other with loss of life. The Comintern in 1923 ordered them to disband in favor of a new grouping. The focus of Korean Communism was in any case shifting to the peninsula itself, where in 1925 the first **Korean Communist Party** (KCP) was established. A treaty with Japan in the same year reduced the Soviet Union's need for allies in the Far East.

Nonetheless, the Comintern still directed doctrine and tactics within the international Communist movement. Persuaded of the necessity of moving through temporary alliances on the way toward communism, it instructed its constituent parties to develop "united fronts" with bourgeois elements. In Korea, this led to the *Shinganhoe*, a left-wing alliance with moderate nationalists, initiated in 1927. A subsequent leftward swing in Comintern tactics caused Korean Communists to withdraw from *Shinganhoe* in 1931 in favor of mobilizing peasants and workers. At around the same time, the Comintern further insisted on the "one country, one party" policy. As a result, all Korean Communists living outside of the peninsula were required to join the national party of their country of residence. This policy, combined with the difficulty of establishing an indigenous party inside Korea, led to the temporary demise of the KCP.

When it entered Korea in 1945, the Soviet Army brought with it a number of "Soviet" Koreans, but they never formed a powerful group. Rather, it was the Soviet protégé **Kim Il Sung**, who had spent the war years in the Soviet Union, who won out.

See also: Korean Communist Party (KCP); Left-Wing Political Factions; Soviet Occupation of North Korea (1945–1948); Soviet/Russian Relations with North Korea.

References: Howard, Pares, and English 1996; Lone and McCormack 1993; Scalapino and Lee 1972; Suh 1970.

SOVIET OCCUPATION OF NORTH KOREA (1945–1948)

On 21 August 1945, troops of the Soviet 25th Army landed at ports on the east coast of Korea to occupy the peninsula north of the **38th parallel** in accordance with a joint U.S.-Soviet agreement on the surrender of Japanese forces in Korea. The main body of Soviet forces reached the main northern city of **P'yongyang** on 24 August and set up military headquarters there. Troops pushed as far as **Kaesong**, just below the 38th parallel, but then withdrew north again. The Soviet occupation army numbered 40,000 and was headed by General Ivan Chistiakov. Political affairs were handled by Major General Nikolai Lebedev, and the civil administration of North Korea by Major General Alexei Romanenko. In its first months in Korea the army gained a bad reputation, with charges of looting, rape, and requisitioning of supplies laid against it. By early 1946, however, discipline had been imposed. A certain amount of industrial plant was removed, but the damage is judged to have been less than that inflicted by the Japanese on their departure from the north. In fact, Soviet sources claimed that as early as November 1945, the Soviet command had taken steps to launch heavy industry in the north, which it had then handed over in August 1946 to the North Koreans, together with power stations and banks. The North Korean provisional administration announced the nationalization of transport, communications, banks, and major industries that same August.

The Soviet forces' main intervention in the years of occupation seems to have been in the areas of politics, administration, and security. One of their first moves on arrival was to insist on equal representation of Communist and non-Communist members in the P'yongyang **People's Committee**. The formation of People's Committees, which had gone ahead in the north as rapidly as in the south of the peninsula, was acceptable to the Soviet authorities. Their policy appears to have been one of nonintervention in the development of local organs of party and administration, provided these did not offer any threat to their interests, while aiming to create a disciplined party structure from above. Soviet army directives issued in mid-September (or mid-October 1945; sources differ on the dates) were relatively mild: they permitted the formation of democratic organizations provided these had no Japanese associations and were registered with the Soviet command, and assured North Korean citizens that their private property would be protected and that religious activities could continue. Unofficial military formations and activities, however, would not be tolerated. The Soviet authorities insisted on disarming members of the Yan'an (Yenan) group of Korean Communists who sought to return to North Korea from China in September–October 1945; and in November of the same year they suppressed student protests in Hamhung and **Shinuiju** directed against Soviet and North Korean Communist control.

After a progressive rundown of troops, the Soviet occupying forces withdrew at the very end of 1948, following the establishment of the Democratic People's Republic of Korea in September of that year.

Scholars differ in their opinions over the intentions of the Soviet occupation army in North Korea. Some believe that the Soviet government, preoccupied with its plans in Eastern Europe, sought no more than a friendly buffer state in that part of East Asia. Others see in the Soviet occupation a determination to implant a particular political form on North Korean society and, more importantly, to impose their choice of leader—**Kim Il Sung**. What is undeniable is that Soviet tutelage allowed North Korea to develop as a viable state.

See also: Korea Peninsula (1945–1948); Shtykov, Terenty Fomich; Soviet/Russian Relations with North Korea.
References: Cumings 1981; Muratov 1985; Suh 1988; Yang 1994; Yi 1973.

SOVIET ROLE IN THE KOREAN WAR

At the time of the outbreak of the **Korean War** in June 1950, it was widely believed in the West that the **Union of Soviet Socialist Republics** (USSR) lay behind what was seen as an example of Communist aggression. The Soviet Union had occupied the northern half of the **Korea Peninsula** in 1945, had refused to cooperate with the United States in bringing about the reunification of the peninsula, and had encouraged the establishment of the Democratic People's Republic of Korea in 1948. The Soviet Union had also begun to train the North Korean armed forces before 1948, and when Soviet troops withdrew from the north in December 1948, they left behind much military equipment. The first Soviet nuclear test in September 1949, and the establishment of the **People's Republic of China** (PRC) on 1 October 1949, following the Chinese Communist Party's victory in the Chinese civil war, had been seen by many in the West as further signs of Soviet aggressive intent. When the war began, therefore, it seemed logical to those taking such views that it was part of a Soviet plan for world conquest. At the same time, there were some puzzling aspects of Soviet behavior. In June 1950, the USSR had been boycotting the **United Nations** (UN) since January of that year, in protest at the refusal of the UN to give the "China" seat to the PRC, and did not immediately return. This absence allowed the passage of the various resolutions condemning North Korea and establishing the **United Nations Command** (UNC) in June 1950. After the Soviet delegates resumed their seats at the UN in August 1950, they consistently supported the North Korean–Chinese position.

The reality seems to be that while close consultation did take place between the North Korean leader, **Kim Il Sung**, and the Soviet leader, **Joseph Stalin**, who was not opposed to the war, it was the North Koreans who decided to attempt reunification by force. Once the war began, Stalin took a close interest in it and continued to supply the North Koreans, but he was careful to limit direct Soviet involvement to relatively low-risk areas, avoiding any direct contact with the UNC. It is clear that some North Korean units had Soviet advisers, that Soviet pilots flew some missions against UNC forces, and that Soviet antiaircraft crews were based in North Korea.

In addition, a few **prisoners of war** and **foreign civilian detainees** reported that they were interrogated by Soviet officers. When the UN forces drove the North Koreans across the **38th parallel** in September 1950, Stalin again refused to provide direct help, although he encouraged the Chinese leader, **Mao Zedong**, to do so.

There is also ambiguity about the Soviet role in ending the Korean War. Although **armistice** negotiations began in summer 1951, they continued until March 1953 with little progress. Then, following the death of Stalin, a broadcast by Jacob Malik, the permanent Soviet representative at the United Nations, indicated there might be a way forward and ultimately led to the end of the war in July 1953.

See also: Blake, George; Geneva Conference (1954); North Korean People's Army (NKPA); Shtykov, Terenty Fomich; Soviet Occupation of North Korea (1945–1948); Soviet/Russian Relations with North Korea.

References: Cold War International History Project Bulletin 1995/1996; Goncharov, Lewis, and Xue 1993; Lowe 1988(a); MacDonald 1990; Petrov 1994; Stueck 1995.

SOVIET/RUSSIAN RELATIONS WITH NORTH KOREA

The Democratic People's Republic of Korea (North Korea) owes its existence to the **Union of Soviet Socialist Republics** (USSR). After the defeat of Japan in 1945, the United States proposed that to take the Japanese surrender, Korea should be divided at the **38th parallel.** Soviet forces would occupy the northern half of the peninsula, the United States the southern half. The Soviet Union installed a young man, known as **Kim Il Sung**, who had fought with their forces during the war, as the head of the provisional government in the north. When U.S.-USSR negotiations on reunification broke down, two separate states emerged on the peninsula in 1948. Kim became the head of government of North Korea, a position he was to hold until his death in 1994. Soon after the establishment of the new state, Soviet military forces withdrew, leaving behind a well-trained army and much military equipment, together with military and political advisers.

The Soviet leader, **Joseph Stalin**, was aware of the North Korean plans to attempt to reunify the peninsula by force. These plans culminated in the **Korean War.** Stalin also remained fully informed of the progress of the war, supplied military equipment to keep it going, and allowed the Soviet military advisers to remain. The Soviet media supported the North's cause, as did Soviet representatives at the **United Nations**. At the same time, Stalin resisted attempts by the North Korean leaders to persuade him to become directly involved, wishing to avoid open confrontation with the United States. Even when the existence of North Korea was threatened after **United Nations Command** (UNC) forces crossed the 38th parallel, Stalin did not move, although he did encourage the Chinese under **Mao Zedong** to come to the North's aid.

After the war, the Soviet Union played an important role in the rehabilitation of the North's shattered economy. So too did the East European countries and the Chinese. This aid allowed Kim Il Sung to begin industrial development on a major scale, and he looked to the Soviet model for inspiration. North Korea's economy, therefore, followed the Stalinist pattern of putting heavy industry first. As in the USSR, this concentration on heavy industry was accompanied by the introduction of collective agriculture, at considerable cost to the peasants who worked the land. However, the emergence of a split within the Communist camp, first evident in 1956 when the Soviet leader Nikita Khrushchev criticized Stalin for the "cult of personality" in a secret speech to the Soviet party congress, caused problems for the North Koreans. Although less developed in the late 1950s than it was to become later, Kim Il Sung's own cult of personality, with the emphasis on the leader and obedience to the leader, was already well established, and Khrushchev's remarks could be seen as indirectly critical of Kim (and of Mao in China) as well as of Stalin. Just as worrying was the steady divergence of views between Moscow and Beijing and the possible need to take sides.

The North Koreans appeared sometimes to favor China, sometimes the Soviet Union, but as far as it was possible, Kim tried to maintain good relations with both countries. The North's general economic development was closely tied to the economies of the Soviet Union and the Eastern European countries, while the Soviet Union's nuclear weapons provided a counterbalance to those of the United States. At the same time, China shared a long frontier with the North and had proved a more reliable ally in the Korean War. Kim now stressed that North Korea was ideologically and spiritually independent of its neighbors, however much it might need them materially. This approach developed into the doctrine of *juche,* or nondependence, which, the North Koreans argued, went beyond Marxism-Leninism, and which for a time attracted a number of newly independent Third World countries as a possible middle way between capitalism and communism.

Although North Korea tried to maintain a balance, the reality was that by the 1970s, it was more dependent on the Soviet Union than on China. From the Soviet Union alone could come the spare parts and new machinery for the factories built in the 1950s. The Soviet Union's nuclear shield was also more important than that of China, and it alone could supply the modern weapons that would allow the North Koreans to keep pace with the South. A sign of the growing importance of the Soviet link came in 1984, when Kim Il Sung paid his first visit to Moscow in 22 years. Soon the USSR was sending MiG-23 jet fighters to North Korea, to match U.S.-supplied F-16s in the South, and over 43 percent of North Korea's trade was with the Soviet Union. By the end of the decade, even more modern MiG-29 and SU-25 aircraft were going to North Korea.

At the same time, the North was concerned at the growing contacts between the Soviet Union and South Korea, especially after Mikhail Gorbachev came to power in 1985. Despite the North's protests, the Soviet Union attended the 1988 Olympic Games in the South Korean capital, **Seoul**. Soviet–South Korean trade grew and was conducted openly. The Eastern European countries were also wooing the South, again despite increasingly desperate protests from the North. When Hungary established diplomatic relations with Seoul in 1988, the message was clear, and the Soviet Union followed in 1990. Even worse, the Soviet Union's economic support drained away almost overnight, and the supply of weapons stopped. In future, the Soviet Union would only trade for hard currency. The North, with little hard currency and declining industries, faced a bleak future. When the Soviet Union itself disappeared in December 1991, the relationship reached rock bottom.

Not all contacts were broken. For some years,

North Korea had rented tracts of land in the Soviet Far East to grow vegetables, and this arrangement continued. North Korean loggers also worked Soviet forests for timber and they too remained, though there was a steady stream of defectors, escaping what appeared to be very harsh conditions. In some circles in the former Soviet Union, it was argued that North Korea should not just be abandoned, although it was difficult for Russia to do much, given its own political and economic problems. Formally, the two sides maintain correct relations, but the old closeness has gone, probably forever.

See also: Diplomatic Recognition; Geneva Conference (1954); Korea Peninsula (1945–1948); North Korean People's Army (NKPA); Rajin-Sonbong Development Zone; Soviet Defense Treaty with North Korea (1961); Soviet Occupation of North Korea (1945–1948); Soviet Role in the Korean War; Soviet/Russian Relations with South Korea.

References: Chung 1978; Kim 1986; Koh 1969; Sanford 1990; Savada and Shaw 1992.

SOVIET/RUSSIAN RELATIONS WITH SOUTH KOREA

From the establishment of the Republic of Korea (South Korea) in September 1948 until the early 1970s, South Korea had no contact with the **Union of Soviet Socialist Republics** (USSR). South Korea, dominated politically by right-wing groups that looked to the United States for support, feared communism and blamed the Soviet Union for perpetuating the 1945 temporary division of the peninsula. When the **Korean War** began in June 1950, South Korea saw it as part of a Soviet plot and thus felt even less inclined to make any attempt to develop relations. Apparent monolithic Soviet support for the Democratic People's Republic of Korea (North Korea) confirmed the South Korean belief that the Soviet Union was an enemy.

Changes in U.S. policies toward the USSR and the **People's Republic of China** in the 1960s led President **Park Chung Hee** to reconsider South Korea's anti-Communist policies. In 1973, Park announced that South Korea would not oppose contacts with "non-hostile" Communist states. There was at first little response. In public, the USSR continued to support North Korea and to criticize the South as a U.S. puppet regime, but some tentative contacts began. A South Korean journalist visited Moscow in 1973. Gradually, South Koreans applying for visas for international conferences in the Soviet Union found they were no longer automatically rejected. In 1978, the health minister became the first South Korean minister to visit the Soviet Union when he attended a World Health Organization conference in Alma Ata. Visits by Soviet officials to South Korea were slower in coming, but eventually they too began. South Korean economic development also attracted Soviet interest, and soon there was small-scale bilateral trade. By 1981, two-way trade amounted to over $30 million and was growing.

Relations then suffered a setback, following the shooting down by Soviet fighter planes of **Korean Air Lines Flight KE007** on 31 August/1 September 1983. For a time, relations seemed likely to return to Cold War levels, especially as the USSR began to improve relations with North Korea. As time passed, however, both sides made moves to renew contact, a process crowned by the Soviet decision to attend the 1988 Olympics held in the South Korean capital, **Seoul**. The new direction in Soviet foreign policy under Mikhail Gorbachev from the mid-1980s, and President **Roh Tae Woo**'s policy of *Nordpolitik*/**Northern Policy** further helped to improve relations. Trade increased, reaching nearly $600 million by 1990. After a determined South Korean campaign, including many promises of economic assistance to the Soviet Union, Roh and Gorbachev met in San Francisco on 4 June 1990. This meeting was followed by an exchange of consular and trade officials, and then by full diplomatic relations in September 1990, much to the fury of North Korea.

Gorbachev's fall and the collapse of the Soviet Union the following year, however, led many in South Korea to argue that their country had paid too high a price for winning over the Soviet Union. Since 1991, relations between South Korea and Russia have developed normally. They are less important, however, than they were in the days of the Soviet Union and are overshadowed by relations with China. In 1998, Russian accusations of "improper behavior" by South Korean diplomats led to a number of expulsions by both sides.

See also: Blake, George; Cross-recognition; Diplomatic Recognition; Geneva Conference (1954); Joint Commission on Trusteeship; Kim Il Sung; Korea Peninsula (1945–1948); Korean Membership of the United Nations; Moscow Agreement (1945); Nixon Doctrine (1969); North Korean Nuclear Program; Rajin-Sonbong Development Zone; Shtykov, Terenty Fomich; Soviet Role in the Korean War; Stalin, Joseph.
References: Koo and Han 1985; Sanford 1990; Savada and Shaw 1992.

STALIN, JOSEPH (1879–1953)

The Soviet leader Joseph Stalin (whose real name was Joseph Vissarionovich Dzhugashvili), a Georgian by birth, was born in Gori in the Caucasus in December 1879. He was educated in church schools and the theological college in Tiflis. There he began to study Marxism and was expelled for revolutionary activities. After periods in prison and exile, he emerged in 1917 as one of the leaders in the Bolshevik revolution. He worked closely with Vladimir Lenin, becoming secretary-general of the Soviet Communist Party in 1922, a post he held until his death in 1953. By the later 1930s, he had disposed of most of his political rivals and emerged as the sole ruler of the **Union of Soviet Socialist Republics** (USSR). He added the post of premier to his titles in 1941. In World War II, he was one of the "Big Three" world leaders with **Franklin Roosevelt** and **Winston Churchill**.

Stalin was not present at the **Cairo Conference** in 1943, which set out the Allied position on a postwar settlement for Korea, but Roosevelt persuaded him to accept this at the Tehran Conference held the same year. Stalin proved equally agreeable to the U.S. proposal in 1945 to divide Korea at the **38th parallel** for purposes of taking the Japanese surrender. At first, the Soviet Union showed signs of willingness to cooperate with the United States in Korea, but as the Cold War developed, it displayed an increasing readiness to allow the separate development of North Korea under **Kim Il Sung**. With the establishment of the Democratic People's Republic of Korea in September 1948, Stalin ordered the withdrawal of Soviet military forces, but not of military advisers. When Kim Il Sung visited Moscow in late 1949, apparently to discuss the question of a forcible reunification of the **Korea Peninsula**, Stalin was encouraging. For the Soviet Union, a united and Communist Korea would help to control any threat from Japan (now heavily under U.S. control), give the Soviet Union a friendly neighbor, and, perhaps, provide some form of balance to the newly established **People's Republic of China.**

Stalin does not seem to have given his final agreement to Kim's plan, however, until the Chinese leader **Mao Zedong** accepted it. After the **Korean War** began in June 1950, it was widely believed in the United States and other Western countries that war was being encouraged by the Soviet Union, but Stalin adopted a cautious attitude. Soviet advisers had to keep well back from front-line engagements, and all direct Soviet participation was avoided. In fact, the Soviet Union supplied much equipment and ammunition both to North Korea and to China, and Soviet pilots flew combat missions against **United Nations Command** forces. In recent years, material from the Soviet archives has shown that Stalin also took a personal interest in the war. Only after his death, on 5 March 1953, did the Soviet Union begin to explore seriously a way to end the conflict.

Stalin's other contribution to North Korea was to provide a model to Kim Il Sung both for the structure and organization of state and party power and for a style of leadership.

See also: Soviet Involvement in Korea (1917–1945); Soviet Occupation of North Korea (1945–1948); Soviet Role in the Korean War; Soviet/Russian Relations with North Korea.

References: Cold War International History Project Bulletin 1995/1996; Stueck 1995; Ulan 1973.

STONE, ISIDOR FEINSTEIN (1907–1989)

The American journalist I. F. Stone was a prolific reporter and writer, editor of the weekly *The Nation,* and creator of *I. F. Stone's Weekly.* His inquiries into the workings of U.S. policies and government practice included one book on the **Korean War:** *The Hidden History of the Korean War 1950–1951,* published in 1952. The volume eventually formed part of Stone's *A Nonconformist History of Our Times.* In it, Stone set out to test U.S. government accounts of what was happening in Korea against official U.S. and **United Nations** documents and reputable press reports. His conclusions led him to doubt official claims that the North Korean attack was unexpected, to challenge the motives of President **Harry S Truman** and General **Douglas**

MacArthur, and to question U.S. good faith in the **armistice** negotiations.

Stone was not an East Asian specialist but a rigorous investigative journalist. His *Hidden History* nonetheless had considerable influence on later Western writers on contemporary Korea.

See also: Histories and Other Studies of the Korean War.
References: Cumings 1992; *Encyclopedia Britannica* 1997; Knightley 1982; Stone 1952.

STRATEMEYER, GEORGE E. (1890–1969)

General George Stratemeyer of the U.S. Air Force was born in Cincinnati, Ohio, in November 1890. He graduated from the U.S. Military Academy in 1915, and later transferred to the Army Air Corps, graduating from its technical school in 1920. Before World War II, he held a variety of instructor posts and also staff appointments. During the war, he was assigned to the China-Burma theater, becoming commander of the U.S. Army Air Force in the China theater, with headquarters at Chongqing, from 1944 to 1946.

In April 1948, Stratemeyer became commanding general of the Far East Air Force. This had originally been established in Australia during World War II but had moved to Japan before the **Korean War** began in June 1950. During the Korean War, it had fighter, bomber, and transport functions. Its commander was the principal air adviser to the **United Nations** (UN) commander, General **Douglas MacArthur,** and in June 1950 had 44 squadrons, 657 aircraft, and nearly 34,000 officers and men under his control. Under orders from MacArthur, Stratemeyer sent bomber aircraft under his command to attack North Korean forces north of the **38th parallel** on 29 June 1950. In August 1950, he ordered a massive air attack on Communist forces near the **Naktong River,** which formed part of the **Pusan Perimeter.** However, although ninety-eight B-29 bombers dropped more than 1,000 tons of explosives in 26 minutes, there was no evidence that this attack had any effect on the Communists. That said, by April 1951, Stratemeyer's forces had effective control of the skies over the battlefield and had inflicted heavy damage on North Korea. On 20 May 1951, Stratemeyer had a serious heart attack and was eventually replaced on 10 June 1951 by General

Otto P. Weyland. Stratemeyer retired from active duty on 31 January 1952 and died in August 1969. *References:* Futrell 1961/1983; Summers 1990.

STUDENT DEMONSTRATIONS AND ORGANIZATIONS

During the 1980s, South Korean students, demonstrating over education policies, in support of reform of political and public life, or against government repression, frequently confronted riot police and were dispersed by police tear gas. Student protest has had a potent history in Twentieth-century Korea, particularly when it has expressed more widely held discontent, from the Declaration of Independence of 1 March 1919 against Japanese colonial rule to the massive demonstrations of 19 April 1960 against **Syngman Rhee**'s electoral fraud. The students killed in those events are still honored. The regimes of **Park Chung Hee** and **Chun Doo Hwan**, however, cracked down on student and worker protest, claiming it was Communist inspired and in contravention of security laws. In response, students organized themselves into cells, to study leftist writings or attempt radical social policies. The death of a student in 1987 during a police interrogation sparked demonstrations that eventually forced Chun's government to concede constitutional change. Radical student organizations, such as Hanchongnyon, are still barred as pro–North Korean groups.

References: Cumings 1997; Eckert et al. 1990; Macdonald 1996; Shaw 1991.

SWEDISH INVOLVEMENT IN THE KOREAN WAR

As a neutral nation, Sweden did not participate as a combatant in the **Korean War** but joined in diplomatic efforts to end hostilities and was eventually nominated by the **United Nations** (UN) to serve as one of four neutral representatives on the **Neutral Nations Repatriation Commission** and **Neutral Nations Supervisory Commission**.

On a practical level, the Swedish Red Cross funded and staffed a medical team and field hospital in Korea. Set up in **Pusan** in September 1950 in permanent and tented accommodations, with a final capacity of 450 beds, the hospital remained in service until April 1957. The heavy fighting and many casualties of the first year of the war made large demands on the Swedish medical services, but from mid-1951 they were able to turn their attention to civilian needs. Swedish medical personnel numbered 154.

The Swedish Hospital functioned in Pusan from September 1950 to April 1957. (Imperial War Museum HU 74992)

See also: Neutral Nations Repatriation Commission; Neutral Nations Supervisory Commission.

References: History: III, 1974 and VI, 1977.

SWITZERLAND

See Neutral Nations Repatriation Commission; Neutral Nations Supervisory Commission.

T'AEBAEK MOUNTAINS

This narrow, extremely rugged range of mountains runs for 155 miles (250 kilometers) in a north-south direction through the province of Kangwon, parallel to the east coast of Korea, from which it is separated by a small coastal strip. The northern end of the T'aebaek ("great white") Mountains, inside what is now North Korea, is formed by the renowned Kumgang or Diamond Mountains. At its southern end, the range extends just into North Kyongsang Province. The mountain area, very steep on its eastern side, has a harsh climate and is sparsely populated. The difficult terrain has always been an obstacle to good road and rail communications between the east and west coasts of Korea, a problem that became very apparent during the **Korean War**.

The T'aebaek Mountains became a refuge for guerrilla fighters, who attempted to set up a base there in late summer of 1949, but they do not appear to have presented the same challenge to the **United Nations Command** and the South Korean forces as the guerrilla fighters operating in the south of the peninsula. Rather, the mountains, being farther north, formed one of the general theaters of conflict in the Korean War. Much later, in the North Korean campaigns of **infiltration** and disruption against the South during the late 1960s and early 1970s, the T'aebaek range became the focus of North Korean agents who had succeeded in landing on the east coast of South Korea. From there they would try to infiltrate the mountain area in the hope of setting up bases and rallying the local population. A U.S.-backed South Korean antiterrorist drive in the T'aebaek during the summer of 1968 rounded up a number of agents. In apparent response, a 120-strong North Korean commando group landed in small detachments at various points on the east coast in November 1968 and headed for the T'aebaek Mountains, with the intention of setting in place new networks of agents. Though they landed undetected, their presence soon became known, and eventually almost all were hunted down by South Korean troops and police, again with U.S. military support.

T

Construction of an expressway across the T'aebaek range to the east coast, the formation of two national parks within the area, and the development of ski resorts are now opening up this formerly remote region.

See also: Chiri Mountains; Infiltration.
References: Bolger 1991; Merrill 1983.

TAEGU

Taegu, the capital of North Kyongsang Province in the southeastern part of South Korea, is an important agricultural and industrial center with a tradition of political activism. In 1946, local students and workers rioted in support of left-wing activists threatened with arrest. In 1948–1949, it was a major center of guerrilla activity. During the first phase of the **Korean War**, it was the temporary capital for a month (16 July–18 August 1950) as President **Syngman Rhee** fled south before the Communist forces. Taegu then formed the center point of the **Pusan Perimeter**, the line along which the North Korean advance was stopped in August–September 1950. For the United States and South Koreans, it became a symbol of their determination to prevent any further Communist gains. After the breakout from the Pusan Perimeter in September 1950, Taegu ceased to play an active role in the war. Taegu students joined in the nationwide protests, which helped to overthrow the **Syngman Rhee** regime. Presidents **Park Chung Hee, Chun Doo Hwan,** and **Roh Tae Woo** all came from the province and attended school in Taegu, which led to a widespread belief that the "T-K (Taegu-Kyongsang) faction" of former classmates played a dominant role in South Korean politics.

See also: Pusan and the Pusan Perimeter.

TAEJON

Taejon, situated in central South Korea, is the capital of South Ch'ungch'ong Province. It is 100 miles (161 kilometers) south of the capital, **Seoul**, and about 130 miles (208 kilometers) northwest of the southern port of **Pusan**. Small and poor before the **Japanese colonial period in Korea**, from 1910 onward, it became an important railway junction. For a brief period (28 June–16 July), following the outbreak of the **Korean War** on 25 June 1950 and the flight of President **Syngman Rhee**'s government from Seoul, it served as the temporary capital of South Korea, but the rapid advance of North Korean forces led Rhee to abandon it, first for **Taegu**, and then for Pusan.

By early July 1950, Taejon was also the main center for both the South Korean army and U.S. forces arriving in Korea to try to stop the North Korean advance. On 3 July, Major General **William F. Dean**, commander of the U.S. 24th Infantry Division, arrived to take command of all U.S. armed forces in Korea. On 12 July, the Taejon Agreement placed South Korean troops under the U.S. forces' operational command. Taejon's role as a command center was brief, and continued North Korean pressure led both the South Korean and U.S. headquarters to move to Taegu. Dean, however, remained in command of the 24th Division, and was ordered to fight a holding action at Taejon to allow newly arrived U.S. forces time to settle in further south. This holding action failed, and on 19 July, a full-scale battle began with the North Koreans for the city. North Korean armored units fought their way into Taejon, and despite heavy fighting, the U.S. forces were unable to stop them. Dean himself became detached from his men and was eventually taken prisoner after 36 days' wandering about. The 24th Division suffered heavy losses as it tried to retreat. For the North Koreans, success at Taejon marked one of the high points of the war, and a huge diorama commemorates the battle in the Fatherland Revolutionary War Museum in **P'yongyang**. The fighting destroyed much of the city, but it was rebuilt in the 1950s and is now an important industrial and educational center.

See also: Taegu.

TAIWAN

Taiwan, also known as Formosa, is an island 100 miles (161 kilometers) off the southeast coast of China. It was a Japanese colony from 1895 to 1945. In 1945, the Republic of China (Nationalist China) took the Japanese surrender on the island and treated it as part of China. Following their defeat in the Chinese civil war (1946–1949), Generalissimo **Chiang Kai-shek** led the Chinese Nationalists to Taiwan, which has been governed as the Republic of China ever since. The **People's Republic of China** (PRC) claims the island as part of China.

In June 1950, PRC forces were preparing to invade Taiwan to end the civil war. However, following the outbreak of the **Korean War**, U.S. President **Harry S Truman** ordered the U.S. Seventh Fleet to patrol the Taiwan Strait to prevent a Communist takeover of Taiwan. The PRC was quick to denounce this development. To the PRC, Truman's action over Taiwan, taken together with the U.S. decision to intervene in Korea—another area of direct concern to China—was clear evidence of unyielding U.S. hostility to the new government of China. The Taiwan intervention, therefore, played an important part in the Chinese decision to send the **Chinese People's Volunteers** to Korea in October 1950.

Chiang Kai-shek also had links to U.S. General **Douglas MacArthur**, who thought that Taiwan was an important anti-Communist outpost and that the Chinese Nationalists should be helped against the PRC. MacArthur visited Taiwan in July–August 1950 and recommended military support for Chiang. In return, Chiang offered to send some 30,000 troops to help the **United Nations** (UN) forces in Korea. The U.S. government eventually decided that this might be too provocative to the PRC and declined the offer. In 1952–1953, many of the Chinese **prisoners of war** in UN hands opted to go to Taiwan, thereby provoking a crisis in the **armistice** negotiations. After the war, Taiwan and South Korea maintained cordial relations, based on strong anti-Communist sentiment. Taiwan also provided support for South Korea at the UN, where Taiwan held the "China" seat until 1971. These good relations ended when South Korea established diplomatic relations with the PRC in 1992. Since then, South Korean–Taiwan relations have been tense, whereas there are occasional reports of trade and other contacts between Taiwan and North Korea, once regarded as bitter enemies.

See also: Chinese Involvement in Korea (1919–1948); People's Republic of China Relations with South Korea; Repatriation of Prisoners of War.
References: Koo and Han 1985; Matray 1991; Stone 1952.

TASK FORCES

During the **Korean War**, a number of task forces were created. These consisted of relatively small, ad hoc groups, brought together from several military units, to perform one clear task. The first, and perhaps the most famous, was Task Force Smith, led by Lieutenant Colonel Charles B. Smith, which was assembled in Japan on 30 June 1950, flown to Korea as part of General **William Dean**'s 24th Division, and immediately sent to meet the advancing North Korean forces at Osan, south of **Seoul**. Ill armed and ill prepared, Task Force Smith proved no match for the North Korean tanks, which swept it aside and continued their advance. Other task forces, such as Task Force Maclean/Faith, which fought in the encounters at the **Changjin Reservoir**, were also defeated. More successful was Task Force Paik, led by General **Paik Sun-yup**, which was engaged in antiguerrilla activities in the south of Korea between December 1951 and April 1952.

See also: Changjin Reservoir (1950); Dean, William Frische; Paik Sun-yup; Taejon.

TAYLOR, MAXWELL DAVENPORT (1901–1987)

Maxwell Davenport Taylor, who succeeded General **James Van Fleet** as commander of the U.S. Eighth Army, was born in Missouri in 1901. He graduated from the U.S. Military Academy in 1922 and served in a variety of positions before becoming a student of Japanese at the U.S. embassy in Tokyo from 1935 to 1939. He graduated from the War College in 1940. During World War II, he took part in the Italian, Normandy, and Western European campaigns.

After the war, Taylor held a series of European and Washington staff appointments before becoming commander of the U.S. Eighth Army in Korea in the final stages of the **Korean War**. Taylor saw his role as primarily to avoid combat or casualties as far as possible as the **armistice** negotiations at **P'anmunjom** slowly drew to a close. This was not an easy task, as the Communist forces pressed the

United Nations (UN) forces hard to gain as much territorial advantage as possible. At the end of the Korean War, Taylor spent much time helping to build up the South Korean army, as well as supervising the armistice agreement. In 1954, he became commander of U.S. Forces, Far East, and in 1955, commander-in-chief, **United Nations Command**. In June 1955, he succeeded General **Matthew B. Ridgway** as U.S. Army chief-of-staff, a post he resigned in 1959, following disagreements with President **Dwight D. Eisenhower**. Under President John F. Kennedy, he was recalled as chairman of the Joint Chiefs of Staff from 1962 to 1964. Following his second retirement from the military, he became U.S. ambassador to South Vietnam, 1964–1965. Thereafter, he served as an adviser to President Lyndon Baines Johnson and was closely associated with the growing U.S. involvement in the **Vietnam War**. He died in Washington, D.C., in 1987.

See also: Pork Chop Hill, Battles of (1951–1953); United States Forces in the Korean War.
References: Taylor 1960, 1972.

TEAM SPIRIT (REPUBLIC OF KOREA–UNITED STATES JOINT MILITARY EXERCISE)

Team Spirit was a major South Korean–U.S. military exercise, first introduced in 1976, designed to improve coordination between the two armed forces. There had been earlier joint service exercises, but Team Spirit was designed to test all aspects of air, land, navy, and marine cooperation, involving troops airlifted from the United States as well as those in country. It was held annually from 1976 until 1991, and each year the North Koreans reacted with hostile propaganda and an enhanced state of military alertness. Following the 1991 **intra-Korean agreements**, it was canceled in 1992 but was reinstated in 1993. Although there was considerable tension in 1994 over the **North Korean nuclear program**, the exercise was again canceled in 1994, and it has not so far been reinstated. However, other joint South Korean–U.S. exercises, such as Ulchi Lens and Foal Eagle, which cover some of the same ground as Team Spirit, still continue.

TELEVISION AND THE KOREAN WAR

In 1950, the year of the outbreak of the **Korean War**, television was available to only a minority of homes in North America and Europe. Coverage of the war came largely through newsreel films, made by companies such as Pathé and Gaumont and shown in cinemas and on television. From the late 1940s, TV newsreel was expanding in reaction to the cinema newsreel companies' reluctance to allow their own products to be used on television. The British Broadcasting Corporation (BBC), for instance, set up a TV newsreel unit in 1948, which had its own cameramen in Korea throughout most of the war and supplied film to Canada, France, and Belgium, among others. But even the material available from television newsreel was shown as an illustration to the spoken news and could not be said to constitute television news. Most people's images of the war came through black-and-white photos, newsreels, and information films, such as the Korean War Combat Bulletins (1950–1951), issued by the U.S. Army, and similar material put out by news corporation—NBC, CBS—and commercial film companies.

Newsreel coverage was fairly constant during the first four months of hostilities and, as might be expected, supported the **United Nations Command** (UNC) and especially the many U.S. troops committed. Emotive descriptions of the stand of the "free world" against the "red tide" bolstered the sense of a confrontation with international communism, judged guilty of launching the war. The nuances of a complicated situation were generally passed over for uncritical reporting of the South Korean scene. Newsreel coverage of hostilities declined from the end of 1950, although separate films were made of outstanding episodes in the fighting. The BBC maintained its newsreel reporting but concentrated on the activities of the British contingent, only a small element in the UNC.

In the three decades following the Korean War, a few documentary films and—as the 16-mm film format passed from use—videos were made on the subject. It was not until the 1980s that extensive interest was renewed. By that time, television and video were established as being among the most effective ways of transmitting arguments backed by visual impact to the public. Scholarly investigation from the late 1970s into the conduct of the war and into the period preceding it, stimulated by the opening of first Western and South Korean archives, then

Soviet and Chinese sources, doubtless contributed in the 1980s and 1990s to encourage historians, journalists, and news companies in the West, Japan, and South Korea toward making television documentaries on the conflict. The readiness of Chinese, Russians, and even North Koreans involved in the war to cooperate with Western television and film companies allowed a wider perspective in these documentaries. Many of them, nonetheless, continued to deal largely with the military aspects of the conflict or with domestic American political differences over the conduct of the war. A few, such as Thames Television's documentary *Korea: The Unknown War* (1988), sought to examine the internal Korean angles and the social consequences of the conflict.

See also: Cumings, Bruce Glen; Histories and Other Studies of the Korean War; Press Correspondents in the Korean War; War Stories and War Films of the Korean War.

References: Cumings 1992; Edwards 1997; Smith 1988.

TERRORISM
See **North Korean Use of Terrorism.**

THAI FORCES IN THE KOREAN WAR
On 20 July 1950, the Royal Thai Expeditionary Forces to Korea, comprising ground troops, air and naval detachments, and medical support staff, were committed to the **United Nations Command** (UNC) by the Thai government.

A Thai infantry battalion, drawn from the 21st Regimental Combat Team, arrived in Korea on 7 November 1950. The battalion came under the operational command of successive U.S. Army divisions. In late November 1950, it advanced to **P'yongyang** but had to withdraw south in January 1951, covering the retreat from **Seoul**. It then faced the two Chinese offensives of spring 1951. From 31 October to 11 November 1952, the battalion joined in the battle of **Pork Chop Hill**, engaging in frequent close combat. In July 1956, it was reduced to company strength and as such remained in Korea until 23 June 1972, when it withdrew, leaving a small contingent for the UNC Honor Guard.

Some 4,000 men passed through the Thai Battalion during the course of the **Korean War**. Its losses during the war were 125 dead, 959 wounded, and five missing in action. The battalion earned the nickname of "Little Tigers" and won numerous citations. By the time the last company left in 1972, a total of 19,000 men had served in Korea.

Between 9 November 1950 and 21 January 1955, a total of five Thai naval vessels—four frigates (one the replacement of a ship damaged in operations) and one transport ship—were based at **Sasebo** in Japan, from where they served with the UNC Naval Command Far East Blockade and Escort Force, largely in the waters off **Wonsan** and Songjin on the east coast of Korea. They undertook bombardment of shore targets and patrol and escort duties. A total of 2,485 personnel served with the Thai naval unit, with the loss of four lives.

Three C-47 Skytrain cargo planes of the Royal Thai Air Force were based from 23 June 1951 to 6 November 1964 at Tachikawa in Japan, operating both within Japan and between Japan and Korea as part of the UNC air command. From 6 November 1964 to 26 July 1976, the Royal Thai Air Transport Detachment maintained two C-123 aircraft at Tachikawa in support of the UN Command (Rear).

Three separate Thai medical service detachments—an air medical team used for evacuation and nursing at UNC hospitals, a Red Cross medical unit based in **Pusan** and staffed by a total of 66 doctors and nurses, and a mobile surgical hospital team serving in UNC hospitals—were all active in Japan or Korea during and after the Korean War.

See also: Japanese Involvement in the Korean War; Korean War (1950–1953); Sasebo Naval Base.

References: Blair 1987; History: I, 1972 and VI, 1977; Summers 1990; Thomas, Abbott, and Chappell 1986.

38TH AND OTHER PARALLELS

Latitude 38 degrees north, known as the 38th parallel, cuts across the **Korea Peninsula** at roughly the midpoint. Since 1945, it has been a symbol of the division of Korea, even though the Military Demarcation Line, which forms the actual "boundary" between the two states, runs a little north of the parallel for much of its length. The parallel is an arbitrary division and does not correspond to a natural frontier.

It was chosen in some haste in August 1945. On 9 August, the **Union of Soviet Socialist Republics (USSR)** declared war on Japan and in the next few days moved troops into **Northeast China** and Korea.

Amid signs of accelerating Japanese collapse, the United States proposed that both it and the Soviet Union should accept the Japanese surrender in Korea. Though military considerations predominated, the Americans were anxious not to see the Soviet Union control the whole of the peninsula. On the night of 10–11 August, two officers in the Operations Division of the U.S. War Department, Colonel Charles Bonesteel and Major **Dean Rusk**, were asked to suggest a line likely to be acceptable to the Soviet authorities, north of which they would take the surrender. The Americans would accept the surrender south of it. The two men, reportedly given thirty minutes for the task, picked the 38th parallel, largely on the grounds that the capital, **Seoul**, lying south of it, would be in the U.S. zone of occupation. Their proposal was incorporated in U.S. General Order No. 1, which was accepted by the Soviet leader **Joseph Stalin** and announced on 2 September 1945 by General **Douglas MacArthur**. It has been suggested that division of Korea along the 38th parallel was discussed at the Yalta Conference (February 1945) and the **Potsdam Conference** (July 1945), but no formal statement was issued on the subject after either conference.

Throughout the **Korean War**, the 38th parallel functioned as a kind of touchstone of intent for the **United Nations Command**. In October 1950, MacArthur crossed the parallel in pursuit of North Korean forces, taking the war to the North. In November 1950, the British suggested a buffer zone below the North Korea–China border, at the 40th parallel. Under the North Korean and Chinese counterattack, UN troops established a new defensive line, first along the 38th parallel, and then, in January 1951, along the 37th. Eventually, with stalemate and negotiation, the 38th parallel emerged again as the line of division.

The concept of a division of the peninsula into (non-Korean) zones of interest was mooted by Russia and Japan as they maneuvered for control in Korea between 1896 and 1904. In at least one secret agreement, in 1896, the two states proposed that should their troops be required in Korea in the event of unrest, they should divide the country north and south of a neutral line along the 39th parallel; i.e., at the level of **P'yongyang**. It is unlikely that the Americans responsible in 1945 for suggesting the 38th parallel knew anything about these earlier proposals.

See also: Demilitarized Zone (DMZ); Korean War (1950–1953); MacArthur, Douglas.

References: Eckert et al. 1990; Giffard 1994; Kim 1990; Lone and McCormack 1993; Macdonald 1996; Sandusky 1983; Schnabel 1972; U.S. State Department 1960.

TRUMAN, HARRY S (1884–1972)

Truman, who was president of the United States from 1945 to 1953, was in office at the outbreak of the **Korean War** on 25 June 1950. He was born in Lamar, Missouri, and served as a captain in the U.S. forces in France during World War I. Before and after the war, Truman engaged in various unsuccessful businesses, until he took up local politics in 1922. He entered the U.S. Senate in 1934 and was President **Franklin Roosevelt**'s somewhat surprising choice for vice-president in 1944. When Roosevelt died in April 1945, Truman became president and then went on to win in his own right in 1948.

Although U.S. statements, in particular one by Secretary of State **Dean Acheson,** had implied that Korea was not a defense concern of the United States, Truman was swift to act when the Korean War began, seeing it as part of a policy of Communist worldwide aggression. He immediately pledged U.S. forces for the defense of South Korea and sought **United Nations** support for his actions. He also decided to appoint the U.S. commander-in-chief, Far Eastern Command, General **Douglas MacArthur,** as commander-in-chief of the newly formed **United Nations Command** (UNC) on 8 July 1950. Truman supported MacArthur's policy of crossing the **38th parallel** and the drive to the **Yalu River.** However, when MacArthur demanded that he should be allowed to attack the **People's Republic of China,** following the intervention of the **Chinese People's Volunteers** and the subsequent retreat of the UNC, and then leaked critical views of the president to a politician, Truman acted swiftly. MacArthur was dismissed on 11 April 1951 and replaced by General **Matthew Ridgway.** Thereafter, Truman had no problems with the military. His main Korean concern after the dismissal of MacArthur was that there should be no forced **repatriation** of North Korean and Chinese **prisoners of war,** a stand that led to stalemate in the **armistice** negotiations.

Truman's popularity fell during the remainder of his period in office. The prolonged armistice negotiations, while the fighting continued, made the Korean War unpopular. Senator Joseph McCarthy's anti-Communist crusade, which attacked the State Department and the administration in general for harboring Communists, also contributed to the president's poor image, as did a number of financial scandals. "Korea, corruption and communism in government" proved a powerful slogan in the 1952 presidential elections. After he left office in 1953, however, Truman's reputation bounced back, and he is now seen by many in the United States as a strong president whose decisions on Korea were mostly the right ones.

See also: Acheson, Dean Gooderham; MacArthur, Douglas.

References: James and Wells 1993; Phillips 1966; Stueck 1995; Truman 1956.

TUMEN RIVER AREA DEVELOPMENT PROGRAM

See **Rajin-Sonbong Development Zone.**

TUNNELS

See **Demilitarized Zone (DMZ).**

TURKISH FORCES IN THE KOREAN WAR

On 25 July 1950, the Turkish Army Command Force was activated to serve under the **United Nations Command** (UNC) in Korea. After the South Korean, U.S., and Commonwealth contingents, the Turks provided the largest national contribution in the **Korean War.** Altogether three brigades, with a peak strength of 5,455 men and a total commitment of 14,936 men, rotated in the fighting. A fourth Turkish brigade arrived on 6 July 1953 and stayed in Korea until May 1954.

On 19 October 1950, the First Turkish Brigade, composed of three battalions and including an artillery regiment, arrived in Korea. It was placed under the operational control of the U.S. IX Corps and attached to the 25th Infantry Division. Its first engagement, at Kunu-ri north of Sunchon in North Korea, in late November 1950, was also its bloodiest. Detailed to help block a Chinese advance, it was beaten back with the estimated loss of 1,000 men, a fifth of its personnel, and retreated south along with U.S. troops. On 3 January 1951, the brigade was reassigned to the U.S. I Corps. It fought with varying success in the two Chinese spring offensives of 1951, operating in the central sector of Korea. For much of 1952, it patrolled in the Heartbreak Ridge area and in May 1953 struggled to retain territory along the line of confrontation north of Munsan.

The Turkish troops had a reputation for hand-to-hand fighting and the use of bayonets and for strong discipline. Those taken prisoner maintained this discipline in captivity and refused cooperation with their captors. Casualties were high: a total of 3,506 (741 killed, 2,068 wounded, 163 missing in action, 244 taken prisoner, and 290 noncombatant casualties). Those killed included four commanding officers or company commanders.

See also: Bloody and Heartbreak Ridges, Battles of (1951); Korean War (1950–1953); Prisoners of War.

References: Blair 1987; History: I, 1972 and VI, 1977; Summers 1990.

UIJONGBU

Uijongbu is a small town some 12 miles (20 kilometers) north of the South Korean capital, **Seoul**. It stands on one of the traditional north-south invasion routes. Before the outbreak of the **Korean War** in June 1950, it was one of the principal South Korean centers for gathering military intelligence about North Korea. North Korean forces passed through it on their way south in June 1950, and it was burned by **United Nations Command** forces retreating from the North in January 1951. It was during this retreat that General **Walton Walker** was killed in a traffic accident at Uijongbu. After the war, it became a major service center for both South Korean and U.S. forces stationed nearby, and since the 1960s it has also developed as a light industry center. It is now linked to Seoul by metro.

See also: United States Military Presence in South Korea since 1953.

UN

See **United Nations (UN).**

UNC

See **United Nations Command (UNC).**

UNCOK

See **United Nations Commission on Korea (UNCOK).**

UNCURK

See **United Nations Commission for Unification and Rehabilitation of Korea (UNCURK).**

UNDERWOOD FAMILY (1885–)

This family of American missionaries and educationists has been involved through several generations with personalities and events central to modern Korean history.

Horace Grant Underwood (1859–1916) arrived in **Seoul** in 1885 as a missionary for the American Presbyterian Church. He took **Kim Kyu-shik**, subsequently a leader in the Korean nationalist movement, into his orphanage as a child and later employed him

U

as his secretary. Underwood's son, Horace Horton Underwood (1890–1951), in 1919 and 1939 had contacts with **Pak Hon-yong**, active in the Korean Communist movement, which were later used in 1955 by **Kim Il Sung** as evidence of Pak's traitorous connections with the Americans. Horace H. Underwood himself was posthumously branded in the charges against Pak as a U.S. spy who had sought to direct Pak's espionage activities. Underwood knew many of the leading figures in Korea during the period from 1945 to 1950. In 1949, his wife was assassinated by Communist agents at her home in Seoul. The Underwood family was seemingly further vilified in the novel *Sarang* ("Love," 1960) by the North Korean writer Han Sor-ya (1900–?1970), for which they may have served as the model for a family of malevolent American missionaries.

Two of Horace H. Underwood's sons, Horace Grant (born 1917) and Richard (born 1927), serving in the U.S. armed forces, interpreted for the **United Nations Command** (UNC) in the **armistice** talks. Horace acted as guide and interpreter in the UNC advance on Seoul following the **Inch'on landing** of September 1950. Another brother, John (1919–1995), was a volunteer civilian interpreter for the U.S. Army.

See also: Armistice; Kim Kyu-shik; Literature of the Korean Conflict; Pak Hon-yong.
References: Caldwell 1952; Kim 1979; Myers 1994; Scalapino and Lee 1972; Underwood 1918/1983; Vatcher 1958.

UNGA

See **United Nations General Assembly Resolutions on Korea.**

UNIFICATION CHURCH
See **Moon Sun Myung.**

UNIFIED COMMAND
See **United Nations Command (UNC).**

UNION OF SOVIET SOCIALIST REPUBLICS (USSR)

The Union of Soviet Socialist Republics (USSR), generally known as the Soviet Union, is the former name of the vast state that extended from the borders of Eastern Europe to the Arctic and Pacific coasts. It was created in 1922, five years after the October revolution of 1917 that established the first Communist state. Eventually the Soviet Union comprised fifteen federated republics, the largest and most powerful of which was always the Russian Soviet Federal Socialist Republic (RSFSR) with its capital at Moscow, which was also the capital of the USSR. From there, the Soviet Communist Party, as the strongest element in Soviet society, controlled the government and economy of the USSR. The party itself was long under the hand of **Joseph Stalin.** His successors followed varying policies, some aimed at a measure of social and economic modernization. Liberalization spreading from Eastern Europe in the late 1980s helped to finally undermine the power of the party and further weakened a shaky economic situation. In December 1991, the USSR gave way to the Commonwealth of Independent States. The RSFSR resumed the name Russia, but it covers a smaller territory than the former Soviet Union.

Through its international front organization, the Comintern, the Soviet Communist Party supported the early Korean Communist groups. It was the backer of the North Korean leader **Kim Il Sung** and played an essential role in the formation of the North Korean state. The Communist bloc it headed provided a wider supportive framework in which the North could flourish.

See also: Korean Communist Party (KCP); Soviet Involvement in Korea (1917–1945).

UNITED KINGDOM AND KOREA

Although the United Kingdom took some interest in Korea during the second half of the nineteenth century (mainly because of its strategic position in East Asia) and for a brief period occupied a group of Korean islands, the peninsula was not a major British concern. China and Japan were always far more important to the U.K., which concluded an alliance with Japan in 1902 and readily accepted the Japanese takeover of Korea in 1910. During the **Japanese colonial period in Korea (1910–1945),** there was always a small British community in the peninsula, but British interests in Korea were far less than those of the United States. The U.K. played a minor role in the wartime discussions of Korea's future—at the 1943 **Cairo Conference** and other high-level meetings—but took no part in the post-war occupation of the peninsula. From 1946 onward, the U.K. had consular officers in South Korea and, soon after the creation of the Republic of Korea (South Korea) in 1948, established diplomatic relations with the new state. Like other Western countries, the U.K. did not recognize the Democratic People's Republic of Korea (North Korea), also founded in 1948.

After the outbreak of the **Korean War** in June 1950, the U.K. government under Prime Minister **Clement Attlee** promptly condemned North Korea. Attlee joined with the United States in encouraging a **United Nations** (UN) response to what was seen as a Soviet-inspired aggression by North Korea against the South. This move was supported by the opposition Conservative Party under the World War II leader **Winston Churchill** and by the British press. At first, Attlee hoped to limit British military involvement to the Royal Navy. The Royal Navy was in action off the coast of Korea within a week of the beginning of the conflict and would fight throughout the war. Of the many ships that took part, HMS *Belfast* (now moored on the River Thames in London as a floating museum) is probably the best known. Before long, U.S. pressure led the U.K. to send land forces to Korea also. On 29 August 1950, men of the 27th Infantry Brigade, together with the Royal Irish Hussars equipped with Cromwell and Centurion tanks, arrived at **Pusan** and took part in the battle of the **Naktong River.** In October 1950, the British 29th Brigade, made up of three infantry battalions and elements of the Royal Artillery, joined them. Later, the Royal Air Force sent reconnaissance aircraft, and so all three British services were represented in Korea. British forces took part in the advance to the **Yalu River** and fought well in the rearguard action that followed the intervention of the **Chinese People's Volunteers** in late October 1950. The best-known British action was the stand of the First Battalion of the Gloucestershire Regiment at Solma-ri in the battle of the **Imjin River** during the Chinese attacks in the **Seoul** region in April 1951. British troops were also in action at **Kap'yong** during the same period. In the summer of 1951, British ground forces became part of the **First Commonwealth Division** and remained so until the end of the war. By then, some 14,000 British troops had served in Korea. Of these, some 700 were killed in action and about 4,000 wounded or captured. In all, 977 were repatriated; one Royal Marine elected to remain in Chinese hands, though he later returned to Britain. British forces remained in Korea until 1957, and a British general was a member of the UN side to the **Military Armistice Commission** until 1962. Thereafter, successive defense attachés at the British embassy assumed the role, which they still held in 1999. Until the early 1990s, Britain also supplied a small contingent of troops to the **United Nations Command** as an honor guard.

The Korean War affected Britain in a number of ways. By 1950, Britain had been fighting a Communist insurgency in Malaya since 1948, and there were other imperial demands that had to be met, including a large garrison in **Hong Kong**. The need to supply troops to Korea led to an extension of compulsory military service ("National Service") for young men and to the recall of reservists, neither of which was a popular decision. The diversion of scarce funds to rearmament programs meant that less money was available for the social welfare policies that the Labour government favored. The decision to impose some health charges to meet increased government expenditure split the Labour Party and contributed to its defeat in the 1951 general elections. Korea also showed that the United States had decisively replaced the U.K. as a world leader. The war was fought as an American war, with strategic decisions being made by American commanders. The U.K. tried to influence the course of the war on a number of occasions. In November 1950, Britain proposed the establishment of a **Demilitarized Zone** from central North Korea to the Yalu. In December 1950, Attlee flew to Washington to express concern about proposals from the UN commander-in-chief, U.S. General **Douglas MacArthur**, for intervention in China and the possible use of the atomic bomb. Although the U.S. government listened to these views, its decisions were made on other considerations than British concern. There was also some tension between the two countries because of the U.K.'s policy toward the **People's Republic of China** and the **embargo** issue. Although in reality there was little change in British policies, relations with the United States improved after Churchill became prime minister in autumn 1951.

After the armistice, the U.K. helped with South Korea's economic reconstruction and supported its efforts to win international recognition. During the 1970s, in particular, the U.K. played an important role in organizing support for South Korea at the UN. Apart from some small-scale trade, British relations with North Korea remained almost nonexistent until both Koreas applied to join the UN in 1991. By voting for its admission to the UN, the U.K. formally recognized North Korea but did not establish diplomatic relations. However, the U.K. began a political dialogue with North Korea in 1992, which has led to the exchange of low-level delegations between the two countries.

See also: Australian Forces in the Korean War; Blake, George; Cameron, Mark James Walter; Foreign Civilian Detainees in the Korean War; Franks, Oliver; Hook, the, Battles of (1952–1953); Literature of the Korean Conflict; Lord, Herbert Arthur; Television and the Korean War; Winnington, Alan.

References: Barclay 1954; Cunningham-Boothe and Farrar 1988; Farrar-Hockley 1990, 1995; Grey 1988; History: II, 1973; Hoare 1983; Lowe 1988(b); MacDonald 1990; Morris 1996; O'Neill 1981.

UNITED NATIONS (UN)

This international organization, of which the majority of the world's states are now members, has its headquarters in New York. Established by charter in June 1945 with a membership of fifty-one, with the aim of providing a framework for the maintenance of world peace and security, it replaced the earlier League of Nations (1918–1946). The origins of the United Nations lay in the 1944 wartime discussions between the United States, the **Union of Soviet**

Socialist Republics, Britain, and Nationalist China on the form of the postwar world. These four powers—later joined by France—have remained at the center of the UN's structure through their permanent membership in the Security Council, the UN's most powerful body. In 1971, the **People's Republic of China** took over the seat previously held by Nationalist China; Russia inherited the Soviet seat in 1991.

The **Korean War** presented an early test for the UN, which responded for the first time in its history with a full-scale military campaign against what it defined as an aggressor. The **United Nations Command** formed the opposition to the North Korean forces, who were joined shortly by Chinese troops. Although the United States was the prime mover against what it saw as Communist aggression, it sought the cooperation of a wider group of states and used its strong position in the UN Security Council and UN General Assembly to maintain pressure on other member states. The absence of the Soviet representative to the Security Council at crucial votes on 25 and 27 June 1950 helped to secure UN backing for military intervention in Korea. A series of resolutions in both the Security Council and the General Assembly provided a formal counterpoint to the fighting on the ground and allowed a greater number of countries to express views or participate in efforts to find solutions to the conflict.

See also: United Nations General Assembly Resolutions on Korea; United Nations Security Council Resolutions on Korea.

References: Nicholas 1962; Robertson 1993.

UNITED NATIONS CEMETERY (PUSAN)

A cemetery to receive the remains of troops killed in the fighting in Korea was established by the **United Nations Command** (UNC) in **Pusan** on 18 January 1951. Remains from six other cemeteries in Korea were transferred there.

In December 1955, the United Nations General Assembly accepted a proposal by the South Korean government that this cemetery should be established as a United Nations Memorial Cemetery. In March 1960, the United Nations assumed charge of it, the land having been granted free in perpetuity by South Korea. Since February 1974, administration

has rested with a commission, which appoints a custodian.

Twenty commemorative plots honor the twenty-two nations, combatant and noncombatant, forming the UNC. Whereas from 1951 to 1954 the cemetery contained about 11,000 bodies, many were later repatriated; it now holds the bodies of 2,299 soldiers of eleven nationalities, four unknown soldiers, and eleven nonbelligerents. Several other monuments have been erected.

See also: Memorials and Museums to the Korean Conflict; United Nations Command (UNC).

UNITED NATIONS COMMAND (UNC)

Following the outbreak of the **Korean War** on 25 June 1950, the United States pledged support for the Republic of Korea (South Korea) against the Democratic People's Republic of Korea (North Korea) and at the same time took the issue to the **United Nations** (UN). In Resolution No. 83 of 27 June 1950, the United Nations Security Council recommended that the member states of the UN should provide assistance to South Korea. Articles 39 and 42 of the UN Charter authorized member states to create international armed forces to combat aggression and restore peace. Based on this authority, the Security Council resolved on 7 July 1950 (Resolution No. 84) to recommend that all member states make available military forces and other assistance to a "unified command" and directed this command to make periodic reports on how well it had achieved its task. The United States was asked to name a commander. U.S. President **Harry S Truman** appointed the Commander-in-Chief Far Eastern Command, General **Douglas MacArthur** (who was also Supreme Commander for the Allied Powers in Japan and Commanding General, U.S. Army Forces Far East), as head of the unified command with the title of Commander-in-Chief, United Nations Command (UNC). A UNC headquarters was established in Tokyo, where MacArthur had his other commands. Sixteen nations sent contingents to the UNC, although the bulk of the forces under its authority were from the United States. On 14 July 1950, South Korean President **Syngman Rhee** placed South Korean forces under the operational control of the UN commander. Overall, the breakdown of ground forces for the UNC was 50.3 percent U.S.,

40.1 percent South Korean, and 9.6 percent others. The United States provided by far the majority of naval and air force units.

In practice, MacArthur delegated his authority as UN commander to the commanding general of the U.S. Eighth Army in Korea, although his successor as UN commander, General **Mark Clark**, signed the 1953 armistice agreement, and the UNC is still represented on the **Military Armistice Commission**. During the Korean War, the headquarters of the UNC and the U.S. Eighth Army were relocated from Tokyo to **Seoul**. Both were moved back to Tokyo after the war, but they were returned to Seoul in 1967 and remain there. The UNC remains in existence today, and its commander makes periodic reports to the UN through the U.S. State Department. Since the establishment of the U.S.–South Korean **Combined Forces Command** in 1978, however, the UNC has been little more than a shell with only a small headquarters staff and an honor guard specifically attached to the UN commander. In theory, should war break out again, the U.S.–South Korean Combined Forces would be immediately available to the UNC, together with such other forces as UN members might furnish. In reality, however, it is hard to see the UNC playing more than a formal role in any such possible conflict.

See also: Australian Forces in the Korean War; Belgian Forces in the Korean War; Canadian Forces in the Korean War; Colombian Forces in the Korean War; Ethiopian Forces in the Korean War; French Forces in the Korean War; Greek Forces in the Korean War; Netherlands Forces in the Korean War; New Zealand Forces in the Korean War; Philippines Forces in the Korean War; Ridgway, Matthew Bunker; South African Forces in the Korean War; Thai Forces in the Korean War; Turkish Forces in the Korean War; United Kingdom and Korea; United States Forces in the Korean War.

References: Bailey 1992; Matray 1991; Summers 1990.

UNITED NATIONS COMMISSION FOR UNIFICATION AND REHABILITATION OF KOREA (UNCURK)

This commission was established by the UN General Assembly on 7 October 1950 to replace the **United Nations Commission on Korea** (UNCOK). Its rehabilitation work was quickly assumed by the **United Nations Korean Reconstruction Agency** (UNKRA),

and UNCURK provided very little in the way of reconstruction funds. However, its continued existence and the task laid upon it to work toward the reunification of the peninsula provided the justification for many countries' refusal to recognize or establish diplomatic relations with North Korea. On 21 November 1973—following various North-South contacts and President **Park Chung Hee**'s statement on 23 June 1973 that South Korea would no longer oppose **diplomatic recognition** of North Korea—the UN made a consensus decision to terminate UNCURK. After this decision, several Western countries, including the Nordic countries and Australia, announced their intention to establish diplomatic relations with North Korea.

See also: Cross-recognition; Red Cross North-South Talks.

UNITED NATIONS COMMISSION ON KOREA (UNCOK)

The United Nations Commission on Korea (UNCOK) replaced the **United Nations Temporary Commission on Korea** (UNTCOK), following the UN General Assembly resolution of 12 December 1948 that recognized the Republic of Korea (ROK) as the only legitimate government on the peninsula. The commission's role was to supervise the dismantling of all non-ROK organizations on the peninsula and to report on progress toward reunification. In September 1949, UNCOK argued that there would be no progress without agreement between the United States and the USSR and criticized the two nations for not achieving this. It was also critical of South Korean President **Syngman Rhee**'s authoritarian rule. A further resolution, on 21 October 1949, reorganized UNCOK, which was to continue to monitor developments in Korea since there was a threat of conflict. In February 1950, this new commission went to Korea, but when it attempted to contact North Korea, it was fired on. UNCOK therefore requested that it should have trained military observers attached. The presence of these observers in June 1950, and their reports on the outbreak of hostilities, formed the basis of later UN resolutions condemning North Korea.

See also: United Nations General Assembly Resolutions on Korea.

Reference: Matray 1985.

UNITED NATIONS GENERAL ASSEMBLY RESOLUTIONS ON KOREA

The General Assembly of the United Nations (UN) is a debating and voting forum open to all members of the UN. The decision of 27 June 1950 to recommend that member states commit armed forces against the North Koreans after their invasion of South Korea on 25 June was taken by the smaller and more powerful Security Council; but the General Assembly had already passed a number of resolutions on the problems of the **Korea Peninsula** in the years before the **Korean War**. It continued to debate developments during the war and subsequent aspects of the Korean problem after the fighting had finished. On most occasions, the General Assembly was responding to proposals submitted by the United States, which took the lead in the UN military and diplomatic campaign against North Korea and its eventual ally, the **People's Republic of China** (PRC). Nonetheless, the open membership of the General Assembly widened the opportunity to express an opinion on Korean issues, sometimes to modify the great powers' proposals, and to participate in subsidiary initiatives to find solutions to the problems of the peninsula.

The General Assembly first debated Korea in late 1947, when the United States, having failed to make any headway in the **Joint Commission on Trusteeship** with the Soviet Union on Korean unification, passed the problem to the UN. On 14 November 1947, the General Assembly accepted a U.S. proposal for free elections in Korea, the withdrawal of foreign troops, and the formation of a **United Nations Temporary Commission on Korea** (UNTCOK) to supervise elections. The failure of this initiative—elections were held only in the southern half of the country—hastened the creation of two separate Korean states during 1948. The United States, by then committed to the South, asked the General Assembly to recognize South Korea as the only legitimate government on the peninsula and to endorse a replacement for the earlier UNTCOK: a **United Nations Commission on Korea** (UNCOK), which would supervise the dissolution of all non-Korean civil and military organizations. The General Assembly passed this request on 12 December 1948. Ten months later, after UNCOK had submitted a report doubting both U.S. and

Soviet commitment to unification, the United States sought UN agreement to new tasks for UNCOK, to include responsibility for reporting any developments that might lead to military conflict. The General Assembly likewise accepted this, on 21 October 1949. Members of UNCOK were present in Korea on 25 June 1950, when the North invaded, and their report was instrumental in securing UN Security Council agreement to commit UN troops.

The headlong course of the Korean War during its first six months left little opportunity for debate. A British proposal on long-term plans for the peninsula, accepted by the General Assembly on 7 October 1950, envisaged reunification, elections, and rehabilitation but barely hinted at military action, even though UN forces had by then crossed the **38th parallel** in pursuit of the enemy. The resolution authorized setting up the **United Nations Commission for Unification and Rehabilitation of Korea** (UNCURK). A further body, the **United Nations Korean Reconstruction Agency** (UNKRA), was voted into being by the General Assembly on 1 December 1950. The initiative passed briefly into the hands of the Arab-Asian group of states, whose proposal for the formation of a three-member Cease Fire Committee to explore ways of achieving the withdrawal of all foreign forces from the peninsula was passed on 14 December 1950. (By then, the participation of Chinese troops in the fighting had been confirmed.) This proposal was rebuffed by the Chinese government. The United States then used the General Assembly for a diplomatic move against the PRC when it launched a proposal early in 1951 condemning China as an aggressor in Korea. The proposal called on China to withdraw its forces from Korea and on all states to continue to support the UN action. Despite some opposition, the General Assembly passed this resolution on 1 February 1951. On 18 May 1951, it further agreed to a U.S. proposal recommending a selective embargo on exports to the PRC and North Korea.

By 1952, when the General Assembly was next called upon to vote on Korea, the subject had moved to **armistice** negotiations. On 3 December 1952, the First Committee of the UN tabled a proposal, which was accepted, aimed at resolving outstanding disagreements between the **United Nations Command** (UNC) and the North Korean/Chinese command on the release of **prisoners of war** (POWs). This resolution incorporated the results of negotiations within the UN on earlier Indian proposals for a **Neutral Nations Repatriation Commission** and argued against forcible repatriation. Though not immediately acceptable to the Communist side, the resolution came to form the basis for the eventual agreements on the release of prisoners. A General Assembly resolution of 18 April 1953 noted the exchange of sick and wounded prisoners in Operation **Little Switch** that month; and a further resolution of 28 August 1953 welcomed the signing of the armistice on 27 July, noted its recommendation for a political conference, and called for the convening of such a conference within three months. (The conference was postponed until April–June 1954, when it met in Geneva, Switzerland.) The POW issue was revived in a resolution of 3 December 1953 that condemned "atrocities" alleged by the United States to have been committed by Chinese and North Korean forces against UNC prisoners. UNCURK reports to the General Assembly in 1954, 1957, and 1958 were the subject of resolutions that reaffirmed UN commitment to the peaceful reunification of the Korea Peninsula. In the same vein, the General Assembly on 17 December 1974 urged the continuation of the North-South dialogue in Korea (which by then had faltered).

See also: United Nations (UN); United Nations Commission for Unification and Rehabilitation of Korea (UNCURK); United Nations Commission on Korea (UNCOK); United Nations Korean Reconstruction Agency (UNKRA); United Nations Security Council Resolutions on Korea; United Nations Temporary Commission on Korea (UNTCOK).

References: History: VI, 1977; Matray 1991.

UNITED NATIONS KOREAN RECONSTRUCTION AGENCY (UNKRA)

This UN agency, established on 1 December 1950, took over the long-range reconstruction tasks in South Korea that theoretically belonged to the **United Nations Commission for Unification and Rehabilitation of Korea** (UNCURK), set up in October 1950. While the **Korean War** was in progress, UNKRA was able to do little except give support for a number of short-term projects, usually carried out with assistance from other UN organizations operating in Korea. After the armistice, UNKRA was less restricted and began a program of providing materials and technical assistance to help rebuild South Korea's shattered economy. Its staff were at one time or another engaged at over 4,000 sites and were involved in crop and livestock development, rehabilitation of agricultural land, restoration of coal mines, health projects, and the repair and reconstruction of schools. Although its total expenditure of $146.5 million was relatively small, by the time it was eliminated in the late 1950s, it had made a substantial contribution to South Korean postwar recovery.

References: Matray 1991; *Rehabilitation and Development of Agriculture, Forestry, and Fisheries in South Korea* 1954.

UNITED NATIONS SECURITY COUNCIL RESOLUTIONS ON KOREA

As the most powerful body of the **United Nations** organization, the Security Council has the authority to call on member states for assistance, including military assistance, in support of its general aim of peacekeeping and security. The council is composed of five permanent members—the United States, Russia (formerly the **Union of Soviet Socialist Republics**), the **People's Republic of China**, Britain, and France—each having power of veto, and ten other members drawn from the general membership of the UN, who hold rotating office. By the time the **Korean War** broke out on 25 June 1950, the United Nations General Assembly, representing all member states, had already considered several proposals—each one tabled by the United States—on aspects of the confused situation in the Korea Peninsula and had authorized the creation of two succeeding commissions to find ways of easing tension.

In June 1950, two members of the **United Nations Commission on Korea** (UNCOK) were in South Korea. They had inspected the **38th parallel** on 24 June and reported they had found the South Korean troops in defensive positions. The North Korean attack across the parallel prompted an immediate meeting of the Security Council at the urging of the United States and UNCOK and with the support of the UN secretary-general, Trygve Lie. The Security Council resolution of 25 June called for an immediate cessation of hostilities and for North Korean forces to withdraw to the 38th parallel. The resolution asked UNCOK to report speedily on the situation and appealed to all UN members to assist the UN and to refrain from giving assistance to North Korea. The resolution was passed by nine votes to one, with one abstention, out of a possible eleven votes. The Soviet member of the Security Council, Jacob Malik, who would have had the power of veto, was absent because of a Soviet boycott of the Security Council in protest at its failure to allot the "China" seat to the People's Republic of China.

Two days later, on 27 June, the Security Council met again and passed a second resolution, by seven votes out of a possible eleven. This resolution noted an UNCOK report that North Korea had not withdrawn its forces and that urgent military measures were needed to restore peace, noted South Korea's appeal for immediate steps by the UN, and recommended that UN members give all necessary assistance to South Korea to repel the North's armed attack.

These two resolutions formed the legal basis for the UN military intervention in Korea. The Soviet Union protested later that the second resolution was invalid, as neither it nor the PRC had voted in favor of it, but its protests were rejected. On 7 July 1950, the Security Council met again to welcome the support already promised to the UN by a number of member states, to propose the setting up of a unified command under the United States, and to request the United States to appoint a commander (General **Douglas MacArthur** was chosen), who should report as appropriate to the Security Council. Apart from this requirement, the Security Council gave itself no further powers of supervision over the unified command.

See also: United Nations Command (UNC); United Nations Commission on Korea (UNCOK); United Nations General Assembly Resolutions on Korea.
References: History: VI, 1977; Matray 1991.

UNITED NATIONS TEMPORARY COMMISSION ON KOREA (UNTCOK)

Following the UN General Assembly's adoption on 14 November 1947 of a resolution to establish a unified government in Korea through nationwide elections, the General Assembly created the United Nations Temporary Commission on Korea (UNTCOK) to carry out this program. The UNTCOK members were Australia, Canada, Nationalist China, El Salvador, France, India, the Philippines, Syria, and the Ukrainian Soviet Socialist Republic, and their task was to implement the General Assembly's resolution. The refusal of the Soviet occupation commander to allow UNTCOK to operate north of the **38th parallel** meant that it was only able to supervise the 10 May 1948 elections in the southern half of the peninsula. Following a U.S.-sponsored resolution on 10 December 1948, it was replaced by the **United Nations Commission on Korea.**

See also: United Nations General Assembly Resolutions on Korea.

UNITED STATES AND KOREA BEFORE 1945

It was probably the trade in ginseng, a plant highly valued for its medicinal use, that first awakened Americans to the existence of Korea. From the middle of the eighteenth century, American ships selling American-produced ginseng on the China coast became aware that they were in competition with ginseng from Korea, a place of which probably few of them had heard. In the mid-nineteenth century, Korea was linked to Japan in American eyes, as places that should be brought into the system of world trade then developing. In 1866, the Boston-owned steamship *General Sherman*, chartered to a British company, made the first attempt to trade with Korea, sailing up the Taedong River to **P'yongyang**, now the capital of modern North Korea. The ship was attacked and burned, and all the passengers and crew, including a British Protestant missionary, were killed. In North Korea, the official account is that the man commanding the Korean attack was the grandfather of President **Kim Il Sung**, North Korea's only leader until his death in 1994.

The U.S. Navy made a number of attempts to find out what had happened to the *General Sherman* and in 1871 sent a force to punish the Koreans for their actions. Although this effort destroyed some forts off Kanghwa Island near the capital, **Seoul**, it failed to achieve its main purpose. Instead, it encouraged the Koreans to believe that they were a match for the West. Japanese efforts at opening

Korea to trade were more successful. Following the Japanese treaty of 1876, U.S. interest revived, and in 1882, Commodore Shufeldt of the U.S. Navy negotiated a treaty that was signed at Chemulp'o (modern Inch'on) on 22 May 1882. From then until 1905, the U.S. presence in Korea was the most important among all the Western countries. More Americans lived in Korea than any other group of Westerners. Some were traders, some teachers, and there was a large missionary presence. Several of South Korea's modern universities owe their origins to American missionary activity in these years, including Yonsei University, closely associated with the **Underwood family**, and Ehwa Women's University. U.S. naval and military officers acted as advisers to the Korean government.

Like other Western countries, however, the United States did nothing when Japan first declared a protectorate over Korea in 1905 and then annexed the country as part of its colonial empire in 1910. The missionaries remained and were vocal in their criticism of Japanese colonial behavior. This was especially true in March 1919, when Koreans rose up in protest against the Japanese, partly inspired by the ideals of U.S. President Woodrow Wilson and the hopes raised by the **Paris Conference and Versailles Peace Treaty** of that year. For most of the colonial period, however, Korea was forgotten in the United States, despite the efforts of Korean exiles such as the Princeton-educated Dr. **Syngman Rhee** to keep the issue of Korean independence alive. It was not until the outbreak of World War II and the beginning of postwar planning at the 1943 **Cairo Conference** that Korea again began to figure in American official thinking.

See also: Assassinations and Attempted Assassinations; Japanese Colonial Period in Korea (1910–1945); Korea Peninsula (1945–1948); Potsdam Conference (1945).

References: Chay 1990; Han 1982(b); Harrington 1961; Koo and Suh 1984; Nahm 1979; Paik 1970; *Reflections on a Centenary of United States–Korean Relations* 1982; Swartout 1980.

UNITED STATES ARMY MILITARY GOVERNMENT IN KOREA (1945–1948)

As it became clear in early August 1945 that the war with Japan would not last much longer, the Americans started working on an agreement with the **Union of Soviet Socialist Republics**, which had declared war on Japan on 9 August, to take the Japanese surrender jointly in Korea, the Russians north of the **38th parallel**, the Americans south of it. Soviet troops had already entered the Korea Peninsula by the time Japan conceded defeat on 15 August and were in the northern city of **P'yongyang** by 25 August. The nearest U.S. troops, however, were on the Japanese island of Okinawa or in the Philippines. Eventually, XXIV Corps, commanded by General **John Hodge,** was sent from Okinawa but did not reach Korea until 8 September.

On arrival, Hodge found that a fledgling political system had been put in place in the southern half of Korea. A provisional administration, the **Korean People's Republic** (KPR), had been established on 6 September, supported by a network of local **People's Committees**. Hodge was under orders, however, to recognize no form of government at that point other than the occupation administration he was tasked with forming. He refused to accept the Korean organizations and on 13 September set up the United States Army Military Government in Korea (USAMGIK). Initially he tried to use Japanese administrators and police still in Korea to keep things running. This policy outraged Koreans. Believing that the KPR and the People's Committees were too much under Communist influence, he looked to a group of conservative advisers for guidance, many of them members of the **Korean Democratic Party**. By February 1946, **Syngman Rhee**, the most forceful of the right-wing South Korean leaders and a familiar figure to the Americans, had formed the South Korean Democratic Assembly as an advisory council to USAMGIK.

Even while North and South Korea were taking the first steps toward two very different societies under Soviet and U.S. tutelage, the two superpowers were in principle committed to exploring ways to achieve unification through the U.S.-Soviet **Joint Commission on Trusteeship** proposed in the **Moscow Agreement** of December 1945. This initiative, the product of consultation between the great powers, was accepted, under Soviet pressure, by the north and by left-wing circles in the south but was immensely unpopular with right-wing Koreans, who felt it would impede national independence.

Soviet and U.S. teams met during 1946–1947 to discuss the trusteeship proposals but made no progress. The U.S. government of occupation had to contend with a strong surge of opposition to the trusteeship proposals and eventually, from mid-1946, with calls for the formation of a separate government in the South. USAMGIK, together with its right-wing Korean supporters, during 1946 moved increasingly against the left, suppressing the People's Committees without necessarily introducing alternative local forms of administration. There was considerable unrest in the south. Agriculture and the economy were in poor shape, aggravated by USAMGIK's initial decision to abolish all wartime economic controls. Food shortages, inflation, and speculation resulted. The United States had to send large amounts of relief supplies, and USAMGIK had to reintroduce some measure of economic control. A flow of people coming from the north or returning from Japan put extra pressure on resources. Toward the end of 1946, riots and strikes broke out, often with Communist participation. USAMGIK responded by taking a harder line with left-wing organizations, and U.S. troops assisted the South Korean police in breaking up insurrection.

As the prospect of unification imposed from without began to recede, motion toward separate forms of government intensified in both the north and south. USAMGIK sanctioned the formation of an Interim Legislative Assembly in **Seoul** in December 1946 and in 1947 pushed through such necessary preliminaries to full elections as voter registration, an election law, and a provisional constitution. With the final failure of the trusteeship talks in the summer of 1947, the United States turned the "Korea problem" over to the **United Nations**. The result was an attempt at nationwide elections monitored by the **United Nations Temporary Commission on Korea**. The North Koreans and the Soviet administration in the north refused to cooperate, and elections were held only in the south, with a number of abstentions. In August 1948, with the establishment of the South Korean state, General Hodge announced the termination of USAMGIK, although U.S. troops did not finally withdraw for another year.

When it arrived, the U.S. government of occupation faced an unfamiliar and confusing scene and lacked the understanding to be able to cope with it. Its instincts were to resist anything that smacked of communism and to choose as allies those whose political approach seemed closer to its own. Thus it fostered the conservative trends and personalities in South Korean society. Its handling of the economy was in the end fairly successful. Among its final measures, in March 1948 it organized the distribution of all land formerly owned by Japanese among the cultivators, and it passed on a balanced budget to its successor. Politically, its chief effects were destroying the Communist power base in the south and turning the country markedly to the right while introducing the principles of an elected government and a plurality of political parties.

See also: Hodge, John Reed; Korea Peninsula (1945–1948); Soviet Occupation of North Korea (1945–1948).
References: Cumings 1981, 1990; Eckert et al. 1990; Henderson 1968; Macdonald 1996; Yi 1973.

UNITED STATES ECONOMIC AID TO SOUTH KOREA

When U.S. forces arrived in the southern half of the **Korea Peninsula** in September 1945, they found it in a sorry condition. For four years, the peninsula had been ruthlessly exploited to help the Japanese war effort. Industry was worn out, much of the forest had been used for fuel or for building, and agricultural land suffered from the unremitting demands of wartime. In addition, Koreans had been forced to work long hours, while high taxation and rising inflation effectively robbed them of much of their earnings. Supplies of electric power and fertilizers, which came mostly from the northern half of the peninsula, were now in Soviet hands. These supplies became increasingly erratic between 1945 and 1948 and were cut off entirely as separate states emerged on the peninsula in 1948.

In these circumstances, the United States could do little except to pour in massive amounts of assistance to keep the economy going. Between 1945 and 1952, the United States provided South Korea with some $852 million in assistance, with the main emphasis on consumer goods, food, and fertilizer. However, any economic gains that South Korea had made by 1950 were wiped out by the **Korean War** (1950–1953), and the process had to restart after the **armistice** in 1953. Again the United States provided large amounts of aid, with other **United Nations** countries adding a little more. As before, at first the urgent need for relief aid dominated, but gradually there was a shift away from providing the means for sheer survival toward support for industrial development. Between 1953 and 1975, South Korea received a total of $3,563.3 million in foreign aid, of which the United States supplied $3,526.3 million, or 99 percent. Most of the U.S. aid was in the form of outright grants until the mid-1960s, when there was a switch to loans. This loan aid was on very favorable terms, with a long lead-in period before payment was due, and very low rates of interest.

By that stage, U.S. aid was generally given at much lower levels, although it continued even after the military coup led by General **Park Chung Hee** in 1961. After reaching a high point of $378 million in 1957, the annual amounts steadily declined to $107.3 million in 1969, and then to $5.1 million in 1972. U.S. aid ended in 1975. By that point, the economic reforms that Park had begun in the 1960s had turned the South Korean economy from one of the poorest in the world in 1948 to one that was being increasingly seen in the non-Communist world as a model for development.

The extent that this was made possible by U.S. aid is a matter for debate. Some argue that U.S. aid was essential in providing the foundation on which Park could build. Others think that the U.S. aid distorted South Korean development to the United States' advantage, and U.S. companies are still prominent in the South Korean economy. For most South Koreans, however, the benefits that U.S. aid brought are seen as outweighing any disadvantages.

See also: Chaebol; Japanese Colonial Period in Korea (1910–1945); Korea Peninsula (1945–1948); United States Army Military Government in Korea (1945–1948).

References: Chung 1979; Hwang 1993; Nahm 1993.

UNITED STATES FORCES IN THE KOREAN WAR

When the **Korean War** began on 25 June 1950, the only U.S. forces in the Republic of Korea (South Korea) were the officers and men of the **Korean Military Advisory Group** (KMAG), a small, specialized unit left behind when most U.S. forces left Korea in 1949. KMAG's task was to provide training for the South Korean army, though it was hampered in this by the limited resources assigned to it. By contrast, by the end of the war in July 1953, units from the Army, Navy, Air Force, and Marines were all serving in Korea, and the U.S. military commitment to South Korea was to continue until the present (1999). In the process, the U.S. military establishment would be transformed, and the political-military organization that has been such a feature of U.S. military life since the 1950s would be created. The U.S. armed forces came out of the Korean War having suffered defeat and recovered. They learned that the advantages of superior equipment and transport could be overcome by a determined enemy armed with relatively simple weapons. They had also learned that there was no inherent difference in fighting qualities between black and white, and Korea marked the beginning of the end of segregation in the U.S. armed forces.

By the outbreak of the Korean War, the United States was well advanced with reducing the large military establishment that had survived World War II. Some have seen this as personal animosity by the president, the Democrat **Harry S Truman**, who had unexpectedly succeeded **Franklin D. Roosevelt** in 1945 and who had, even more unexpectedly, won the 1948 presidential election. In reality, however, the United States longed for peace after four years of fighting, while many believed that U.S. possession of atomic weapons meant that conventional forces were no longer required. For whatever reasons, by the summer of 1950, cutbacks were well in hand. Even where units were not formally reduced, in practice they were rarely up to anything like fighting strength or combat readiness.

Once the political decision was made by President Truman to commit U.S. forces to the defense of South Korea, and following an early visit to Korea by General **Douglas MacArthur**, supreme commander of the Allied Forces in Japan, U.S. involvement was swift. The Air Force launched attacks on North Korea, while the U.S. Navy moved to begin a blockade of North Korean ports that would last until the end of the war some three years later. In addition, units of the U.S. Eighth Army in Japan were sent to supplement the meager—and by now retreating—resources of KMAG. The first detachment to arrive was part of the 24th Division,

Marilyn Monroe struts for the U.S. troops stationed in Korea, 26 February 1954. (Corbis-Bettmann)

under the command of General **William F. Dean.** Unfortunately, like all U.S. forces in Japan, it was understrength, and, after garrison duties, ill pre-pared for battle. The first unit from this force to go into action in Korea was the first of the **Task Forces,** Task Force Smith. On 5 July 1950, at Osan, south of

Suwon, the men of this unit found that they were ill equipped to deal with North Korean T-34 Soviet-made tanks, and, equally surprising, that the North Koreans stood and fought. Task Force Smith was wiped out, with little obvious effect on the enemy. U.S. forces in Korea were to recover from the ignominy of this failure, but not before they had suffered other blows to their pride.

After the failure at Osan, U.S. forces, like their South Korean counterparts, retreated to the **Pusan Perimeter**, where they regrouped and, joined by other **United Nations Command** (UNC) forces, held off the advancing North Koreans, thus allowing breathing space to prepare for a counterattack. This came both with the **Inch'on landing** in September 1950 and the simultaneous breakout from the Pusan Perimeter. Meanwhile, UN air forces, but principally four U.S. air forces, established air superiority over the peninsula, which they would maintain until the end of the war. UN naval forces, again principally U.S. forces, largely commanded the seas, although they found North Korean mining operations difficult to handle. The bulk of the fighting was borne by land forces, and the U.S., South Korean, and other UN forces had great success following Inch'on until the intervention of the **Chinese People's Volunteers** in October–November 1950. Faced with a new and determined enemy, U.S. forces broke and ran in what became known as the "**bug-outs.**" There were exceptions to this, especially the fighting retreat of the U.S. 1st Marine Division and the 3rd and 7th Infantry Divisions from the **Changjin Reservoir**, but the headlong nature of the retreat came as a surprise to other UN forces.

From the spring of 1951, after the recapture of the South Korean capital, **Seoul**, the war settled down to one of attrition. The fighting could occasionally be savage, but the war of movement that had marked the period June 1950–June 1951 was over. Generally, U.S. forces in the Korean War consisted of three army corps, one marine division, three naval groups, four air force groups, and other supporting units. At the end of the war, some 360,000 personnel were present in Korea. The headquarters of the UNC and of the U.S. Eighth Army were relocated from Tokyo to Seoul. (After the end of the war, both were moved back to Tokyo but returned to Seoul in 1967 and remain there.) U.S.

casualties in the war were 33,625 dead, 105,785 wounded, and 7,852 missing. Most of the latter are presumed dead, although there are persistent rumors that some remain alive in either North Korea, China, or Russia. All three countries have denied this.

U.S. forces in South Korea were reduced in 1954 and again in 1970. Plans under President **Jimmy Carter** to reduce them further were abandoned, and some 32,000 land troops still remain in South Korea. There are also substantial U.S. air and naval forces in the country. All come under the U.S.–South Korean **Combined Forces Command**, created in 1978. In the United States, Korean War veterans often feel that they have been overshadowed by the later **Vietnam War** and that Korea is the "forgotten war." The dedication of a Korean War memorial in Washington in 1995 has helped to persuade the veterans that they are not forgotten.

See also: Aerial Bombing; Blockade of Korean Coasts; Clark, Mark Wayne; Home for Christmas (1950); Hook, the, Battles of (1952–1953); Invasion and Counterinvasion (1950–1951); Korean Augmentation to the United States Army (KATUSA); Military Equipment Used in the Korean War; Naktong River; Nixon Doctrine (1969); North Korean People's Army (NKPA); Pork Chop Hill, Battles of (1951–1953); Prisoners of War; Pusan and the Pusan Perimeter; South Korean Armed Forces; United States Military Presence in South Korea since 1953; United States Mutual Defense Treaty with South Korea (1953).

References: Appleman 1961; Blair 1987; Hastings 1987; Hermes 1966; History: IV, 1975 and V, 1976; Matray 1991; Mossman 1990; Nahm 1993; Schnabel 1972; Summers 1990; Whelan 1990; Williams 1993.

UNITED STATES MILITARY PRESENCE IN SOUTH KOREA SINCE 1953

The most tangible evidence of U.S. commitment to the protection of South Korea is in the large number of American troops still stationed on its territory, numbering around 40,000 infantry, naval, and air force personnel. They are there by virtue of the 1953 Mutual Defense Treaty. Their conditions of living and their relations with the surrounding society are controlled through the Status of Forces Agreement (SOFA) of 1965. A detailed system of committees and regular meetings aims to support the relationship and sort out problems. Since 1970, a number of

U.S. troops have been withdrawn from South Korea. Nonetheless, the continued presence of a large number of military personnel within the country enjoying special status and not always under South Korean jurisdiction has come to offend sections of the South Korean population. Koreans show considerable ambivalence, since many in the South would not wish to lose the shield provided by these U.S. forces, but they resent the implied challenge to South Korea's sovereignty and the impact of the U.S. presence on Korean society. They often regard U.S. troops as disruptive elements and are particularly harsh on African American soldiers.

Korean grievances have ranged from political to social issues. The most serious complaint against the U.S. military command has concerned the possible extent of U.S. acquiescence in the role of South Korean troops under the control of the **Combined Forces Command** (CFC) in suppressing the 1980 popular uprising in **Kwangju**. The charge of U.S. complicity boils down to the responsibilities of the U.S. commander of the CFC, who at that time had operational control of the South Korean army units sent to Kwangju. The incident gave the North Koreans and left-wing critics in the South much material for propaganda, but it also disturbed large segments of the South Korean population.

More enduring problems have centered around U.S.-Korean relations, especially in areas around the U.S. bases. In late 1997, the U.S. Forces, Korea (USFK) reportedly still occupied 96 locations throughout South Korea as military camps, training sites, and shooting ranges. Sometimes, as with the Yongsan base in **Seoul**, land that when originally leased to the United States lay on the outskirts of a city has over time become a central site. South Korean government pressure has led to the return of some U.S. military sites to Korean use. A source of particular dissatisfaction and embarrassment to both Korean and U.S. authorities is the prevalence of prostitution around the camps. This has been a problem since the **Korean War**, when poverty and homelessness forced many women into prostitution. According to one estimate, one million Korean women have engaged in providing sexual services to U.S. military personnel since the war. A further irritation is the legal immunity of the USFK in areas such as customs and tax exemptions, use of vehicles,

and the provision of a forces' radio and television network. Minor offenses committed by U.S. military personnel while on official duty have generally been handled within the U.S. system, but serious crimes such as murder are handed over to the South Korean judiciary.

See also: Combined Forces Command (Republic of Korea–United States); Kwangju; Uijongbu; United States Mutual Defense Treaty with South Korea (1953).
References: Macdonald 1996; Moon 1997.

UNITED STATES MUTUAL DEFENSE TREATY WITH SOUTH KOREA (1953)

Signed on 8 August 1953, this treaty was ratified in January 1954. Its origins lay in South Korean President **Syngman Rhee**'s threat to disrupt the **armistice** agreement that had ended the **Korean War** on 27 July 1953 unless the United States provided South Korea with a guarantee of assistance in case of attack. Although the United States was reluctant to enter into an open-ended agreement with South Korea, it could see advantages in imposing some restrictions on Rhee's ability to operate independently. The most important clause of the treaty provided that each party would view an armed attack on the other as dangerous to its own peace and security and would act, in accordance with its constitutional processes, to meet the common danger. The treaty remains in force as of 1999.
References: Matray 1991; Pollack and Cha 1995.

UNITED STATES NAVY RECONNAISSANCE PLANE EC-121 (1969)

On 15 April 1969, two MiG interceptor aircraft of the North Korean Air Force without warning shot down an EC-121M Constellation reconnaissance aircraft of the U.S. Navy over the East Sea, 95 miles (153 kilometers) south of Ch'ongjin, a town on the northeast coast of North Korea. The unarmed plane was carrying 31 men. It was operating out of Atsugi Naval Air Station in Japan and was equipped to gather information from both electronic sources (ELINT, electromagnetic intelligence) and radio and telephone signals (SIGINT, signals intelligence). The United States asserted that the plane was over international waters. The late 1960s were marked by persistent North Korean aggression against South Korean and U.S. targets. The United States responded to the shooting down of the EC-121 with a show of naval force in the East Sea and a protest to the North Korean side of the **Military Armistice Commission**. U.S. reconnaissance flights in the region continued.

See also: Aerial Surveillance; North Korean Use of Terrorism.

References: Bermudez 1988; Bolger 1991.

UNITED STATES RELATIONS WITH NORTH KOREA

Having fought the **Korean War** against the Democratic People's Republic of Korea, and with a close treaty relationship with the Republic of Korea (South Korea) from 1953, the United States displayed little interest in contacts with North Korea until the late 1980s. For its part, North Korea argued that the United States rather than the **United Nations** had been its real enemy in the war and regularly demanded that the United States engage in direct talks. Since this proposal excluded South Korea, the United States declined. However, in the lead-up to the 1988 Olympic Games in the South Korean capital, **Seoul**, and amid fears about possible North Korean terrorist actions to disrupt the games, the United States decided to begin talking directly to the North Koreans. The first contacts were in the Chinese capital, Beijing. Concern about the **North Korean nuclear program**, related issues such as missile exports, and U.S. domestic concerns over the question of U.S. forces **missing in action** since the Korean War meant that by the late 1990s, the United States and North Korea were engaged in discussions on a wide range of subjects.

See also: Korean Peninsula Energy Development Organization (KEDO); Military Armistice Commission (MAC); North Korean Use of Terrorism.

References: Cumings 1997; Oberdorfer 1997; Sigal 1998.

UNITED STATES RELATIONS WITH SOUTH KOREA

Since 1948, the Republic of Korea (South Korea) has maintained the closest links to the United States of any state, except perhaps for Japan. Many Koreans remember that the United States was the first Western country to open relations with the kingdom of Korea in 1882, an event that was marked in 1982 with a great deal of ceremony and the publica-

tion of many books. Most older South Koreans believe that the United States saved them from being controlled by the Communist **Union of Soviet Socialist Republics** (USSR) in 1945 and supplied the economic aid without which they would not have survived. They also believe that the U.S. intervention in 1950 at the start of the **Korean War,** and its rallying of other **United Nations** (UN) forces to help, saved the young state from being taken over by the Communist Democratic People's Republic of Korea (North Korea). After the end of the war, the United States again provided massive aid, which prevented widespread hunger and eventually formed the basis for modern South Korean economic development. As continued assurance of U.S. support, should there be another attack from the North, the United States and South Korea signed a Mutual Defense Treaty in 1953, which is still in force, and U.S. military units have been stationed in South Korea since the end of the Korean War. The United States has consistently supported South Korea in the UN and other international organizations. Many South Koreans have studied and lived in the United States, where there is a large Korean community, and the two countries are major economic partners. Managing this relationship is important to the South Koreans, and the country's largest embassy is in Washington. South Korea is also aware of the need to maintain good relations with Congress, even if this has occasionally gotten out of hand, as in the **Koreagate** scandal.

Like all such close relationships, however, there are problems. Since the beginning, South Koreans have been aware that their interests come second to those of the United States. The disillusion goes back a long way. Many Koreans still believe that the United States was obliged by the terms of the 1882 treaty to help Korea in 1910, when the United States did nothing to prevent the Japanese takeover. Some argue that the United States could have prevented the communization of North Korea by insisting in 1945 that the United States take over the entire peninsula. These Koreans believe that, since the Soviet Union did not enter the war against Japan until the very last days, it would not have objected to being excluded from Korea. Others claim that the United States sent the wrong signals to North Korea and the USSR in 1949–1950, allowing them to think that the United

States would take no action if there was conflict on the Korea Peninsula. Once the Korean War began, many thought that the United States should continue it, whatever the cost, until the peninsula was unified. Whether or not the United States should maintain troops in South Korea has also been a source of tension, especially during the Nixon and Carter presidencies, and conflicts over trade have marked the 1980s and 1990s. U.S. concerns about nuclear weapons proliferation and the **North Korean nuclear program** have worried South Koreans, who see the willingness of the United States to talk directly to North Korea on this issue as a threat to the U.S.–South Korean relationship. On the whole, however, the relationship between South Korea and the United States seems to have more strengths than weaknesses, with advantages for both sides, and, despite moments of tension, it is likely to last.

See also: Carter, James (Jimmy) Earl; Combined Forces Command (Republic of Korea–United States); Dulles, John Foster; Eisenhower, Dwight David; Korea Peninsula (1945–1948); Koreagate (1977); Korean Peninsula Energy Development Organization (KEDO); North Korean Nuclear Program; Roosevelt, Franklin Delano; Rusk, David Dean; South Korean Nuclear Program; Truman, Harry S; United States and Korea before 1945; United States Army Military Government in Korea (1945–1948); United States Economic Aid to South Korea; United States Forces in the Korean War; United States Relations with North Korea.

References: Han 1982(a), 1982(b); Koo and Suh 1984; Kwak et al. 1982; Nahm 1979; Nam 1986.

UNKRA
See **United Nations Korean Reconstruction Agency (UNKRA).**

UNOFFICIAL CONTACTS BETWEEN NORTH AND SOUTH KOREANS
South Korea's **National Security Law** (NSL) specifically prohibits "unauthorized" journeys by South Korean citizens to the North. The 1990 South-North Exchange and Cooperation Law stipulates government permission for travel to North Korea and meetings with North Koreans in third countries, and a number of businessmen and officials have made such trips. However, those anxious to discuss issues such as reunification with colleagues in the North may not obtain authorization. From 1988, members of formal and informal opposition groups—including church workers, a National Assembly opposition member, labor activists, writers, journalists, teachers, and students—have visited North Korea in support of reunification, traveling via China, Japan, and Europe. On return to the South, they have been charged under the NSL and often imprisoned. Others have remained abroad, fearful of arrest on return. They have now been promised leniency on return, provided they admit their error. The number of authorized visits by South Koreans, representing many professions, to the North rose considerably in 1998.

International gatherings in third countries have occasionally allowed North and South Koreans to meet on neutral ground.

See also: Chung Ju-yung; Pro-unification Activities.

References: Amnesty International 1989, 1995; *Newsreview,* 13 June 1998, 2 January 1999.

UNTCOK
See **United Nations Temporary Commission on Korea (UNTCOK).**

USAMGIK
See **United States Army Military Government in Korea (1945–1948).**

USSR
See **Union of Soviet Socialist Republics (USSR).**

V

VAN FLEET, JAMES ALWARD III (1892–1992)

General James Van Fleet succeeded General **Matthew Ridgway** as commander of the U.S. Eighth Army in Korea on 11 April 1951, after Ridgway took over from General **Douglas MacArthur** as commander-in-chief of the Unified Command. Van Fleet came from New Jersey and graduated from the U.S. Military Academy in 1915. He served in the Mexican border campaign of 1916–1917 and in both world wars. When he arrived in Korea, **United Nations** (UN) forces were under attack in what proved to be the last major Chinese offensive of the **Korean War**. Van Fleet organized the counterattack that led to the effective stabilization of the battle line around the **38th parallel**, where hostilities had begun. Thereafter, the war ceased to be one of movement and became bogged down into lines of trenches. Despite occasionally heavy fighting, the gains were small. During this period, Van Fleet devoted much energy to building up the South Korean army. Although the lack of action was partly because Van Fleet instructed his troops not to engage the enemy more than was necessary, he eventually grew frustrated with this policy and left Korea in February 1953, retiring from the army the following April. Criticism of his handling of the revolt in the **Koje Island prisoner of war camp** in 1952 and the loss of his son, an air force captain, in a bombing raid on North Korea in April 1952 may have contributed to his sense of resentment. In retirement, he wrote articles critical of the failure to pursue the war to a final victory.

See also: United States Forces in the Korean War.

VIETNAM WAR (1954–1975)

Between October 1965 and March 1973, some 300,000 South Korean troops were committed to the Vietnam War in support of U.S. military forces. Backed by support and naval and air force units, three South Korean Army divisions took part: the 2nd Marine Brigade, the Capital Division, and the 9th Division. These divisions had tactical responsibility for pacification of Vietcong guerrillas in the provinces of Phu Yen, Binh Dinh, and Khanh Hoa.

In return for its support in a common struggle against a Communist enemy, South Korea received considerable military and civilian aid from the United States; contracts for the delivery of military supplies, services, and equipment to U.S. troops in Vietnam; and the opportunity to participate in construction projects in South Vietnam. The South Korean economy benefited from this impetus to its export trade. Several conglomerates or *chaebol*, such as Hyundai, date their expansion into overseas transportation and construction work from the Vietnam War.

References: Eckert et al. 1990; War Memorial Service (n.d.).

WALKER, WALTON HARRIS (1889–1950)

Walton H. Walker, who was born in Texas in 1889, graduated from the U.S. Military Academy in 1912 and served in Europe in both world wars. In 1948, he took command of the U.S. Eighth Army in Japan. When the **Korean War** broke out on 25 July 1950, he was immediately designated commander of the U.S. forces in Korea. In July 1950, the Eighth Army moved to Korea, and Lieutenant General Walker established his headquarters at **Taegu**, where he remained until being forced to retreat to the **Pusan Perimeter**. He led the breakout from Pusan in September 1950, pursuing the North Korean forces to the **Ch'ongch'on River** south of the **Yalu River**. While organizing the Eighth Army's retreat following the intervention of the **Chinese People's Volunteers,** he was killed in a traffic accident at **Uijongbu** on 23 December 1950. He is commemorated at the Walker Hill resort area in eastern Seoul. *See also:* United States Forces in the Korean War.

WAR STORIES AND WAR FILMS OF THE KOREAN WAR

Fiction and films of the **Korean War** were largely an American genre. This is not surprising, given the extensive U.S. military and political commitment to the Korean conflict. Moreover, the Hollywood film industry, which had already produced a long run of popular war films of World War II, was well placed to use the new themes suggested by the Korean War. The predominant American interest meant that fiction and films were primarily directed at U.S. readers and film audiences and often reflected U.S. preoccupations with the conduct and progress of the war and U.S. interpretations of its significance.

From the period of hostilities (1950–1953) up to the mid-1980s, around 40 Korean War novels were published, largely by American authors. About half appeared in the 1960s, some earlier. Many nonfictional accounts were also published in the form of memoirs and journalistic reports. After a lull, interest in the war as a theme for fiction revived in the 1980s. In the years from 1950 to the early 1990s,

somewhat under 100 Korean War films were made. The highest output was between 1951 and 1957. About 36 films were produced during the war itself. The long time span of 30 to 40 years during which the war has yielded material for fiction and film has been reflected in a shifting choice of themes and considerable differences in the handling and interpretation of the material. The immediacy and realism of novels and films produced up to the early 1960s tended to give way from the late 1960s to a more detached and critical approach. The great transforming factor was the **Vietnam War** and the American public's response to it.

Combat fighting provided good material for both fiction and films, particularly the close engagements at the **Changjin Reservoir (1950)**, the fighting of 1950–1951 during the active phase of the war, and the frequent patrols from late 1951. The exploits of the more "glamorous" branches of the U.S. armed forces—the Air Force, the Navy, and the Marine Corps—were popular for stories of the 1950s. The elite and highly professional standing of these services licensed the expression in such novels of dissatisfaction with the way the war was being conducted, criticism of tactics and strategy, and resentment over public indifference to the conflict. (The majority of writers of war novels, as scholars in the field have pointed out, have had military experience as regular or enlisted soldiers, or have been press correspondents and journalists.) The dispute at the highest level between General **Douglas MacArthur** and President **Harry S Truman** over the decision to move from an offensive strategy to a policy of containment was reflected in both fiction and films.

One of the great issues of the Korean War, the treatment and conduct of **prisoners of war** (POWs), provided abundant material for novels and films produced after the conflict had ended, as conditions in the camps and the varying behavior of prisoners became more fully known. Between 1956 and 1976, about one-quarter of Korean War novels dealt with the subject. No films about the POW camps were released during the war itself, but they were popular immediately afterward. The questions raised particularly by the perceived conduct of some captured U.S. soldiers greatly unsettled American public opinion. Reports of detainees succumbing to "brainwashing," cooperating with the enemy, and betraying fellow prisoners fueled fears that the Communist enemy may have broken American morale. The Cold War was already under way, and in the United States, Senator Joseph McCarthy (1909–1957) from 1950 to 1954 was running his campaign against alleged Communist infiltration of public life. These anxieties seeped into literature and the cinema, in works in which the "enemy" was not so much the obvious Chinese or Korean interrogator, whose inquisitorial skills were acknowledged, as the "progressive" U.S. prisoner of war who chose to collaborate. Among the most powerful evocations of these fears is the film *The Manchurian Candidate* (1962), based on Richard Condon's novel of 1959. There is little that is specifically Korean in many stories and films of the war; rather, a domestic agenda predominates. As Edwards (1997: 4) suggests, Korean War films tell us mostly about the United States in the 1950s.

The other way of coping with a war that to many seemed marked by irrationality and absurdity was through dark humor. Richard Hooker's novel *M*A*S*H** (1968), together with the film (1970) and television series (1972–1983) based on it, have perhaps had the greatest success of any Korean War fiction. Yet it owes its sense of ironic detachment, in place of the realism and commitment of 1950s work, to the doubts and reservations that surrounded the later Vietnam War.

The Korean War was and remains an issue of enormous complexity. In terms of literary and cinematic representation, it fit into existing Western genres of "war novel" and "war film"; but the absence of familiar signposts that had guided the reader or filmgoer of World War II products—clearly defined enemy, large-scale epic action, visible heroes—deprived novels and films of a clear impact. Unexpected reverses—the **United Nations** (UN) forces routed by seemingly inexperienced and ill-equipped enemy troops; the likelihood that some American soldiers had cracked under pressure in captivity; high-level disagreement over the conduct of the war; above all, confusion among the **United Nations Command** (UNC) combatants over the purpose and objectives of the fighting—led to ambiguity and uncertainty that was not the stuff of which truly heroic novels and films could be fashioned.

Nonetheless, the big names of Hollywood starred in the Korean War movies: Humphrey Bogart, Marlon Brando, James Cagney, Kirk Douglas, Clint Eastwood, Rock Hudson, Alan Ladd, Lee Marvin, Robert Mitchum, Gregory Peck, Sidney Poitier, Ronald Reagan, and Robert Redford. Only John Wayne refused. A few films came from British, Dutch, French, and (in co-productions) South Korean sources. Laurence Olivier made one appearance, and Michael Caine's film debut was in *A Hill in Korea* (1956). Among British novels dealing with Korea, *The Dead, the Dying and the Damned*, by D. J. Hollands (1956; London, Cassell & Co. Ltd.), which presented a bleak picture of young conscripts and military life, enjoyed some popularity in the 1950s.

See also: Histories and Other Studies of the Korean War; Literature of the Korean Conflict; *M*A*S*H** (Film and Television Series); Television and the Korean War.
References: Axelsson 1990; Edwards 1997.

WILLOUGHBY, CHARLES A. (1892–1972)

At the time of the outbreak of the **Korean War** in 1950, Major General Charles Willoughby was the U.S. assistant director of intelligence in the Pacific. He was born in Heidelberg, Germany, and became a U.S. citizen in 1910. After completing university studies, he joined the army and was commissioned in 1915. He saw service in Mexico, and in France in World War I. After a series of military attaché appointments, he attended infantry school and staff college and later taught at staff college. In 1941, he was U.S. Army General **Douglas MacArthur**'s chief of intelligence in the Philippines, and he served with MacArthur throughout the war, transferring with him to Tokyo on Japan's defeat in 1945.

During the Korean War, his assessments proved

consistently wrong. He first thought that the North Koreans would not attack the South. When they did attack, he argued that the South would hold. Later, despite much evidence to the contrary, he rejected the view that the Chinese would intervene in the war. When they did, he regularly underestimated their strength. It is not clear whether he was an incurable optimist, or whether he did not feel able to give MacArthur bad news, but the result was the same: MacArthur tended to downplay the difficulties he faced. When MacArthur was recalled in April 1951 by U.S. President **Harry S Truman**, Willoughby resigned. He spent much of his time in retirement defending his former boss.
References: Matray 1991; Schnabel 1972.

WINNINGTON, ALAN (1910–1983)
The British journalist Alan Winnington was born in London, where he joined the British Communist Party and was involved with the party's newspaper, the *Daily Worker* (now called the *Morning Star*) from its inception in January 1930, first on the production side and from 1942 as a deputy chief sub-editor. In 1948, he traveled to China as correspondent for the *Daily Worker* and adviser to the Chinese Communists on their information services. After two years, he went to North Korea to cover the **Korean War** for the *Daily Worker* and the Communist **New China News Agency** (NCNA). Not long after the end of the war, his request for renewal of his passport was refused, a result, Winnington maintained, of U.S. pressure on the British government in retaliation for his reporting activities in North Korea. In 1955, he returned to the **People's Republic of China** to work again for NCNA and at Beijing University and as *Daily Worker* correspondent. Stateless, in 1960 he left China, where he was coming under criticism, for the German Democratic Republic (East Germany). His British nationality was eventually restored to him, but he remained settled in Berlin, where he died in 1983.

Winnington drew heavy criticism from the U.S. and British governments for his reporting in the *Daily Worker* on a number of issues: the massacre of politically suspect South Korean civilians near **Taejon** in the summer of 1950; U.S. tactics of saturation and napalm bombing; the treatment of North Korean and Chinese **prisoners of war** in

camps run by the **United Nations Command** (UNC) on **Koje Island**; the alleged U.S. use of germ warfare against the North Koreans in 1951–1952 and his interviews with two U.S. airmen accused of having participated in such warfare; and his visits to British POWs in the prison camps in the north of the peninsula. He and **Wilfrid Burchett**, as the only two English-speaking correspondents attached to the Communist side in the **armistice** negotiations at **Kaesong** and **P'anmunjom**, were often better briefed than the journalists credited to the UNC and were consequently used by the latter as a source of information. Winnington, presumably in a spirit of feeling for a fellow journalist, apparently reported back to Britain the capture of Philip Deane, correspondent for the London *Observer*, who was held along with other **foreign civilian detainees** in the war, and visited Deane in confinement in **P'yongyang.**

Winnington's activities were denounced as "treasonable" by sections of British society, an accusation of which he made much, but action against him was confined to depriving him of his passport. There is no doubt, however, that he contributed much to the general propaganda accompanying the Korean War. He explained and defended himself in an autobiographical volume, *Breakfast with Mao* (1986), and with Burchett coauthored exposés of UNC policies and tactics in *Koje Unscreened* (1952) and *Plain Perfidy* (1954).
See also: Bacteriological and Chemical Warfare; Burchett, Wilfrid; Press Corespondents in the Korean War.
References: Deane 1953; Knightley 1975; Lone and McCormack 1993; Winnington 1986; Winnington and Burchett 1952, 1954.

WONSAN
A major seaport and railway center on the east coast of North Korea, some 95 miles (153 kilometers) east of the capital, **P'yongyang**, across the narrowest width of the northern half of the peninsula. It is the capital of South Pyongan Province. In October 1950, Wonsan was the planned site of a two-pronged attack by land and sea, which was to follow the successful landing at **Inch'on** in early September. The U.S. Eighth Army under General **Walton Walker** was to attack by land, while the U.S. Tenth Corps would land at Wonsan, join up with Walker,

and move north to encircle P'yongyang. In preparing for the landing, U.S. minesweepers, assisted by Japanese vessels, began clearing the area on 10 October. While this operation was partially successful, many mined areas were undetected, and the U.S. Navy lost two ships. Wonsan had in any case already fallen to South Korean forces on 10 October, and P'yongyang itself fell on 19 October, thus reducing the importance of the Wonsan landing by the time the minesweeping exercise was completed. Wonsan was hastily evacuated in December 1950 as forces under the **United Nations Command** (UNC) retreated before the **Chinese People's Volunteers'** advance down the peninsula. When the UNC counterattacked in the spring of 1950, Wonsan came under a naval siege that lasted until the end of the war in July 1953, tying down large numbers of North Korean troops. During the siege, the city was under constant bombardment and was largely destroyed. It was rebuilt after the war and developed as a fishing and industrial center. Since the 1970s, the captured American intelligence-gathering ship, the **USS *Pueblo***, has been periodically open for display in the city harbor.

See also: Japanese Involvement in the Korean War; United States Forces in the Korean War.

Reference: Cagle and Mason 1957.

WU XIUQUAN (1908–)

The Chinese diplomat Wu Xiuquan (Wu Hsiuch'uan) was born in Hubei Province in 1908 and studied in the Soviet Union from 1926. On return in 1931, he taught at Shanghai's Fudan University. He later joined the Red Army and was a member of **Peng Dehuai**'s group on the Long March, 1935–1936. After various appointments in **Northeast China**, 1945–1949, he became head of the Soviet Union and East European department of the Chinese Ministry of Foreign Affairs. In this role, he joined **Mao Zedong** and **Zhou Enlai** in Moscow to negotiate the 1950 Sino-Soviet treaty. In November 1950, he led the Chinese delegation to the **United Nations** (UN), the only time until the 1970s that the **People's Republic of China** (PRC) was represented there. Wu set the tone for the PRC's attitude toward the UN with a savage attack on U.S. policy toward Korea and especially **Taiwan**. He failed to sway the UN, and the delegation departed after twelve days. He became vice-minister of foreign affairs on his return and later ambassador to Yugoslavia. He disappeared during the Cultural Revolution, resurfacing in the mid-1970s, and he remained active until the early 1990s.

See also: United Nations General Assembly Resolutions on Korea.

References: Klein and Clark 1971; Matray 1991.

XIE FANG (1904–1984)

Xie Fang (Hsieh Fang), a senior member of the Chinese military, participated in the **armistice** negotiations at **Kaesong** and **P'anmunjom** in 1951–1952. Born in China's Jilin Province in 1904, he was commissioned as an officer in the Guomindang (Chinese Nationalist) army and studied in Japan. In the late 1930s, he joined the Chinese Communist Party (CCP) while remaining a Guomindang officer, defecting to the Communists in 1939. He subsequently studied in the Soviet Union and taught at the CCP Central Party Academy. After 1945, he played an important role in organizing Korean guerrilla fighters in **Northeast China**. Appointed chief of the Chinese 13th Army Group in June 1950, his task was to develop links between the North Korean and Chinese armies. From July 1951 until October 1952, he was one of the **Chinese People's Volunteers'** representatives at the armistice negotiations, establishing a reputation as a tough and uncompromising negotiator who could be "harsh, browbeating [and] name-calling" (Hermes 1966: 505). In 1955, he became a major general and then headed the Chinese Military Academy from 1959 until the Cultural Revolution (1966–1976).

References: Hermes 1966; Matray 1991.

Y

YALU RIVER

The Yalu River (in Korean, the Amnok), which flows for some 490 miles (789 kilometers), has long formed the major part of the border between China and the Korea Peninsula. It rises on Mount Paektu and flows westward into the Yellow Sea. South Korean and U.S. troops reached the Yalu in October–November 1950 during the **Korean War**, but they were driven back following the intervention of the **Chinese People's Volunteers.** For much of the war, the Yalu was the site of camps, where both the Chinese and the North Koreans held civilian prisoners captured in South Korea and soldiers of the **United Nations Command** (UNC) and South Korean forces taken **prisoners of war.** The importance of the Yalu bridges as a source of supply for Chinese and Korean forces and of the hydroelectric power stations along the river led General **Douglas MacArthur** to demand that they be a target for UNC bombing. Although some damage was done, the attacks made no noticeable difference to the outcome of the war.

YANBIAN

See **Northeast China.**

YANG DEZHI (1911–1996)

Yang Dezhi, a senior member of the Chinese military, was born in Henan Province in 1911 to a peasant family. From 1927, Yang served in the Red Army, and at the end of the civil war in 1949 he was commander of the Ningxia Military District. In October 1950, he led the 63rd, 64th, and 65th **Chinese People's Volunteers'** (CPV) armies into Korea. From 1951 to mid-1953, he was chief-of-staff of the CPV, and from late 1952 he was also concurrently a deputy commander of the CPV under **Peng Dehuai.** In October 1954, after the **armistice,** Yang assumed command of the CPV, a post he held until March 1955. On return to China, he became a colonel general in 1955, and was commander of the Jinan Military Region from early 1958. He disappeared during the early stages of the Cultural Revolution

(1966–1976) but reemerged in 1971 and held military, state, and party roles until his death in 1996.
References: Klein and Clark 1971; *Who's Who in China* 1989.

YI SONG-MAN

See **Rhee, Syngman.**

YONHAP NEWS AGENCY

Yonhap has been South Korea's only general news agency since 1980. The first South Korean news agency, Kukje News, was formed in October 1945 from the office of the former Japanese agency Domei. In December 1945 it was replaced by the Hapdong News Agency. Other agencies emerged in the 1950s but all had financial problems, leaving only Hapdong and the Orient Press by the early 1970s. Following the military takeover under President **Chun Doo Hwan** in 1979–1980, these two were disbanded and replaced by the Yonhap News Agency. While nominally independent, and in reality far less controlled than the North Korean **Korean Central News Agency**, Yonhap has tended to follow the government line on both domestic and, to a lesser extent, international news. This is done by suppressing news rather than falsifying stories.
See also: Korean Central News Agency (KCNA); Naewoe News Agency.

YOSU-SUNCH'ON REBELLION (1948)

In the autumn of 1948, following the uprising on **Cheju Island**, the newly formed government of President **Syngman Rhee** took determined measures to reestablish control. However, when the 14th Regiment of the newly organized South Korean army was ordered to Cheju in October 1948, it refused to go. Instead, encouraged by a large group of local Communist sympathizers, the troops mutinied, seizing control of Yosu and the nearby important rail junction town of Sunch'on. There was much destruction of property and many people were killed. Although pro-Communist groups were involved, the main causes of the rebellion were dissatisfaction with the decision to establish a separate South Korean state and the order to suppress the Cheju uprising. After a week, troops loyal to Rhee restored order, at a heavy cost. Some of those involved in the rebellion fled to the **Chiri Mountains** to the north and established guerrilla bands that continued fighting until the mid-1950s.

See also: Cheju Island; Chiri Mountains.
References: Halliday and Cumings 1988; Merrill 1989.

YU JAE-HUNG (1921–)

At the outbreak of the **Korean War** in June 1950, Brigadier General Yu Jae-hung commanded the South Korean 7th Division guarding the **Uijongbu** corridor, a traditional invasion route providing easy access to the South Korean capital, **Seoul**, 30 miles (48 kilometers) to the south. Yu had attended the Japanese Military Academy, reaching the rank of major in the Japanese army. After 1945, he headed the South Korean Constabulary, the forerunner of the South Korean army. In June 1950, he was ordered to move northwest of Uijongbu, with the intention that the 2nd Division would support him on the northeast. Yu made his move, but the 2nd Division was well under strength, and its commander did not obey his orders, with the result that Yu's exposed forces broke in the face of the North Korean attack. He attempted to regroup south of Seoul, but the capital was left to the North Koreans. Promoted to major general, he commanded II Corps, leading them into North Korea following the **Inch'on landing** in September 1950. General **Paik Sun-yup** replaced him in October 1950, just before the **Chinese People's Volunteers** smashed II Corps. Yu held no further wartime commands, but he attended the **armistice** negotiations at **P'anmunjom**. After the war, he held senior staff appointments before retiring in 1960. Under President **Park Chung Hee**, he served as an ambassador and was for a time minister of defense.

See also: South Korean Armed Forces.
References: Matray 1991; Noble 1975.

YUN I-SANG (1917–1995)

Yun I-sang was perhaps the most famous Korean composer of the twentieth century, but, in a tragic illustration of the division of Korea, his music was banned in South Korea and honored in the North. Born in Tongyong, South Kyongsang Province, in what is now South Korea, Yun studied in Japan, where he was active in Korean revolutionary groups. In 1955, he won a major award from the **Seoul** city government and went to study in West Germany. There he acquired an international reputation, but in 1967, along with other South Koreans, including his wife, he was kidnapped by South Korean agents and brought back to Seoul, accused of spying for North Korea. He was sentenced to life imprisonment, but following an international outcry, he was released after two years and returned to Germany. Thereafter, his music began to reflect a more political position. He visited the North several times, where his works were regularly performed, while they were banned in the South. After his death in 1995, and in the changed political climate of South Korea, his reputation has revived in the South, and his music is performed. It continues to be popular in the North. A Yun I-sang musical festival was held in **P'yongyang** in November 1998.

See also: Abductions; Espionage.
References: Hwang 1998; Nahm 1993; Shaw 1991.

YUN PO-SUN (1897–1990)

A former president of South Korea, Yun Po-sun was born in Seoul in 1897 into a noble family and was educated at Edinburgh University in Scotland. After 1945, he was associated with the **Korean Independence Party** and was appointed mayor of Seoul in 1948. He served as minister of trade and industry, 1949–1950, but he soon resigned and thereafter opposed President **Syngman Rhee**. Following the overthrow of Rhee in 1960, Yun was elected president by the National Assembly. Despite his personal opposition to Major General **Park Chung Hee**'s military coup in 1961, Yun remained as president until March 1962, thus giving legitimacy to the military regime. In 1962, he objected to Park's political purges and resigned. He ran unsuccessfully for the presidency in 1963 and 1967. He opposed the **Yushin Constitution**, and received a five-year suspended sentence in 1976. His antigovernment protests also led to a two-year jail sentence in 1979. After 1980, under President **Chun Doo Hwan**, he was treated as an elder statesman who posed no threat to the regime.

YUSHIN CONSTITUTION

After the 1961 military coup in South Korea, Major General **Park Chung Hee**'s regime proposed a new Constitution, which was approved in December 1962. Park became president in 1963 and 1967 under this Constitution. Elected by popular vote and wielding strong powers, Park amended the Constitution in 1969 to allow him a third term. In December 1971, after his narrow victory over **Kim Dae Jung**, Park introduced sweeping measures of control. In October 1972, he proclaimed martial law, the suspension of the National Assembly, and the closure of schools and universities. A few days later, he introduced the Yushin or "revitalizing" Constitution. He could now succeed himself indefinitely and appoint one-third of the National Assembly members, thus giving the government a built-in majority. The president would be elected by a nonpartisan National Conference for Unification. Thus began the South Korean "Fourth Republic." Park justified these measures because of the dialogue with North Korea, which had begun in 1971. A modified form of the Yushin Constitution survived until 1987. It was widely criticized internationally and domestically and was attacked by North Korea.

See also: Chun Doo Hwan; National Security Law.

References: Hoare and Pares 1988; Macdonald 1996; Yang 1994.

ZHOU ENLAI (1898–1976)

When the **Korean War** began on 25 June 1950, Zhou Enlai (Chou En-lai) had been premier and foreign minister of the **People's Republic of China** (PRC) since its creation on 1 October 1949. Zhou had well-established credentials as a long-standing member of the Chinese Communist Party (CCP), as a revolutionary leader, and, above all, as a negotiator for the CCP, first in its civil wars with the Guomindang (Chinese Nationalists) from the 1920s, and then with the United States during World War II. Until his death in 1976, Zhou was one of the top three or four leaders of the CCP.

He was born in Jiangxi Province, to a reasonably well-off family. He attended Nankai Middle School in Tianjin from 1913 to 1917 and later studied in Japan. He returned to Tianjin, was arrested in 1920, and went to France on a work-study program on his release. He returned to China in 1924 and was active in the Guomindang National Revolution, until its leader, **Chiang Kai-shek**, turned on the Communists in 1927. Thereafter, Zhou worked with the CCP. From 1934, Zhou supported **Mao Zedong** in a partnership that would last until Zhou's death.

With the establishment of the PRC, Zhou's skills as a negotiator were augmented by those of a bureaucrat. In January 1950, he joined Mao in Moscow, to negotiate and sign a 30-year treaty of alliance with the Soviet Union. He also probably became aware around that time of plans by **Kim Il Sung**, the leader of the Democratic People's Republic of Korea (DPRK) to attempt the reunification of Korea by force. As premier and foreign minister, Zhou played a prominent public role during the Korean War, supporting the DPRK's position and attacking the United States for its hostility both to the DPRK and to China. Mao may have made the broad policy decisions, but Zhou translated them into action. In August 1952, Zhou led a delegation to Moscow to negotiate more aid for the PRC, which

was bearing the brunt of the Korean fighting. In November 1952, he signed an agreement with Kim Il Sung to provide for postwar aid to North Korea. Zhou attended the funeral in Moscow of the Soviet leader **Joseph Stalin** in March 1953, at which time the Chinese and Soviet leaders appear to have decided that it was time to end the Korean War. As a result, the **armistice** negotiations at **P'anmunjom** began to make headway. Following the end of the war in July 1953, Zhou led the PRC delegation to the 1954 **Geneva Conference**. Although the Chinese achieved a satisfactory solution to the Indochina problem at Geneva, the Korean problem, despite Zhou's efforts, proved more difficult to settle.

From 1954 until his death, Zhou was regarded by the North Koreans as a good friend, even though he became particularly associated with the improvement of Sino-U.S. relations under Henry Kissinger and President Richard Nixon. Zhou survived the Cultural Revolution, and although he was quite ill at the time, he received Kim Il Sung in Beijing in April 1975, soon after the North Vietnamese final victory in the **Vietnam War**. Zhou appears to have advised Kim that the time was not ripe for another Korean war. Since Zhou's death in April 1976, the North Koreans have regarded his widow, Deng Yingchao, whom he married in 1925, as one of their supporters.

See also: Chinese Involvement in Korea (1919–1948); Chinese People's Volunteers; People's Liberation Army (PLA); People's Republic of China Relations with North Korea; Taiwan.

Reference: Encyclopedia Britannica 1997.

Bibliography

Books

Abramovitz, Morton. 1971. *Moving the Glacier: The Two Koreas and the Powers.* Adelphi Paper No. 80. London, International Institute of Strategic Studies.

Acheson, Dean. 1969. *Present at the Creation: My Years at the State Department.* New York, W. W. Norton.

———. 1971. *The Korean War.* New York, W. W. Norton.

Amnesty International. 1989. *South Korea: Return to "Repressive Force and Torture"?* London, Amnesty International, International Secretariat.

———. 1995. *Republic of Korea (South Korea): International Standards, Law and Practice: The Need for Human Rights Reform.* London, Amnesty International, International Secretariat.

Appleman, Roy E. 1961. *The United States Army in the Korean War.* Vol. 1, *South to the Naktong, North to the Yalu.* Washington, DC, U.S. Government Printing Office.

———. 1987. *East of Chosin: Entrapment and Breakout in Korea, 1950.* College Station, TX, Texas A&M University Press.

———. 1990. *Ridgway Duels for Korea.* College Station, TX, Texas A&M University Press.

Attlee, Lord. 1961. *A Prime Minister Remembers.* London, Heinemann.

Axelsson, Arne. 1990. *Restrained Response: American Novels of the Cold War and Korea, 1945–1962.* New York, Greenwood Press.

Bailey, Sidney D. 1992. *The Korean Armistice.* London, Macmillan.

Barclay, Cyril N. 1954. *The First Commonwealth Division: The Story of British Land Forces in Korea, 1950–53.* Aldershot, UK, Gale and Polden.

Bartz, Patricia McB. 1972. *South Korea.* Oxford, Clarendon Press.

Bedeski, Robert E. 1992. *The Transformation of South Korea: Reform and Reconstruction in the Sixth Republic under Roh Tae Woo 1987–1992.* London, Routledge.

Bergot, E. 1983. *Bataillon de Corée: Les Volontaires français 1950–1953.* Paris, Presses de la Cité.

Bermudez, Joseph S. Jr. 1988. *North Korean Special Forces.* Coulsdon, UK, Jane's Publishing.

Blair, Clay. 1987. *The Forgotten War: America in Korea 1950–1953.* New York, Anchor Books.

Blake, George. 1990. *No Other Choice: An Autobiography.* London, Jonathan Cape.

Bolger, Daniel P. 1991. *Scenes from an Unfinished War: Low-Intensity Conflict in Korea, 1966–1969.* Leavenworth Papers No. 19. Fort Leavenworth, KS, Combat Studies Institute.

Brune, Lester H. 1996. *The Korean War: Handbook of the Literature and Research.* Westport, CT, Greenwood Press.

Bucher, Lloyd M., with Mark Rascovich. 1970. *Bucher: My Story.* Garden City, NY, Doubleday.

Bullock, Alan. 1983. *Ernest Bevin: Foreign Secretary 1945–51.* London, Heinemann.

Buzo, Adrian. 1981. "North Korea—Yesterday and Today," *Transactions of the Korea Branch of the Royal Asiatic Society* 56: 1–25.

Cagle, Malcolm W., and Frank A. Mason. 1957. *The Sea War in Korea.* Annapolis, MD, U.S. Naval Institute.

Caldwell, John C., in collaboration with Lesley Frost. 1952. *The Korea Story.* Chicago, Henry Regnery.

Cameron, James. 1967. *Point of Departure: Experiment in Biography.* London, Arthur Barker.

———. 1974. *An Indian Summer: A Personal Experience of India.* London, Macmillan.

Chay Jongsik. 1990. *Diplomacy of Asymmetry: Korean-American Relations to 1910.* Honolulu, University of Hawaii Press.

Chen Jian. 1994. *China's Road to the Korean War: The Making of the Sino-American Confrontation.* New York, Columbia University Press.

Chinese Academy of Social Science (ed.). 1989. *Information China,* 3 vols. Oxford and New York, Pergamon Press.

Cho Soon Sung. 1967. *Korea in World Politics, 1940–50.* Berkeley, University of California Press.

Choi In-Hoon [Ch'oe In-hun]. 1961. *The Square.* Trans. Kevin O'Rourke, 1985. Barnstaple, UK, Spindlewood.

Chung, Chin O. 1978. *Pyongyang between Peking and Moscow: North Korea's Involvement in the Sino-Soviet Dispute*. Mobile, AL, University of Alabama Press.

Chung Young-iob. 1979. "US Economic Aid to South Korea after World War II," in *The United States and Korea: American-Korean Relations, 1866–1976*, ed. Andrew C. Nahm. Kalamazoo, MI, Center for Korean Studies, Western Michigan University, 187–217.

Clark, Donald N. (ed.). 1988. *The Kwangju Uprising: Shadows over the Regime in South Korea*. Boulder, CO, Westview Press.

Clark, Donald N., and James H. Grayson. 1986. *Discovering Seoul*. RAS Guidebook Series, No. 4. Seoul, Seoul Computer Press for the Royal Asiatic Society Korea Branch.

Clark, Mark. 1954. *From the Danube to the Yalu*. New York, Harper.

Cohen, Warren. 1980. *Dean Rusk*. Totowa, NJ, Cooper Square Publications.

——— (ed.). 1996. *Pacific Passage: The Study of American–East Asian Relations on the Eve of the Twenty-First Century*. New York, Columbia University Press.

Cold War International History Project Bulletin 1995/1996. Issues 6–7 (Winter): 30–125. "New Evidence on the Korean War," articles and translations by Kathryn Weathersby, Chen Jian, Evgueni Bajanov, Hyun-su Jeon with Gyoo Kahng, Alexandre Y. Mansourov, Bruce Cumings and Kathryn Weathersby, and Laurence Jolidan. Washington, DC, Woodrow Wilson International Center for Scholars.

Commission on Theological Concerns of the Christian Conference of Asia (CTC-CCA). 1981. *Minjung Theology: People as the Subjects of History*. Singapore, CTC-CCA. 1983, revised edition. Maryknoll, NY, Orbis Books; London, Zed Press; Singapore, CTC-CCA.

Conroy, Hilary. 1960. *The Japanese Seizure of Korea: 1868–1910: A Study of Realism and Idealism in International Relations*. Philadelphia, University of Pennsylvania Press.

Cotton, James. 1998. "Defection of North Korea's Ideologist a Sign of Regime Crisis," *Pacific Review* 11/1: 107–118.

——— (ed.). 1993. *Korea under Roh Tae Woo: Democratization, Northern Policy and Inter-Korean Relations*. Saint Leonards, NSW, Allen and Unwin.

Cowdery, Albert E. 1987. *United States Army in the Korean War: Medic's War*. Washington, DC, Chief of Military History.

Crahay, Albert. 1967. *Les Belges en Corée*. Brussels, La Renaissance du livre.

Crosbie, Philip. 1954. *Pencilling Prisoner*. Melbourne, The Hawthorn Press.

Crusader for Democracy: The Life and Times of Kim Young Sam. 1993. Seoul, Yonhap News Agency.

Cumings, Bruce. 1981 and 1990. *The Origins of the Korean War*, 2 vols. Princeton, NJ, Princeton University Press.

———. 1992. *War and Television*. London, Verso.

———. 1997. *Korea's Place in the Sun: A Modern History*. New York, W. W. Norton.

——— (ed.). 1983. *Child of Conflict: The Korean-American Relationship, 1943–53*. Seattle, University of Washington Press.

Cunningham-Boothe, Ashley, and Peter Farrar (eds.). 1988. *British Forces in the Korean War*. Halifax, UK, British Korean Veterans Association.

Cutforth, René. 1952. *Korean Reporter*. London, Allan Wingate.

Danchev, Alex. 1993. *Oliver Franks: Founding Father*. Oxford, Clarendon Press.

Davies, S. J. 1954. *In Spite of Dungeons: The Experiences as a Prisoner of War in North Korea of the Chaplin to the First Battalion, the Gloucestershire Regiment*. London, Hodder and Stoughton.

Dean, William F. 1954. *General Dean's Story, As Told to William L. Worden by Major General William F. Dean*. New York, Viking.

Deane, Philip. 1953. *Captive in Korea*. London, Hamish Hamilton.

———. 1976. *I Should Have Died*. London, Hamish Hamilton.

Dockrill, Michael L. 1989. "The Foreign Office, Anglo-American Relations and the Korean Truce Negotiations July 1952–July 1953," in *The Korean War in History*, ed. James Cotton and Ian Neary. Manchester, Manchester University Press.

Documents and Materials Exposing the Instigators of the Civil War in Korea: Documents from the Archives of the Rhee Syngman Government. 1950. P'yongyang, Foreign Languages Publishing House.

Duus, Peter. 1995. *The Abacus and the Sword: The Japanese Penetration of Korea, 1895–1910*. Berkeley, University of California Press.

Eberstadt, Nicholas. 1995. *Korea Approaches Reunification*. Armonk, NY, M. E. Sharpe.

Eckert, Carter J., Ki-baik Lee, Young Ick Lee, Michael Robinson, and Edward W. Wagner. 1990. *Korea Old and New: A History*. Seoul, Ilchokak, Publishers, for the Korea Institute, Harvard University.

Eden, Anthony. 1960. *The Memoirs of Sir Anthony Eden: Full Circle*. London, Cassell.

Edwards, Paul M. 1990. *The Inchon Landing, Korea, 1950: An Annotated Bibliography*. Westport, CT, Greenwood Press.

———. 1997. *A Guide to Films on the Korean War*. Westport, CT, Greenwood Press.

Encyclopedia Britannica CD-ROM edition, 1997.

Facts Tell. 1960. P'yongyang, Foreign Languages Publishing House.

Fairbank, John King. 1992. *China: A New History*. Cambridge, MA, Harvard University Press.

Farrar-Hockley, Anthony. 1954. *The Edge of the Sword*. London, Frederick Muller. 1985, 2nd ed. London, Buchan and Enright.

———. 1990 and 1995. *The British Part in the Korean War*, 2 vols. London, HMSO. [U.K. official history.]

Field, James A. Jr. 1962. *A History of the United States Naval Operations: Korea*. Washington, DC, U.S. Government Printing Office.

Foley, James. n.d. "Korean Divided Families: The Surviving Generation." Unpublished article.

Foot, Rosemary. 1985. *The Wrong War: American Policy and the Dimensions of the Korean Conflict*. Ithaca, NY, Cornell University Press.

———. 1990. *A Substitute for Peace: The Politics of Peacemaking at the Korean Armistice Talks*. Ithaca, NY, Cornell University Press.

Foreign Relations of the United States: Diplomatic Papers: The Conferences at Cairo and Tehran, 1943. 1961. Washington, DC, U.S. Government Printing Office.

Forty, G. 1982. *At War in Korea*. London, Ian Allan.

Futrell, Robert F. 1961, rev. 1983. *The United States Air Force in Korea, 1950–53*. New York, Duell, Sloan and Pearce. [U.S. official history.]

Giffard, Sydney. 1994. *Japan among the Powers 1890–1990*. New Haven, CT, Yale University Press.

Gills, B. K. 1996. *Korea versus Korea: A Case of Contested Legitimacy*. London, Routledge.

Gittings, John. 1967. *The Role of the Chinese Army*. London, Oxford University Press for the Royal Institute for International Affairs.

———. 1968. *Survey of the Sino-Soviet Dispute*. New York, Oxford University Press for the Royal Institute for International Affairs.

Goncharov, Sergei N., John W. Lewis, and Xue Litai. 1993. *Uncertain Partners: Stalin, Mao and the Korean War*. Stanford, CA, Stanford University Press.

Goodman, Allan E. (ed.). 1978. *Negotiating While Fighting: The Diary of Admiral C. Turner Joy at the Korean Armistice Conference*. Stanford, CA, Stanford University Press.

Grajdanzev, Andrew I. 1944. *Modern Korea*. New York, Institute of Pacific Relations. Reprinted 1975, Seoul, Kyung-in Publishing.

Grayson, James. H. 1989. *Korea: A Religious History*. Oxford, Clarendon Press.

Grey, Jeffrey. 1988. *The Commonwealth Armies and the Korean War*. Manchester, Manchester University Press.

Halliday, Jon, and Bruce Cumings. 1988. *Korea: The Unknown War: An Illustrated History*. London, Viking.

Hallion, Richard. 1986. *The Naval Air War in Korea*. Baltimore, MD, Nautical & Aviation Publishing Company of America.

Hammel, Eric M. 1994 (paperback edition). *Chosin: Heroic Ordeal of the Korean War*. Novato, CA, Presidio Press.

Han Su-yin. 1994. *Eldest Son: Zhou Enlai and the Making of Modern China*. New York, Hill and Wang.

Han Sungjoo. 1982(a). "The Korean-American Relations during the Post–World War II Period," *Korea Journal* 22/12 (December): 4–32.

——— (ed.). 1982(b). *After One Hundred Years: Continuity and Change in Korean-American Relations*. Seoul, Asiatic Research Centre, Korea University.

Hao Yufan and Zhai Zhihai. 1990. "China's Decision to Enter the Korean War: History Revised," *China Quarterly*, March.

Harrington, Fred Harvey. 1961. *God, Mammon and the Japanese: Dr Horace Allen and Korean-American Relations, 1884–1905*. Madison, University of Wisconsin Press.

Harris, Keith. 1982. *Attlee*. London, Weidenfeld and Nicholson.

Hastings, Max. 1987. *The Korean War*. London, Michael Joseph.

Hayes, Peter. 1991. *Pacific Powderkeg: American Nuclear Dilemmas in Korea*. Lexington, MA, Lexington Books.

Henderson, Gregory. 1968. *Korea: The Politics of the Vortex*. Cambridge, MA, Harvard University Press.

Her Majesty's Stationery Office (HMSO), Korea No. 1 (1952), June 1952. *Korea: A Summary of Developments in the Armistice Negotiations and the Prisoner of War Camps, June 1951–May 1952*. London, Her Majesty's Stationery Office (cmd. 8596).

Hermes, Walter G. 1966. *The United States Army in the Korean War*. Vol. 2, *Truce Tent and Fighting Front*. Washington, DC, U.S. Government Printing Office.

Higgins, Marguerite. 1951. *War in Korea: The Report of a Woman Combat Correspondent*. Garden City, NY, Doubleday.

Highsmith, Carol M., and Ted Landphair. 1995. *Forgotten No More: The Korean War Veterans Memorial Story*. Washington, DC, Chelsea Publishing.

Hinshaw, A. L. 1989. *Heartbreak Ridge: Korea, 1951*. New York, Praeger.

History of the Just Fatherland War of the Korean People. 1961. P'yongyang, Foreign Languages Publishing House.

The History of the United Nations Forces in the Korean War, 6 vols. 1972–1977. Seoul, Ministry of National Defense, Republic of Korea. [Abbreviated in text citations to History, with relevant volume number and year of publication.]

Hoare, James. 1983. "The Centenary of Korean-British Relations: Aspects of British Interest and Involvement in Korea 1600–1983," *Transactions of the Korea Branch of the Royal Asiatic Society* 58: 1–34.

———. 1997. "North Korean Foreign Policy," in *The Korean Peninsula in Transition*, ed. Daw Hwan Kim and Tat Yan Kong. New York, St. Martin's Press, 172–195.

Hoare, James, and Susan Pares. 1988. *Korea: An Introduction*. London, KPI.

Hopkinson, Tom (ed.). 1970, reprinted 1979. *Picture Post 1938–50*. Harmondsworth, Middlesex, UK, Penguin Books.

Howard, Keith, Susan Pares, and Tessa English (eds.). 1996. *Korea: People, Country and Culture*. London, SOAS.

Hoyt, Edwin P. 1984. *The Pusan Perimeter: Korea 1950*. New York, Stein and Day.

———. 1985. *The Bloody Road to Panmunjom*. New York, Stein and Day.

———. 1990. *The Day the Chinese Attacked: Korea 1950: The Story of the Failure of America's China Policy*. New York, McGraw-Hill.

Hwang Eui-gak. 1993. *The Korean Economies: A Comparison of North and South*. Oxford, Clarendon Press.

Hwang Jang-jin. 1998. "Memoirs Shed Light on Composer Yun Isang," *Korea Herald*, 16 September.

Hyun, Peter. 1981. *Darkness at Dawn: A North Korean Diary*. Seoul, Hanjin Publishing.

An International Terrorist Clique: North Korea. n.d. Seoul, Korean Overseas Information Service.

Intra-Korean Agreements. 1992. Seoul, National Unification Board, Republic of Korea.

Jackson, Robert. 1973. *Air War over Korea*. New York, Scribner's.

———. 1998. *Air War in Korea, 1950–53*. Shrewsbury, UK, Airlife.

James, D. Clayton, with Anne Sharp Wells. 1993. *Refighting the Last War: Command and Crisis in Korea*. New York, The Free Press.

Johnson, R. W. 1986. *Shootdown: The Verdict on KAL007*. London, Chatto and Windus.

Joy, C. Turner. 1955. *How Communists Negotiate*. New York, Macmillan.

Kang Myung Hun. 1996. *The Korean Business Conglomerate: Chaebol Then and Now*. Berkeley, University of California Press.

Kapur, K. D. 1995. *Nuclear Diplomacy in East Asia: US and the Korean Nuclear Crisis Management*. New Delhi, Lancer Books.

Keith, Ronald C. 1989. *The Diplomacy of Zhou Enlai*. New York, St. Martin's Press.

Kenyon, Albert. 1966. *Valiant Dust: Graphic Stories from the Life of Herbert A. Lord*. London, Salvationist Publishing and Supplies.

Kiernan, Ben (ed.). 1986. *Burchett Reporting the Other Side of the World 1939–1983*. London, Quartet Books.

Kim Chi-ha. 1980. *The Middle Hour: Selected Poems of Kim Chi Ha*. Trans. David R. McCann. Standfordville, NY, Human Rights Publishing Group.

Kim Chong-un (trans. and ed.). 1974. *Postwar Korean Short Stories: An Anthology*. Seoul, Seoul National University Press.

Kim Choong Soon. 1988. *Faithful Endurance: An Ethnography of Korean Family Dispersal*. Tucson, University of Arizona Press.

Kim Chum-kon. 1973. *The Korean War*. Seoul, Kwangmyong Publishing.

Kim Dae Jung. 1985. *Mass-Participating Economy: A Democratic Alternative for Korea*. Lanham, MD, University Press of America.

———. 1987(a). *Philosophy and Dialogues: Building Peace and Democracy*. New York, Korean Independence Monitor.

———. 1987(b). *Prison Writings*. Trans. Choi Sung-il and David McCann. Berkeley, University of California Press.

Kim, Dae Young, and John E. Slobada. 1981. "Migration and Korean Development," in *Economic Development, Population Policy, and Demographic Transition in the Republic of Korea*, ed. Robert Repetto, Tai Hwan Kwon, Son-Ung Kim, et al. Cambridge, MA, Council on East Asian Studies, Harvard University Press, 36–138.

Kim Gye-Dong. 1990. "The Legacy of Foreign Intervention in Korea: Division and War," *Korea and World Affairs* 14/2 (Summer): 275–302.

Kim Hak-chun [Kim Hak-joon]. 1981. "Sino-North Korean Relations before the Outbreak of the Korean War," *Korea Journal* 21/6 (June): 4–17.

Kim Hak-joon. 1986. *Korea in Soviet East Asian Policy*. Seoul, Institute of International Peace Studies, Kyung Hee University.

———. 1990. "International Trends in Korean War Studies: A Review of the Documentary Literature," *Korea and World Affairs* 14/2 (Summer): 326–370.

———. 1992. *Unification Policies of North and South Korea, 1945–91: A Comparative Study*, 3rd ed. Seoul, Seoul National University Press.

Kim Han Gil. 1979. *Modern History of Korea*. P'yongyang, Foreign Languages Publishing House.

Kim Il Sung. 1965– . *Selected Works of Kim Il Sung*. P'yongyang, Foreign Languages Publishing House.

Kim, Ilpyong J., and Kihl Young Whan (eds.). 1988. *Political Change in South Korea*. New York, The Korean PWPA.

Kim Jong Il. 1989. *On the Juche Idea*. P'yongyang, Foreign Languages Publishing House.

Kim Jung-ik. 1996. *The Future of the US–Republic of Korea Military Relationship*. New York, St. Martin's Press.

Kim, Richard. 1969. *The Martyred*. Seoul, Si-sa-yong-o-sa Publishers.

Kim Se-Jin (ed.). 1976. *Problems of Korean Unification*. Seoul, Research Centre for Peace and Unification.

King, Ross. 1997. "Language, Politics, and Ideology in the Postwar Koreas," in *Korea Briefing: Toward Reunification,* ed. David McCann. Armonk, NY, M. E. Sharpe, 109–144.

Kirkbride, Wayne A. 1984. *DMZ: A Story of the Panmunjom Axe Murder*. Elizabeth, NJ, Hollym.

———. 1985. *Panmunjom: Facts about the Korean DMZ*. Elizabeth, NJ, Hollym.

———. 1994. *North Korea's Undeclared War: 1953– .* Elizabeth, NJ, Hollym.

Klein, Donald W., and Anne B. Clark. 1971. *Biographic Dictionary of Chinese Communism 1921–1965*, 2 vols. Cambridge, MA, Harvard University Press.

Knightley, Phillip. 1982. *The First Casualty: The War Correspondent as Hero, Propagandist and Mythmaker*. London, Quartet Books.

Koh Byung Chul. 1969. *The Foreign Policy of North Korea*. New York, Frederick A. Praeger.

———. 1993. "The War's Impact on the Korean Peninsula," in *A Revolutionary War: Korea and the Transformation of the Postwar World*, ed. William J. Williams. Chicago, Imprint Publications.

Kolko, Joyce, and Gabriel Kolko. 1972. *The Limits of Power: The World and United States Foreign Policy, 1945–1954*. New York, Harper and Row.

Koo Youngnok and Han Sung-joo (eds.). 1985. *The Foreign Policy of the Republic of Korea*. New York, Columbia University Press.

Koo Youngnok and Suh Dae-sook (eds.). 1984. *Korea and the United States: A Century of Cooperation*. Honolulu, University of Hawaii Press.

Ku Dae-yeol. 1985. *Korea under Colonialism: The March First Movement and Anglo-Japanese Relations*. Seoul, Seoul Computer Press for the Royal Asiatic Society, Korea Branch.

Kumatani, Akiyasu. 1990. "Language Policies in North Korea," *International Journal of the Sociology of Language* No. 82: 87–108.

Kwak Tae-han et al. (eds.). 1982. *US-Korean Relations 1882–1982*. Seoul, Institute for Far Eastern Studies, Kyungnam University.

Kwak Tae-han, Kim Chongchun, and Kim Hong Nack (eds.). 1984. *Korean Reunification: New Perspectives and Approaches*. Seoul, Institute for Far Eastern Studies, Kyungnam University.

Kwak Tae-han, Wayne Patterson, and Edward A. Olsen (eds.). 1983. *The Two Koreas in World Politics*. Seoul, Kyungnam University Press.

Kwon, Tai Hwan. 1977. *Demography of Korea: Population Change and Its Components, 1926–66*. Seoul, Seoul National University Press.

Lautensach, Hermann. 1945. *Korea: A Geography Based on the Author's Travels and Literature*. Trans. Katherine Dege and Eckart Dege, 1988. New York, Springer-Verlag.

Lee Chae-jin, with Park Doo-bok. 1996. *China and Korea: Dynamic Relations*. Stanford, CA, Hoover Institute Press.

Lee Chong-sik. 1965. *The Politics of Korean Nationalism*. Berkeley, University of California Press.

Lee Hyun-bok. 1990. "Differences in Language Use between North and South Korea," *International Journal of the Sociology of Language* No. 82: 71–86.

Lone, Stewart, and Gavan McCormack. 1993. *Korea since 1850*. Melbourne, Longman Cheshire/St. Martin's Press.

Lowe, Peter. 1988(a). *The Origins of the Korean War*. London, Longman.

———. 1988(b). "The Settlement of the Korean War," in *The Foreign Policy of Churchill's Peacetime Administration*, ed. John W. Young. Leicester, Leicester University Press, 207–231.

MacArthur, Douglas. 1964. *Reminiscences*. London, Heinemann.

MacDonald, Callum. 1986. *Korea: The War before Vietnam*. London, Macmillan.

———. 1990. *Britain and the Korean War*. Cambridge, MA, Basil Blackwell.

Macdonald, Donald Stone. 1996. *The Koreans: Contemporary Politics and Society*, 3rd ed. Ed. and rev. by Donald L. Clark. Boulder, CO, Westview Press.

Macksey, Kenneth. 1993. *The Penguin Encyclopedia of Weapons and Military Technology: Prehistory to the Present Day*. London, Viking.

Marshall, S. L. A. 1956. *Pork Chop Hill: The American Fighting Man in Korea*. New York, William Morrow.

Marton, Andrew, Terry McGee, and Donald G. Paterson. 1995. "Northeast Asian Economic Cooperation and the Tumen River Area Development Project," *Pacific Affairs* 68/1 (Spring): 9–33.

Matray, James. 1985. *The Reluctant Crusade: American Foreign Policy in Korea, 1941–1950*. Honolulu, University of Hawaii Press.

———. 1991. *Historical Dictionary of the Korean War*. Westport, CT, Greenwood Press.

Mazaar, Michael J. 1995. *North Korea and the Bomb: A Case Study in Non-proliferation*. New York, St. Martin's Press.

McCormack, Gavan. 1983. *Cold War, Hot War: An Australian Perspective on the Korean War*. Sydney, Hale and Iremonger.

———. 1993. "Kim Country: Hard Times in North Korea," *New Left Review* No. 198 (March–April).

McCune, George M. 1947. *Korea's Postwar Political Problems*. New York, International Secretariat, Institute of Pacific Relations.

———, with the collaboration of Arthur L. Grey. 1950. *Korea Today*. Cambridge, MA, Harvard University Press.

McGibbon, Ian. 1992 and 1996. *New Zealand and the Korean War*, 2 vols. Auckland, Oxford University Press. [N.Z. official history.]

McKenzie, Frederic Arthur. 1929. *Korea's Fight for Freedom*. New York, Fleming H. Revell; 3rd ed., 1975, Seoul, Yonsei University Press.

Melady, John. 1983. *Korea: Canada's Forgotten War*. Toronto, Macmillan of Canada.

Merrill, John. 1982. "The Cheju-do Rebellion," *Journal of Korean Studies* 2: 139–198.

———. 1983. "Internal Warfare in Korea, 1948–50: The Local Setting of the Korean War," in *Child of Conflict: The Korean-American Relationship*, ed. Bruce Cumings. Seattle, University of Washington Press, 133–162.

———. 1989. *Korea: The Peninsular Origins of the War*. Newark, NJ, University of Delaware Press.

Michener, James. 1953. *The Bridges at Toko-ri*. New York, Random House.

Middleton, Lawrence. 1997. "South Korean Foreign Policy," in *The Korean Peninsula in Transition,* ed. Daw Hwan Kim and Tat Yan Kong. New York, St. Martin's Press, 149–171.

Millett, Allan R. 1995. "Remembering the Forgotten War: Anglo-American Scholarship on the Korean Conflict," *Transactions of the Korea Branch of the Royal Asiatic Society* 70: 53–70.

Montrose, Lynn, and Nicholas A. Canzona. 1957. *US Marine Operations in Korea 1950–53.* Vol. III, *The Chosin Reservoir Campaign*. Washington, DC, U.S. Government Printing Office.

Moore, Dermot, and Peter Bagshaw. 1991. *South Africa's Flying Cheetahs in Korea*. Johannesburg, Ashanti Publishing.

Morris, Warwick. 1996. "UK Policy Towards North Korea," in *North Korea in the New World Order,* ed. Hazel Smith et al. London, Macmillan, 86–92.

Mossman, William. 1990. *The United States Army in the Korean War*. Vol. 4, *Ebb and Flow*. Washington, DC, U.S. Government Printing Office.

Muratov, A. 1985. "The Friendship Will Grow Stronger: The 40th Anniversary of the Liberation of Korea by the Soviet Army from the Japanese Colonial Rule," *International Affairs* [USSR] 9 (September): 22–28.

Myers, Brian. 1994. *Han Sorya and North Korean Literature: The Failure of Socialist Realism in the DPRK*. Ithaca, NY, Cornell University.

Nahm, Andrew C. 1993. *Historical Dictionary of the Republic of Korea*. Metuchen, NJ, The Scarecrow Press.

——— (ed.). 1973. *Korea under Japanese Colonial Rule*. Kalamazoo, Center for Korean Studies, Institute of International and Area Studies, Western Michigan University.

——— (ed.). 1979. *The United States and Korea: American-Korean Relations 1866–1976*. Kalamazoo, Center for Korean Studies, Western Michigan University.

Nam Joo-hong. 1986. *America's Commitment to South Korea: The First Decade of the Nixon Doctrine*. New York, Cambridge University Press.

Nam Koon Woo. 1989. *South Korean Politics: The Search for Political Consensus and Stability*. Lanham, MD, University Press of America.

National Unification Board. 1989. *To Build National Community through the Korean Commonwealth: A Blueprint for Korean Unification*. Seoul, National Unification Board.

Nicholas, H. G. 1962. *The United Nations as a Political Institution*, 2nd ed. London, Oxford University Press.

Nineteen Contemporary Korean Novelists. 1985. Seoul, Korean Culture and Arts Foundation.

Noble, Harold J. (ed. Frank Baldwin). 1975. *Embassy at War*. Seattle, University of Washington Press.

Oberdorfer, Don. 1997. *The Two Koreas: A Contemporary History*. Reading, MA, Addison Wesley Longman.

Oliver, Robert T. 1954. *Syngman Rhee: The Man behind the Myth*. New York, Dodd Mead; 1955, London, Robert Hall.

———. 1978. *Syngman Rhee and the American Involvement in Korea, 1942–60*. Seoul, Panmun.

O'Neill, Robert. 1981 and 1985. *Australia in the Korean War 1950–53*, 2 vols. Canberra, The Australian War Memorial and the Australian Government Publishing Service. [Australian official history.]

Paik Lak-Geoon George. 1970. *The History of Protestant Missions in Korea*. Seoul, Yonsei University Press.

Paik Sun Yup. 1992. *From Pusan to Panmunjom*. New York, Brassey's.

Pang Hwan Ju, and Hwang Bong Hyok. 1991 and 1997. *A Sightseeing Guide to Korea: Collection of Materials, Photographs and Maps*. P'yongyang, Foreign Languages Publishing House.

Park Choon-ho. 1983. *East Asia and the Law of the Sea*. Institute of Social Science Seoul National University International Studies Series, No. 5. Seoul, Seoul National University Press.

Park Chung Hee. 1979. *Korea Reborn: A Model for Development*. Englewood Cliffs, NJ, Prentice-Hall.

Peacock, Lindsay. 1991. *North American F-86 Sabre*. New York, Salamander Books.

Pelser, Frederick, and Marcia E. Pelser. 1984. *Freedom Bridge*. Fairfield, CA, Fremar Press.

Peng Dehuai. 1984. *Memoirs of a Chinese Marshal*. Beijing, Foreign Languages Publishing House.

Perret, Geoffrey. 1996. *Old Soldiers Never Die: The Life of Douglas MacArthur*. London, Andre Deutsch.

Petrov, Vladimir. 1994. "Soviet Role in the Korean War Confirmed: Secret Documents Declassified," *Journal of Northeast Asian Studies* 13/3 (Fall): 42–67.

Phillips, Cabell. 1966. *The Truman Presidency*. New York, Macmillan.

Pihl, Marshall. 1993. "Contemporary Literature in a Divided Land," in *Korea Briefing, 1993: Festival of Korea*, ed. Donald N. Clark. Boulder, CO, Westview Press.

Pihl, Marshall, Bruce Fulton, and Ju-Chan Fulton (trans. and eds.). 1993. *Land of Exile: Contemporary Korean Fiction*. Armonk, NY, M. E. Sharpe/UNESCO Publishing.

Pollack, Jonathan D., and Cha Young-koo. 1995. *A New Alliance for the Next Century: The Future of US-Korean Security Co-operation*. Santa Monica, CA, RAND.

Provocations from North Korea. ca. 1988. Seoul, Korean War Veterans Association.

Pusan History Compilation Committee. 1998. *The History and Culture of Pusan*. Pusan, City of Pusan.

Rees, David. 1964. *Korea: The Limited War*. London, Macmillan.

———. 1984. *The Korean War: History and Tactics*. New York, Crescent.

Reflections on a Centenary of United States–Korean Relations. 1982. Ed. Academy of Korean Studies and the Wilson Center. Washington, DC, University Press of America.

Rehabilitation and Development of Agriculture, Forestry, and Fisheries in South Korea. 1954. Report prepared for the United Nations Korean Reconstruction Agency by a mission selected by the Food and Agriculture Organization of the United Nations. New York, Columbia University Press.

Republic of Korea National Red Cross. 1977. *The Dispersed Families in Korea*. Seoul, Republic of Korea National Red Cross.

Ri In Mo. 1997. *Memoirs: My Life and Faith*. P'yongyang, Foreign Languages Publishing House.

Ridgway, Matthew B. 1956. *Soldier: The Memoirs of Matthew B. Ridgway*. New York, Harper and Brothers.

———. 1967. *The Korean War*. New York, Doubleday.

Riley, John W., and W. Schramm, narratives translated by Hugh Heung-wu Cynn. 1951. *The Reds Take a City: The Communist Occupation of Seoul, with Eyewitness Accounts*. New Brunswick, NJ, Rutgers University Press; reprinted 1973, Westport, CT, Greenwood Press.

Robertson, David. 1993. *A Dictionary of Modern Politics*, 2nd ed. London, Europa Publications.

Robinson, Michael Edson. 1988. *Cultural Nationalism in Colonial Korea, 1920–1925*. Seattle, University of Washington Press.

Roh Tae Woo. 1990. *Korea: A Nation Transformed; Selected Speeches*. Oxford, Pergamon Press.

Rusk, Dean. 1991. *As I Saw It*. New York, W. W. Norton.

Ryang, Sonia. 1997. *North Koreans in Japan: Language, Ideology and Identity*. Boulder, CO, Westview Press.

Sakurai, Hiroshi. 1998. "A Survey: Studies on the Korean War in Japan," in *Social Science Japan Journal* 1/1 (April): 85–89.

Sandusky, Michael C. 1983. *America's Parallel*. Alexandria, VA, Old Dominion Press.

Sanford, Dan C. 1990. *South Korea and the Socialist Countries: The Politics of Trade*. Basingstoke, Macmillan.

Savada, Andreas Matles, and William Shaw (eds.). 1992. *South Korea: A Country Study*, 4th ed. Washington, DC, Federal Research Division, Library of Congress.

Sawyer, R. K., and W. G. Hermes. 1962. *Military Advisers in Korea: KMAG in War and Peace*. Washington, DC, Office of the Chief of Military History, Department of the Army.

Scalapino, Robert, and Chong-sik Lee. 1972. *Communism in Korea*, 2 vols. Berkeley, University of California Press.

Schnabel, James F. 1972. *The United States Army in the Korean War*. Vol. 3, *Policy and Direction: The First Year*. Washington, DC, U.S. Government Printing Office.

Schoenbaum, Thomas J. 1988. *Waging War and Peace: Dean Rusk in the Truman, Kennedy and Johnson Years*. New York, Simon and Schuster.

Segal, Gerald. 1993. *The World Affairs Companion: The Essential One-Volume Guide to Global Issues*, rev. ed. New York, Simon and Schuster.

Shaw, William (ed.). 1991. *Human Rights in Korea: Historical and Policy Aspects*. Harvard University Studies in East Asian Law 16. Cambridge, MA, Harvard University Press.

Shin Yong-ha. 1990. *Formation and Development of Modern Korean Nationalism*. Seoul, Dae Kwang Munhwasa.

Sigal, Leon V. 1998. *Disarming Strangers: Nuclear Diplomacy with North Korea*. Princeton, NJ, Princeton University Press.

Sigur, Christopher J. (ed.). 1992. *Democracy in Korea: The Roh Tae Woo Years*. New York, Carnegie Council on Ethics and International Affairs.

Simmons, Robert. 1975. *The Strained Alliance: Peking, Pyongyang, Moscow and the Politics of the Korean Civil War*. New York, The Free Press.

Smith, Howard. 1988. "The BBC Television Newsreel and the Korean War," *Historical Journal of Film, Radio and Television* 8/3 (November): 227–252.

Sohn Hak-kyu. 1991. *Authoritarianism and Opposition in South Korea*. London, Routledge.

Sohn Ho-min. 1997. "Orthographic Divergence in South and North Korea: Toward a Unified Spelling System," in *The Korean Alphabet: Its History and Structure*, ed. Young-key Kim-Renaud. Honolulu, University of Hawaii Press, 193–217.

Spurr, Russell. 1988. *Enter the Dragon: China at War in Korea*. New York, Newmarket Press.

Stone, Isidor F. 1952. *The Hidden History of the Korean War 1950–51*. New York, Monthly Review Press.

Stueck, William W. 1981. *The Road to Confrontation: American Policy towards China and Korea, 1947–50*. Chapel Hill, University of North Carolina.

———. 1983. "The March to the Yalu: The Perspective from Washington," in *Child of Conflict: The Korean-American Relationship*, ed. Bruce Cumings. Seattle, University of Washington Press, 195–238.

———. 1995. *The Korean War: An International History*. Princeton, NJ, Princeton University Press.

Suh Dae-Sook. 1967. *The Korean Communist Movement, 1918–1948*. Princeton, NJ, Princeton University Press.

———. 1970. *Documents of Korean Communism 1918–1948*. Princeton, NJ, Princeton University Press.

———. 1981. *Korean Communism 1945–1980: A Reference Guide to the Political System*. Honolulu, University Press of Hawaii.

———. 1988. *Kim Il Sung: The North Korean Leader*. New York, Columbia University Press.

Suh Dae-Sook and Edward J. Schultz (eds.). 1990. *Koreans in China*. Honolulu, Center for Korean Studies, University of Hawaii.

Summers, Harry G., Jr. 1990. *Korean War Almanac*. New York, Facts on File.

Swartout, Robert R., Jr. 1980. *Mandarins, Gunboats, and Power Politics: Owen Nickerson Denny and the International Rivalries in Korea*. Honolulu, University Press of Hawaii.

Taylor, Maxwell D. 1960. *The Uncertain Trumpet*. New York, Harper.

———. 1972. *Swords and Plowshares*. New York, W. W. Norton.

Tennant, Agnita (trans.). 1996. *The Star and Other Korean Short Stories*. London, KPI.

Thomas, Nigel, Peter Abbott, and Mike Chappell. 1986. *The Korean War 1950–53*. Men-at-Arms Series 174. London, Osprey.

Truman, Harry S. 1956. *Memoirs*. Vol. 2, *Years of Trial and Hope*. Garden City, NY, Doubleday.

Ulan, Adam. 1973. *Stalin*. New York, Viking.

Underwood, Lilias H. 1918. *Underwood of Korea*. Seoul, Yonsei University Press. Reprinted 1983, *A Series of Reprints of Western Books on Korea*, No. 8. Seoul, Yonsei University Press.

The US Imperialists Started the Korean War. 1977. P'yongyang, Foreign Languages Publishing House.

U.S. State Department. 1960. *The Record on Korean Unification 1943–1960: Narrative Summary with Principal Documents*. Far Eastern Series 101. Washington, DC, Department of State.

Vatcher, W. H. Jr. 1958. *Panmunjom*. New York, Frederick A. Praeger.

The Victorious Fatherland Liberation War Museum. 1979. P'yongyang, Foreign Languages Publishing House.

War Memorial Service. n.d. *War Memorial: A National Defence Sanctuary*. Seoul, Military Art Publishing.

Welsh, Frank. 1993. *A History of Hong Kong*. London, HarperCollins.

Whan, Kihl Young. 1994. *Korea and the World: Beyond the Cold War*. Boulder, CO, Westview Press.

Whelan, Richard. 1990. *Drawing the Line: The Korean War 1950–53*. Boston, Faber and Faber.

White Paper on Human Rights in North Korea. 1997. Seoul, Korea Institute for National Unification.

Whiting, Allen S. 1960. *China Crosses the Yalu: The Chinese Decision to Enter the Korean War*. New York, Macmillan. Reprinted 1968, Stanford, CA, Stanford University Press.

Whitney, Courtney. 1956. *MacArthur: His Rendezvous with History*. New York, Knopf.

Who's Who in China: Current Leaders. 1989 and subsequent editions. Beijing, Foreign Languages Press.

Who's Who in Korean Literature. 1996. Korean Culture and Arts Foundation. Elizabeth, NJ, and Seoul, Hollym.

Williams, William J. (ed.). 1993. *A Revolutionary War: Korea and the Transformation of the Postwar World*. Chicago, IL, Imprint Publications.

Wilson, Dick. 1984. *Chou: The Story of Chou En-lai 1898–1976*. London, Hutchinson.

Winnington, Alan. 1986. *Breakfast with Mao: Memoirs of a Foreign Correspondent*. London, Lawrence and Wishart.

Winnington, Alan, and Wilfrid Burchett. 1954. *Plain Perfidy*. London, Britain-China Friendship Association.

Wood, Herbert Fairlie. 1966. *Strange Battleground: The Operations in Korea and Their Effects on the Defence Policy of Canada*. Official History of the Canadian Army in Korea. Ottawa, R. Duhamel.

Yang Sung Chul. 1994. *The North and South Korean Political Systems: A Comparative Analysis*. Boulder, CO, Westview Press; Seoul, Seoul Press.

Yasuda, Jun. 1998. "A Survey: China and the Korean War," *Social Science Japan Journal* 1/1 (April): 71–83.

Yi Kyongsik. 1973. "Korea Chronology 1901–1960," *Transactions of the Korea Branch of the Royal Asiatic Society* 48: 104–193.

Yoon Taek-Lim. 1992. "The Politics of Memory in the Ethnographic History of a 'Red' Village in South Korea," *Korea Journal* (Winter): 65–79.

Annuals, Newspapers, and Periodicals

Korea Annual. Published annually by Yonhap News Agency, Seoul.

Newsreview: Korea's Weekly News Magazine. Published weekly by *The Korea Herald*, Seoul.

The People's Korea. Published weekly by Chosen Shimposha, Tokyo.

The Pyongyang Times. Published weekly, P'yongyang.

Transactions of the Korea Branch of the Royal Asiatic Society (TKBRAS). Published annually by the Korea Branch of the Royal Asiatic Society, Seoul.

World Wide Web Sites

"Canadians in Korea."http://www.vac-acc.gc.ca/historical/koreawar/korea.htm

"The Chinese Failure at Chosin." http://www.koreanwar.org./html/units/frontline/chosin.htm

"Second Squadron SAAF (Flying Cheetahs) in Korea." http://ourworld.compuserve.com/homepages/RAllport/Korea.htm

"Selected Reunification Policy of DPRK." http://www.korea-np.co.jp/pk/27th_issue/98012101.htm

Yue Dongxiao. 1998. "Korean War FAQ." http://centurychina.com/history/krwarfaq.html

Chronology

1910

22 August   Annexation of Korea by Japan.

1912

15 April   Birth of Kim Il Sung (1912–1994) near P'yongyang.

1919

1 March   Declaration of Independence.

10 April   Provisional Korean National Assembly established in Shanghai.

11 April   Provisional Korean Government adopts Taehan Min'kuk as name of Korea.

9 November   Formation of Korean Independence Fighter Corps in Jilin, China.

1920

January   Delegation from Provisional Korean Government visits Moscow. Russians give one million rubles' donation.

February   Korean Independence Army formed in Manchuria.

5 March   *Chosun Ilbo* newspaper founded in Seoul.

1 April   *Donga Ilbo* newspaper founded in Seoul.

1923

2 June   Provisional Korean Government splits; formation of the Korean Republic in Shanghai.

1924

17 August   Formation of the Korean Labor Party in Seoul.

1925

17 April   Organization of the Korean Communist Party in Seoul.

18 April   Organization of the Korean Communist Youth Association.

1926

8 January   Japanese Government-General moves to Capitol Building in Seoul.

1932

29 February   Establishment of Japanese puppet state of Manzhouguo.

1935

5 July   Various Korean groups come together in Nanjing in China to form Nationalist Revolutionary Party.

1937

7 July   Marco Polo Bridge incident near Beijing—outbreak of the Sino-Japanese War.

1941

16 February   Birth of Kim Jong Il, son of North Korean guerrilla leader Kim Il Sung.

7 December   Japanese attack on U.S. fleet at Pearl Harbor—beginning of the war in the Pacific.

9 December   Provisional Korean Government in China declares war on Japan.

1943

November–December   Cairo Conference. Korea to be independent "in due course."

1945

February   Yalta Conference.

8 August   Union of Soviet Socialist Republics (USSR) declares war on Japan and sends troops to Korea.

11 August   USSR-U.S. agreement to divide Korea at the 38th parallel for Japanese surrender.

15 August   Japan sues for peace.

20 August   USSR forces land at Wonsan. USSR army commanding general issues General Order No. 1, ordering formation of People's Committees.

22 August   Arrival of USSR forces in P'yongyang.

2 September   Formal Japanese surrender.

6 September   Establishment of Korean People's Republic in Seoul.

8 September   Arrival in Korea of U.S. troops under General John R. Hodge.

28 December   Moscow Conference proposes a period of trusteeship for Korea.

1946

2 January   Korean Communist Party declares for trusteeship.

8 February   Establishment in North Korea of Provisional People's Committee, with Kim Il Sung as chairman.

5 March   Provisional People's Committee announces land reform.

20 March   First meeting of Joint U.S.-USSR Commission in Seoul to discuss future of Korea.

8 May   Adjournment of Joint USSR-U.S. Commission after failing to agree on implementation of the Moscow Agreement.

12 December   South Korean Interim National Assembly established in Seoul.

1947

19 July   South Korean Interim Government established in Seoul.

17 September   United States refers Korean problem to the UN General Assembly.

14 November   UN General Assembly decides to establish a unified government in Korea after a general election supervised by the UN Temporary Commission on Korea (UNTCOK).

1948

24 January   USSR occupation commander refuses to allow UNTCOK north of the 38th parallel, thus preventing all-Korea elections.

3 April   Beginning of rebellion on Cheju Island in South Korea.

19–21 April   Southern political leaders Kim Ku and Kim Kyu-shik attend political conference in P'yongyang.

10 May   Elections in South Korea under UNTCOK supervision.

31 May   Constituent Assembly opens in South Korea.

15 August   Establishment of the Republic of Korea (ROK) (South Korea).

9 September   Establishment of the Democratic People's Republic of Korea (DPRK) (North Korea).

19 October   Mutiny of South Korean 14th regiment at Yosu.

12 December   UN resolution recognizes the Republic of Korea as the only legitimate government on the Korea Peninsula, calls for USSR and U.S. withdrawal, and establishes a UN Commission on Korea (UNCOK).

31 December   USSR forces leave Korea.

1949

16 February   North Korean application to join the UN rejected.

8 April   South Korean application to join the UN vetoed.

29 June   Completion of U.S. troop withdrawal.

1 July   U.S.-Korean Military Advisory Group (KMAG) established.

1 October   Establishment of the People's Republic of China (PRC).

29 October   Communist Party and affiliated organizations outlawed in South Korea.

1950

12 January   U.S. Secretary of State Dean Acheson, in a speech to the National Press Club, excludes South Korea from U.S. defense perimeter.

26 January   Signing of U.S.–South Korea Defense Support Agreement.

14 February   Sino-Soviet Treaty of Friendship and Alliance signed.

25 June   Outbreak of Korean War, with North Korean attacks at 4 A.M. across the 38th parallel. UN Security Council resolves that the North Korean attack is a breach of the peace, calls for end of hostilities and withdrawal of North Korean forces to the 38th parallel.

27 June   UN Security Council calls on UN member states to provide assistance to South Korea. South Korean government retreats to Taejon, later to Taegu.

28 June   Fall of Seoul to North Korean forces.

30 June   U.S. President Harry Truman commits U.S. ground forces to Korea.

5 July   Failure of Task Force Smith to stop the North Korean advance at Osan.

8 July   U.S. President Harry Truman appoints General Douglas MacArthur commander of UN forces in Korea.

13 July   As commander of all U.S. and South Korean forces, U.S. General Walton Walker establishes his headquarters at Taegu.

20 July   Taejon abandoned to North Korean forces.

4 August   Establishment of the Naktong River (Pusan) Perimeter.

15 August   South Korean government establishes its wartime capital at Pusan.

15 September   UN forces land behind North Korean lines at Inch'on in Operation Chromite.

22 September   U.S. Eighth Army breaks out from Pusan Perimeter.

27 September   UN forces recapture Seoul.

1 October   Third ROK Division crosses the 38th parallel.

2 October   Chinese premier, Zhou Enlai, issues warning to the Indian ambassador in Beijing that, if U.S. forces cross the 38th parallel, China will enter the war.

7 October   U.S. forces cross the 38th parallel. UN General Assembly authorizes UN forces to cross the 38th parallel. Establishment of United Nations Commission for Unification and Rehabilitation of Korea (UNCURK).

19 October   South Korean forces capture P'yongyang. Chinese forces cross the Yalu River.

26 October   South Korean forces reach the Yalu River.

27–31 October   Chinese launch first offensive.

8 November   UN forces bomb bridges at Shinuiju on the Yalu River.

24 November   U.S. Eighth Army launches drive to the Yalu River.

25–26 November   Chinese second offensive.

30 November   U.S. President Truman refers to possible use of atomic bombs in Korea.

4 December   British Prime Minister Clement Attlee flies to Washington for talks on Korea.

5 December   UN forces abandon P'yongyang.

23 December   Eighth Army commander, General Walton Walker, killed in a road accident. Replaced by General Matthew Ridgway.

24 December   All UN forces withdrawn from North Korea.

31 December   Chinese launch third offensive south of 38th parallel.

1951

4 January   Fall of Seoul to Communist forces.

1 February   UN General Assembly condemns People's Republic of China as an aggressor.

15 March   UN forces recapture Seoul.

3 April   UN forces at the 38th parallel.

11 April   Dismissal of General MacArthur, appointment of General Ridgway as UN commander.

23 June   USSR broadcast suggesting truce talks.

10 July   Armistice negotiations begin at Kaesong, behind North Korean/Chinese lines.

23 August   Armistice talks suspended.

25 October   Armistice talks resume at P'anmunjom.

12 November   Operation Ratkiller begins against suspected guerrilla groups in South Korea.

1952

18 February   USSR claims UN Command (UNC) is using biological warfare in Korea.

28 April   General Mark Clark replaces General Ridgway.

7 May   Prisoner of war uprising on Koje Island.

25 May   President Syngman Rhee declares martial law in Pusan.

5 August   President Syngman Rhee reelected president by popular vote.

1 October   Prisoner of war uprising on Cheju Island.

1953

5 March   Death of Soviet leader Joseph Stalin.

20 April   Operation Little Switch begins, with the release of sick and wounded POWs; release of civilian diplomatic and other detainees by North Korea.

8 June   North Korean–Chinese People's Volunteers accept principle of voluntary repatriation of POWs.

18 June   27, 000 Communist POWs released by President Rhee.

10 July   President Rhee refuses to sign, but agrees not to disrupt, the armistice agreement.

13 July   Final Chinese offensive in Kumsong region against South Korean forces.

27 July   Signing of the armistice at P'anmunjom.

28 July   First meeting of the Military Armistice Commission.

15 August   South Korean government partially returns to Seoul.

1 October   U.S.-ROK Mutual Defense Treaty.

1954

26 April–June   Geneva Conference on Korea and Indochina.

15 June   Announcement of the failure of the Geneva Conference to solve the Korean problem.

1955

8 December   South Korean application to join the UN vetoed.

1956

15 May   Reelection of Syngman Rhee as South Korean president; Chang Myon elected vice-president.

1957

2 July   UN Command headquarters moves from Tokyo to Seoul.

9 September   South Korean application to join the UN vetoed.

1958

16 February   (South) Korean National Airlines plane hijacked to North Korea.

8 December   South Korean application to join the UN vetoed.

1959

15 February   Japanese government agrees to repatriate Koreans in Japan to North Korea. Repatriation begins in December.

1960

15 March   Reelection of Syngman Rhee as president of South Korea.

19 April   Student uprising in South Korea.

27 April   Syngman Rhee resigns as president and goes into exile.

15 June   South Korean National Assembly replaces executive presidential system with a cabinet system; Chang Myon becomes prime minister on 23 August.

6 July   USSR–North Korea Treaty of Friendship, Cooperation, and Mutual Assistance.

11 July   PRC–North Korea Treaty of Friendship, Cooperation, and Mutual Assistance.

12 August   Yun Po-sun becomes president of South Korea.

1961

16 May   Military coup d'état in South Korea led by Major General Park Chung Hee overthrows Chang Myon government.

1962

22 March   Resignation of President Yun Po-sun; General Park Chung Hee becomes acting president.

1963

15 October   Park Chung Hee elected president of South Korea.

1965

22 June   Japan–South Korea Basic (i.e., normalization) Treaty.

19 July   Death of former South Korean President Syngman Rhee in Hawaii.

13 August   South Korean National Assembly approves the dispatch of combat divisions to South Vietnam.

1966

2 November   One South Korean and six U.S. soldiers killed in a shooting incident on south side of the Demilitarized Zone (DMZ).

1967

18 January   Chinese Red Guard newspapers and wall posters claim that a coup has taken place in North Korea.

19 January   South Korean frigate PCE-56 sunk by North Korean shore battery while on fishery protection duties. Twenty-eight killed.

26 January   Chinese stories denounced as "intolerable slanders" by North Korea.

3 March   Park Chung Hee reelected president of South Korea.

31 March   First broadcasts of the clandestine "South Korea Liberation Radio", apparently based in North Korea.

12 April   After a number of earlier shooting incidents in which seven North Korean soldiers were killed, there occurs the heaviest clash since 1953, in which South Korean forces use artillery. Three North Koreans and one South Korean are killed.

17 April   North Korean gunboat sunk.

12 December   End of the Japanese–North Korean repatriation arrangements, in operation since 1959.

13 December   Conviction in Seoul of thirty-four alleged North Korean spies, kidnapped from West Germany.

1968

6 January   North Korean naval vessels capture five South Korean fishing boats.

21 January   Unsuccessful North Korean commando raid on South Korean presidential palace, the Blue House.

23 January   U.S. intelligence ship USS *Pueblo* seized by North Korean naval vessels.

9 April   U.S. and North Korean security personnel clash in the Joint Security Area at P'anmunjom.

14 April   North Koreans ambush a UN truck in the Joint Security Area at P'anmunjom; two U.S. and two South Korean soldiers killed.

28 August   Capture of 50-ton North Korean spy boat off Cheju Island. Boat sinks as it is being towed in.

4 November   North Korean guerrilla raid on South Korean east coast.

23 December   Release of the surviving crew of USS *Pueblo*.

1969

15 April   U.S. EC-121 reconnaissance aircraft shot down by North Korean aircraft over the Sea of Japan (East Sea).

8 June   "Infiltration boat" sunk off South Korean east coast.

13 June   "Commando ship" captured off South Korean southwest coast.

17 August   U.S. helicopter strays over Military Demarcation Line and is shot down.

24 September   "Armed ship" sunk off South Korean west coast.

14 October   "Armed ship" sunk off South Korean west coast.

3 December   Release of U.S. helicopter crew.

11 December   Korean Air Lines YS-11 turboprop aircraft with 51 passengers and crew hijacked to North Korea.

1970

31 March   Japanese Red Army terrorist group hijacks Japan Airlines "Yodo" airliner to North Korea.

5 June   South Korea announces capture of a ship; North Korea announces sinking of "U.S. spy ship."

23 June   Two North Korean agents killed setting explosives at Seoul National Cemetery.

30 June   South Korea announces capture of a "fast infiltration ship"; six crew killed.

15 August   South Korean President Park offers to open contact with North Korea if North Korea renounces the use of force.

24 December   South Korean trade law amended to allow trade with Communist countries.

1971

12 March   South Korean troops take over defense responsibility along the DMZ.

27 April   Park Chung Hee reelected president of South Korea, defeating Kim Dae Jung.

20 September   Preliminary North-South Red Cross meetings at P'anmunjom.

1972

4 July   Signing of the North-South Joint Communiqué and establishment of the North-South Coordinating Committee.

29 August   First round of full North-South Red Cross Talks at P'yongyang to discuss family reunions.

12 October   First round of official North-South Coordinating Committee meetings at P'yongyang.

27 December   New North Korean state Constitution; Kim Il Sung becomes executive president.

1973

30 March   Nordic foreign ministers announce that their countries will establish diplomatic relations with North Korea.

23 April   South Korea announces breaking up of thirteen-member spy ring.

1 June   North Korea, on joining the World Health Organization, gains observer status at the UN. (South Korea has had such status since 1949.)

23 June   South Korean President Park Chung Hee announces that South Korea will no longer oppose other countries' establishment of diplomatic relations with North Korea and expresses the hope that countries hitherto recognizing only North Korea will now establish relations with the South.

8 August   South Korean opposition leader Kim Dae Jung kidnapped in Tokyo and brought to Seoul.

28 August   North Korea suspends Red Cross and North-South Coordinating Committee meetings in protest at Kim Dae Jung kidnapping.

21 September   First official Australian delegation, led by Trade Minister Jim Cairns, visits North Korea.

21 November   UN agrees by consensus to end UNCURK.

1974

31 July   Australia and North Korea establish diplomatic relations.

15 August   Assassination attempt on South Korean President Park Chung Hee by pro–North Korean from Japan. Park's wife killed.

15 November   UNC announces the discovery of an alleged infiltration tunnel in the southern part of the DMZ.

1975

26 February   Clash between North and South Korean ships in the West Sea.

19 March   UNC announces discovery of second tunnel under the DMZ.

April   Fall of Saigon to North Vietnamese forces. North Korean leader Kim Il Sung visits Beijing.

15 September   Visit to South Korea by some 700 pro–North Koreans from Japan.

30 October   North Korea withdraws its diplomatic mission from Australia.

6 November   North Korea expels Australian embassy staff from P'yongyang.

19 November   UN General Assembly passes pro–South Korean and pro–North Korean resolutions on future of the Korea Peninsula.

1976

9 March   U.S. President Jimmy Carter announces plan to withdraw U.S. forces from Korea.

22 July   U.S. Secretary of State Henry Kissinger proposes a conference of North and South Korea, the United States, and China to discuss Korea.

18 August   Ax murders of two U.S. Army officers at P'anmunjom.

1977

9 March   U.S. President Jimmy Carter announces that U.S. ground combat forces will be withdrawn from Korea in five years.

3 May   South Korean soldier killed in firefight in the DMZ.

21 June   North Korea declares 200-mile maritime zone.

14 July   U.S. helicopter shot down on northern side of DMZ.

1 August   North Korea proclaims a "military sea boundary" that extends 50 miles from its territorial sea in the Sea of Japan (East Sea) and 200 miles in the West Sea and that is closed to all foreign shipping.

12 October   Two South Korean civilian workers steal a South Korean army aircraft and fly it to North Korea.

1978

30 April   South Korea declares a 12-mile territorial sea.

27 October   UNC announces discovery of third tunnel under DMZ.

7 November   Establishment of the U.S.–South Korean Combined Forces Command.

1979

18 July   Korean Central Intelligence Agency announces breakup of eleven-member North Korean spying ring.

9 August   Twenty-four-member North Korean spy ring discovered at Sokcho.

26 October   Assassination of South Korean President Park Chung Hee.

27 October   Nationwide martial law proclaimed in South Korea.

12 December   South Korean General Chun Doo Hwan stages coup and arrests Martial Law Commander General Chung Sung-hwa.

1980

17 May   Proclamation of martial law and banning of all political activities in South Korea.

12–21 July   Representative Stephen Solarz becomes the first member of the U.S. Congress to visit North Korea.

1 September   General Chun Doo Hwan becomes South Korean president.

14 September   Kim Il Sung offers to abandon 1961 treaties with China and Russia if the United States begins negotiations for a peace treaty.

17 September   Kim Dae Jung sentenced to death.

24 September   North Korea breaks off all dialogue with South, refusing to deal with the "military fascist clique."

10 October   At (North) Korean Workers' Party Congress, Kim Il Sung repeats his proposal for a "Confederation" as a final form for a future unified Korea: the South Korean government would withdraw, leaving Korea as one country, two systems, and nonaligned.

1981

12 January   South Korean President Chun Doo Hwan proposes a North-South summit meeting; North rejects it on 19 January.

23 January   Kim Dae Jung's sentence commuted to life imprisonment.

1982

5 January   Lifting of the South Korean curfew, in force since 1952.

12 January   South Korean President Chun Doo Hwan proposes a North-South summit meeting.

12 February   South Korea arrests a seven-member North Korean spy network.

15 February   North Korean Central People's Committee appoints Kim Jong Il "Hero of the DPRK."

13 April   Three North Korean spy rings found in South Korea.

5 May   Hijacked Chinese passenger aircraft lands in South Korea.

18 May   North Korea accepts the body of an alleged infiltrator for the first time since 1953.

5 June   President Chun repeats his summit proposal; North Korea rejects it.

9 June   Breakup of two spy rings in South Korea.

19 June   North Korea accuses U.S. SR-71 reconnaissance aircraft of violating its airspace.

12 August   Japan announces the arrest of a prominent North Korean spy.

13 August   South Korea announces the arrest of two North Korean spies.

26 August   North Korea fires a surface-to-air missile at a U.S. SR-71 aircraft.

28 August   U.S. Private Joseph T. White defects to North Korea.

2 September   First known visit to South Korea since 1949 of a Sino-Korean couple from the People's Republic of China.

29 September   South Korea arrests twenty-nine spies, some with a twenty-five-year history of operating in South Korea.

16 October   Defection to South Korea of a Chinese pilot flying a MiG fighter aircraft.

23 December   Kim Dae Jung leaves South Korea for medical treatment in the United States.

1983

5 August   South Korea sinks alleged North Korean spy ship near Wolsong nuclear power station; North Korea subsequently denies involvement.

7 August   Defection to South Korea of a Chinese pilot flying a MiG fighter aircraft.

3 September   Shooting down of Korean Air Lines Flight KE007 by Soviet fighter aircraft.

8 October   North Korea passes secret proposal via Chinese officials to the United States, suggesting North, South, and U.S. meeting.

9 October   Bomb attack at Aung San memorial in Rangoon, just before arrival of South Korean President Chun Doo Hwan, kills seventeen senior South Korean leaders.

4 November   Burmese government announces that it has "firmly established" that North Korea was behind the Rangoon bombing, breaks off diplomatic relations, and withdraws recognition of the North Korean government.

4 December   South Korea announces capture of two North Korean spies and the sinking of their vessel.

19 December   South Korea announces the arrest of members of three North Korean spy rings.

1984

11 January   North Korea announces that it has sent letters to the U.S. and South Korean governments proposing three-way talks.

9 April   First meeting at P'anmunjom to discuss joint North-South team for the Los Angeles Olympics.

May   Kim Il Sung makes first visit to USSR since 1975.

2 June   North Korea announces boycott of Los Angeles Olympics.

20 September   First family reunions since 1953 in Seoul.

29 September   Arrival of North Korean flood relief goods in South Korea.

6 October   North suggests three-party talks (United States and North and South Korea) on withdrawal of U.S. troops and a nonaggression pact.

15 November   First round of North-South economic cooperation talks at P'anmunjom.

20 November   Preliminary meeting on resumption of North-South Red Cross talks.

23 November   A Russian defects through P'anmunjom; three North Koreans killed in the resulting shoot-out.

1985

9 January   North postpones full-scale Red Cross talks because of joint South Korean–U.S. exercise Team Spirit.

28–29 May   Eighth round of Red Cross talks held in Seoul.

23 July   Preliminary discussions at P'anmunjom on interparliamentary talks.

18–23 September   Exchange of North-South artistic troupes/home visit groups.

1987

11 November   North proposes five-point plan for reunification, including cohosting 1988 Olympics.

29 November   Korean Air Flight 858 blown up over Andaman Sea.

1988

15 January   Kim Hyon-hui, arrested in connection with airliner bombing, confesses to being a North Korean agent.

16 January   The (South) Korean Chamber of Commerce and Industry signs an agreement on promoting economic cooperation with the Hungarian Chamber of Commerce.

20 January   U.S. State Department adds North Korea to its list of terrorist states because of the November 1987 aircraft bombing.

7 July   South Korean President Roh sets out his *Nordpolitik,* his policy of developing links with Communist countries.

1989

1 February   South Korea and Hungary establish diplomatic relations.

1990

4 March   UNC announces discovery of fourth tunnel under the DMZ.

4 September   First round of North-South prime ministers' talks in Seoul.

1991

25 March   South Korean Major General Hwang Won-tak is named as first non-U.S. head of United Nations Command Military Armistice delegation at P'anmunjom; North Korea says that it will boycott meetings.

19–20 April   Summit meeting on Cheju Island between South Korean President Roh Tae Woo, and Soviet President Mikhail Gorbachev.

11 May   Death of long-serving North Korean Foreign Minister Ho Dam.

17 May   First commercial flight between North Korea and Japan.

28 May   North Korea abandons opposition to separate North-South entry to the UN.

24 June   North Korea hands over remains of eleven U.S. servicemen killed in the Korean War.

17 September   North and South Korea join the United Nations.

27 September   U.S. President George Bush announces worldwide withdrawal of U.S. tactical nuclear weapons.

1 October   South Korean forces take over last section of DMZ, south of P'anmunjom, from U.S. troops.

30 November   Unification Church leader Moon Sun Myung in North Korea.

13 December   North-South Agreement on Reconciliation, Non-aggression, Exchanges and Co-operation. North-South Joint Declaration on Denuclearization of the Korea Peninsula.

18 December   South Korean President Roh Tae Woo announces that there are no nuclear weapons in South Korea.

1992

6 January   U.S. President Bush visits South Korea.

30 January   North Korea signs International Atomic Energy Safeguards Agreement.

18 December   Ruling party candidate, former opposition leader Kim Young Sam, elected president of South Korea.

1993

25 March   North Korea announces its withdrawal from the Nuclear Non-proliferation Treaty (NPT).

11 June   U.S.–North Korea joint statement in New York; neither side to use force against the other and North Korea suspends NPT withdrawal.

3 August   North Korea allows International Atomic Energy Authority (IAEA) inspectors in for the first time since May.

4 August   Japanese government's first official admission of the existence of "comfort women" for military prostitution in World War II.

19 August   South Korean government formally asks Russia for compensation for the shooting down of KE007 in 1983.

30 November   North Korea hands over remains of thirty-three UN soldiers killed in the Korean War.

7 December   North Korea hands over remains of thirty-one UN soldiers killed in the Korean War.

1994

5 January   United States and North Korea reach agreement "in principle" on inspection of North Korea's seven declared nuclear sites.

24 January   First Seoul-Beijing direct air route agreed upon.

27 January   U.S. evangelist Billy Graham makes second visit to North Korea.

28 April   North Korea announces its intention to withdraw from the Military Armistice Commission, to end the Neutral Nations Supervisory Commission, and to seek a peace treaty with the United States.

13 June   North Korea withdraws from the IAEA.

15 June   Former U.S. President Jimmy Carter in North Korea to discuss nuclear issue.

18 June   Carter returns to Seoul with a proposal for a North-South summit and a freeze on North Korean nuclear development. South Korean President Kim Young Sam offers to hold a summit meeting with Kim Il Sung without preconditions.

28 June   North-South preliminary contact on summit agrees that Kim Young Sam will visit North Korea 25–27 July.

8 July   Death of Kim Il Sung. North postpones the summit.

19 July   Kim Il Sung's funeral.

2 September   North Korea announces that the Chinese will withdraw their members from the Military Armistice Commission.

10 September   Led by Lynn Turk, first U.S. diplomatic mission to North Korea since the Korean War.

13 September   North Korea hands over remains of fourteen U.S. soldiers killed in the Korean War.

16 October   First known public appearance of Kim Jong Il since the death of Kim Il Sung.

21 October   North Korean and U.S. delegates in Geneva sign an Agreed Framework on the supply of light-water nuclear reactors to North Korea.

28 November   IAEA confirms that North Korean nuclear program is halted.

6 December   U.S.–North Korean talks in Washington on opening of diplomatic offices in each country.

10 December   South Korean government allows Samsung, LG (formerly Lucky Goldstar), and four other groups to visit North Korea for business consultations.

11 December   U.S. Senators Frank Murkowski (R-Alaska) and Paul Simon (D-Illinois) arrive in P'yongyang on the first U.S. military aircraft to fly into North Korea since the end of the Korean War in 1953.

17 December   U.S. Eighth Army OH-58 helicopter with two crew crashes north of DMZ; one killed.

22 December   North Korea returns remains of killed helicopter crew member.

30 December   North Korea repatriates live helicopter crew member.

1995

20 January   United States lifts some economic sanctions against North Korea.

26 January   Martin Luther King Peace Prize awarded to South Korean President Kim Young Sam.

16 February   Kim Jong Il's birthday becomes "Greatest Festival of the Nation."

9 March   Formal establishment in New York of Korean Peninsula Energy Development Organization (KEDO) to supply light-water nuclear reactors to North Korea.

27 July   Opening of Korea War Memorial in Washington, D.C.

31 July   Inaugural general conference of KEDO in New York.

11 September   First round of North Korea–KEDO talks in Kuala Lumpur, Malaysia.

3 December   Arrest of former South Korean President Chun Doo Hwan on corruption charges; mutiny and treason charges later added.

5 December   Arrest of former South Korean President Roh Tae Woo on corruption charges; mutiny and treason charges later added.

21 December   Indictment of former South Korean Presidents Chun and Roh on a variety of charges, including mutiny.

1996

23 January   Former South Korean Presidents Chun and Roh charged with treason.

5–7 April   Several hundred North Korean troops enter prohibited areas along the DMZ.

16 April   U.S. President Bill Clinton and South Korean President Kim Young Sam propose four-party talks (United States, China, and North and South Korea) to establish a permanent peace settlement on the Korea Peninsula.

7 May   North Korean foreign ministry requests a briefing on the four-party talks.

15 June   U.S.–North Korea agreement on joint searches for missing-in-action (MIA) remains.

17 August   First joint venture between North Korea and a South Korean company begins operation at the North Korean port of Namp'o.

26 August   Conviction of former South Korean Presidents Chun and Roh.

18 September   North Korean submarine on espionage mission runs aground on South Korea's east coast. South Korea suspends all aid to the North.

25 November   Detention of U.S. citizen E. C. Hunziker in North Korea as a spy. Later released; commits suicide.

29 December   North Korean foreign ministry spokesperson expresses "deep regret" for submarine incident.

1997

12 February   Hwang Jang-yop, secretary of the Central Committee of the North Korea Supreme People's Assembly and former tutor to Kim Jong Il, becomes the highest-ranking defector from North Korea.

5 March   Briefing session of four-party talks held in New York.

16–21 April   Second briefing session of four-party talks. North Koreans walk out because of lack of food aid.

16 July   Heavy exchange of fire in the DMZ.

5–7 August   Preliminary four-party talks held in New York. Two more rounds held in September and November also in New York.

19 August   Ground-breaking ceremony for the light-water reactors to be built in North Korea by KEDO.

8 October   Kim Jong Il becomes secretary general of the (North) Korean Workers' Party.

9–10 December   Four-party talks begin in Geneva.

18 December   Election of South Korean veteran opposition leader Kim Dae Jung as president of South Korea.

22 December   Release from jail of former South Korean Presidents Chun Doo Hwan and Roh Tae Woo.

1998

19 February   South Korea announces it is cutting its diplomatic missions from 145 to 125, to reduce costs.

25 February   Veteran opposition leader Kim Dae Jung becomes president of South Korea.

1 March   Cathay Pacific Airways cargo aircraft becomes first non-Communist aircraft to fly through North Korean airspace.

2 March   Spokesperson for the North Korean Flood Damage Rehabilitation Committee releases detailed statement on flood and other damage to crops.

14 March   North Korea announces that it is cutting its overseas missions by 30 percent.

7–11 April   Catherine Bertini, executive director of the World Food Program, visits North Korea to assess food needs.

9 April   Former Seoul National University professor, Ko Yong-bok, receives seven-year jail sentence for engaging in spying for North Korea for thirty-six years.

8–16 May   European Union humanitarian/technical mission to North Korea.

28–29 May   United Nations Development Program Round Table on North Korea in Geneva.

16 June   South Korean industrialist, Chung Ju-yung, delivers 501 head of cattle and other relief goods to North Korea via P'anmunjom. He also reaches agreement on opening tourist traffic between South and North Korea.

22 June   North Korean Yugo-class miniature submarine trapped in nets of a South Korean fishing boat off Sokcho on the South Korean east coast. All occupants subsequently found dead.

23 June   First "General Officer" meeting at P'anmunjom since 1991.

3 July   Return of the bodies of North Korean crew of the submarine at P'anmunjom.

12 July   Body of a suspected North Korean frogman found on east coast.

27 July   Elections for the Tenth North Korean Supreme People's Assembly, the first since 1990.

31 August   North Korean rocket launch. North Korea claims it is a satellite launch.

5 September   After a change in the North Korean Constitution, the chair of the National Defense Commission becomes the highest post; Kim Jong Il is reelected to this position. His father, Kim Il Sung (d. 1994), is declared "president in perpetuity."

2 October   South Korean prosecutors allege that aides of then government party candidate Lee Hoi-chang, in 1997 presidential election, had contact with North Korean agents in Beijing to stage incident at P'anmunjom during the election.

27 October–2 November   South Korean industrialist, Hyundai Group honorary chair Chung Ju-yung, takes second batch of 501 cattle and trucks to North Korea. He meets Kim Jong Il and gets final agreement on tourist trips by South Koreans to the Diamond Mountains (Kumgang-san).

17–19 November   South Korean President Kim Dae Jung attends Asia-Pacific Economic Council meeting in Kuala Lumpur, then visits China and Hong Kong.

18 November   First Hyundai tourist ship sails for Diamond Mountains.

20–23 November   U.S. President Bill Clinton visits South Korea.

2 December   First European Union–North Korean working-level talks, Brussels.

7 December   Delegation of the European Parliament visits North Korea.

19 December   North Korean "spy boat" sunk by South Korean navy.

Index